Land of the
Oneidas

Land of the Oneidas

Central New York State and the Creation of America, from Prehistory to the Present

DANIEL KOCH

SUNY PRESS

Cover map inset: Taken from "A general map of the middle British colonies, in America. Containing Virginia, Maryland, the Delaware counties, Pennsylvania and New Jersey. With the addition of New York, and the greatest part of New England, as also of the bordering parts of the province of Quebec, improved from several surveys made after the late war, and corrected from Governor Pownall's late map 1776." Library of Congress Geography and Map Division.

Published by State University of New York Press, Albany

© 2023 State University of New York

All rights reserved

Printed in the United States of America

No part of this book may be used or reproduced in any manner whatsoever without written permission. No part of this book may be stored in a retrieval system or transmitted in any form or by any means including electronic, electrostatic, magnetic tape, mechanical, photocopying, recording, or otherwise without the prior permission in writing of the publisher.

For information, contact State University of New York Press, Albany, NY
www.sunypress.edu

Library of Congress Cataloging-in-Publication Data

Name: Koch, Daniel Robert, author.
Title: Land of the Oneidas : Central New York State and the creation of
   America, from prehistory to the present / Daniel Koch.
Other titles: Central New York State and the creation of America, from
   prehistory to the present.
Description: Albany : State University of New York Press, 2023. | Includes
   bibliographical references and index.
Identifiers: LCCN 2022035143 | ISBN 9781438492698 (hardcover : alk. paper) |
   ISBN 9781438492704 (ebook) | ISBN 9781438492711 (pbk. : alk. paper)
Subjects: LCSH: New York (State)—History. | Oneida Indians—History. | Finger
   Lakes Region (N.Y.)—History. | Mohawk River Valley (N.Y.)—History.
Classification: LCC F119 .K63 2023 | DDC 974.7/01—dc23/eng/20220722
LC record available at https://lccn.loc.gov/2022035143

10 9 8 7 6 5 4 3 2 1

To Laura, Samuel, and Jacob

Contents

List of Illustrations	ix
Acknowledgments	xi
Preface	xiii
Introduction	1
Chapter 1 Origins, The Ice Age to 1635	15
Chapter 2 The Age of the French, 1635–1763	35
Chapter 3 Rebellion, 1763–1784	59
Chapter 4 Removal, 1784–1835	81
Chapter 5 Reckoning, 1835–1865	129
Chapter 6 Consummation, 1865–1917	169
Chapter 7 Boom and Rust, 1917–2000	201
Epilogue: 2000–2023	245
Conclusion	257

Notes	261
Bibliography	307
Index	325

List of Illustrations

Figure I.1	The Oneida Homeland in Central New York State.	xvi
Figure 1.1	Pre-Eighteenth-Century Archaeological Sites in Central New York.	18
Figure 1.2	Depiction of Samuel de Champlain's siege of an Oneida or Onondaga village in 1615 in his *Voyages et descouvertures faites en la Nouvelle France, depuis l'année 1615, jusques à la fin de l'année 1618*.	24
Figure 2.1	New York, Iroquoia, and New France During the Seventeenth and Eighteenth Centuries.	34
Figure 2.2	Detail from Guillaume de l'Isle, "Carte de la Louisiane et du cours du Mississippi" (1718).	45
Figure 3.1	John Trumbull, "Good Peter" (1792).	76
Figure 4.1	"A Map of the Oneida Reservation Including the Lands Leased to Peter Smith, ca. 1810."	84
Figure 4.2	"Oneida County, Showing Original Patents, Grants, &c. from Surveyor General's Map, 1829," from Samuel Durant's *History of Oneida County*.	91
Figure 4.3	Detail from "Map of lands bordering Oneida Lake with references to Indian purchases, 1798–1817."	106
Figure 4.4	Detail from "Plan of a Village at Oneida Castle, in Vernon in the County of Oneida" (1813).	109

Figure 4.5 Detail from Gurdon Evans, A. D. Byles, and Robert Pearsall Smith, "Topographical Map of Madison County, New York" (1853).   126

Figure 5.1 Detail from Sylvanus Sweet, "Map of the Rail-roads of the State of New York."   143

Figure 5.2 Portrait of Rev. Jermain W. Loguen (1859).   155

Figure 6.1 Albert Bierstadt, *Evening on Oneida Lake*.   168

Figure 6.2 Detail from D. G. Beers, "Utica, 2nd, 3rd, 6th, and 9th Wards" in D. G. Beers's *Atlas of Oneida County, New York*.   181

Figure 6.3 Portrait of Julius M. Goldstein in *Notable Men of Central New York*.   183

Figure 6.4 Clinton Square, Syracuse (circa 1905).   187

Figure 6.5 The Oneida Community Mansion House (1870).   189

Figure 6.6 Photograph of Matilda Joslyn Gage (1871).   193

Figure 7.1 Alison Mason Kingsbury, "The Onion Fields" (1942).   206

Acknowledgments

I am grateful to many people for their help and support with this project, or for their inspiration and example. In no order, I am indebted to the late Professor Warren Roberts and his wife Anne, Jo Godfrey, Milton Sernett, Anthony Anadio, Harry Schüler, Matthew Urtz, Laurence Hauptman, Michael Oberg, Karim Tiro, Doug George-Kanentiio, Phil Bean, Richard Carlin, James Peltz, Michael Colangelo, Jonathan Lothrop, Joel Barkin, Bob Davidson, Leah Shenandoah, Norm Dann, Daniel Rück, Anthony Wonderley, Mike Myers, and Jack Henke. I am also greatly obliged to my New York family, who inspired my interest in this land from a young age, and to my UK one—particularly my wife, Laura, and our two children, Samuel and Jacob—for their love and patience.

Preface

This is a history of the land where I grew up, the central part of the state of New York. It is a land of immense natural beauty and a complex past. Some of its history is uplifting and some of it tragic.

My parents, grandparents, and great-grandparents all grew up here, too. Most branches of my family reach back even farther than that in this region. Some of my ancestors were Palatine Germans, the first non-Native people to settle here. Others came in the "Yankee invasion," when New England farmers flooded the region after the American Revolution. Some came in later waves of immigration. None of them rose to any particular prominence. They were ordinary people, and I have mainly left them, as individuals, out of this book. Nonetheless, it has been an enriching and rewarding experience for me to discover all I could about their home in central New York as it was in their times.

I have been captivated by the history of this land since I was a boy. I began reading about it in my grandparents' book collections. I became conscious of the importance of what happened here to the broader course of North American history. But there was not a book I could find there or in any of the libraries I've haunted over the years that brings the story together in an accessible way. That is what I hope this book will do.

I started writing parts of this book over twenty years ago, as a history student working with Professor Warren Roberts at the State University of New York at Albany. I have lived abroad since then, briefly in France and Germany, and, since 2003, in the UK. But every year I return home, and my interest in central New York and its history has only become stronger. As Ralph Waldo Emerson wrote, "We go to Europe to be Americanized."

I call the book *Land of the Oneidas* for a few reasons that are discussed in the Introduction, but mainly, it's because that's what this land is. Long before Europeans came here, it was the home of the Oneida Haudenosaunee (Iroquois) people. The land was taken from them in a series of treaties between the 1780s and the 1840s that violated federal law. Many Oneida people left the area—not because they wanted to but because the pressure they were put under by the state and, later, the United States government to leave their homeland became unbearable. They started new lives on land they acquired in Wisconsin or in Canada. A minority remained in New York.

I am not a Native American historian by background. I reached out to two of the best while writing this book, Laurence Hauptman and Michael Oberg. They gave me excellent advice. The thing that I really took away was a better understanding of where the limits of this piece of writing lie. This book is a history of central New York and the people that made their homes in it—both Native and non-Native—across the centuries. But it is very far from being a complete history of the Oneida Haudenosaunee people.

That history deserves to be written. I hope it will be someday and that the contents of this book will be helpful to its authors. I am fascinated by the Oneida people's history, their beliefs, and traditions. I have read most of what has been written about them. But a history of the Oneida people—particularly one that goes up to the present day—would need greater focus and far more Oneida voice than I have been able to present in this history.

The Oneida people are, of course, central in much of the story this book tells. Some of it is difficult and painful. There are places where I give quotes or paraphrase sources by non-Native people in previous centuries that use terms that would be completely unacceptable today. I also show the shameful language that more recent opponents of the Oneidas have used in their campaigns. I do so to allow readers to understand the way people spoke and wrote (as indicators of how they thought), not to show approval. I would like all Oneida Haudenosaunee people to know that I come from a place of respect.

This book also discusses African American people in central New York in previous centuries and in our own time. Some Black people were forced to endure slavery in this land. Some traversed it or settled on it as "fugitive slaves," to use the language of the time. Similarly, I refer to words in quotations that were spoken or written by people in the past that are hateful and wrong. Again, I do so to expose the kind of abuse that Black people have had to endure, not to condone it.

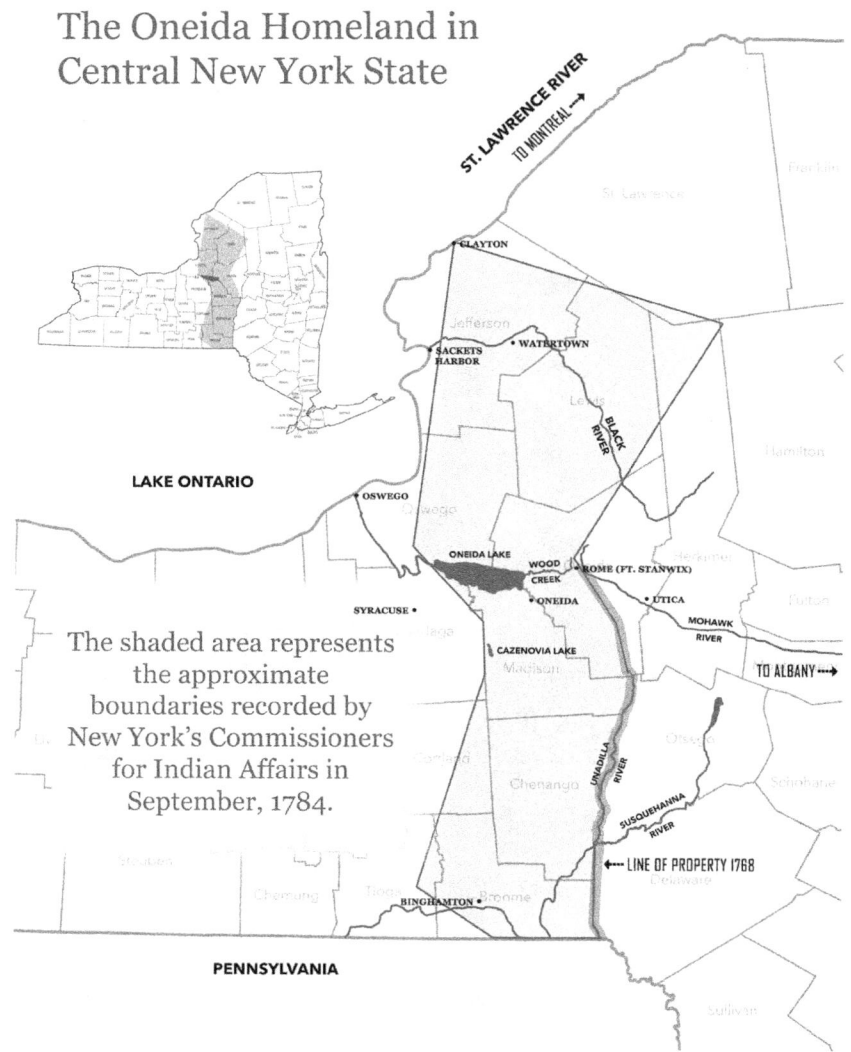

Figure I.1. The Oneida Homeland in Central New York State.

Introduction

The first attempt to formally mark out the boundaries of the lands of the Oneida Haudenosaunee occurred within a few years of the dispossession of millions of acres of it. In September 1784, commissioners from New York asked the Oneidas to describe the extent of their territory. It was in preparation for an upcoming conference to be held in the charred ruins of Fort Stanwix. The Oneidas offered the Americans vital assistance in their War of Independence, which concluded the year before, and suffered greatly because of their participation. Yet they feared that the state would attempt to gain control over their land, in spite of all they had done to help the colonists achieve their victory.

Sensing that good relations with the Oneidas would strengthen his hand in negotiating with the other Haudenosaunee nations at Stanwix, Governor George Clinton sent a delegation to meet them. They addressed the Oneida leaders, saying they wished to know the precise boundaries of their homeland "in order to prevent any Intrusions thereupon."[1]

The Oneidas knew that the state wasn't the only danger to the continued possession of their homeland. It could be overrun by squatters or bought up by intriguing private speculators. They had seen it happen in the Mohawk lands to the east in the decades before the Revolution. The Oneidas had nothing to fear from the state, the commissioners told them. They posed as protectors. The Oneidas agreed to describe their boundaries. Knowing them would at least give the state a moral imperative to respect and keep their people on the right side of them, even if few Oneidas had much confidence that it would.

The Oneidas told the commissioners that their territory extended from the St. Lawrence River in the north to the Susquehanna in the south. Their lands to the southeast had already been bound by a previous treaty with the British in 1768, which set a "Line of Property" across the New York colony beyond which no Indian land could be bought or sold. To the east of that line lie thousands of acres of Oneida land that had already been transferred to white ownership, including the 1705 Oriskany Patent upon which Fort Stanwix was built. But some six million acres to the west of the line belonged to the Oneidas alone. The Line of Property's northernmost point was on Wood Creek, just west of Fort Stanwix. The Oneidas told the commissioners that from there, the eastern boundary of their territory extended up to Canada. It followed

> the Canada Creek till it comes to a certain Mountain called Esoiade or Ice Mountain, under which Mountain that Canada Creek opposite to old Fort Hendricks heads; from thence running Westerly to an old Fort which stood on the Creek called Weteringhra Guentire, and which empties into the River St. Lawrence about twelve Miles below Carleton's or Buck's Island, & which Fort the Oneidas took from their Enemies a long time ago.

They then described the western boundary separating their land from that of the Onondagas. From the old fort, the line ran

> Southerly to a Rift upon the Onondaga River called Ogontenayea or Aquegontenayea (a Place remarkable for Eels) about five Miles from where the River empties out of the Oneida Lake and from thence runs to the Creek called Cogshunto, to that part or Point of the said Creek which lays about six Miles East of Onondago and where the Water runs over a Ledge of Rocks and from thence runs up the said Creek to a Lake out of which it empties called Anagwolas and from thence to the head of the Owego River which heads in a Swamp nearly at the same Place where the said Cogshunto River heads, and from thence down the said Owego River to where it empties into the Susquehannah.

Making sense of this description is difficult, and plotting the area onto a current map of New York State cannot be done without making some approximations and interpretations. Some of the landmarks mentioned are identifiable. The junction of Canada Creek and Wood Creek is just west of Rome, New York. When the treaty text was published in *Proceedings of the Commissioners of Indian Affairs* (1861), the editor consulted Rev. Eleazar Williams—a St. Regis Mohawk who lived and preached among the Oneidas—about the locations of some of the places mentioned. Williams placed Ice Mountain in the central Adirondacks, Weteringhra Guentire at the present location of Clayton, New York, and the "Place remarkable for Eels" at the great bend in the Oneida River a few miles west of the outlet of Oneida Lake at Brewerton. The place where the "Water runs over a Ledge of Rock" is almost certainly Chittenango Falls in Madison County, and Anagwolas is Cazenovia Lake.[2]

Other landmarks can be guessed at but not pinpointed. The reality is, no one can say with certainty where Ice Mountain is. It is unclear if the Owego River referred to is what is currently known as Owego Creek. No corresponding map was made at the time that survives today.

Even if all the places mentioned were clearly identifiable, using this description as a set of boundaries for the ancestral Oneida homeland would still be problematic. The description only covers lands west of the Line of Property, and so it does not capture the full extent of the Oneida domains prior to 1768. The context in which the description was given, when the Oneidas were in a vulnerable position at the conclusion of a devastating war, is important. It is conceivable that the commissioners wrote down what they wanted to hear from the Oneidas rather than what they said. The record of New York's land negotiations and treaties with its Native people abounds with examples of this kind of tactic being used. In the period after the Revolution, legislators were keen to make sure that the borders with British Canada did not remain under Native American control. This may explain why land along the St. Lawrence River that the Oneidas frequently used in the eighteenth century is not within the boundaries recorded in 1784.

What is clear, however, is that the Oneidas inhabited, hunted, and traveled over a homeland that stretched up through the center of what is now New York State. To the west lay the easternmost of the Great Lakes, Ontario, and to the east, the peaks of the Adirondacks. In the heart of the country is Oneida Lake. To the north of Oneida Lake is a comparatively flat corridor running up to Canada (except for the elevated region known as the Tug Hill Plateau) through which the Salmon River, Sandy Creek, and the Black River run before pouring into Lake Ontario, the lattermost through a wide bay guarded by Sackets Harbor. To the south is a hilly plateau, with long rounded-top highlands, divided by creek and river valleys flowing north into Oneida Lake or south to the Susquehanna River.

§

The Oneidas' main villages for centuries lay in the hilly country just south of the Oneida Lake plain. Before the appearance of Europeans, and in the early centuries of colonization, they lived together in matrilinear families in wooden longhouses. They were members of the confederacy called the League of the Iroquois, or the Five Nations by Europeans. They called themselves the Haudenosaunee, the People of the Longhouse. The confederated nations controlled most of what is now known as upstate New York. From east to west, the Mohawks, Oneidas, Onondagas, Cayugas, and Senecas worked together, seeking consensus with one another in times of war and peace. The Onondagas in what is now the Syracuse area hosted the council fire, where delegations from each of the nations met to discuss matters of mutual concern. The peace with the peoples to the east and west allowed the Oneidas to push the area they controlled to the north and south, explaining the sliver-like shape of their homeland.

A process of change began in the sixteenth century, when European traders began arriving on the Atlantic seaboard and exploring the Hudson and St. Lawrence Rivers. From their strong inland position, the Haudenosaunee became a dominant force in the fur trade and in the so-called Beaver Wars it spawned, even if they were at times far from unified in a political or military sense. Native American tribes (backed by European allies) vied for control over vital hunting grounds and trade hubs. European products began appearing in Oneida villages, and before long, Dutch and French visitors arrived in their homeland, on missions to woo or to punish, depending on the tides of trade and war. A poisonous cocktail of guns, disease, violence, and alcohol staggered the Oneidas in the seventeenth century, but still they remained a powerful force capable of launching devastating raids against European and Native enemies. Non-native witnesses recorded that torture, cannibalism, and captive-taking were commonplace in these years. (A few missionaries even reflected on their own people's guilt in causing it. Seventeenth-century Europe was also a cauldron of war, the scene of atrocities on a far greater scale.) Christianity and European-made goods changed the Oneidas' way of life. Competing colonial forces divided loyalties.

Across the center of the Oneida lands there is a great valley that runs west to east, through which the Mohawk River flows. This corridor is what explains the vast importance that the region would later have in the making of America. The Mohawk River carried goods from the interior of the continent east to Albany where it connects to the Hudson River and thence to the Atlantic. At present-day Rome, a few miles of dry, flat land separate the Mohawk River from Wood Creek, a meandering stream that flows westward until reaching Oneida Lake. The water route then proceeds along the Oneida and Oswego Rivers to Lake Ontario. It is the only significant break in the Appalachian Mountains that stretch from Maine to Georgia, and it remains the flattest route by which to traverse that thousand-mile barrier separating the Atlantic seaboard from the interior of North America. This valley was the key to a continent. Apart from the St. Lawrence River, which was firmly in the hands of the French, any hopes of westward expansion from the coast would depend on control of the Mohawk to Ontario corridor. The British, who controlled the Atlantic seaboard and supplanted the Dutch in the Hudson Valley during the 1640s, grasped the significance.

In the eighteenth century, European relations with the Haudenosaunee became less about pelts and more about land. British colonists bought huge tracts from the Mohawks along the river bearing their name. They wooed the Oneidas into selling the so-called "Oneida Carry"—the portage on the Mohawk-to-Ontario water route—and into allowing British forts to be erected deep in the wilderness of Iroquoia along that vital artery. For the eastern Haudenosaunee, now linked inextricably to the British in trade, there were benefits in British military presence, for they, too, feared raids from the French and their Native allies. Another plague of violence engulfed the region in the eighteenth-century wars between Britain and France, known in North America as the French and Indian Wars.

Thanks in large part to their Haudenosaunee allies, the British prevailed in that conflict. They gained control of the St. Lawrence in 1763 and knocked France out of contention for control of the Great Lakes. But within fifteen years, they were at war once again, this time against their own colonial subjects. The American War of Independence was perhaps the most destructive conflict in the two hundred years of European-backed warfare to disturb Iroquoia. The Oneidas primarily sided with the American colonists, while the other Haudenosaunee nations backed the British, or so goes the simplified version of events. In fact, it was far more divisive even than that. Individual Oneidas fought on both sides, though on balance the help they offered the American side was more significant, particularly in the Siege of Fort Stanwix and Battle of Oriskany in 1777. Haudenosaunee leaders who attempted to tread a path of neutrality found themselves drawn into the conflict as their warriors often ignored elders and rushed off to fight. Raiding parties destroyed nearly every village in Iroquoia, including the Oneida capital of Kanonwalohale (Oneida Castle on today's map). By the end of the war, most of the Oneidas lived in dismal conditions as refugees in Schenectady or Massachusetts. Most other Haudenosaunee people were also refugees, in camps supplied by the British at Niagara.

Central New York's wilderness battles were of the utmost importance in explaining the outcome of the war. The great three-pronged thrust that the British planned to destroy the rebellion in the summer of 1777 was thwarted in large part by the Oneida and American resistance at Stanwix and Oriskany. Barry St. Leger's army, which had come across Lake Ontario to Oneida Lake, was supposed to proceed down the Mohawk Valley and meet with General Burgoyne's army marching down the Champlain corridor to Albany. Instead, they were forced to retreat after a failed siege and a bloody battle that pitted Haudenosaunee against Haudenosaunee at Oriskany. Without hope of reinforcement from the west, Burgoyne was also defeated at Saratoga. These victories prompted France to join the war, paving the way to the final British surrender at Yorktown in 1781.

In the aftermath of the war, the Oneidas returned and rebuilt Kanonwalohale, but nothing was ever the same. They were feted, to some extent, by American leaders who acknowledged their key role in the conflict. Compared to other Haudenosaunee nations, who were treated as defeated enemies, the Oneidas were given promises in a treaty with the United States at Fort Stanwix in October 1784 that they would be "secured in the possession of the lands on which they are settled." But with a small, weakened, and impoverished population, voracious Americans knew that the Oneidas would not be able to guard a six-million-acre homeland against westward-spreading settlers and speculators; nor did the state of New York feel it in their own interest to help them do so. Quite the contrary, the state wanted to acquire as much of Iroquoia as it could to stave off rival claims to the area and pay its debts by selling the land on at much higher prices. In 1788, New York signed treaties with the Onondagas, Cayugas, and Oneidas in which they paid relatively small sums for huge expanses of land. The Onondagas and Cayugas kept 64,000-acre reservations. The Oneidas kept a 250,000-acre reservation in what are now Oneida and Madison Counties. Some of the Oneidas' leaders were fed lies and told that the transfer of land was a lease rather than a sale.

To prevent states taking advantage of Indians in treaties such as these, the United States government (with a new Constitution in 1789) passed the Indian Nonintercourse Act in 1790. It stipulated that federal representatives must be present at any treaty signing where Indian land was sold. New York officials nevertheless persisted in chipping away at the Oneidas' reservation, procuring sale after sale, ignoring the law. The largest of these sales was in a 1795 treaty where 132,000 acres were sold by a faction of Oneidas to the state with no federal oversight. The United States government was aware of the sale but was not prepared to enforce its own law, despite having pledged again at the 1794 Treaty of Canandaigua to protect the Indians on their land.

Over the next four decades, further parcels were sold off to the state of New York at first in large pieces and, when there were no large pieces left, in transactions as small as seventy-five acres. With their land base and chance at self-sufficiency dwindling, most Oneidas reluctantly emigrated out of New York State to Wisconsin and Ontario. Those who remained lived mainly in poverty on small plots hidden away in rural Madison and Oneida Counties, or as guests on the Onondaga Reservation near Syracuse, until the final decades of the twentieth century.

The land of the Oneidas was sold by the state, mainly to wealthy speculators and land companies who then sold it on to settlers. In the pioneer era, thousands of land-hungry sons of New England built log cabins to see them through their first years, then set up farms and homesteads. They cut down the seemingly infinite forest, burned the timber, and sometimes sold the ashes down the Hudson or the St. Lawrence after turning them to potash. Many of them interacted with the Oneidas—some as friends, some as swindlers, some as traders, and others as squatters on their remaining land. Non-Native Americans and Oneidas fought the British and their Indian allies again during the War of 1812 on the shores of Lake Ontario, and once again events there had a crucial bearing on the outcome of the war.

Peace with Britain in 1815 ushered in a new era of westward expansion. The long-held prediction that the Mohawk-to-Ontario corridor would be the key to unlock the vast interior of the continent proved true. Engineers dug canals, first to make transport on the existing route easier, then to circumnavigate its most challenging features entirely, including the Oneida Carry. In the 1820s, the state directed the construction of the Erie Canal straight across what had only recently been the Oneida Reservation. It transported passengers from the east and freight from the expanding west. Later the New York Central Railroad, the Barge Canal, and finally the New York State Thruway occupied that vital corridor.

America was shaped by it. Today millions of Americans in the Midwest and beyond have ancestors who came there by canal or rail. Millions more in cities from Buffalo to Albany and, most of all, in New York City, live in urban environments that grew to preeminence due to the Erie Canal's success. Had the Oneidas remained in possession of their original reservation and the state not obtained and dug through it, the subsequent development of the United States would have played out much differently. Had they received rent or tolls for allowing the canal to pass through their land, the Oneidas' history may not have been marked by two mass emigrations and multigenerational poverty.

Instead, in the first half of the nineteenth century, the former Oneida lands, including nearly all areas of the former reservation in Oneida and Madison Counties, were rapidly populated with new American settlements. They became a unique and highly important part of the United States. Waves of religious revivalism crashed with tremendous force there in the 1820s and '30s. Preachers like Charles Grandison Finney set church buildings and meeting halls ablaze with evangelical passion. The Oneida Community—religious perfectionists from Vermont who practiced a form of free love—started a new life there in the cabins left behind by the emigrant Oneida Indians in 1848. It became the most successful utopian experiment in American history. The factory they started continued manufacturing operations on the former Oneida Reservation until 2004.

The sectional tensions of antebellum America and the advent of the Civil War arguably had as much to do with events and people in this central part of the most powerful state in the Union as it did with the plantations of the south. Abolitionists like Gerrit Smith from Madison County spoke and campaigned ceaselessly about the evils of slavery. Hundreds of central New Yorkers housed fugitive slaves escaping to freedom on the Underground Railroad. Anti-slavery conventions in places like Utica, Peterboro, and Cazenovia brought together the nation's most prominent abolitionists, Black and white, male and female. John Brown found a welcome reception and financial support there on his path to Harper's Ferry. During the Civil War, it was one of the most solidly pro-Lincoln areas of the nation. Thousands of young men joined the Oneida regiments and other forces that went by rail or by ship to fight in the South, many never to return.

On the nineteenth-century map, the region that had once been the Oneida homeland was bracketed by two of the North's most important cities: Syracuse and Utica. Strictly speaking, the land upon which they were built had not been Oneida Indian possessions, or at least not exclusively so. The former was in the domain of the Onondagas rather than the Oneidas, and the latter was near where Oneida lands gave way to those of the Mohawks. The term "central New York" is a confounding one, which has been defined differently by various writers and agencies at different times. But for the purposes of this book, it will refer to the ancestral homeland of the Oneidas plus the two large cities that bookend it. In the canal and railroad era in which these cities experienced exponential growth, they became major industrial centers and entrepots, the host cities of thousands of immigrants who came to live and work there first before moving into smaller towns and villages in between. Many New York Oneidas themselves lived mainly in the Syracuse area for nearly a century between the Civil War and the 1960s.

From the mid-nineteenth century onward, Welsh, Irish, and German immigrants changed the cultural and religious profile of the region. Later waves of Italians, Poles, Jews, and Russians arrived around the turn of the twentieth century. Finally, before, during, and after World War II, thousands of African Americans came, not as immigrants but as migrants from the south looking to start new lives in cities with better economic prospects, free of Jim Crow laws. They moved into neighborhoods that were being evacuated by previous immigrant groups who joined the so-called "white flight" to the suburbs in the post-war era.

After 1970, the cracks in central New York State's economy and social fabric became fissures. The manufacturing jobs that had underwritten the area's prosperity for decades started disappearing by the thousands. Black neighborhoods in urban areas were plunged into poverty. The entire region struggled with economic stagnation and depopulation as one major employer after another left for reasons ranging from global competition to the end of the Cold War.

§

This is the story of a people's homeland, a biography of the land of the Oneidas from the earliest times to the present day. To the Oneida Haudenosaunee, it is sacred ground.[3] It is a homeland in which they have been, since the early nineteenth century, a minority, but in which they have always maintained a presence.

For decades this Indian presence would have gone completely unnoticed to most people passing through it. The Oneida people residing on their ancestral homeland lived mainly in poverty. But in the last three decades all that has changed. New legislation allowed the Oneidas to open a casino which has been phenomenally successful, bringing in millions of dollars and fundamentally changing the fortunes of the original occupants of this land.

The Oneidas of New York, Wisconsin, and Ontario also gained the right to pursue land claims in federal courts through a stunning test case victory in the US Supreme Court in 1974. For nearly four decades, they vigorously pursued two different land claims in court called the "pre-1790" and "post-1790" claims respectively. The post-1790 claim was for the

250,000 acres of the Oneida Reservation as defined in the 1788 Treaty of Fort Stanwix. It hinged on the fact that the 1790 Indian Nonintercourse Act forbade the state from purchasing Indian land without federal oversight or authority. The pre-1790 claim was for the much larger six-million-acre area that the Oneidas possessed before the 1788 sale of land to New York State, which most Oneida leaders thought at the time was a lease.

Other Indian land claims were also filed in federal courts from the 1970s onward, but the Oneida case was particularly prominent. Not only was it the oldest and largest of the cases, but there was a bitter irony in that the people who had done so much to help the Americans to win their independence, and who had been promised repeatedly by the United States government that their lands would be protected, were so badly defrauded. The fact that these lands, through which the Erie Canal was dug, were of such immense value to the expansion of the American Republic lent support to the argument that if the law had been adhered to, the Oneidas would have remained strong and prosperous on their own lands.

This book tells the story of the Oneida lands in central New York both before and after they were coveted and settled upon by Euro-Americans. The title, *Land of the Oneidas*, conveys two truths. The first is that this was and is the ancestral land of the Oneida Indians, lands that were sold to the state of New York in treaties that were exploitative and mainly illegal. The second is that there are other Oneidas, entities that appropriate the Indian name but are American rather than Native American in character. There is a city of Oneida and a village of Oneida Castle, the latter built atop the site of Kanonwalohale. There is Oneida County in which Utica, Rome, and dozens of towns, villages, and rural crossroads grew up, each with a history of its own. The "Oneida woods" was a name familiar in pioneer days for any part of the highly sought-after former Oneida Indian land that was being opened for settlement. The Oneida Community was a utopian commune, famous and notorious for its sexual practices. Its successor, Oneida Limited, became a household name as one of the world's largest silverware producers in the twentieth century.

The Oneida Carry, Oneida Lake, Oneida Creek, and the Oneida River shaped the destinies of both the Oneida Indians and of the state of New York. Indeed, insofar as they exist at a critical point on what was the most strategically important route from the Atlantic coast to the Great Lakes and beyond, these places and the battles fought over them exerted a determining impact on the history of the United States and of the entire North American continent.

§

This is a land that has captured the imagination of great American writers from James Fenimore Cooper in his *Leatherstocking Tales* to Walter D. Edmonds, whose 1936 novel *Drums along the Mohawk* became a beloved classic as well as a Hollywood smash hit. The Haudenosaunee Confederacy, the New York frontier in the American Revolution, and the Erie Canal figure in most broad-scoped histories of the United States. It is difficult to describe the nation's origins and its spread westward without them. Some historians have provided detailed studies of certain aspects of the Oneida lands and their history. Iroquoian studies emerged in the nineteenth century beginning with L. H. Morgan's *League of the Iroquois* (1851). In the twentieth century, archaeologists and ethno-historians conducted extensive studies of Haudenosaunee prehistory. Since the 1970s, some of these studies have focused on the early Oneida sites, meaning we now have a better picture than ever before of how and where Oneidas and other peoples lived on this land before contact with Europeans began changing their way of life.[4] In the last three decades, historians have written important studies of the Haudenosaunee, including the Oneidas, during the early years of colonization, the French and Indian Wars, the American Revolution, and in the era of dispossession that followed it.[5]

The land as it existed after the balance tipped towards white settlement in the pioneer era has also received some scrutiny from historians. Starting in second half of the nineteenth century, great tomes of county history were produced for all the counties of central New York beginning with Pomroy Jones's *Annals and Recollections of Oneida County* (1851). Some of these number in the thousands of pages and cover the early histories of every town, village, bank, industry, and church that existed at the time of writing. The earliest of these were written while many of the first white settlers in the area were still alive. Later ones, published in the final quarter of the nineteenth century and first decade of the twentieth, focused extensively on the region's leading men, particularly those who patronized local institutions and championed charity in a pre-income tax era.

Recently, historians reassessed the period in which the wilderness of Iroquoia was first opened to white settlement, divided up, and provided with American political structures, judges, officials, and dignitaries. The realities of life in Oneida's pioneer days were as much about dealing with murders and crimes between Indians and non-Indians, controlling unruly squatters, and dealing with rum-fueled feuds at frontier taverns as they were about planting the seeds of American democracy on new and fertile ground.[6]

Historians of the nineteenth century have studied central New York as a hotbed of religious fervor and social progressivism that exerted enormous influence in the antebellum North.[7] The Oneida Community has a historiography all its own. Scores of books and scholarly articles dissect the sexual and spiritual life of the several hundred men and women that lived and breathed a philosophy of "Bible Communism" in central New York for over thirty years.[8] But detailed studies of central New York as an industrial powerhouse, a land in which immigrants became Americans in an era of vast social change, are fewer and farther between.[9] Even rarer are studies of the agricultural regions in which the vestiges of the original Yankee invasion of the "Oneida woods" can still be found.

The boom and devastating bust of the central New York economy in the twentieth century has had few in-depth chroniclers. The Oneida Indian land claims and growth of the Oneida Indian Nation's business enterprises received extensive coverage from journalists in the local and national press. But the way they shaped the politics and tested the social fabric of the region since 1970, and particularly since the opening of the Turning Stone Casino in 1993, is a fascinating story of its own and worthy of greater attention.[10]

Despite the rich body of historiography, no attempt at a complete history of this region has been written in over eighty years, and none have focused specifically on Oneida land.[11] Since William F. Galpin's four-volume *Central New York: An Inland Empire* (1941), new ways of understanding the region's past have emerged, and of course eight additional decades have been added to the story—decades that transformed the region in ways that could hardly have been foreseen in 1941. The Oneida land claim has gained the attention of Supreme Court justices and made national news since the 1970s. The Oneida Indian Nation of New York's current leader, Ray Halbritter, received widespread media attention, first for his role in building up the nation's businesses and more recently for spearheading a "Change the Mascot" campaign that led to the renaming of the Washington Redskins NFL franchise in 2020–21. The Oneida land claims and the long process of reckoning with them since 1970 have shown that this part of New York State has a complicated relationship with the past—one that shapes its present and will continue to impact its future.

This book has two central arguments. The first is that what happened in the land of the Oneidas, before and after it was exclusively the home of the Oneida people, is of great significance—locally, of course, but also nationally and internationally. This has always been a key strategic battleground in the most significant struggles for power—whether military, political, or moral—in North American history. The competition for control in the age of empires, the battle for freedom in the American Revolution, the struggle for the interior of the continent that culminated in the engineering triumph of the Erie Canal, and the war for America's soul in the fight against slavery all had front lines that ran across this land.

The making of an industrial nation fueled by immigrant labor and the descent of once-thriving urban centers into racially divided rustbelt cities happened here, too. Today, the region is a major political battleground where recent elections have been among the most bitterly contested in the nation. This book shows how America was created on Indian land and argues that, to a significant extent, what happened on *this* Indian land created America as we know it. This process continues.

The second is that in central New York, perhaps more than in any other region in the United States, the past has never remained neatly in the past. It resurfaces constantly in the present, in ways that can range from thrilling to upsetting to uncanny. DeWitt Clinton passed through the region in 1810 scouting the route for the future Erie Canal that would connect New York to the great west but found himself face to face with an ancient Indian people in Oneida whose continuing existence he found both fascinating and problematic. Settlers in the region encountered the skeletons of Indians as they plowed their fields—some thought they found the remains of an ancient race of giants.[12] Gerrit Smith ran a philanthropic business empire that he used to finance abolitionist activities but struggled to come to terms with its origins in his father's less-savory procurements of vast expanses of Oneida Indian land. James Fenimore Cooper's *Leatherstocking Tales* sought to recapture aspects of central New York's past, to preserve and contrast them with what he saw as a more dismal, less-heroic present.

Since the nineteenth century, each transport line across Oneida lands has run alongside the one that proceeded it; the I-90 Thruway is yards away from the New York Central line, the Erie Canal, the Seneca Turnpike Road (once an Indian trail), and the Mohawk River in many places. Waves of immigrants moved into neighborhoods only recently dominated by the previous wave. Rural villages center around deteriorating wooden Protestant churches built by New Englanders in the early days of white settlement, reminders of a pioneer past. In the post–World War II era, Oneida Limited company executives burned an entire truckload of nineteenth-century documents pertaining to the Oneida Community to erase a problematic history. A swathe of urban Rome was demolished to make way for a reconstruction of eighteenth-century Fort Stanwix, erected on its original site in the middle of the city in the 1970s. Today, it is still there, the wooden battlements a short walk away from boarded-up nineteenth-century factory buildings and twentieth-century strip-malls.

More recently, battles raged over events that took place decades or even centuries ago. The assistance offered by the Oneida Indians to the Americans in the War for Independence was described repeatedly to explain their sense of betrayal over the loss of their land, as they sought compensation for it in federal courts and in talks with state officials. Opponents to the land claims, meanwhile, likened themselves to patriots of the Revolutionary War era, protesting an unfair tax system. The details of treaties signed between 1785 and the 1840s have been scoured in legal case after legal case. Rows erupted in 2015 when a new Oneida Indian-owned casino was built in the hometown of the celebrated author L. Frank Baum, best known for his *Wonderful Wizard of Oz*, who made viciously anti-Indian statements while editing a South Dakota newspaper in the 1890s.

The role of central New York as a hotbed of abolitionist activity has also been reexamined and celebrated with a statue commemorating the 1851 rescue of a fugitive slave from slavecatchers in Syracuse. At the same time, the ways in which Syracuse became an unofficially segregated city in the interwar and post–World War II years are being rediscovered. Recent Black Lives Matter protests against the unfair treatment of African Americans locally and nationally have used the statue as their meeting point, calling out the contrast between central New York's past and present.

Most of all, the continued presence of the Oneida Indians on this land links its present (and future) inextricably to its earliest history. Although that presence was hidden from view for over a hundred years, between the departure of large parties of Oneidas to Wisconsin and Canada and the emergence of the land claims cases in federal courts, there is no mistaking it now. The Turning Stone Casino attracts thousands of visitors per year. Its twenty-story hotel tower is visible from the New York State Thruway and from the high hills where the Oneidas built their villages centuries ago.

America is built on land that once belonged to Native peoples. This book shows how this happened on the land of one Indian tribe, the Oneida Haudenosaunee. The story told here raises questions about social justice, of how people living in the present should reckon with wrongs done in a distant or not-so-distant past. In this way it is part of much bigger story, one that is playing out all over America now. There are no easy answers, but it does show what attempts have been and are being made.

Chapter 1

Origins, The Ice Age to 1635

Long before the advent of the Haudenosaunee and longer still before it was surveyed by Euro-Americans, central New York State lay under thousands of feet of ice. About twenty-five thousand years ago, a great glacier known as the Laurentide Ice Sheet reached down from the Arctic, covering most parts of present-day New York State. Its retreat around fifteen thousand years ago marked the end of the Ice Age. Melted ice pooled in Glacial Lake Iroquois, an enlarged version of current Lake Ontario. That enormous lake also covered the flat central corridor of what later became the Oneida peoples' homeland, including Oneida Lake and the upper Mohawk Valley. It drained not via the St. Lawrence River (which had yet to form, still covered with ice) but rather via the Mohawk and Hudson to the Atlantic.

The first humans entered present-day New York State just under thirteen thousand years ago. The land at that time was slowly changing from tundra to forest. It was home to mastodons, woolly mammoths, and giant beaver.[1] These Paleoindian hunters carried stone tools. Their spearheads have been found in places like Bouckville in Madison County—near where the Oneida Indians established their main villages thousands of years later—with the distinctive fluted shape that characterized the weapons of these roaming peoples. Three Paleoindian sites known as the Owlville Cluster have recently been discovered near the drained marshes called the "muckland" around Canastota in northern Madison County, providing evidence of seasonal encampments and tools made from chert stone that were probably carried into the area from further down the Mohawk Valley.[2]

As the ice sheet retreated further north into Canada, Lake Iroquois's water levels dropped by hundreds of feet then rose again, before finally taking on the shape and shoreline of the Lake Ontario of the present day.

Cataclysmic flooding occurred as the waters of the great lakes shifted outlets, eventually finding a permanent route to the sea via the St. Lawrence. Some archaeologists have suggested that there was little if any human activity during this period of grand-scale environmental changes, but more recent evidence suggests that hunter-gatherer populations maintained a presence in the area, albeit in extremely small numbers.[3]

A change to a warmer climate by 4000 BCE made for a more inviting environment in which to hunt, fish, and gather food. Nomadic peoples may have roamed the woodlands of central New York in the Late Archaic Period (c. 4000–1500 BCE). There were human settlements in the Finger Lakes region, notably at Lamoka Lake, around 2800–2200 BCE. In the 1920s, archaeologists unearthed hundreds of artifacts from the period there, including fishhooks made of bone, notched stones used to anchor fishing nets, and cooking hearths. A later hunter-gatherer culture established a home near Brewerton at the outlet of Oneida Lake.[4]

These cultures may have disappeared as other prehistoric groups penetrated the region or changed as new ideas and cultural practices came in through association or trade with people further south in the period known as the Frost Island Phase (c. 1250 BCE). The west end of Oneida Lake was used once again by hunter-gatherers in the Meadowood Phase, about 998 BCE. Later groups of people from the Point Peninsula culture also lived on the west end of Oneida Lake around 240 CE. One skeleton from this period was uncovered near Norwich in Chenango County that had been buried with a necklace of five shark teeth, suggesting wider connections to the Atlantic, nearly two hundred miles away.[5]

Twentieth-century archaeologists led by William A. Ritchie argued that the ancestors of the Haudenosaunee probably came into New York State around 900 CE and lived in the Broome County area, near Binghamton. These members of the Owasco Culture lived in longhouses, used pottery, and practiced agriculture. They farmed corn, beans, and squash to supplement their hunting and fishing—all clear links to the practices of the later Haudenosaunee. They wove baskets and sewed with bone needles.[6] Some archaeologists, notably Richard MacNeish, took this interpretation further, arguing for an "in situ" model by which the Owasco developed from the widespread Point Peninsula culture. This interpretation supports the view that the Haudenosaunee developed in broadly the same region for over a millennium.

That explanation of the origins of the Haudenosaunee has come under attack more recently, however, from archaeologists disputing the

Point Peninsula link. Dean Snow argued in the 1990s that the ancestors of the Haudenosaunee came to New York sometime after 900 CE and displaced the Point Peninsula people who lived there. In his analysis, the Owasco people migrated north from the Appalachian region. Archaeological sites dating from 775 CE in central Pennsylvania show that people there grew maize and squash and produced pottery that closely resembles later Iroquoian styles. These groups lived in more densely populated, semipermanent settlements than the nomadic Paleoindians of New York. They had a matrilocal settlement system in which men would join and live with their wife's family, like the later Haudenosaunee, and probably spoke a proto-Iroquoian language. But the "in situ" and the "migration" hypotheses need not be mutually exclusive. The Owasco culture could have been formed through a fusion of people who migrated into the region with peoples who were already residing in the area.[7]

Groups of Owasco people splintered off over several centuries from about 1000 CE, moving into new areas and taking their proto-Iroquoian language with them. Some settled along the eastern shore of Lake Ontario and the St. Lawrence River. The Iroquoian group that later became known as the Hurons or Wyandots migrated to southern Ontario. Other groups went south to the Carolinas. As the groups separated, their language evolved into separate and distinct dialects. It is from the groups that settled along the east-west axis in what is now New York State, from the Finger Lakes to the Mohawk Valley, that the "Five Nations" or Haudenosaunee—the Seneca, Cayuga, Onondaga, Oneida, and Mohawk—descend.

Late Owasco Period (1275–1350 CE) artifacts include pots with castellated collars and smoking pipes, sometimes decorated with inlaid human faces or animal shapes. Owasco settlements tended to be small and were scattered over a wide region, but in the fourteenth century, their longhouses grew larger, sometimes up to 39 meters in length (large enough for six nuclear families) and were typically 6 meters wide. One extreme example from this period at the Howlett Hill site, southwest of Syracuse, was 102 meters long. Some Late Owasco villages in Onondaga County held between 330 and 500 people. They were fortified. Two, or in some cases three, rings of palisades made of tall saplings twisted deep into the ground wrapped around the village in an oval shape.[8]

By the fourteenth and fifteenth centuries, the Owasco culture in central New York faded, or rather transformed into what Europeans later called the Five Nations. Settlement patterns continued towards clustering into ever-closer communities, probably for better defense in war. Each of the Five Nations established large villages with hundreds of inhabitants. Their languages became more distinct from one another, and each took up permanent residence in a separate geographic area. The Senecas grouped along the Genesee River, the Cayugas to the east of Cayuga Lake. The Onondagas came together near present-day Syracuse, and the Mohawk nation inhabited two main sites in the Mohawk River valley (see Figure 1.1).[9]

The origins of the Oneidas are the most mysterious of the Five Nations. They were the last of the nations to form. They came to inhabit the area between the Onondaga settlements and the Mohawk villages ninety miles to the east. They almost certainly started as a splinter group, either of Onondagas or of Mohawks (or some combination of the two), who moved away from the rest, probably around the fifteenth century. Early Oneida pottery samples are closer to Mohawk than Onondaga in style, and the Oneida language is more closely related to Mohawk.[10] Geographically, however, the earliest Oneida sites were closer to the Onondagas. Around 1500 CE, the main

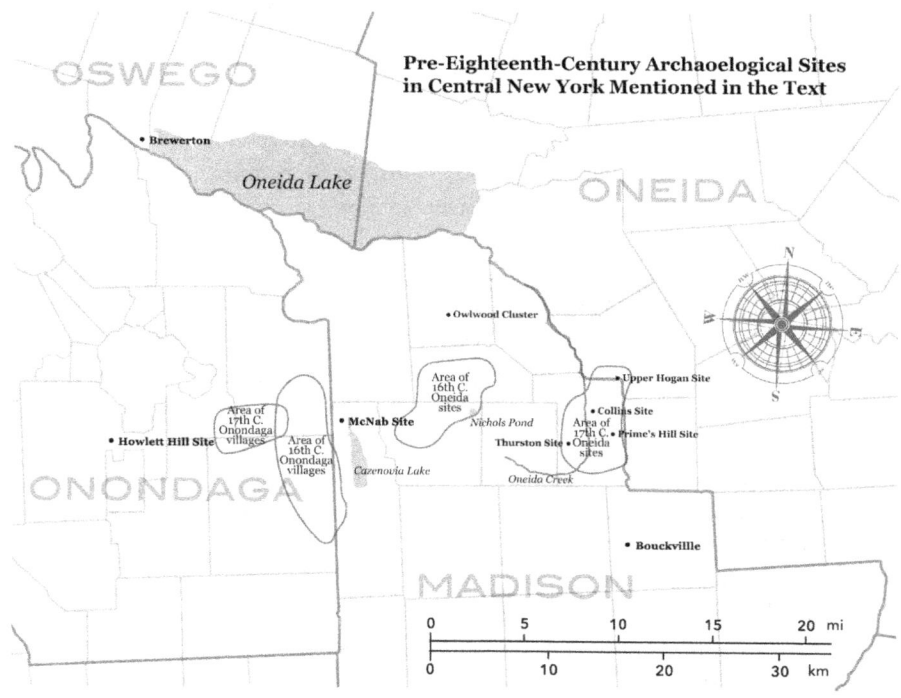

Figure 1.1. Pre-Eighteenth-Century Archaeological Sites in Central New York.

18 | Land of the Oneidas

Onondaga villages were in the Pompey area west of Cazenovia Lake. They also had a settlement on the north end of the lake known to archaeologists as the McNab site.[11] The earliest known Oneida villages at the Dougherty, Nichols Pond, Tuttle, Buyea, Goff, and Moon sites were all less than ten miles away.[12] Later Onondagas built their villages further to the west and Oneidas further to the east, gradually becoming two separate nations.

The Oneidas hunted and roamed a vast area, but their main villages from the fifteenth century onward were located south of Oneida Lake, mainly along Oneida Creek and in the hilly country of what is now Madison County. Before the eighteenth century, it was normal to move village locations every five to twenty years. The Oneidas call themselves *Onyota'a:ka*, meaning "the People of the Standing Stone"—an allusion, perhaps, to a sacred stone that they carried with them each time they relocated.[13] In the sixteenth century, the Oneida population may have numbered between one thousand and fifteen hundred, similar in size to the Mohawks to the east, though estimates vary widely. The overall population of the Five Nations may have been as large as twenty or thirty thousand by the early seventeenth century.[14]

The Haudenosaunee all spoke various dialects of a common language family, markedly different from and unintelligible to the Algonquin languages spoken by most of the non-Iroquoian tribes of the northeast and eastern Canada. The Haudenosaunee also differed from their Algonquin neighbors in that they were comparatively stationary, living in semipermanent villages as opposed to nomadic camps. Their longhouses were large and sturdy structures, built of bent saplings covered with elm bark. Like the earlier settlements to the west, the Oneidas surrounded their villages with high palisades that protected them from attack. Often these were multilayered with a complex maze-like path leading from the outer to the inner gates. Within the longhouses several families lived together. Society within the tribe revolved around matrilineal clans. In Oneida, the three clans—the Wolf, Bear, and Turtle—were headed by clan mothers. When a man married a woman, he would join her clan and the couple's children would be brought up in the mother's longhouse. The tribes did not have an all-powerful chief, but rather a group of senior sachems who were chosen (and could be removed) by the clan mothers.[15]

Prior to contact with Europeans, the Oneidas used the materials around them to structure their lives in their woodland environment. Their bows and flint-headed arrows were strong enough to pierce human bone. Men used them to hunt deer, bear, and turkey—and as weapons of war.

Their hatchets and axes were made of stone and were strong enough to cut down trees and shape timber. Knives, spearheads, and fishhooks were made of bone. The famous "three sisters" of corn, beans, and squash were sown and cultivated in clearings. Nearly all agricultural work was done by women. Corn and beans were not native to the forests; they were brought into to the area from southern regions between 800 and 1300 CE, around the time that the Haudenosaunee nations and the way of life that prevailed at the time of European contact were taking shape. They also grew sunflower and harvested tobacco, which they smoked in pipes made of clay, antler, or bone. The Haudenosaunee did not hold livestock, though they did on occasion capture bear cubs and feed them until ready to slaughter. They grew hemp, which they used to make rope. Their clothing, moccasins, blankets, and snowshoe webbings were made of animal skins. Combs made of bone and antlers were used for hair. An example from an Oneida site in Madison County of a three-pronged comb from approximately 1550 sits alongside clay pots and a range of other precontact Haudenosaunee artifacts in the New York State Museum in Albany. Men's hair was long, and parts of the head were kept free of hair, not by razors but by plucking.[16] The Oneidas, like other Haudenosaunee people, made canoes, carved pestles and mortars for grinding corn, and fashioned bows, arrows, clubs, flutes, ladders, and lacrosse bats from the various hardwood trees of the forest.[17]

War was part of life in Iroquoia, though it seems to have intensified during the fifteenth century. Archaeological finds show evidence of torture and cannibalism—discarded fingers, for instance—in sites from this period, where previously there had been none. War parties painted themselves and went in search of captives and scalps. Some wore body armor and helmets made of tightly woven reeds that were thick and strong enough to stop an arrow penetrating. Some captives, usually men, would be killed, their heads placed on poles. Others, usually women, were "requickened," or adopted by the tribe to replace one of the dead; they would often be given the same name as the deceased. The Five Nations had not united at that time. They fought neighboring peoples as well as each other. Burials were important. Elaborate condolence ceremonies took place when a loved one died. Bodies were washed and greased in preparation for burial. Precontact graves contained pipes, bowls, and food that were interred with the bodies.[18] Burial offerings became even more elaborate when valuable European-made goods and wampum beads began entering Haudenosaunee villages in the sixteenth and seventeenth centuries.

The Haudenosaunee lacked a writing system. But oral tradition and archaeological information allows us to understand a great deal about what happened in Iroquoia before the arrival of Europeans. By the time of first contact, the Oneidas were part of a strong confederation with their neighboring peoples, which kept the peace between them and strengthened their hand in dealing with surrounding tribes. Before this, however, there was a period remembered in Haudenosaunee lore as a dark time of suffering and endless war between the nations. Killings and kidnappings were avenged by further killings and kidnappings in a cycle of violence that threatened to destroy the Haudenosaunee altogether.

In the incessant war, a tyrannical chief came to power among the Onondagas. Named Tadodaho, he was alleged to have feasted on human flesh and worn snakes in his hair. Among the Onondaga warriors was a particularly able and fierce young man called Hiawatha who, after raid upon raid on the neighboring tribes, grew tired of the violence and disillusioned with Tadodaho's cruel leadership. He encountered a prophet on the shore of Lake Ontario named Deganawido. Later called The Great Peacemaker, Deganawido was a Huron. Said to be born of virgin birth, he left his home on a mission to stop the incessant fratricidal war that he knew was raging among the Haudenosaunee on the other side of the great lake. Deganawido and Hiawatha traversed the Oneida lands and travelled to the chief village of the Mohawks, then back via Oneida to the other Haudenosaunee nations, before finally arriving back at Onondaga to confront the sorcerer chief Tadodaho. They carried with them a vision of peace and unity, which would bring the five nations together in a confederation, where disputes could be settled and mutual decisions made at a council fire. Tadodaho was won over to their vision, partly due to the influence of one of his most trusted female supporters, Jigonhsasee. The five nations agreed to "bury the hatchet" at the Great Tree of Peace in Onondaga territory. The Confederacy of the Haudenosaunee, or the Great League of the Iroquois, was the result. It probably formed between 1450 and 1520, just prior to the arrival of the first white explorers on the north Atlantic coast of the Americas.[19]

The Confederacy brought together people who already had common traditions, beliefs, myths, and legends. The Haudenosaunee shared a creation story, albeit with local differences. They believed that the earth was created when a woman called Atahensic (Sky Woman) fell from a world in the sky down to our own world, which at the time was covered in water. As she fell, animals tried to find a place for her to land. They gathered earth from the sea floor onto the back of a great turtle for her, allowing her to land safely. The land on the turtle's back continued to expand. Sky Woman was pregnant when she fell and soon gave birth to a daughter. The daughter then became pregnant herself and gave birth to twins, one good and one evil. The good twin (Sky Holder) and evil twin (Flint) worked against each other. For all good things that Sky Holder made, such as food, crops, rivers, and animals to eat, Flint (working with his grandmother, who favored him) created an associated evil or obstruction. Later Sky Holder fought and killed his brother, but it was too late to undo Flint's work. In one version of the creation story, when Flint died, the ancestors of the Haudenosaunee sprouted up from the ground on the land they inhabited.[20]

The League was a useful institution. It brought representatives from each of the nations around a council fire, hosted by the Onondagas, to discuss their most important problems, to seek consensus and devise a collective response. It meant that each nation was free from the constant threat of war with each other, allowing them to concentrate instead on fighting their enemies from outside the Confederacy. The Haudenosaunee envisioned their League as a longhouse—the Senecas held the western door, the Mohawks the eastern one, and the Onondagas maintained the central fireplace. Their men could roam much further from home, pushing the limits of their hunting territory northwards and southwards.

Thus, at about the time that the first Europeans began exploring the Americas, the Haudenosaunee were in a powerful position. They would become the scourge of their Algonquin-speaking neighbors to the east and south, the Mahicans of eastern New York and Delawares of the Hudson valley. They were equally dangerous to Iroquoian-speaking people who were not part of the League: the Susquehannocks of the river valley that bears their name, the Hurons of Ontario, the St. Lawrence Iroquoians to the north, and the Wenro, Neutrals, and Erie to the west. Some of these would disappear altogether in the centuries that followed, victims of a combination of diseases brought by Europeans and wars with the Haudenosaunee.

§

The first Europeans to venture into Oneida lands came to bring war. Samuel de Champlain came from the north, landing on the shores of Lake Ontario before venturing into the heart of Iroquoia. It was 1615. Champlain had travelled from Quebec up the St. Lawrence River by canoe, via the Thousand Islands and onto the great lake. With him were a few Frenchmen and a group of allied Huron warriors. Somewhere on the southern shore, they hid their canoes and began traveling on foot into the "territory of the enemy."

They marched for four days covering what he estimated to be sixty or seventy miles. Champlain noted of Oneida Lake that it "contains some fine islands, and is the place where our enemies, the Iroquois, catch their fish, in which it abounds." He recounts that on October 9, the Hurons encountered a group eleven Haudenosaunee, probably Oneidas or Onondagas, who had gone fishing four leagues (about ten miles) from their fort. They took the whole group—four women, three boys, one girl, and three men—prisoner. A Huron chief chopped off the finger of one of the women. Champlain, protesting this brutality, threatened to withdraw his participation in the war party. The Huron explained that the enemy treated their people the same.[21]

The raiders reached a Haudenosaunee settlement on October 10. Some male inhabitants sallied forth to defend it. After an initial skirmish betwixt the "savages," as he called Hurons and Haudenosaunee alike, Chaplain and the few Frenchmen drew firearms. It was the first time a gun was fired in central Iroquoia. Champlain wrote: "We showed them what they had never seen nor heard before; for, as soon as they saw us and heard the arquebus shots and the balls whizzing in their ears, they withdrew speedily to their fort, carrying the dead and wounded in this charge." Champlain and his men then withdrew to build a *cavalier*, a wooden platform that could be lifted above the palisades with "four or five arquebusiers" on top, so that they could rain shots down upon the longhouses below. They also built a large wooden *mantelet*, or shield, that they could use to shelter behind as they advanced to a close enough distance to set the village on fire.

A reinforcement contingent of five hundred Hurons failed to arrive, but Champlain urged them to attack again before the Haudenosaunee could increase their defenses—they had already "begun to barricade themselves and cover themselves with strong pieces of wood." The siege began: "We approached to attack the village, our cavalier being carried by two hundred of the strongest men, who put it down before the village." Three arquebusiers were atop shooting. The Haudenosaunee inside shot arrows and threw stones from the palisade galleries at the advancing force (see Figure 1.2).[22]

Champlain was determined to win and did his utmost to direct the attack. He complains repeatedly in his account that the Indians made blun-

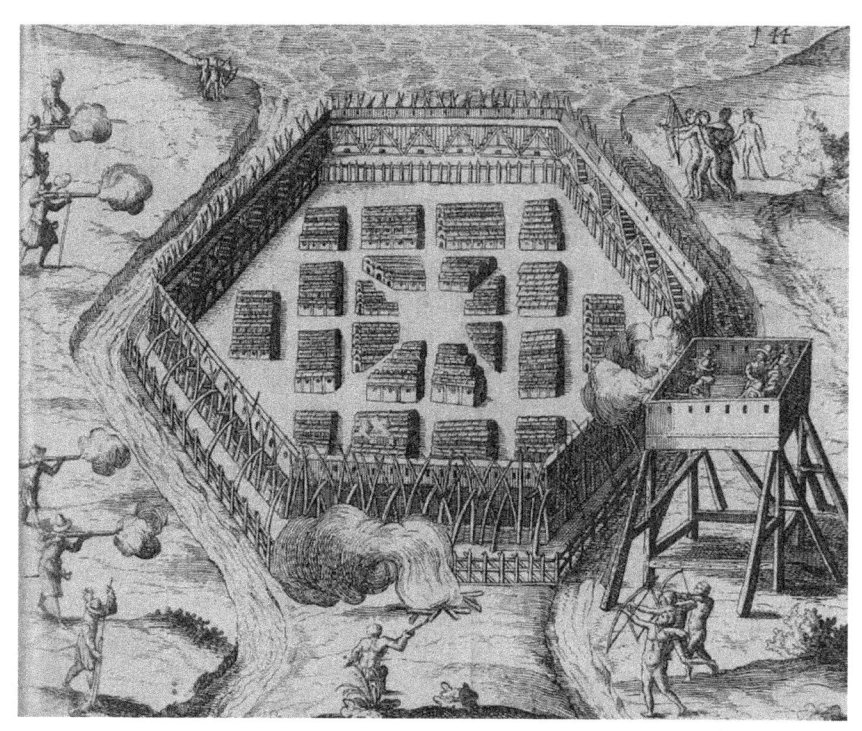

Figure 1.2. Depiction of Samuel de Champlain's siege of an Oneida or Onondaga village in 1615 in his *Voyages et descouvertures faites en la Nouvelle France, depuis l'année 1615, jusques à la fin de l'année 1618.*

ders whenever they failed to follow his orders. In the initial encounter, they blew their cover by attacking too hastily, against Champlain's advice. In the siege, they failed to proceed towards the fort in a quiet and orderly fashion behind the mantelet, but instead pounced, screaming and shooting their arrows indiscriminately into the palisade. Champlain insists that despite being told the best way to set fire to the fortifications, they failed to do it his way and as a result the fire was easily extinguished by the Haudenosaunee, who had a water source within their village that they had diverted from a nearby pond. As a result, enemy arrows "fell upon us like hail." After two Huron chiefs and fifteen warriors were wounded, they retreated, "a disorderly rabble." Champlain himself had been hit by two arrows, one in the leg and one in the knee which, he said, "caused me great inconvenience, aside from the severe pain." Champlain told the Indians it was their duty to attack again, but they only agreed that they would wait a further four days to see if the reinforcements would arrive.

Some further skirmishes took place over the following days, which Champlain reported were only broken up when the arquebusiers came to the Hurons' rescue. Finally, on October 16, when the five hundred reinforcements had still not arrived, they decided to leave. Champlain couldn't walk and had to be carried in a speedily woven basket, again complaining that the way the Indians carried him caused more pain than the wound itself. On their return to the place where they had hidden their canoes, they were caught in an early snow and pelted with hail. Champlain was then ferried by canoe back to Canada for the winter.[23]

The site of the battle has been hotly debated. For decades it was thought that the Oneida village at Nichols Pond south of Canastota in Madison County is where Champlain and his men attacked. In the 1970s, the archaeologist Peter Pratt argued that the battle couldn't have been fought there because the site was abandoned well before 1615.[24] Champlain does not say whether it was an Oneida village; it may have been an Onondaga one. It was certainly somewhere in the vicinity of Oneida Lake, and the encounter with the fishing party after crossing the outlet suggests they may have skirted the lake's south shore from west to east. Archaeologists place the Oneidas' main village in 1615 at the Cameron site near Oneida Creek and the Onondagas' at Pompey Center, but there have been no attempts to locate the battle at either location.

The only other clue is that Champlain says that the village was "near a pond where the water was abundant, and was well supplied with gutters, placed between each pair of palisades, to throw out water, which they had also under cover inside, in order to extinguish fire." This was one of the leading arguments behind the placement of the battle at Nichols Pond. Others have suggested it was in fact Onondaga Lake, but there was no known Onondaga village near that lake at the time either.[25] The word Champlain used to describe the body of water in his original account was *estang* (*étang* in modern French), which clearly suggests a pond rather than a lake. Signs at Nichols Pond—part of a country park owned by Madison County—still proudly proclaim that this was the site of Champlain's siege, the target destination in the first incursion of white men into the land of the Oneidas.[26]

Wherever the attack took place, the significance for the Oneidas (and the Onondagas) could not have been clearer. Their enemies the Hurons now had powerful allies in the French, who were not afraid to bring war to their very doors. Guns and European-style methods of war had been used against them. The war party tried to burn their village to the ground, with them in it. They would be back. Survival would require a change of course.

But what explains Champlain's decision to launch the attack? The entire expedition took him away from Quebec for months, and he was clearly risking life and limb. In part, it was a voyage of exploration. Champlain was an expert explorer, and this was an opportunity to chart new territory for France—one of Champlain's personal passions. Champlain wrote of the expedition that it would "facilitate my undertakings and explorations which, as it seemed, could only be accomplished by [the Hurons'] help," and that he was "glad to find this opportunity for gratifying my desire of obtaining a knowledge of their [the Iroquois'] country."

However, Champlain went not just as an observer but as an active participant, a commander in his own eyes, in war—one he was determined to win. It was not his first time taking sides in a war between the Natives of Canada, with whom the French had formed alliances, and their Haudenosaunee enemies. In 1609, he and his Native companions encountered some Mohawks while exploring Lake Champlain. Champlain himself killed two with one shot of his musket. He fought them again and was wounded by an arrow piercing his ear and entering his neck in 1610. Champlain felt that helping his allies in their wars would "put them the more under obligations to love us." He also saw it as a "preparatory step to their conversion to Christianity."[27]

But above all, there was a great deal to be gained both for Champlain personally and for the colony of New France. Champlain repeatedly petitioned the king to allow his company a monopoly on the fur trade in new areas he discovered. Several monopolies had been granted to Frenchmen since 1599, one of whom was Champlain's partner, the Sieur De Mons, who held it from 1603 to 1607. Champlain's *Compagnie du Canada* trading company finally got it in 1613.[28] The French-allied Indians' greatest value to the French was that they procured and traded pelts, especially beaver pelts. These were by far the most highly prized export from New France to Europe; fur was Canada's cash crop. The Haudenosaunee, by warring on them, disrupted that trade. The Iroquois "were always on the road disrupting their passage," wrote Champlain—fur routes along the St. Lawrence and Ottawa Rivers had been repeatedly targeted by Oneida and Onondaga raiders. Furthermore, the Dutch were now trading with the Haudenosaunee and assisting them in making war with the French-allied Indians.[29] Iroquoia was becoming key battleground in an economic and territorial war between European empires in America, a war that would shape, and eventually destroy, the Indians' way of life over the next two centuries.

§

Although a white man in the heart of Iroquoia was unknown before 1615, the presence of Europeans was felt there much earlier. When Columbus landed and explored the islands of the Caribbean in 1492, he was convinced that he had found India, hence the name he gave to the Native people, "Indians." Sensing the commercial opportunities that a new trade route to the East would create, Henry VII of England was keen to get in while the striking was hot. He sent an Italian navigator, Giovanni Caboto (called John Cabot by the English), to traverse the Atlantic and find Asia, taking a more northerly route than the one taken by Columbus. Sailing from Bristol, Cabot reached the coast of Canada in 1497. He too was sure he had reached Asia and returned to England with tales of the abundant fishing waters he had traversed off the coast of Newfoundland. Fishing boats from England, Portugal, and France followed the route to those waters to fill their holds with cod to bring back. Fishermen sometimes met with Natives on the coast of Newfoundland and traded furs for European-made objects. Indians from far inland began bringing pelts to the coast. In Iroquoia, hundreds of miles away, European objects began to appear in villages in the mid-sixteenth century, particularly glass beads, iron axes, and copper kettles.[30]

The first European to come within five hundred miles of Oneida was Giovanni da Verrazzano, a Florentine navigator sailing for the king of France who explored the Atlantic coast of North America in 1524. His ship, *La Dauphine*, had gone in search of a route to the Pacific. Coming up the coast from present-day North Carolina to the mouth of the Hudson, his men kidnapped a Native boy to carry back to France. In New York Harbor, Verrazzano encountered the Haudenosaunees' near neighbors, the Algonquin-speaking Lenape. The Lenape, he said, "came toward us joyfully, uttering very great exclamations of admiration, showing us where we could land with the boat more safely." Further along the coast, he induced Natives to board his ship by offering "little bells and mirrors and many trinkets" and marveled that the Natives were uninterested in cloth and gold.[31]

Jacques Cartier was the first European to sail up the St. Lawrence River in 1534, claiming it for France. He encountered the Iroquoian people who lived between present-day Quebec and Montreal. The St. Lawrence Iroquoians (and others further south along Lake Ontario, sometimes called the Jefferson County Iroquois) dwelled in longhouses and likely spoke a language related to those of the Five Nations but were not a part of the confederation. Little is known of them, as they disappeared between Cartier's visit and Champlain's voyages—most likely the victims of disease, war, or both.

Cartier went back to France with the children of an Iroquoian chief, promising to return with European goods to trade. He returned the following year to search for the Kingdom of Saguenay, which the Indians told him lay to the north and was rich in gold. He sailed as far as Hochelaga (present-day Montreal). Cartier kidnapped more Indians, including the Iroquoian chief Donnacona, before departing. The captives all died in France. In 1540, Cartier made another voyage to establish a colony on the St. Lawrence called Charlesbourg-Royal. However, his failure to return the Indians he had stolen soured his relations with the Iroquoians and the colony was repeatedly attacked. In 1543, it was abandoned.[32]

From these experiences, the Oneidas and their Haudenosaunee allies would have known enough of Europeans by 1600 to be wary but also interested in the commodities they possessed, which could bring prestige, ease, military power, and trade value in intertribal markets. This might have motivated the Five Nations (and other surrounding tribes) to attack and destroy the Iroquoians of the St. Lawrence. The goods being traded with the French by this time included steel knives, hatchets, and axes that were far superior to Native tools and weapons.[33] Gaining and maintaining control of large hunting grounds that gave access to a larger number of pelts to trade and securing preferential links at new European trading posts were the main drivers of the so-called Beaver Wars that raged throughout the seventeenth century. The Haudenosaunee fought the Algonquin and Huron tribes of northeastern North America over nine decades in a spiral of violence that Europeans stoked for their own purposes. Europeans from France, the Netherlands, England, and Sweden all established colonies on the Atlantic coast in the seventeenth century and began penetrating closer to Haudenosaunee lands. They sought the most advantageous positions in the fur trade. Treaties, food, firearms, friendship, alcohol, and religion all served as weapons in the fight for fur.

The Dutch, recently liberated from Hapsburg domination in Europe, were keen to build an empire of their own. They commissioned the English-born explorer Henry Hudson to traverse the Atlantic on the *Halve Maen* (*Half Moon*) in search of the northwest passage to Asia. In 1609 he sailed into New York Harbor and up the Hudson River, trading for furs with Native Americans along the way. The Dutch returned in 1614 to build permanent trading posts at Fort Orange (now Albany) and New Amsterdam on the island of Manhattan. When Champlain launched his attack on central Iroquoia, he was preoccupied with the Dutch threat, for they seemed to be doing exactly what the French had done in Canada—backing Indians in their vicinity in their wars with old enemies to win their loyalty and, with it, an abundance of pelts and furs to sell on to Europe for immense profit.

§

To travel from Albany to Oneida in the dead of winter can be dangerous even driving a modern car with airbags along the smoothly paved and frequently plowed New York State Thruway. It is a 120-mile journey—about two hours on a good run. But upstate New York winters can be treacherous. Heavy snow brings occasional whiteouts most winters. Temperatures can plunge to –20°F (–30°C) and high winds can make for deadly conditions. In 1634, a Dutchman decided to walk it. His name was Harmen Mendertsz van den Bogaert, an employee of the Dutch West India Company and a barber-surgeon at the colonial outpost. He departed Fort Orange on December 11.

The reason: "trade was going very badly." The Haudenosaunee to the west were saying they had made a truce with the French-allied Indians and were now complaining that the French were paying more for pelts than the Dutch were. They wanted the same price. Worse still, peace with the French and their allied tribes could prompt the French to establish a trading post at Oneida Lake, which would starve the Dutch of pelts from all points west of Mohawk country. That would spell disaster for Fort Orange. The future of the colony was at stake. Van den Bogaert brought two companions with him to investigate and negotiate with the Oneidas on the price of furs. "May the Lord bless our journey," he wrote as he set off. Divine good will would be needed. There was more to fear than just the weather. Only six years earlier, the Haudenosaunee had dismembered and burned a Dutch prisoner who had supported their Mahican enemies to the east.[34]

After eight days' march, in a Mohawk village, they enticed an Indian named Sqorhea to guide them to the Oneidas in exchange for "one half piece of duffel, two axes, two knives, and two awls." There were no bridges over the rivers that flow into the Mohawk. They waded through thigh-deep water on December 22, causing their shoes and stockings to freeze "hard as armor plate." They were marooned on Christmas day in a Mohawk village due to heavy snow. Two days later another two and a half feet fell overnight, making walking the next day extremely difficult. After leaving Mohawk country, they needed to camp out each night. They built fires, but Van den Bogaert wrote that "it was so cold in the night I could barely sleep two hours." On one occasion Van den Bogaert said he had to walk all through the night to keep from freezing. One of his companions slept so close to a fire that it badly burned his trousers.[35]

They arrived at the Oneida village on December 30, nineteen days after setting off. It was high up on a hill in what is now Madison County, most likely at what archaeologists call the Thurston site south of Munnsville.[36] The Oneidas formed a peaceable gauntlet through which the visitors entered. Above the entrance, three scalps of slain enemies fluttered in the wind—a symbol of the fate that awaited those who crossed the Haudenosaunee. From the hill, looking northwest, Van den Bogaert noted that he could see "a very large body of water" in the distance—Oneida Lake. Upon inquiring, the Indians told him this was where the French had come to their country to trade.[37] The French controlled Lake Ontario, and they had sailed up the Oneida River the previous summer. The fears of the Dutch were confirmed.

Inside the village, Van den Bogaert found "many acquaintances," presumably Oneidas who had ventured to Fort Orange previously to trade. But the atmosphere was tense. One Indian asked the Dutchmen what presents they had brought them and was disappointed when Van den Bogaert said he had nothing to give. The Indian replied that the group of six Frenchmen who had come in August brought "good gifts" with them. Van den Bogaert saw "good timber axes, French shirts, coats and razors" in the Oneida village. The Oneidas derided the Dutch as "worthless" and "scoundrels." Van den Bogaert recorded that Oneida men surrounded him and his companions, sitting so close to them that if they attacked, they would not have been able to fight back. This continued over several days. On one occasion there were nearly fifty who sat so close they "could have easily grabbed with their hands and killed us without much trouble."

The French, they were told, had given the Oneidas "six hands of seawant [wampum] for one beaver, and all sorts of things in addition."[38] The French were clearly on a charm offensive, attempting to woo the Oneidas away from the Dutch. Wampum beads, made from shells on the Atlantic coast, had symbolic significance for the Haudenosaunee as well as a trade value. Decorative shell beads were traded with coastal Indians before Europeans arrived, but when large-scale trade began, wampum became a sort of currency in the Atlantic colonies. Strung together, they became works of art, tokens of peace and friendship, and visual representations of stories, as well a way of keeping track of price.[39]

The Oneida chief Arenias had just returned from brokering a four-year truce with the French-allied Indians, bringing back wampum as a sign of the deal. On January 1, the Dutch visitors presented Arenias what they could as gifts: "two knives, two scissors, and some awls and needles that we had with us." Although communication was limited due to lack of fluency in a common language, Van den Bogaert did have some basic Iroquois vocabulary and was able to understand when the Oneidas inquired about trade arrangements with the Dutch. They asked in the future for "four hands of seawan and four hands of long cloth" for each large beaver skin. They promised: "If we receive four hands then we shall trade our pelts with no one else." Van den Bogaert promised to relay the proposal to the Dutch governor in Manhattan. The hostility of the first few days subsided and the travelers were given a collection of pelts as a goodwill gesture and a feast of bear meat.[40] Van den Bogaert's journey was difficult in the extreme, but he achieved his main objective. The Dutch were able to secure Haudenosaunee trade and alliance for decades to come.

Van den Bogaert's journal is the first written account of a visit to an Oneida village. He was a careful observer. He noted the dimensions of the village, which had a double palisade and sixty-six longhouses, many of which had fronts that were "painted with all sorts of animals." He was impressed with a gravesite outside the village. The graves were surrounded by palisades and neatly painted red, white, and black. Above the chief's grave was a large wooden bird, and there were paintings of "dogs, deer, snakes, and other animals."

The Oneidas seemed to be prospering, with an abundance of food, particularly fish: "six, or seven, or even eight hundred salmon are caught in one day." In some of the houses he saw "60, 70, and more dried salmon" hanging.[41] The Oneidas fed the guests pumpkin, dried salmon, and bear. Van den Bogaert observed a healing ritual and met some Onondagas who came to visit. The account offers a rare glimpse of Oneida life as it existed before permanent European presence in their lands. But even in 1635, the signs of change were clear. There were a range of non-Native items in the village. The Oneidas had not obtained guns yet but were familiar enough with firearms that they asked the Dutchmen to entertain them by firing their pistols.

Most telling of all, perhaps, was that on his return journey, he came to a Mohawk village in the initial throes of a smallpox epidemic. In the next few decades, the European disease would decimate the Haudenosaunee. With incessant grief and suffering came further reason to fight—boosting population through captive-taking was a prime aim in the spiraling violence of the Beaver Wars. Alcohol and firearms found their way into Indian villages, "gifts" from their European allies.

As for Van den Bogaert and his companions, they reached Fort Orange on January 21, a month and a half after they left. Van den Bogaert was only twenty-three at the time of his mission. He married, had four children, and worked in Manhattan. In 1645 he returned to Fort Orange. In 1647 he was charged with sodomy with his servant, a Black man called Tobias. First, he fled to a Mohawk village but was found there, arrested, and brought back to Fort Orange. He managed to escape from jail. In his flight, he attempted to cross the frozen Hudson River. He fell through the ice and drowned.[42]

§

In 1635 the Oneidas were nearing the height of their power and yet they were at a point of maximum vulnerability. With their Haudenosaunee allies, they were a scourge to rival nations in all directions. In the decades that followed, they would defeat and obliterate some of those that remained. Both the French and the Dutch realized their significance in the fur trade and were vying against each other to win the Oneidas' favor. They seemed to be prospering and thriving. Their first Dutch visitor was amazed with the abundance of food they had in their village, even in the middle of a brutally cold winter. A few European-made goods could be found, but traditional ways of life prevailed in a close-knit, cohesive community.

Yet within several decades all that would change. The Oneidas remained a fearsome fighting force, but food would become scarcer, guns and alcohol would change their lives, and diseases would rack their population. It was about to dawn on Europeans that the Oneidas inhabited a land of immense value to trade and control in North America. The French had discovered the water route from Ontario to Oneida Lake and the Dutch (soon to be supplanted by the English) were aware of the furs from hundreds of miles west that were coming down the Mohawk to Fort Orange. The stage would soon be set for a clash of empires on Oneida lands that would divide the Haudenosaunee and decide the future of a continent.

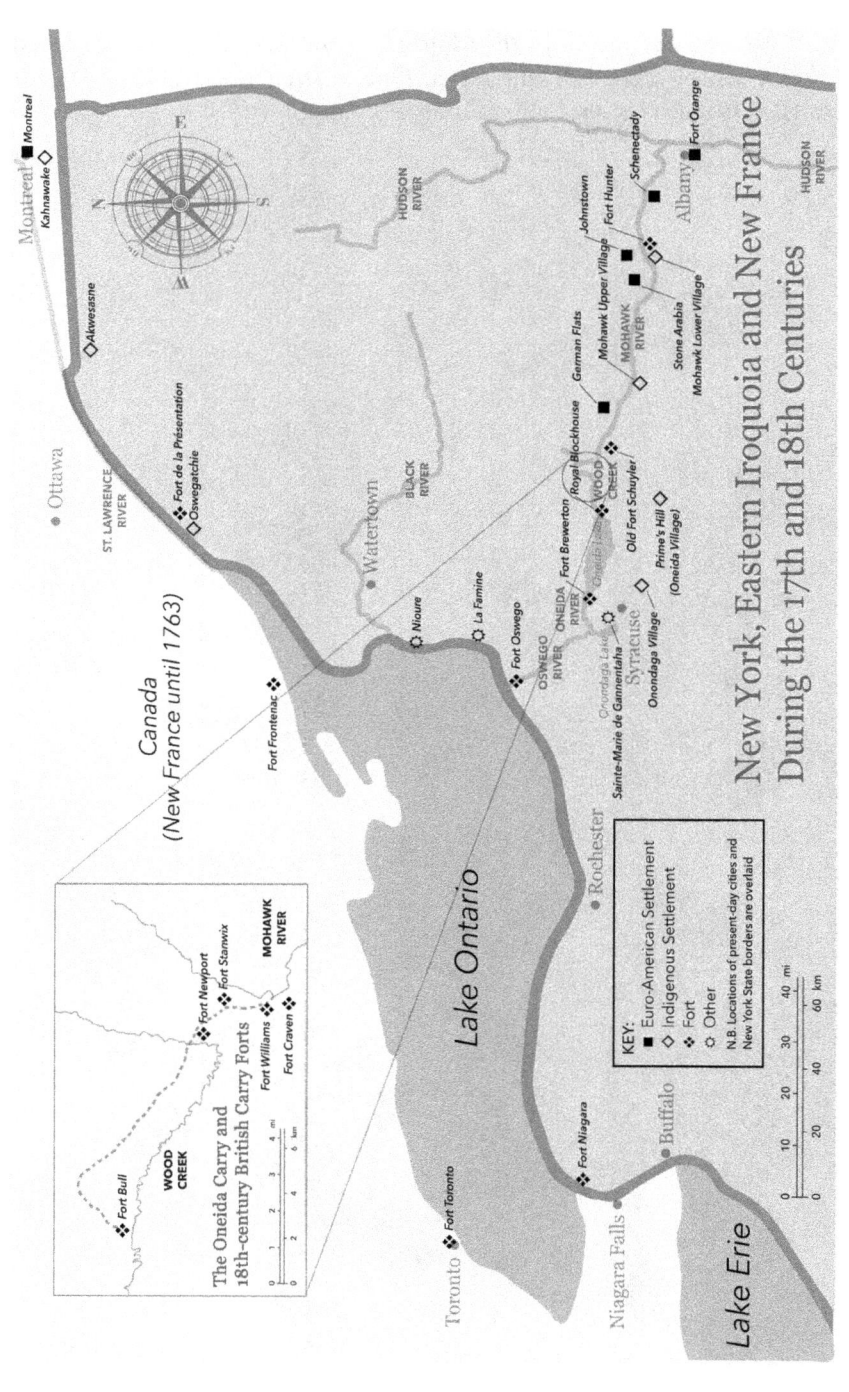

Figure 2.1. New York, Eastern Iroquoia, and New France During the Seventeenth and Eighteenth Centuries.

Chapter 2

The Age of the French, 1635–1763

Thwarted by the Dutch in trade, the French tried a new tack with the Haudenosaunee. One tool they had at their disposal which the Dutch could never match was the Society of Jesus, otherwise known as the Jesuit order. Jesuit priests, ready to suffer all sorts of deprivation to gain souls for Christ, were happy to assist the Catholic French in their colonial efforts. They had been successful in missions among the Hurons and other Native groups in Canada. They lived with the Indians, sharing in their suffering when times were hard. As the Natives of Canada died from smallpox and in incessant war, the priests' spiritual—and sometimes material—support was valuable. They learned Indian languages. They earned genuine converts to Roman Catholicism and grudging respect from many Native people who wanted nothing to do with their religion. The Protestant Dutch, and the English who began colonizing Massachusetts from 1620, were certainly preoccupied with religion. But they did not have the missionary zeal, the ecclesiastical manpower, or the vast resources of the Catholic Church behind them that underwrote the success of the Jesuit mission in Canada.

The truce of 1635 was a distant memory in the early 1650s. Violence raged again between the Haudenosaunee, supplied by the Dutch, and the French-allied Indians. The Hurons had nearly been annihilated by disease and disastrous Haudenosaunee raids into Canada between 1648 and 1650. Increasingly, French Canadian settlers were being targeted. In 1653, the Onondagas stunned the French with overtures of peace. With their main competitors in Canada subdued, they could hope to dominate trade with the French if peace were established. The idea of a French trading post on Oneida Lake was revived. The Haudenosaunee were still bound to the Dutch, but they might have sensed that New Netherland was in trouble. The Dutch had been at war with the English since 1652. The French, by contrast, had just emerged from the Thirty Years' War as the most formidable power in Europe. The Onondagas signaled that the door was open for the French to set up a new settlement in their territory. The Mohawks strongly objected, for they would lose their privileged place as the vital link connecting the western Haudenosaunee nations to the Dutch at Fort Orange. The French (and Jesuits) were delighted, and even hoped the western four Haudenosaunee nations would renounce their ties to the Mohawks, who were determined to carry on with war against the French.[1]

The Oneidas were caught in the middle. In April 1654, the Oneidas made a raid near Montreal and took a young Frenchman prisoner. Some Onondagas arrived in Montreal the following month, unaware of the kidnapping. They told the French that they would ensure the safe return of the prisoner and sent a delegation to Oneida, probably with some "gifts" procured from the French. The Oneidas delivered him up.[2] Sensing that the time was right, the Jesuit father superior dispatched two priests to live with the Onondagas. Father Claude Dablon and Father Joseph Chaumonot were picked. Chaumonot was an experienced Indian missionary with a strong command of the Huron Iroquoian language. He was able to learn the dialects of the Five Nations with relative ease. Dablon was fresh from France, an excellent musician and flautist. The Onondagas had asked specifically for priests. They had learned from Huron and Algonquin captives of their usefulness. A convert to Christianity called Madeleine Teotonharason invited the missionaries to offer Mass in November to a group of Indians who, the next day, helped to construct a chapel. Surrounded by palisades, this chapel called Sainte-Marie de Gannentaha, overlooking Onondaga Lake a few miles from the Indian village, became the hub of the Jesuit mission to the Haudenosaunee.[3]

Early in 1656, the Onondagas held a council that resulted in them asking Dablon to return to New France to seek more missionaries and a colony of Frenchmen to live nearby. Dablon walked on snowshoes in midwinter from the Onondaga lands back to Quebec. The governor sent Dablon back in May with a party of seven, who reached Onondaga in July. By the summer there were over fifty Frenchmen living in the Onondaga mission.[4] The priests began branching out, visiting other Haudenosaunee people, including the Oneidas (called the *Onneiouthronnon* in their writings) in 1656, and delivering "presents" of European-made goods to them. The priests used the present-giving as an opportunity to preach the Gospel. They also sent information back to the French about the Haudenosaunee to help them in their dealings with the various nations.

Before going to Oneida, the priests had been warned that there were plots to kill them. They proceeded just the same. When they arrived, the Oneidas assembled and listened intently as the priests spoke of the Christian faith and of the "bright light of the Gospels, that came to enlighten them." The Jesuits felt that there "was reason to hope for a good harvest" of Oneida souls. They baptized two old men there and several children.[5] Chaumonot was the first Christian missionary in the Oneida lands. His mission was to end dramatically, but he would not be the last.

On October 25, 1657, a group of Oneida warriors shot and killed three Frenchmen in Montreal, "taking the scalps of two of them and bearing them in triumph to their own country." This was almost certainly done without the backing of their sachems and probably with the support of the Mohawks and Dutch. When another group of Oneidas turned up at Montreal on the twenty-ninth to say it hadn't been their people but rather the Cayugas who murdered the French, the governor received gifts from them. But he did not believe their words, particularly after they disappeared in the middle of the following night.[6]

Later that winter, in February 1658, three Mohawk representatives approached the governor to say that they did not know who murdered the Frenchmen, while simultaneously demanding the release of some Mohawk hostages. With a veiled threat, they declared, "The Iroquois and the Dutch are united by a chain of iron, and their friendship cannot be broken."[7] The French governor had had enough and gave them a blunt response, determined not to release the Mohawk prisoners. But there was substance to the Mohawks' warning. The Anglo-Dutch war had ended. New Netherland now had a strong governor, Peter Stuyvesant, who had shown his military strength by taking over New Sweden on the Delaware River in 1655. Furthermore, there was growing resistance to the Jesuits in Iroquoia. Factions within the tribes distrusted the priests, who encouraged converts to dissociate from traditional ways. Non-Christian captives from Canada warned their adoptive tribes that the priests practiced witchcraft and spread disease.[8]

The *Jesuit Relations*, a compendium of the activities of the Jesuits in Canada mainly in the form of letters to the headquarters in France, suggests that the Mohawks held a "very secret council" of anti-Jesuits from all the Haudenosaunee nations. They agreed to murder the missionaries at Gannentaha and to keep the rest as hostages to exchange for their own prisoners held in Canada. A spy among them warned the French. The missionaries in Onondaga, fearful of an imminent slaughter, decided to abandon their post, quoting Jeremiah 51:9 as they fled: "*Curavimus Babylonem, et non est sanata; derelinguamus eam.*" ("We would have healed Babylon, but she is not healed: forsake her.") The entire French colony made an escape in the middle of the night and fled back to Quebec in horrendous winter conditions in March 1658.[9]

War between the Haudenosaunee and French then spun further and further out of control, with Oneida warriors again playing a major part in the hostilities. They acquired a reputation as the "most cruel of all the Iroquois." François Le Mercier, the father superior at Quebec, called them "the proudest and most insolent" nation, despite being the smallest in number.[10] The depictions of hideous torture inflicted on the French by the Oneidas in the *Jesuit Relations* advanced those claims. In June 1658, a band of roughly thirty Oneidas captured three Frenchmen at Three Rivers. French sources say they burned one of the three straight away, then carried the other two off to "put to death at a slow fire."[11] The Dutch were arming the Haudenosaunee with guns, the father superior wrote back to France, enabling them to "hold dominion for five hundred leagues around."[12] We have no balancing sources that tell the Oneidas' side of the story and must approach the Jesuits' stories with caution. Acts of violence and cruelty were almost certainly committed by both sides. It is impossible to say for certain what is fact and what is fiction, but they certainly paint a grotesque picture.

The Onondagas tried to restore peace and invited the Jesuit Father Simon Le Moyne back to their village in 1661. The *Relations* tell us that their efforts were frustrated by further actions by Oneida warriors. One French captive wrote a letter to Le Moyne at Onondaga pleading, "There are two of us prisoners from Montreal at Onneiout [Oneida]. Monsieur Vignal was killed by these Barbarians. . . . My comrade has already had two fingernails torn out. For the love of God, we pray you, repair hither and do your utmost, with presents, to rescue us and take us with you; and then we shall care no longer whether we die or not." Le Moyne himself was nearly taken prisoner by an Oneida war party who threatened him with "hatchets and knives with which they made as if they would cut my throat." Another French prisoner escaped from Oneida to Onondaga, where he was united with Le Moyne. Angry Oneidas attempted to recover their captive seven times before the situation was "adjusted" by the priest, probably by paying them off.[13]

A group of mainly Oneida warriors with some Mohawks made another attack on a group of Frenchmen near Montreal in 1662. According to the *Relations*, they killed some in the fighting, cooked and ate a priest (after removing his scalp), and took three prisoners—one to Mohawk country and two, René and Brignac, to Oneida. In their village, the Oneidas stripped the two Frenchmen and painted their faces. They then made them run the gauntlet, forcing them to "pass between two hedge-rows, so to speak, each person giving them a blow with a stick." Then they were taken to the middle of the village, where they were made to mount a scaffold. René was beaten with a stick and his fingernails were plucked out. They decided to burn Brignac slowly, over two days, before "cutting the body in pieces, putting these into a kettle, and eating them." René, we are told, managed to escape and make his way to New Netherland, eating nothing but herbs along the way.[14]

§

In 1677 the Oneidas received a new type of visitor: an Englishman. Wentworth Greenhalgh was on a tour of Iroquoia. Of the "Onyades" (Oneidas) he wrote: they "have butt one towne which lys aboutt 130 miles westward of ye Maques [Mohawks]." They had recently moved their village. Greenhalgh said it was "newly settled, double stockadoed, but [had] little cleared ground, so thatt they are forced to sent to ye Onondago's to buy corne." There were one hundred houses, and new crops were growing "around about the towne."[15] Exactly like Van den Bogaert before him, he had been sent to investigate rising French influence among the Haudenosaunee and to do what he could to counteract it. He carefully assessed the size and strength of each of the Five Nations and brought his findings back east to the colonial headquarters. But the Dutch administration of New Netherland was no more. Greenhalgh was working for Edmund Andros, the governor of the English colony of New York. His mission was to conclude for England a trade agreement and anti-French alliance with the Haudenosaunee similar to those the Dutch had forged in the 1630s.[16]

Despite its brief resurgence in the 1650s, New Netherland had met its nemesis. Since 1620, it had had to contend with not only New France to the north but also the growth of the English colonies to the south and east. Massachusetts, Rhode Island, and Connecticut grew far more rapidly in population than New Netherland. English settlers constantly impinged on what the Dutch considered to be their territory, but with New Netherland's tiny population—about five and a half thousand in 1660 compared to thirty-three thousand in New England—there was no way to hold them back. The Dutch colony had its own Indian wars with Algonquin-speaking tribes in the Hudson Valley that drained its resources and resolve. The English first captured New Amsterdam in 1664 by sailing four frigates into New York harbor (as it is now known) and demanding surrender. The Dutch took the colony back in August 1673, but then returned it to England in the Treaty of Westminster in 1674. Many Dutch New Netherlanders stayed and lived in the colony that was renamed New York, with some, like the Schuyler and Rensselaer families, becoming part of an Anglo-Dutch elite in the province.[17] The colony's new English administrators turned their attention to the French.

There was reason for the English to worry. Despite decades of war, the French had stepped back into Iroquoia during the precarious transition from Dutch to English rule along the Hudson. It was an ideal power vacuum situation from which they sought to gain. Pro-French and pro-Jesuit factions existed among all the Haudenosaunee nations. Even at the height of war, chroniclers in the *Jesuit Relations* were sure that although the Oneidas and Mohawks were against them, the rest of the Haudenosaunee considered themselves "friends and allies" of the Jesuit cause. Christian converts wanted priests back. The baptisms that they performed for those dying with smallpox gave some comfort in the thought that the departed's soul would find peace in the afterlife. With Dutch trade lagging, Mohawk and Oneida sachems, and even some warriors, could see sense in turning back to the French. In July 1667, a delegation of Oneidas and Mohawks went to New France to request three priests—two for the Mohawk villages and one for Oneida.[18]

The father superior obliged. Father Jacques Bruyas was sent to Oneida with a mission to establish a church there. Bruyas sent his first letter from Oneida on January 8, 1668. In it he reports on the land and people. Oneida Lake was teeming with salmon, he wrote, enough that it "furnishes fish to nearly all the Iroquois." There were trees of apple, plum, and chestnut, and "mulberries and strawberries are so abundant that the ground is all covered with them." But "the nature of the onneiouts," he said, is "altogether barbarous, – that is to say, cruel, secret, cunning, and inclined to blood and Carnage." Worst of all, they had become drunkards. The Dutch were supplying them with brandy, giving them "as much of It as they can carry." When drunk, he wrote, they behaved demonically. One drunken Oneida came to him at the chapel saying he would kill the "black gown . . . who forbids us to have several wives." When he couldn't get into the door, he went home "shouting like a mad man." Bruyas wrote that his greatest sorrow was witnessing four female Andastogué captives being burned alive. He was prevented from baptizing them. In the following year, rumors that Oneidas had been killed and tortured by Frenchmen in Montreal turned the Oneidas against Bruyas. When "sixty kegs of Brandy brought from New Holland" were added to the mix, Bruyas ran away temporarily to avoid being killed. Despite the abundance of food in the village, other missionaries noted that Bruyas was forced to survive on eating nothing but "dried frogs."[19]

The smallpox epidemic was raging. The priest gained some respect by attending to the sick and dying. Some entries in 1670 show the horror. On September 10, "I found a child dead." On the September 20: "There are a great many sick people. A Child that has been baptized goes to Paradise, to join the innocent band of those already there; it is the twentieth since my coming to Onneiout." On October 3: "a woman aged thirty years"; on October 4, "a child'; on October 5: "another little angel"; on October 25: "an old Christian"; and the list goes on. Meanwhile, war parties continued to go out. Bruyas relates the executions by fire of two more captives in the village in the new year 1671, and in April, the arrival of "forty more kegs of brandy."[20] Recent research suggests that the Oneida village Greenhalgh visited in 1677 was at the Collins site in the town of Stockbridge, which was discovered in the 1970s. It likely had a population of about eight hundred based on Greenhalgh's report of a warrior strength of two hundred. That was half the population of a hundred years earlier.[21]

Things began to improve for Bruyas in 1670. While the warriors were away hunting, the priest began holding daily conferences with village elders, who listened attentively. To the west, an influential Onondaga chief named Garakontié had converted to Christianity with the missionary Father Pierre Millet and fully backed the Jesuits' activities among the Haudenosaunee. At the same time a venerated Oneida "whose reputation and example retard[ed] the progress of the Faith during his lifetime" died. Bruyas continued baptizing children in 1671 "most of whom . . . have gone to swell the number of the predestined in Heaven."[22] During the 1670s, some Oneidas joined Christians from other Haudenosaunee nations in moving to a new settlement opposite Montreal. It was called Saint François Xavier du Sault by the French and Kahnawake by the Haudenosaunee.[23] A young Mohawk woman called Kateri Tekakwitha, known for saintly piety, joined them in 1677 and remained there until her death in 1680 at age twenty-four. A chapel was built by her grave and became a pilgrimage site for Christian Haudenosaunee. In 2012 she was canonized as a saint of the Roman Catholic Church.

After five years in Oneida, Bruyas moved on to the Mohawk mission and Father Millet replaced him at Oneida. Baptisms and deaths continued to be the main topics in his letters. He described how even among non-baptized Oneidas, the fear of hell and hope of paradise were perceptible and how some Oneidas had come to see parallels between his teachings and their own spiritual traditions. They believed, for example, that "their souls have come down from the sky; that they will return thither when they are separated from their bodies." Even some non-Christians felt that the presence of the priest at a child's death would help their soul into heaven. Millet won over some of the chiefs who used their influence to encourage Christian practices.[24] In 1675, the superior wrote that the "Onneiouts . . . have always been considered the most cruel of these barbarians; but they are now so changed through Father Millet's care that it may be said that from wolves they have become lambs." In 1676 Soenrese was the first Oneida chief to officially convert to Christianity. Millet wrote that he "renounced all the superstitions of the country," and was baptized.[25] The *Jesuit Relations* of the early 1680s portray the Oneidas as peaceful, turning away from drink, and becoming converted Christians, or at least having great respect for the cross.

§

Father Pierre Millet left Oneida in 1684. When he returned in 1690, it was as a prisoner of war. He expected to be burned upon arrival and not without reason. He knew it was customary to burn the first prisoner taken in a new campaign. He was beaten, mocked, stripped, and bound with rope along the way. When he arrived at Oneida there was a great debate among the sachems. Chief Manchot argued that Millet was there "not as a Prisoner, but . . . a missionary who returned to visit [his] flock." Another chief, "a great friend of the English," argued that Millet was a Frenchman, the same as those who were killing and burning Haudenosaunee villages.

Millet recorded that he was taken to a cabin where he had to be protected from drunkards who wanted to set it ablaze. They hurled stones at the building. The council deliberated about what to do with him and for several weeks Millet was spoken of in the village as *Genherontatie*, the dead man who walks. When a war party of Oneidas returned with some more

French prisoners, the council decided to burn them. The Oneidas painted Millet's face red and black in preparation for execution, to satisfy (in his words) "the demon of war and Iroquois wrath."[26]

The governor of New France had determined to punish the Haudenosaunee in 1684. Father Millet and all the French missionaries were recalled from Iroquoia to spare them from the wrath that was about to be inflicted on the Five Nations. They knew a renewal of war would undermine and destroy three decades of progress in their missionary work. But Antoine Lefèbvre de la Barre was fed up with the Haudenosaunee. Despite the increasing warmth shown to the Jesuit missionaries, they continued to be a scourge to New France's Native allies. Worse still, they had aligned themselves with the English. Greenhalgh's 1677 trip had been successful. With trade flowing and a new stable partner in Albany, the Haudenosaunee (particularly the Mohawks and Oneidas) saw it in their interest to replace their Dutch alliance with an English one, known as the Covenant Chain.[27]

The Onondagas managed to hold off war temporarily by hosting a peace conference with De la Barre at La Famine, near the mouth of the Salmon River. But by 1687 the situation reached a breaking point. De la Barre was replaced by the Marquis de Denonville as the governor general of New France. Denonville was even more determined to suppress the Haudenosaunee. In the summer of 1687, the French lured two hundred Onondaga, Oneida, and Cayuga people to a trading post called Cataraqui in Ontario, stole their pelts, and took them all prisoner. Denonville then launched an invasion of Seneca country at the head of an army of more than 1,600 French and Indian allies. They burned four Seneca villages and destroyed all their corn and livestock. In August 1689 the Five Nations hit back with fifteen hundred or so warriors raiding French Canada. The settlement at Lachine near Montreal was the site of a particularly brutal massacre. By 1689 England was at war with France. The French and their allies launched a retaliatory raid on the Dutch-English settlement at Schenectady in 1690, killing or capturing most of its population.[28]

It was in this frenzy of killing and hostage-taking that Father Millet ended up a Haudenosaunee prisoner. He was captured in a Haudenosaunee raid on Cataraqui in October 1689. But unlike his fellow captives, he was spared execution. Christian women intervened with the sachems and recommended him for requickening. He was given a new name, Otassete, and given his rosary back. He was made an adopted Oneida and even given an elevated position as a sachem of the tribe.

The English were infuriated by the adoption of a Frenchman by the Oneidas and tried discrediting him. When that didn't work, they tried to have him released. An English emissary came to Oneida, promising to Millet that he would be given back to the French in a prisoner exchange. Millet replied, "After the obligations I was under to the Onneiouts, I could not leave them." Even Pieter Schuyler, the mayor of Albany, and the top Protestant missionary in New York, Godefridus Dellius, could not convince Millet to leave his "captivity."[29] In 1693, Benjamin Fletcher, the governor of New York, told the Oneidas that "all their designes will be destroyed soe long as he [Millet] is kept among them" and "advised them speedily to remove that dangerous Person." Schuyler admonished the Five Nations to pressure the Oneidas to give up Millet, whom he called "a pest in your Countrey . . . who betrays all your actions."[30] The English were highly concerned with keeping the Five Nations' enmity against the French strong, to prevent them from making a separate peace or even switching sides. Millet was disrupting that. Finally—probably against his will, for he seems to have become fully dedicated to his Oneida identity—he was brought back to Quebec in 1694 with fifteen other captives during peace talks that proved to be futile.[31] The war raged on.

The villages of the Mohawks were the next to burn in winter raids early in 1693, with three hundred prisoners taken. Raids continued and peace initiatives failed. In August 1696, an army of 1,434 French and Indians launched another invasion of Iroquoia, cannon and artillery in tow. New France's governor, the Comte de Frontenac, led a division that went by canoe and bateaux to Onondaga Lake. The Onondagas had fled after burning their own village to prevent the French capturing it. An Oneida warrior appeared with a French man whom they had held prisoner for seven years and a wampum belt, requesting peace. Frontenac rejected the offer unless, he said, the Haudenosaunee would be willing to abandon their homeland and move to New France where they could be kept under control. Frontenac intimated in a letter to King Louis XIV that the Oneidas agreed to this condition but that he decided to torch their village anyway.[32]

The French plundered the supply stores of the Onondagas that they found and destroyed their entire crop of grain until "not a single head remained." Their Indian allies burned alive an old man they found hiding, who shouted as he died, "Learn, French dogs! and ye, savages! their allies—that ye are the dogs of dogs."[33]

Meanwhile, Frontenac's lieutenant, Philippe de Rigaud de Vaudreuil, went to Oneida with a force of six or seven hundred. When they reached it, only thirty-five or so of the Oneida chiefs were there. The rest had fled. Vaudreuil left the village only "after having seen it burned and the corn entirely cut." He returned with the thirty-five chiefs as captives to the French camp on Onondaga Lake, and they all returned from there to Montreal via Fort Frontenac (now Kingston, Ontario). The chronicler responsible for conveying the most significant news from New France back to Paris concluded that "the Iroquois will be reduced to the necessity of dying of hunger, or accepting peace on the conditions we may think proper to impose on them."[34]

The primary Oneida, Onondaga, Mohawk, and Seneca villages—and all their crops—had been burned within nine years. The Cayugas, too, had suffered defeats against the French as well as in their wars against the Miami Indians to the southwest. Hundreds of Haudenosaunee, from a population already depleted in the plague years, had been killed or taken prisoner. Their population probably halved in those nine years. The English at Albany gave the Indians enough corn to survive the winter, but the Haudenosaunee were resentful that the English had done nothing to stop the French striking such devastating blows on them. England's own attempts to attack New France during King William's War, as it was known in the colonies, had

Figure 2.2. Detail from Guillaume de l'Isle, "Carte de la Louisiane et du cours du Mississippi" (1718).

The Age of the French, 1635–1763 | 45

been unsuccessful. In 1697 more than thirty Oneidas defected to Montreal. Many Mohawks, too, joined the Catholic Indians at Kahnawake. The English reckoned in 1700 that two-thirds of the Mohawks were living in Canada. An Oneida and Onondaga delegation tried to make peace with Frontenac, unsuccessfully, angering the English in the process.[35]

After Frontenac's death, the French were more willing to negotiate. Two hundred representatives from the Five Nations went to Montreal to meet the French and French-allied Indians and sign a grand peace compact in 1701. The Haudenosaunee agreed to remain neutral in future conflicts between England and France. The most destructive war in the Oneidas' history to that point was over. They left the ashes of their old village behind. Archaeologists who discovered the site in the 1970s found scraps of copper, brass, glass, and iron, European-made fishhooks, gun parts, musket balls, Jesuit rings, and scissors there. The lives of the Oneidas were now intimately influenced by the material culture and customs of the Euro-Americans to the north and east. European weapons and religion had more than a foothold in the Oneida village; they were now realities of life, as was alcohol. The Oneidas built a new village at Prime's Hill, just east of the present-day village of Munnsville in Madison County. It was to be the last traditional Haudenosaunee village they would ever build.[36]

§

Robert Livingstone, the new secretary for Indian affairs in New York, had big dreams for Oneida lands. It was a vision that would shape their destiny over the next three centuries. As he travelled to Onondaga in 1700, he contemplated turning the Mohawk River and Oneida Lake into a great corridor for trade and migration that would link the Atlantic seaboard to the vast interior of the continent. He looked to the west, to the "place calld [sic] by the French De Troett [Detroit] . . . where there is arable land for thousands of people," and where there were "millions of Elks, Bears, Deer, Swans, Geese, and all sorts of fowl." He wanted to build a chain of forts across Iroquoia to secure the route there. The "Great Carrying Place" between the Mohawk River and Oneida Lake would be crucial. Livingstone urged that Wood Creek should be cleared and a dam built to increase water levels. This would enable supplies to easily flow from east to west from Albany to Oswego. Agricultural settlements could be established in the interior. The whole region would be linked to Albany by the presence of a contingent of "bushlopers," young men stationed along the route.

Livingstone's vision was prescient. But the immediate problem for the English was that the Haudenosaunee were nearly as distrustful of them for having done so little to help as they were of the French who had torched their villages. Hundreds were defecting and joining their relatives under French protection at Montreal. The two main reasons for this, Livingstone wrote, were fear of further French attacks on those who remained allied with the English and "our neglect of sending ministers among them." The answer was to secure the route from Oswego to Albany with forts and to counteract the Jesuit influence by sending Anglican Christian missionaries among the Haudenosaunee. If this were accomplished, Livingstone wrote, "it would be no difficult matter in time to perswade the Oneydes & Onnondages to desert their habitations and remove nearer us."[37]

The English tried their best to charm and reassure the Haudenosaunee. Pieter Schuyler passed through Oneida country on horseback and stayed in the Oneida village in 1701. He presented a gift of "seven hands of wampum."[38] England went to war against France again just as the Great Peace of Montreal secured peace between the French, their Indians allies, and the Haudenosaunee. In the colonies, the new conflict was known as Queen Anne's War. The Haudenosaunee remained neutral but were targeted with threats from the French about what would happen if they helped the English: "[We] will not only come ourselves but sett the farr nations upon you to destroy you your wifes and Children Root & Branch." With memories of Frontenac's raids still fresh among the Onondagas and Oneidas—and with knowledge that the French could strike just as easily along the same route they had taken in 1696—the chiefs asked the English "to build a Fort and Garrison it well in their Castle, or where they thought fitt in their Countrey which would prevent all the French intragues." They also asked for blacksmiths, one to "to mend their Arms at Onnondage and another at Oneyde." The English didn't promise a smith, but they committed to fixing their weapons and gave blithe assurance to the Oneidas and Onondagas that "they need not fear of Her Majesty's assistance & protection."[39]

The colony of New York tried to limit its involvement in Queen Anne's War, though they did lend support to two major expeditions against Quebec in 1709 and 1711 respectively, both of which failed.[40] New England was more active, and in response their colonies were raided repeatedly by French and Indians. Deerfield, Massachusetts, was burned to the ground, with 47 killed and 112 captives forced to march to Montreal in the freezing winter. The Oneidas were not satisfied with Governor Hunter's vague assurances. The Oneida chiefs met again with Hunter, Schuyler, and Livingstone to repeat the request for a blacksmith. They told them that due to the French threat, they were building extra defenses around their village in case of attack and repeated that the presence of a smith was necessary for continuing the work. The governor again brushed them off with flattering words but little action. He told them "he had a particular regard for ye nation of Oneyde whom he was informed by every body had always been ready and willing to obey what was commanded them by this Province." He made no promises but said he would make "all endeavors" to fulfil the request.[41]

What endeavor he made is unknown, but no smith was sent to live with the Oneidas. The fact that France and Britain made peace in 1712 would have lessened the urgency of it from the British point of view. In the Treaty of Utrecht that ended Queen Anne's War, France recognized that the British side had prevailed in the wider world conflict known as the War of the Spanish Succession. The French recognized British suzerainty over the Haudenosaunee, effectively accepting that they were not subjects of France. However, Lake Ontario became a contested area. The French had forts on either end of the lake and continued to claim right to all lands in the Ontario basin, despite acknowledging British suzerainty over the Haudenosaunee who lived there.[42] This prompted the British to make a push for power and control over the lake and routes west.

The Haudenosaunee attempted to strike a balance that would allow them to maintain their neutrality in any conflict between the British and the French, while also benefiting from both in the meantime by putting them—to some degree at least—into competition for Haudenosaunee custom and affection. To balance the French post at Niagara (which they allowed to be rebuilt and developed), they gave the British the right to build a fort at Oswego. It angered the French (who had proposed building their own fort at Oswego in 1724) but also forced them to be generous—it meant that they had to ensure their prices and gifts kept pace with those of the British. The Haudenosaunee also hoped that in allowing naval bases to be built on the lakeshore, if war did erupt between the two European powers, it could be fought out on the waters of Lake Ontario rather than in the Haudenosaunee heartland.[43]

Following Livingstone's logic, the British began establishing missions among the Haudenosaunee during Queen Anne's War. The Society for the Propagation of the Gospel in Foreign Parts sent Church of England missionaries to the Mohawks in 1702, with some success. In 1710 a group of Mohawk leaders went to England to meet Queen Anne, who resolved to build a chapel on the Mohawk River. The construction of Fort Hunter at the confluence of the Mohawk and Schoharie Creek, and St. Anne's

Church within it, began the following year. Rev. William Andrews was the first to reside at Fort Hunter between 1712 and 1719. He began baptizing Mohawk children as Anglican Protestants. His main opposition came from Albany traders, who benefited from selling the Indians alcohol. Andrews tried to have the sale of liquor to Indians banned. His successor, Rev. Henry Barclay, arrived in 1735 and Rev. John Ogilvie began work there in 1749. These missionaries developed a written form of the Mohawk language and used it to translate the Book of Common Prayer.[44] The missionaries' main achievement was to secure the loyalty of the New York Mohawks to the Church of England. Their loyalty to the British crown during the American Revolution was in part due to their legacy.

The Mohawks agreed to allow the British to settle a group of German refugees on their lands. These "Palatine Germans," it was thought, would be a good buffer to stand between New France and the Hudson. They had fled to England after Louis XIV's armies devastated their home in western Germany. Their anti-French feelings could be relied upon. About two thousand Palatine Germans journeyed across the Atlantic. They resided first in internment camps in New York Harbor and labor camps on the Hudson. Hunter's successor as New York governor, William Burnet, negotiated for their resettlement along the Mohawk River in the 1720s. One group went to Stone Arabia and the other to a new land patent known as Burnetsfield—later called German Flats and now known as Herkimer (it bears the Anglicized name of a grandson of Georg Herchheimer, one of the original Palatine immigrants).[45] For the first time, a permanent white settlement existed within a day's walk of the Oneidas' main village.

The man who would have as large an impact as any single white person on the Haudenosaunee in the eighteenth century arrived from Ireland in 1738. William Johnson came with twelve Irish Protestant families to settle a vast tract of Mohawk land that had been acquired by Johnson's uncle, the famous naval officer Peter Warren. Johnson soon established himself as a trader with the Mohawks near Fort Hunter and later at Johnstown, New York.[46] Unlike the unscrupulous Albany traders the Haudenosaunee were used to, Johnson cultivated his relationships and enmeshed himself into Mohawk life, eventually becoming trusted as a friend and advisor to the nation. Later, he would be adopted by the Mohawks and would lead them in war and peace, not without enriching himself in the process. His star also rose within the colonial administration. He became superintendent of Indian affairs in 1756 and exerted enormous influence with the Haudenosaunee and on British policy in America.

The Oneidas were not untouched by any of these developments further down the Mohawk valley. British presence on Oneida lands steadily increased throughout the century. The Oneidas allowed the British to make improvements at the Oneida Carry starting in 1724. It was a move that benefitted both parties. For the British, it secured their access to Lake Ontario and enabled trade to pass from Iroquoia and beyond more easily into Albany. It would improve trade opportunities for the Oneidas as well. As traffic increased, a village called Oriska was established on the Carry route where Oneidas could procure goods in exchange for helping with transport from the Mohawk River to Wood Creek. This brought them into frequent contact with Europeans on their own lands.[47]

Some Oneidas traveled to join the Mohawks at the chapel at Fort Hunter. Rev. Barclay baptized at least one. Rev. John Ogilvie visited Oneida, baptizing six adults and fourteen children, and marrying nine couples in a single day. The effects of Christianity at Oneida were reported back to Ogilvie by General Amherst, who visited Oneida in 1760. When he arrived there, "he found the Indians at worship, and expressed a vast pleasure at the decency with which the service of our Church was performed by a grave Indian Sachem."[48] A minister, this one a Presbyterian named Rev. William Kirkpatrick from New Jersey, was with Amherst at the time. He recounted, "In our march . . . to the Oneida Lake, we happened to meet with a number of the Oneida Indians, who seemed to pay a great deal of respect to that sacred character, which, from my apparel, they easily imagined I sustained." They told Kirkpatrick that they wished to have a minister settle among them and that they had set aside $300 to build a house of worship.[49]

The artifacts discovered by archaeologists at the Oneidas' last traditional village site on Prime's Hill were nearly all of European manufacture: iron nails, brass bangles, gun flints, glass beads, European ceramic, Jew's harps, brass points, and rum bottle glass, to name a few. European imports, both spiritual and material, were now completely pervasive; even dances and traditional ceremonies that were frowned upon by Christians were infused with non-Native items, as were hunting, agriculture, and war.[50]

Although the Oneidas were drifting ever further into the British sphere of influence, their acceptance of the Tuscaroras onto their lands from 1714 onwards, which went strongly against the wishes of New York's colonial government, is an example of their persisting autonomy. Throughout the seventeenth and early eighteenth centuries, the Haudenosaunee had been involved in fighting for hunting rights for the fur trade as far south as

Virginia and the Carolinas. Their primary enemies in this southern war were the Catawba and Choctaw, often called the "Flatheads." When these tribes, allied with the British, fought the Iroquoian-speaking Tuscaroras in the Carolinas during the 1711–1713 Tuscarora War, the Five Nations supported the latter. When they were routed by Anglo-Flathead forces, the Tuscaroras were allowed to move north and settle in the Susquehanna Valley on the lands of the Oneidas and Onondagas. They were adopted by the Haudenosaunee as the sixth nation in their confederation.

For the Oneidas, still recovering from the destruction of 1696, the Tuscarora presence provided a buffer to the south that would help protect their core lands from settlers and enemy Indian raids alike. It boosted their overall numbers and potential military strength. It also provided a counterbalance against the British (towards whom the Tuscaroras remained hostile), which pleased those Oneidas who were wary lest the tribe become too enamored of their new suzerains. The Oneidas continued to fight the Catawba after the Tuscaroras arrived. In one particularly bloody day in 1729, fifty-four Oneida warriors were killed.[51]

The Oneidas were on good enough terms with the New York British colony that they allowed them easy passage over the Oneida Carry, continued using them as their key trade partner, and allowed Anglican Christian missionaries into their villages. But they were not willing to do Britain's bidding when war broke out again between Britain and France in 1744. King George's War, which lasted until 1748, broke the uneasy peace that had reigned since the signing of the Treaty of Utrecht in 1713. French and Indian raids again became a feature on the New York frontier. The British settlement at Saratoga, north of Albany, was burned and its inhabitants killed or taken prisoner in a violent raid in November 1745. Although some Haudenosaunee warriors (mainly Mohawks) made their own decision to fight on the British side during the war, the League Council succeeded in maintaining a strict neutrality, despite the supplication (and increasing frustration) of New York's new governor, George Clinton. It was Clinton who appointed William Johnson as Indian commissioner, hoping to leverage his influence with the Haudenosaunee. The Oneidas were worried about potential raids and built up the defenses around their village, but in the end French penetration into Haudenosaunee country was limited to small scale (violent though they were) raids on white-Palatine settlements in Mohawk territory. Stone Arabia was attacked in May 1746 and Burnetsfield on July 21, 1747.[52]

When trade boomed again after King George's War, Oswego and the route between it and Albany became increasingly important for the British. Indians from all parts of the Lake Ontario region, not only western Haudenosaunee but also Mississaugas from the north shore, brought their wares there for trade. The French tried to counter this by increasing their own presence around the lake, with new forts at Toronto, Little Niagara, and Oswegatchie. The latter, known as Fort de la Présentation on the St. Lawrence at present-day Ogdensburg, New York, also included a new Catholic mission to attract Haudenosaunee converts and settlers. The French even attempted to negotiate again for the building of a new trading post on Oneida Lake, though without success. Présentation, however, turned out to be a triumph, in the short term at least. Five hundred Haudenosaunee families had resettled there by 1756, especially from Onondaga. For many, it was a conscious choice to move away from the old villages where, by virtue of increased trade, alcohol had become a pervasive aspect of life. Another mission village at Akwesasne (Saint Regis) was founded in 1754.[53] With large groups of recently resettled Haudenosaunee firmly in the French camp, any Anglo-French war would—if the Haudenosaunee joined with their respective neighbors—also become a civil war pitting closely related Indian families against each other to the death.

§

War between France and Britain did break out in 1754, this time on a grander scale than ever before. In this conflict, known as the French and Indian War in America and the Seven Years' War in Europe, the Haudenosaunee heartland would be scarred on a scale not seen since 1696. It would strain the Haudenosaunee Confederacy and lead to bloodshed by Europeans and Natives on Oneida lands. For both France and Britain, control of the lands west of Iroquoia, in the Ohio Valley and beyond, were the prize. When war broke out, five of the six nations tried to maintain neutrality. The Mohawks joined the British despite increasing tension due to encroachments on their land. It took thirty wagonloads of presents and all of William Johnson's cajoling influence, exerted in a major conference at his house, to convince them to join in.[54]

In 1755, the British prepared to assault French Canada by sea and via the Champlain corridor. They also sent men and supplies across Oneida territory to Oswego. During that summer they began building ships there for a waterborne attack on Fort Niagara. The French had another naval port on Lake Ontario at Frontenac (now Kingston, Ontario) and built a staging post at Henderson Bay (called Nioure) on the lake's eastern shore from which they could launch raids.[55] The supply line between Albany and Oswego took on prime importance. For the British it was the only route by which they could supply their sole base on Lake Ontario and maintain any significant presence west of Mohawk country. Their hopes of winning land in the interior of the continent hinged on it. All canons, shipbuilding material, and personnel passed that way. For the French, it was a strategic target.

Due to the sudden urgency of maintaining control of the Oswego-Albany route, Britain immediately set to building a chain of defenses to protect it. The most vulnerable position along that route was the Oneida Carry. Here supplies moving from east to west needed to be unloaded and carried a mile on land before being reloaded onto bateaux on Wood Creek. The British sought the consent of the Oneidas to construct fortifications there, promising them an "extensive trade" and assuring them that they would demolish the forts after the war.[56] In 1755 they began building three forts—Fort Williams at the place where boats heading west came off the Mohawk, Fort Newport at the point where boats could enter Wood Creek when water levels were high, and Fort Bull at the "lower landing" where boats would enter the creek in dryer periods. These were simple square structures with corner bastions and wooden stockades. Fort Williams had high pickets, "four pieces of Cannon," and "a garrison of 150 men." Fort Bull had four interior buildings that were used to store powder and supplies. It had "a garrison of 60 soldiers, commanded by a lieutenant" and packed with "a considerable quantity of munitions of war and provisions." Fort Bull was star-shaped and surrounded by fifteen- to eighteen-foot heavy pickets. It "had no cannon, but a number of grenadoes."[57] The French determined to raid the Carry in a winter assault in March 1756. They knew a heavy blow there would disrupt preparations at Oswego for the summer campaigns and could even knock the British out of Iroquoia altogether.

Gaspard-Joseph Chaussegros de Léry left Montreal with a force of four hundred French, Canadians, and Indians on March 17, 1756, to strike the Oneida Carry. The Indian contingent included members of traditionally French-allied Algonquin peoples such as Abenakis and Nipissings. But it also included Haudenosaunee of the Five Nations who had moved to the settlements at Oswegatchie and Akwesasne. They provided vital intelligence to the French about the buildup at the Oneida Carry and were essential guides through the snow-laden forest. A contemporary account tells us the war party proceeded down on foot from modern-day Ogdensburg to Rome, over ice and "along the mountains, by paths known only to the savages." Their lead guide was an Oswegatchie Oneida spy who had obtained knowledge of the fort during a visit back to his native village the previous November.[58]

In the early morning hours of March 27, 1756, fifteen batteaux of supplies were at Fort Bull, ready to enter Wood Creek for shipment to Oswego, with nine more loads of supplies arriving by sled. De Léry and the Indians captured the sleds on their way to Fort Williams and took the transport party prisoner. Hearing from them that Fort Bull was less well fortified but had greater stores than Fort Williams, they chose to strike there. Initially all but two Indian guides refused to go, being satisfied with the success of the raid on the sleds. However, "encouraged by some drams of brandy," twenty decided to follow the French while the rest guarded the prisoners. In an echo of Champlain's attack in 1615—according to a French account—the silent advance towards the fort was given away by the "whoop of the savages, notwithstanding the prohibition [De Léry] had issued." They rushed forward, battering down the gates while the English within shot their muskets and threw grenades.

Once the gate was broken through, "the whole detachment with a cry of *Vive le Roi* rushed into the Fort and put every one to the sword they could lay hands on." They began throwing the barrels of gunpower into the creek, but a fire began to spread and before the entire group could get to a safe distance, the powder store was lit, causing an explosion. Meanwhile, a British sortie left Fort Williams to defend Fort Bull, but the Indians who had stayed with the prisoners on the road fought them and killed seventeen, causing them to turn around.[59]

It was a humiliating and costly defeat for the British. De Léry had only two dead and two wounded. British losses were far heavier. A French-Canadian report said that the day had "cost the English 90 men of whom 30 are prisoners," alongside the loss of thirty horses. The French claimed to have destroyed "40 thousand weight of powder" along with "a number of Bombs, grenades, and balls of different calibre" and substantial British food and clothing stores. Reports like these were prone to exaggeration, but Fort Bull was certainly a scene of devastation. When the British returned to the site, the bodies of the dead were laid in heaps and burnt. Many of those killed were from old Dutch families in and around Albany. Their names were spelled out in the *New York Mercury* of April 12, 1756. Those of "three Servants & five Negroes," also killed there, were not.[60]

The Oneidas were forced to play a delicate game to keep their neutrality. With both British and French forces on their home soil, they would face attack from either if they were seen to be too far in the other side's camp. Two days prior to the French and Indian attack on Fort Bull, De Léry went to the Oneidas' village with a gift of wampum, and to make assurances that the victims of their raid would be exclusively British, not Indian. Aware that the British would piece together that the Oneidas would have been consulted prior to any attack on their soil, the Oneidas did give them a tip-off of the impending raid, though it was with too little notice to change the outcome.[61]

The devastation at Fort Bull would have left no doubt in the Oneidas' minds that the French were still a powerful force, and—in this theatre of the war, at least—the one with the upper hand. This view would only have been strengthened in the summer of 1756 when the British were besieged and eventually defeated at Oswego. The survivors scurried back towards Albany, burning down their own recently built fortifications along the way—including Fort Bull and Fort Williams—to prevent them falling into the hands of the French. The French, for their part, were content to turn their attention to other theatres in the war, knowing that at least for the foreseeable future they controlled all access into and out of Lake Ontario.

When the French returned the following year, it was to attack the "British" settlement of German Flats. Once again, the good will of the Oneidas was sought before making an attack via their territory. The commander of this expedition, François-Marie Picoté de Belestre (sometimes spelled Belletre), sent "four influential Indians" to the Oneidas ahead of the attack. Once again, Haudenosaunee who had moved to the Canadian settlements were among the raiding party of some two hundred Indians and sixty-five French-Canadian troops.[62] Six Oneida warriors voluntarily returned with them to join in the expedition. In November 1757, after ascending the Black River and passing by the destroyed forts at the Oneida Carry, Belestre's men let loose on the German village. Over forty-eight hours they burned over sixty houses, as well as their barns and water mill, killing over forty (some drowned) and taking one hundred fifty prisoners.

In a boastful French-Canadian summary of the attack, it was recorded that—without a single Canadian or Indian killed—the tally of damages was "a much larger quantity [of grain] than the Island of Montreal has produced in years of abundance," plus a vast number of hogs, "3000 horned cattle, 3000 sheep [and] 1500 horses." They also claimed to have destroyed "furniture, wearing apparel, merchandize and liquor [equaling] a capital of 1,500,000 livres," and taken large quantities of "Wampum, silver-bracelets &c, scarlet cloth and other Merchandize." Whilst this report almost certainly exaggerated the damages, the financial losses at German Flats were enormous, and so, too, was the moral blow. Britain had failed to display any ability to repel the French, not only in Onondaga and Oneida country, but even in the Mohawk valley. On his return from German Flats, Belestre sent another envoy to Oneida by whom "he communicated to them the success he experienced" and "invited them to persevere in their good Sentiments and not to fear the English."[63]

William Johnson, infuriated, sent his deputy, George Croghan, to the Oneidas and Tuscaroras "to Explain themselves why they had not given more timely notice to the Germans of the designs and approach of the Enemy." Johnson suspected the Oneidas had deployed the same maneuver as they had used at Fort Bull, giving notice of an impending attack, but only—in this case—"the same morning the attack was made." At this time there were two Oneida villages—the "Upper Castle" at Prime's Hill and a smaller settlement called the "Castle at [Oneida] Lake." The Oneida chief Conaghquieson explained that he had tried to warn the Germans two weeks before the attack, having heard rumors of a coming French force, but they refused to listen: "[They] laughed at me, slapping their hands on their buttocks, saying they did not value the Enemy." He then admitted that the French, on their way to attack, had stopped at the Castle at the Lake and told the Oneidas there what they were going to do, but told them not to tell the Oneidas at the main Upper Castle village. He said that a loyal Oneida did, however, run to the Upper Castle, and then the news was passed directly to German Flats, where even still they did not believe it. Croghan noted that the Germans agreed that this had been the case.[64]

The raid on German Flats was a turning point in the Six Nations' position on the war. Unlike the attack on Fort Bull, this had been a brutal and aggressive strike on a nonmilitary target within their territory. The Oneidas had grown close to their German neighbors. There were several mixed-race Oneida-Palatine families by the mid-eighteenth century, a fact to which the common Oneida surname Doxtator (from the German name Dochstädter) owes its origins. The Palatines, like the Oneidas, had tried to maintain neutrality in the war.[65] The French had given the Oneidas some notice, but in a cursory way, particularly if they only went to the smaller Oneida village on Oneida Lake and besought them not to alert the others. And it had certainly landed them in a sticky situation with Johnson, the powerful superintendent of Indian affairs. The following May, in 1758, the French made another raid on German Flats. An Oneida warned Captain Nicholas Herkimer, a Palatine himself and in charge of Fort Herkimer on the south bank of the Mohawk, that they were coming. This time they were better defended, but still thirty-three inhabitants were killed.[66]

By 1758, the tide of the war was starting to turn. Britain laid siege on Louisbourg at the Atlantic gateway to the St. Lawrence in June and began to pose a major threat to Quebec. While New France's eyes turned eastward, they also faced a humiliating sting from behind. It came in the form of a British attack on Fort Frontenac in August. Lieutenant Colonel John Bradstreet had come with over three thousand men in bateaux from Schenectady up the Mohawk, across the overgrown Oneida Carry, and to the abandoned fort Oswego. They sailed across Lake Ontario and captured the French fortress at the gateway to the St. Lawrence.

The British again set to building forts along the Albany-Oswego corridor. At an important ford of the Mohawk where Utica now stands, they built Old Fort Schuyler. At the Carry, Fort Stanwix and Fort Craven were erected in 1759. They also built two royal military blockhouses on either end of Oneida Lake—one near Fish Creek's entry into the lake and the other at Brewerton. Along this route, thousands of British and colonial soldiers would pass in 1759 and 1760 for assaults on Fort Niagara and, finally, Montreal. The Haudenosaunee view of French invincibility crumbled. Quebec fell in 1759.

In the major expeditions of 1759 and 1760, Haudenosaunee warriors from across the confederacy joined with the British. A thousand New York Haudenosaunee participated in the assault at Niagara, and seven hundred in the capture of Montreal. They also used diplomacy to persuade the Canadian Haudenosaunee in the mission towns to stay out of the fighting on the St. Lawrence. Thus, by the time the war ended in 1760, the Oneidas, despite having had their loyalty questioned at German Flats, had shown more than strict neutrality and could rightly point out that their cooperation had been vital to British victory.[67] A peace treaty finally formally ended the war between Britain and France in 1763. France ceded Canada and all lands east of the Mississippi to Britain. Quebec was handed over to the British.

The end of the war brought momentous change to Iroquoia. After two centuries of French power and influence in the region, New France was no more. Britain was the supreme and undisputed power in all areas surrounding Iroquoia. The Haudenosaunee practice of playing imperial forces against each other would no longer be possible in a new era of monolithic British control. The age of the French in northeastern America was over. The commodity that Euro-Americans desired most from the Haudenosaunee changed as well. American colonists became less interested in their furs and more in their land. The threat of French and Indian raids on frontier settlements had kept expansion in check before 1763. With that threat removed, colonists began eyeing Indian land in Iroquoia and elsewhere in a new light. From 1763 on, Oneida territory stood at the border between Native and non-Native realms. The Oneidas continued to be key players in the most important power struggles in North America, but these struggles were no longer between competing imperial powers. The forces that vied increasingly for control were two sides of the same British imperial entity—the colonies and the Crown.

Chapter 3

Rebellion, 1763–1784

At the conclusion of the French and Indian War, the Oneidas' most pressing worry was that they would lose their lands to speculators and squatters. With no further threat from the French and their allied Indians, they feared there would be nothing to restrain settlers moving onto their lands. When Sir William Johnson passed through in 1761, he met the Oneida chief Conaghquieson with upwards of thirty other Oneidas and Tuscaroras at German Flats. Conaghquieson said to Johnson, while presenting rows of ceremonial wampum, "This land which was given us by the Divine Being, we love as our lives, and therefore hope you will secure the possession of it to us, which has been ours from the beginning by preventing any more of your people from settling higher in the Country." The Oneidas at Oquaga—a mixed Indian village in the southern reaches of Oneida lands that grew up in the eighteenth century—also petitioned Johnson to protect their lands from white settlers in 1762.[1]

Britain was buoyed by its victory in North America but also burdened by it. Its war debts were enormous and nearly as soon as the war with France ended, a new one against Native American adversaries began as they tried to take control of the Ohio Territory. In 1763 the Ottawa chief Pontiac launched an attack on now-British Detroit, the opening act in a widespread offensive against nearly all of Britain's trans-Appalachian forts. Protecting these frontier outposts from Indian raids over nearly the entire eastern half of North America, from Hudson Bay to the Gulf of Mexico, would be a mammoth, expensive task. Protecting hundreds or thousands of new colonial settlements over the same area would be impossible.

It was not in Britain's interest to allow an unchecked, chaotic spread into Indian territory. Although the Mohawk Joseph Brant and some Oneidas fought on the side of the British against the Indian alliance, others—particularly the Senecas, geographically closest and therefore most vulnerable to attack if seen by anti-British tribes to be aligned with the enemy—were wavering. Many of their warriors joined the rebellion.[2] The British were aware that the western five (at least) of the Six Nations could join the ranks of their enemies if something were not done to alleviate their most urgent concern.

In 1763, King George III signed a royal proclamation declaring that all lands west of the Appalachians would be off-limits for settlement. The proclamation also stipulated that land east of the boundary line could no longer be bought directly from Indians; only the British government via its royal governors or the superintendent for Indian affairs could buy land from Indians. Land purchasers and speculators would thenceforward need to buy from the government. Theoretically, this would protect Indians from the sort of exploitative land sales they had been forced to accept in years past. This irked both land speculators and settlers looking to move west. However, it made Britain and its superintendent for Indian affairs, Johnson, look to some Indians like the best hope of protecting their lands against ravenous colonists. It helped turn the Six Nations more clearly to Britain's side in the later stages of Pontiac's War. In the end, however, it would contribute to turning many whites in the colonies against the King.

The 1763 line was ill-defined and needed clarifying to make it legitimate in the eyes of settlers. For one thing, there were already some settlements and patents west of the Appalachians in Pennsylvania and Virginia. A revised line, henceforward known as the Line of Property, was drawn up by Johnson and proposed to a grand conference of representatives from Indian nations throughout eastern North America at Fort Stanwix on the Oneida Carry in 1768. The line was moved westward in most places, in exchange for a range of presents and promises that royal enforcement of the boundary would be rigorous.[3] It ran right through Oneida territory.

§

Although no white settlers lived west of the Palatine Germans in 1763, some of the Oneida lands had already been sold—not to hardy pioneers but to wealthy speculators who had no intention of living on them. Even before 1763, the process of securing a patent to take ownership of Indian land was laborious and expensive. The first step was to petition the governor for the right to buy a set number of acres in a given location. If the petition was successful, the prospective buyer would then have to extinguish the Indian title to the land. This would involve paying a translator to propose it at a tribal council. If they approved, a price would be set. A deed would then be drawn up. Then a request needed to be put to the governor and council (the upper house of the Province of New York's legislature) for a survey, which, if approved, would be arranged by the surveyor general. Once the survey was carried out, a certificate would be drawn up and signed by several colonial officials. That done, a further approval from the governor and council must be given. A warrant would then be made out to the attorney general to draft a patent.

There were costs at every step—a fee for the initial petition to the governor, the cost of the translator, the price of the land itself (normally paid in goods rather than money), the surveyors' fees, a fee for writing the warrant, and another for drafting the patent.[4] In effect, buying land that had never belonged to white men before was impossible unless one had abundant wealth or connections to government officials. Those who bought tended to have both, and indeed many of them were government officials themselves. The speculator would then be free to divide up the parcels and sell them via intermediaries to settlers, normally at a hugely inflated price per acre compared to what they had paid for the patent, thereby recouping their costs and making a handsome profit.

The first parcel of Oneida land ever to be sold was the thirty-thousand-acre Oriskany Patent of 1705, which consisted of the entire Oneida Carry from the bend in the Mohawk River to the entry points on Wood Creek. The buyer was Pieter Schuyler, the influential former mayor of Albany (and future governor), working with a group of four other politically powerful and well-connected investors. There were several things that made it an unusual purchase. At the time, it was an island of land deep in Indian country, nearly one hundred miles from the nearest white settlement. It would be several decades before any other land in the vicinity was patented and nearly a century before the area surrounding it was settled in by whites. Second, the cost was extremely low, and the conditions attached to the purchase were few. Normally, patents would come with a substantial quit rent to be paid annually and clauses obliging the patentee to develop the land within a certain number of years. In the case of the Oriskany Patent, the quit rent was fixed at a scandalously low ten shillings with no obligation for development.[5]

It was a risky investment for Schuyler and his associates. The French had ravaged the area in the 1690s, and it lay defenseless against future incursions. It was hardly clear at the time whether it was in the British or the French realm in North America; both powers laid claim, and even after the peace at Utrecht it was unclear which imperial domain had the upper hand there. But Schuyler would have been aware of Livingstone's report in 1700 in which he envisioned the clearing of Wood Creek and the opening of a crucial water route between Albany and Oswego. Schuyler knew that the value of that piece of land would skyrocket as soon as the waterway was clear. It was the ultimate insider deal.

Between 1705 and the outbreak of the French and Indian War, land along the Mohawk River between Schenectady and the eastern edge of the Oriskany Patent was patented off, large piece by large piece. First, parcels of land between Schenectady and Fort Hunter, where Schoharie Creek flows into the Mohawk, were sold or gifted to predominantly Dutch patentees. After the end of Queen Anne's War, patents were sold further west, mainly to wealthy speculators. The German Palatines began settling patented land in Stone Arabia from 1723 and Burnetsfield (German Flats), in what is now Herkimer, in 1725. After the construction of Fort Oswego, there was further demand for patents on the remaining areas between Burnetsfield and Fort Hunter. Construction began on a road to allow travel from Albany west to the new frontier settlements. In 1734, the 43,000-acre Cosby Patent was purchased from the Oneidas and issued to William Cosby, the British governor of New York. It contained the vital ford of the Mohawk River at present-day Utica. It was not settled before the revolution, apart from the construction of Old Fort Schuyler during the French and Indian War.[6]

The Mohawks sold nearly all land along the Mohawk River by the 1760s, but the patented land was still very sparsely populated by whites. The impact of white settlement before the revolution on the Mohawks was far greater than on the Oneidas. The Mohawks retained just two enclaves in the valley for their villages—one known as Canajoharie and the other as Tiononderoge, called the "Upper Castle" and "Lower Castle," respectively. Tiononderoge was on Schoharie Creek, opposite Fort Hunter, while Canajoharie was further upriver near where the Nowadaga Creek meets the Mohawk River (not in the location of today's village of Canajoharie).

Not all transactions went seamlessly; indeed, some were strongly disputed when, for example, the tract of land deeded seemed far larger than the one the Indians thought they had sold due to botched or (more likely) intentionally aggrandizing surveys. Squatters, like George Klock, who moved onto Mohawk land and refused to budge, were another pervasive problem. However, the Mohawks felt that Sir William Johnson was their protector from the greediest colonists. He often ruled in the Mohawks' favor in boundary disputes. Johnson was also a distributor of royal gifts and a fluent speaker of the Mohawk language. He had a Mohawk common-law wife, Molly, the sister of Joseph Brant. In the struggle against France, he dressed as a Mohawk when leading Indian warriors into battle. Although he accumulated vast expanses of Mohawk land himself, he was nonetheless seen by many of the Mohawks as someone with their interests at heart.[7]

The most difficult part of the 1768 proceedings at Fort Stanwix was the placement of the Line of Property in Oneida country. For Johnson it was imperative that the line be placed to the west of Oneida Carry, so that the now-crucial route to the continent's interior could be secured for the future. The sticking point was that the Oneidas were arguing the legitimacy of the 1705 patent. At Stanwix, the Oneidas "said they had the greatest reason to doubt [that] an Indian Deed" had been legitimately made in 1705, given that only one name had been signed to it. Johnson argued that the patentees were men of good character, but the Oneidas dug in. If the Line of Property were set at the western end of the Oriskany Patent, large areas of the Oneidas' ancestral hunting ground that had not yet been patented would be east of the line and vulnerable to squatters.

Most annoyingly of all for Johnson (foreshadowing troubles to come), two "New England Missionaries who attended the Congress . . . used everry means in their power with the Oneidaes . . . to prevent their parting with [the Oriskany Patent], poisoning their Minds with a thousand Storys."[8] The missionaries had been sent by Eleazar Wheelock, a Connecticut Congregationalist preacher who hoped to build a grand Indian school there, and aggressively advised the Oneidas not to give up any ground.[9] The Presbyterians, Congregationalists, and other nonconformists of New England—dissenters from the official Church of England—would come increasingly into conflict with the Crown and with Johnson as its major representative west of Albany.

In the end, Johnson prevailed in getting the Oneidas to forfeit the Oriskany Patent, drawing the boundary just to the west of it. From there it ran southeastward to the west branch of the Unadilla River, near present-day Bridgewater. The Oneidas were paid an extra one thousand British pounds for making this concession, and nine Oneida families living on the tract who earned money by helping transport goods across they carry were allowed to remain.

After 1768 the gaps between existing patents and the Line of Property were filled almost immediately. A tract of forty-seven thousand acres was patented to William Coxe in May 1770 bordering the Line of Property.[10] Johnson set about procuring a tract of 127,000 acres of Oneida land east of the Line "for Some of my friends," as he wrote in a letter to another colonial official, Goldsbrow Banyar. Among them were Lord Holland, General Gage, William Walton, and Peter Hasenclever, all wealthy and well-connected gentlemen.[11] A 25,000-acre tract called Servis's Patent was nominally made out to a group of settlers led by Peter Servis, but in fact it was paid for by William Johnson and the deed was transferred to the superintendent almost immediately after the patent was written in exchange for a roast dinner.[12]

Johnson's work to secure the Line of Property was a success in the short term. It made King George III's 1763 proclamation a reality. But for many American colonists, the proclamation itself felt like a high-handed decree forbidding their movement west onto land they felt they had helped Britain to win. Land purchases from Indians would still be the preserve of high-ranking royal officials and aristocrats. For the Oneidas, the Line of Property cut across their hunting grounds. A repetitive cycle of land sales that constantly divided the nation between pro- and anti-sale factions had begun.

§

The centuries-old Oneida tradition of living in a single main village, in longhouses, had changed completely by the time of the Fort Stanwix Treaty. Their last traditional village site at Prime's Hill housed between eleven hundred and twelve hundred people in 1714. It was surrounded with traditional twelve-foot palisades. Diffusion began after Queen Anne's War, partly driven by factionalism within the tribe and partly due to the influx of other Native groups onto traditional Oneida lands. By the 1730s, the Oneidas, like most of the Haudenosaunee, had divided themselves into several smaller hamlets and homesteads. Officials still referred to the most densely populated of their settlements as "castles," but by the middle of the eighteenth century, the traditional Oneida village was no more.[13]

While most Oneidas stayed within about twenty miles of the Prime's Hill site, some scattered further afield. The village of Oquaga was established far to the south of the main Oneida settlements, on the Susquehanna

River near the Pennsylvania border. It started as an Oneida village in the 1730s but soon became a mixed community with Tuscarora and a range of other groups including refugee Algonquins from the Hudson River tribes, Shawnees, Nanticockes, and several others living there by the 1750s. Many of the Oneidas who left were tired of the political disputes raging between sachems and warriors in the old settlements. Later, many Mohawks moved to Oquaga too. European styles of agriculture were practiced there, alongside hunting and fishing. It had a population of about three hundred in 1769, of whom about half were Oneidas.[14]

In the 1750s, at the time that Belestre launched his raid on German Flats, a group of Oneidas was living near Oneida Lake, ten or twelve miles from Chief Conaghquieson and the main group of Oneidas. Archaeologists refer to this location near the lake as the Sterling Site. Another small village called Oriska existed near the Oneida Carry where Oneidas worked transporting materials.[15]

By mid-century, the main Oneida settlement itself had split in two. The larger village was Kanonwalohale, at a ford of Oneida Creek where the village of Oneida Castle is today. It was founded in the 1740s by warriors who had grown more powerful within the nation. Its name, meaning "enemy's head on a pole," cast a fear-inspiring picture. But the Oneidas at Kanonwalohale did not build palisades and had moved down from the defensive positions afforded by the high hills, where the Oneidas had lived for centuries, onto the main east-west land route from Albany to Oswego. They were generally accepting of Euro-Americans. The village resembled a colonial settlement more than a traditional Haudenosaunee one in most ways. There was no longhouse. Some sixty houses with one or two families each sat spread apart from each other, with orchards and enclosures for livestock in between. About seven hundred Oneidas lived in Kanonwalohale, roughly half the population.

A smaller but significantly sized settlement known as Old Oneida was in the hills several miles south of Kanonwalohale, in the vicinity of the old Prime's Hill village site. Probably a scattered group of about forty homesteads rather than a concentrated village, it was the stronghold of the traditionalist faction of the tribe—Oneidas who wanted as little as possible to do with colonists and who largely rejected Christianity, particularly when it gained a greater hold in Kanonwalohale during the 1760s. This is where Chief Conaghquieson held sway. The views of the sachems, as opposed to the warriors (led by Tagawaron at Kanonwalohale), carried more weight at Old Oneida.[16]

Maps from the 1750s show two Tuscarora villages to the west of Kanonwalohale, also along the main east-west path. Nearer Oneida was Canastota, and several miles further west was Canaseraga, near where the village of Chittenango is today. Later, probably after the American Revolution, the Tuscaroras founded another village between Kanonwalohale and Old Oneida. When the first white settlers moved into the area between the present-day towns of Vernon (in Oneida County) and Stockbridge (in Madison County), they found an old orchard that was believed to have been planted by the Tuscaroras and a large burial ground.[17]

Just as the nature of Oneida settlements was changing indelibly, Protestant Christianity was becoming firmly entrenched. The Anglican missionaries at Fort Hunter had been successful in the Mohawk settlements and had made some inroads among the Oneidas, but it was Presbyterianism that would make the biggest impact. Presbyterianism, like the other variants of Protestantism that flourished in New England, had its origins in the puritanical rejection of the Church of England's preservation of some Roman Catholic practices. The Presbyterians, with their main base in Scotland, created their own organization, which sent missionaries to the American Indians called the Society for the Propagation of Christian Knowledge.

Presbyterian missionaries found their first success among the Oneidas at Oquaga. Elihu Spencer was the first to arrive, in 1748. He started writing an Oneida vocabulary but left within a few months. Although he was already married, he impregnated an Oneida woman while he was in Oquaga and had a son born in 1749, who later died at the Battle of Oriskany.[18] He did succeed—or rather, his interpreter Rebecca Kellogg, an adopted Mohawk who spoke a number of languages fluently did—in converting two prominent men who were central to the spread of Christianity among their people in the years following Spencer's mission: Dekayenensere Isaac (called "Old Isaac") and Agwrondougwa ("Good Peter"). Another Presbyterian, Gideon Hawley, went to Oquaga in 1753, bringing with him the fiery New England preacher Jonathan Edwards's ten-year-old son; his father wanted him to learn the language of the Haudenosaunee. Hawley learned the Oneida language himself and became a well-established figure. Visitors noted that his services were being attended by over one hundred Indians. Old Isaac and Good Peter, wearing black coats, helped to lead them. Psalms were sung and sermons delivered in both English and Oneida. Services were solemn and dignified, but Hawley was less strict than other Presbyterian missionaries. Dancing and feasting were not prohibited, though alcohol and war were preached against strongly.[19] He and young Edwards left in 1756; Old Isaac and Good Peter ran the Christian community at Oquaga until 1762 when Eli Forbes came, though he stayed for only a few months.

Although the Oquaga mission was flourishing, the Christians in the Oneida heartland did not have a minister of their own. Some went to Fort Hunter or to Oquaga and participated in Christian services there, but these were long and difficult journeys. Christianity was embedded enough in the main Oneida villages that it survived, at least among a significant faction within the tribe, between the visits of the Anglican missionaries in the 1750s and the arrival of a new and different kind of missionary, Samuel Kirkland, in 1766. This may be attributed in part to the visit of Samson Occom, a Mohegan Indian who trained for the Presbyterian ministry under Eleazar Wheelock in Connecticut in 1761.

Rev. Kirkpatrick, as noted previously, had encountered Oneidas in 1760 on his way to Niagara. He witnessed a Native-led Christian service. He learned that the Oneidas wished to have a missionary and had money to build a place of Christian worship. Kirkpatrick wrote to Occom, urging him to make his first mission to the Oneidas. Occom arrived in Oneida country with David Fowler, his brother-in-law.[20] Sir William Johnson—probably with some degree of wariness about seeing a Presbyterian as opposed to an Anglican moving into Iroquoia—agreed to accompany him.

Occom's short visit was a success, seemingly both at Old Oneida and Kanonwalohale, though he did irritate some by suggesting that Indians should dress and wear their hair in styles more like the whites and by disallowing dancing after a baptism. A farewell ceremony was held when he left with gifts of wampum presented. The fact that this was at traditionalist Old Oneida (where Occom saw that hunger was pervasive) shows his achievement. One thing that likely united even the non-Christian sachems of Old Oneida with the Presbyterian missionary was the desire to see Oneida rid of alcohol. As Occom left, they said, "Father . . . We request the great Men would forbid Traders bringing any more rum among us; for we find it not good; it destroys our Bodies and Souls." They also asked that the great men "protect us on our Lands, that we may not be encroached on by any People." When Occom returned to Connecticut in 1762, he reported to Wheelock that "by an untimely Frost last fall their Indian Corn was all cut off—that the Onoyadas are almost Starved having nothing to live upon but what they get by Hunting." He also reported that his mission turned some Oneidas away from drunkenness. Wheelock commended Occom for the "good Effects of his Labours."[21]

Thus, some groundwork for a Presbyterian mission had been laid before the arrival of Samuel Kirkland in 1766. Like Occom, Kirkland's faith had been forged in the Great Awakening, a period of evangelization in the American colonies, that inspired him to spread the Gospel even if it meant martyrdom. He was also trained by Wheelock and studied alongside the Mohawk leader Joseph Brant.[22] When Kirkland came to Kanonwalohale, he built a small cabin, tilling his own garden and surviving on very little food in his first year there. This, he said, earned him "contempt" from villagers who saw his way of life as unprofitable and effeminate. Agriculture was still seen as women's work. However, in 1767 he began to win some ground in the community. He mastered the Oneida language and began teaching Indians to read and write it. He worked with Good Peter and Old Isaac, creating a Christian bond between Kanonwalohale and Oquaga. He also visited the Tuscarora settlements in the Oneida lands. He showed courage in standing up to alcohol abuse, even wrestling to the ground an Oneida man who tried to strangle him after he destroyed a cache of rum.

Food became scarcer in the 1760s, partly due to settlers' encroachments on traditional Oneida hunting grounds and partly due to failed harvests. Kirkland stayed close to the people and saw their suffering, offering kindness and what charity he could. He gained new status with the Oneidas as someone who knew and understood their problems (much like the Jesuits of the century before). By 1771, he reported that three or four hundred Indians were attending his worship services at Kanonwalohale. Although there were fluctuations in faithfulness and very few conversions among the traditionalists at Old Oneida, Kirkland had become a powerful and respected presence among the People of the Standing Stone. He baptized respected warriors, including one in 1767 who would be a lifelong follower, Shenandoah. Kirkland gave him the Christian name John.[23]

In the years between 1766 and 1774, the Oneidas' relationship with Kirkland deepened, just as their relationship with William Johnson became more and more strained. Johnson, although beloved by the Mohawks, had already tangled with the Oneidas at Stanwix. To the latter it was obvious that while he promised to protect their lands, he was simultaneously keenly interested in buying large pieces for himself and for wealthy friends, as he had done in 1769. Kirkland, by contrast, showed no interest in procuring land and indeed promised the Oneidas that he never would attempt to buy or take a single acre. The Oneidas began to resent what looked like Johnson's preferential treatment of the Mohawks. Blacksmiths, always in short supply, were provided close to the Mohawk villages but not to Oneida. In 1771, when the Oneidas petitioned him for their own blacksmith, Johnson ended up caught in a lie. He gave the Oneidas and the governor different reasons for rejecting the proposal, but the Oneidas discovered the deception.

When Johnson tried to block the building of a place of worship that would be financed by Presbyterians in Boston rather than via him (representing the king and the Anglican Church), the Kanonwalohale village council, backed by Kirkland, insisted they would go forward with building it anyway. The new meeting house was constructed in 1774. It was a two-story structure with glass windows, thirty-six by twenty-eight feet with a steeple towering sixty feet high; the most impressive western-style building in Iroquoia. Johnson was incapable of stopping it. To save face, he donated a church bell. Johnson and his Mohawk protégé, Joseph Brant (brother of Johnson's mistress and Kirkland's former classmate), were also meddling in Oquaga in 1773, trying to turn as many Indians as possible away from Presbyterianism and towards the Church of England.[24]

Kirkland and Johnson themselves became representative of the two increasingly polarized camps in the political life of colonial America—those unwaveringly loyal to the Crown and those for whom Britain's control over the colonies seemed increasingly intolerable. Kirkland was a New England Presbyterian whose immediate employers were in Boston, the epicenter of anti-British agitation in the American colonies. It was the site of the Boston Massacre in 1770, in which colonial protestors were killed by British troops who had been sent to occupy the city. In 1773, Bostonians destroyed thousands of pounds of tea in Boston Harbor to protest British taxation. Just as tensions were beginning to crest, Sir William Johnson died in 1774. His nephew, Guy Johnson, equally committed to the British Crown, succeeded him as superintendent of Indian affairs. Johnson tried to downplay the tensions to the Haudenosaunee as a dispute over tea that would "soon be over." Kirkland, however, interpreted the proceedings of the Continental Congress to Oneidas who were keen to understand the issues more fully.[25] The missionary was one influence drawing the Oneidas' interest to the colonial cause, but not the only one. The Oneidas were dependent on their colonial neighbors, particularly at German Flats, for vital trade. The Palatine Germans resented British taxation, and when fighting broke out, they would take the side of the rebels.[26]

In April 1775, British soldiers marched to Lexington and Concord, Massachusetts, where colonial militia were building stockpiles of arms. The first gunfire of the battle there was later called by Ralph Waldo Emerson "the shot heard round the world." It began America's War of Independence. In some eyes, it was a just war against imperial tyranny. In others, it was a treasonous rebellion. Soon after Lexington and Concord, Guy Johnson attempted to argue the virtues of George III with some Mohawk Valley patriots and ended up in a brawl. Palatine Germans drew up a petition to the king and declared solidarity with the people of Boston, where further battles between British forces and colonial militia were taking place.[27] The Johnsons sensed their time was up and evacuated to Canada.

§

The Oneidas and most of the Haudenosaunee attempted to stay neutral in the conflict for as long as possible. Some individuals chose their own way. There was no coercive control within the nations to stop them doing so. Many warriors were keen to gain reputations that would come with fighting. Some went to Montreal, eager to join in campaigns on the British side against the rebellious Americans. Others, like the half-Oneida Thomas Spencer, advocated strongly in favor of fighting against the British. Many Oneidas sympathized with Kirkland, who saw the Americans' conflict as just, but they knew they had little to gain, and much to lose, by taking sides in this war between "two brothers," as they saw it. They promoted neutrality vigorously among the Haudenosaunee. For the Haudenosaunee nations to the west, there was little to endear them to the American side. Their trade was less dependent on the Mohawk Valley and Albany (which became a rebel-controlled city in 1775). They could trade with the British via the Great Lakes, Niagara, and the St. Lawrence, and they had not been influenced by a "patriot" figure like Kirkland. The Mohawks, too, were drawn far more to the British than to the American side. Their most prominent figure, Joseph Brant, was intensely loyal to the Johnsons and carried many warriors with him.

When Johnson fled to Canada via the Oneida Carry, he attempted to give gifts to the Oneidas, sensing that they would be the biggest obstacle in tipping the balance in Iroquoia towards the British. The Oneida chief Shenandoah refused to accept them, and the Oneidas did not meet with Johnson at a conference he held with Indians at Oswego.[28] However, in response to petitions for support from rebels of Massachusetts, the Oneidas sent forth clear declarations of neutrality. In a speech translated by Kirkland and directed to the Provinces of New England, the Oneida chiefs and sachems said, "You are two brothers of one blood. We are unwilling to join on either side in such a contest, for we bear an equal affection to both of you, Old and New England. Should the great King of England apply to us for our aid, we shall deny him. If the Colonies apply, we will refuse." They asked that all Indians be left out of the conflict: "Let us Indians be all of one mind, and live in peace with one another, and you white people settle your own disputes betwixt yourselves." An Oneida delegation also went to Kahnawake in 1775 to urge their relatives there to remain neutral.[29]

Other Haudenosaunee began accusing the Oneidas of being too sympathetic to the colonists in 1776. Kirkland had clearly attached himself to the rebellion, becoming an Indian agent for the Continental Congress. Shenandoah accompanied Kirkland on a visit to the patriot forces in Boston the year before, where he met George Washington. The Cayugas were outraged that to demonstrate their neutrality, some Oneidas had handed over to the patriot leader Philip Schuyler a war belt that Johnson had presented to Haudenosaunee warriors in Montreal. In 1776, successful colonial attacks in Canada meant the western Haudenosaunee were deprived of their usual trade with the British and took out their anger on the Oneidas. It was clear by the end of a Grand Council meeting in Onondaga in March 1776 that Haudenosaunee neutrality was hanging by a thread and that the Oneidas were clearly the odd one out. That summer, Philip Schuyler (on behalf of the Continental Congress) and John Butler (on behalf of the British) held rival conferences at German Flats and Fort Niagara, respectively, each giving gifts and trying to gain the trust and partnership (or in Schuyler's case, neutrality, at least) of the Haudenosaunee nations.

The Americans, at the same time, reoccupied Fort Stanwix as a means of protecting the Mohawk Valley settlements from potential British incursions via Oswego. By tolerating American presence on their soil (even if the Oriskany Patent, on which the fort stood, was not owned by them), the Oneidas knew that both British and Indian observers would see it as yet another sign of pro-American leanings. However, they also felt a need for protection. The Oneidas and American officers at Stanwix, which was rechristened Fort Schuyler during the war, built up a positive relationship. Captain Joseph Bloomfield of New Jersey and some of his men visited Kanonwalohale. The Oneidas were able to trade and buy supplies at Fort Schuyler, and the American fortress offered at least some hope of refuge if Kanonwalohale were to come under attack.

Not all Oneidas were pleased with this perceived drift into the Americans' camp. Knowing that most of the Haudenosaunee to the west (and east) were leaning heavily toward the British, some chiefs, particularly in Old Oneida and Oquaga, dissented. When the Mohawk leader Joseph Brant visited Oquaga in the winter of 1776–77, he was able to capitalize on the Indians' frustration with further unauthorized white colonists' encroachment into their territory and tell stories of his martial prowess in the Battle of Long Island earlier that year, where he and the British had routed the Americans.[30]

By 1777, even while the Oneidas were still technically united in neutrality, it was clear who favored which course. On the pro-American side were prominent sachems, chiefs, and warriors, including Shenandoah, Good Peter, Grasshopper, White Skin, Hann Yerry, and Thomas Sinavis; on the pro-British side were Old Isaac, Jimmy Tayaheure of Kanonwalohale, and Niklasko and Kanaghwaes of Old Oneida. A delegation of Oneidas, including William Kayendalongwea, Beech Tree, and Hendrik, toured the patriot armies in New England and New York to investigate rumors spread by Brant and others that they were not strong enough to fight against the British reinforcements that were expected to arrive that summer. Meanwhile Brant returned to Oquaga and hoisted the Union Jack there. A few Oneida warriors went their own way, following Brant as he gathered pro-British Mohawks to fight on the British side in the 1777 summer campaign, while others continued to gather intelligence about both the British and the Americans' next moves.[31]

The British plan for 1777 was to destroy the revolution with a three-pronged attack, converging at Albany. General Burgoyne would head south from Montreal with eight thousand men. General Howe would proceed north from British-controlled New York City. Barry St. Leger would lead a force of ships from Canada down the St. Lawrence and across Lake Ontario to Oswego. There they would meet up with Joseph Brant and his Indian force, which would bring together a combined total of sixteen hundred fighting men. From there they would traverse Oneida country, take Fort Schuyler (Stanwix), and proceed down the Mohawk. This would cut New England off from the southern colonies, while a naval blockade would starve the colonists of supplies and force capitulation by the end of the summer. At the height of summer, Burgoyne's offensive appeared to be going successfully. They took Fort Ticonderoga on Lake Champlain in July. John Butler convinced large numbers of Senecas, Cayugas, and Onondagas—and even a few Tuscaroras and Oneidas—to join with Brant and St. Leger at Oswego. St. Leger arrived at Oswego with seven hundred Indians, four hundred British army regulars, and six hundred American loyalists. An Oneida spy called Thomas relayed the news to Fort Schuyler and urged the Americans to prepare for battle.[32]

In June and July, Mississauga and Haudenosaunee war parties hid in Oneida lands surrounding Fort Schuyler, capturing and killing soldiers who walked away from the fort on work details or to hunt. Knowing that the main attack was on its way from Oswego, the Oneidas attempted one last time to persuade the Haudenosaunee there to remain neutral. As expected, they could not be convinced. With the battle coming to their home soil, Oneida warriors were left to choose their own path. Technically the nation was still neutral, but several hundred went to Fort Schuyler to fight or to seek protection. Brant and his group of Indians was the first to arrive on foot, on August 2, while St. Leger's main force sawed its way through the trees the Americans had felled along Wood Creek to slow them and their artillery down. When they arrived, they surrounded the fort, and the siege began. Seven hundred fifty American soldiers were in the fort, far outnumbered by the siege party. An Oneida woman called Two Kettles Together and Powless, a young Oneida man known for his speed, raced down the Mohawk River to call for reinforcements. Nicholas Herkimer had assembled a militia force in German Flats composed of Mohawk Valley farmers and settlers. He began marching them towards Fort Schuyler on August 4, reaching the Indian village of Oriska the following day, where he was joined by somewhere between sixty and one hundred Oneida warriors.

On August 6, Herkimer and the Oneidas set out from Oriska on the final leg of their journey to Fort Schuyler. Several miles in, they were ambushed by a combined force of British and Haudenosaunee who fired at them from both sides of the road. Herkimer himself was wounded and the American advance towards the fort was halted. Fighting continued throughout the day, often in intense hand-to-hand combat using spears, tomahawks, swords, and rifle butts. By the end of the Battle of Oriskany, as it came to be known, hundreds of dead bodies littered the road. Most of them were white members of Herkimer's militia. But there were significant numbers of Haudenosaunee dead, including several dozen Seneca warriors who fought on the side of the British.

The remnants of the British forces retreated to their camps around Fort Schuyler, where the siege continued. While the battle was raging at Oriskany, an American sortie had gone out of Fort Schuyler and looted the campsites of the British and Haudenosaunee who were involved in the fighting, meaning that when the weary fighters returned, their food, blankets, and possessions were gone. Messengers reported that a powerful new force of battle-hardened patriot soldiers under Benedict Arnold was coming up the Mohawk from Albany, striking fear into the increasingly demoralized British and Indians. They abandoned the siege and retreated towards Oneida Lake, but not before making a raid on Oriska, stealing what they could and burning the village to the ground.[33]

By the end of August, British forces were gone from the Oneida heartland, but there was no saying whether they'd be back. At Oriskany, Haudenosaunee of the Six Nations on opposite sides of the Revolutionary War had fought and killed each other. The Oneidas received a bloody hatchet from Onondaga, signifying that they were now at war with the rest of the Haudenosaunee Confederacy.[34] But the offensive that would have cut the colonies in half and almost certainly ended the war if had succeeded was stopped. St. Leger's retreat killed the British pincer movement's momentum. It meant that Burgoyne's force was now on its own, deprived of vital support from the west that might have resulted in a triumphant occupation of Albany by the autumn. Instead, he was defeated at Saratoga in October 1777. It was the key battle in the preservation of the revolution. The French, seeing that the colonists had a chance of winning, decided to throw their support behind the Americans, eager as they were to get back at their old rivals who had ruined their own North American empire fifteen years earlier. The soldiers, militiamen, and Oneidas who fought at Stanwix and Oriskany had laid the foundation for America's victory.

§

In September 1777, Oneidas and Tuscaroras met in another council with Philip Schuyler. He offered a war belt to confirm that that they would fight side by side against the British. It was accepted. The fighting with the other Haudenosaunee, however, weighed heavily. The Oneidas declared their objective in future fighting would be to capture British prisoners, which they would exchange for Haudenosaunee warriors who had been captured by the Americans. About one hundred fifty Oneida warriors then went to Saratoga, where the decisive phase of the battle between Schuyler's and Burgoyne's armies was underway.[35] The Battle of Saratoga was a disaster for the British. On October 17, 1777, Burgoyne surrendered, ending all hope of success in the New York campaign.

The Oneidas were understandably worried about attacks from other Indians and asked for fortifications at Kanonwalohale. The Marquis de

Lafayette, a French aristocrat who had enlisted to fight with the Americans against Britain at the rank of major general (despite his age, twenty in 1777), was in Albany. After a meeting with the Oneida chief Grasshopper at Johnstown in March 1778, he sent three Frenchmen to Kanonwalohale to engineer a fort. The Americans' hope was that if they were able to provide the Oneidas enough security, they would in turn send warriors to Valley Forge to help Washington, who requested the help of the Oneidas, knowing that their skills would be of particular use against small British raiding parties that were harrying the countryside in Pennsylvania.

In April, forty-seven warriors, nearly all Oneidas, met at Fort Schuyler and began their trek with Louis de Tousard to Valley Forge. When they arrived, Washington met them personally. Alongside Lafayette, they fought, and at least six of them died at the Battle of Barren Hill in May 1778. The fort building at Kanonwalohale stalled, however. The three Frenchmen stayed for a month in April 1778, but the project was abandoned due to lack of manpower.[36]

During the summer of 1778, patriot settlements at Cobleskill and German Flats were raided by a pro-British band of Haudenosaunee and loyalists led by Joseph Brant. The predominantly loyalist town of Unadilla was raided by Oneida warriors in September. American soldiers raided and burned down the mixed Indian village of Oquaga, which Brant had been using as a base, sending refugees either to the British camp at Niagara or to the Oneidas at Kanonwalohale, depending on the side to which their sympathies leaned. A final raid by Brant and Butler's Indian-loyalist force on the village of Cherry Valley in November turned into a massacre, with women and children among the victims. Given the escalating violence in and near Oneida territory, Congress reinitiated the plan to help fortify Kanonwalohale. Fifty troops led by Captain John Copp from Fort Schuyler were sent to help the Oneidas build a picketed wooden fortification big enough for the residents to shelter in if attacked. It was completed between January and February 1779.[37]

To prevent further massacres on the frontier, Washington determined to destroy the Haudenosaunee. A large force under General John Sullivan began to assemble in Pennsylvania. A plan coalesced whereby General James Clinton would march his forces through New York to meet Sullivan's troops in Tioga, bringing the total number of soldiers to some four and a half thousand. They would then take the war into the Cayuga and Seneca homelands. An initial strike against the Onondagas was led by Goose Van Schaick from Fort Schuyler. This was carried out in April 1779. The Oneidas were not consulted and indeed the arrangements were deliberately kept from them. After the destruction of the Onondagas' village, refugees again fled to Niagara or to Kanonwalohale, as had happened after the burning of Oquaga. Clinton and Sullivan began their tour of destruction. Throughout the month of September 1779, the Sullivan-Clinton expedition destroyed every Cayuga and Seneca village, home, field, and food store they came across. Brant's small group of volunteers were unable to challenge an army of over four thousand. Four Oneida warriors accompanied the expedition, but the majority stayed away, citing that they would be needed to defend their own homes in case of an attack on Kanonwalohale.[38]

By October, nearly all the Seneca, Cayuga, and Onondaga people were living as refugees at Fort Niagara, dependent on the British Crown for the food and clothing needed to survive the winter. With so many warriors thirsting for revenge, the Oneidas knew Kanonwalohale would be under attack as soon as the spring weather in 1780 would permit. Two of the most respected Oneidas, Shenandoah and Good Peter (Figure 3.1), went, along with two neutral Mohawks, to Niagara to try once more to persuade the Haudenosaunee there to stop fighting on the side of the British. They

Figure 3.1. John Trumbull, "Good Peter" (1792).

76 | Land of the Oneidas

were not only ignored but imprisoned and lowered into a dungeon beneath the fort, where they languished for five months in four-foot by four-foot cells. One of the Mohawks died.

As summer came and the delegation did not return, the Oneidas knew that Kanonwalohale would be targeted. The fortress there was small and had no cannons, so there was a final choice to be made. Those who wished were permitted to go to join the British and the Haudenosaunee at Fort Niagara. Some did, for a range of reasons. Shenandoah's family went to be closer to him. Some Onondagas and Tuscaroras and thirty-two Oneidas, including the sachem White Skin, joined the British, perhaps for self-protection and perhaps out of fear of, or loyalty to, the greater body of Haudenosaunee. The rest of the Oneidas in Kanonwalohale and Old Oneida fled and set up temporarily outside Fort Schuyler.[39]

In July 1780, Brant set out with three hundred men, including Shenandoah and Good Peter, who had been released from the dungeon on the condition that they try to persuade the Oneidas to turn their back on the rebels and join the Haudenosaunee at Niagara. When they found Kanonwalohale empty, they burned it to the ground. They then went to Fort Schuyler where they convinced 132 Oneidas, including twenty warriors, to join them, while the rest rushed into the fort for protection. The six hundred or so Oneida refugees then went to Schenectady, where they were promised housing in former barracks. They passed a miserable winter there amidst shortages of food, fuel, and clothing. In town, despite what they had done to help the American cause, they were subjected to anti-Indian sentiments that had been stirred up over the murderous raids of the previous year.[40] In that winter there was no substantial Indian habitation anywhere in the Oneida lands nor—for the first time in centuries—nearly anywhere between Schenectady and Niagara.

Several skirmishes occurred in the Mohawk Valley in 1780 as Brant and Sir John Johnson continued to harry the area around their former homes. In 1781 another British-Indian raid on Cherry Valley crossed the vacated Oneida lands. But the focus of the war that year was in Virginia, where Washington's forces, including three Oneidas who had been meeting patriot leaders in Philadelphia earlier in the summer, forced the surrender of Cornwallis's troops at Yorktown. This decisive showdown made it clear that Britain was not going to win the war. The Oneidas spent another winter in Schenectady. They celebrated the arrival of George Washington when he visited the area in June 1782. In London, Parliament had already signaled that they would seek peace, though it would take months of deliberations before the final Treaty of Paris was signed, officially ending the war. The Americans attempted one final strike to dislodge the British from Fort Oswego in February 1783, traveling from Fort Herkimer through the frozen Oneida country. Two soldiers died in the freezing temperatures and the assault was abandoned after becoming lost in the woods near the fort.[41]

Washington visited Fort Schuyler and inspected the carry over to Wood Creek. It was shallow and narrow—"as unprepossessing a waterway as one can imagine" in the words of Michael Berleth—but Washington already knew this muddy river was essential to America's future. No grand vista, as anyone who has seen Wood Creek will know, but in Washington's mind he contemplated "the vast inland navigation of these United States," and saw the distant bounds "to a New Empire."[42] Washington's great preoccupation in his post-war life and presidency would be the binding together of America as it began to expand across the Appalachians and away from the eastern cities. The great channel formed by the long-disappeared outlet of Lake Iroquois was about to take center stage.

§

The Treaty of Paris that ended America's grueling War of Independence was signed on September 3, 1783. A boundary line separating British Canada from the United States was drawn through Lake Ontario. Britain also recognized American control of lands west of the Appalachian Mountains, extending all the way to the Mississippi River. Exhausted by eight years of war, both sides had accumulated heavy debts and lost thousands of men in the struggle. The Haudenosaunee were not mentioned in the treaty and indeed, there had been no official end to their war. They still lived as refugees, either in Schenectady or at Niagara, and it was unclear when or if they would ever return to their homes.

Two conferences were held at Fort Stanwix (as it was called again after the war) in 1784 with representatives from each of the Six Nations to make peace. The first was a meeting with commissioners from the state of New York. New York's Governor George Clinton was keen to get his state involved quickly, initially hoping to secure some land cessions from the Haudenosaunee to strengthen New York's claim over the area. They were competing against Massachusetts, who had a rival claim to Iroquoia based on its 1630 Royal Charter, which in theory entitled it to all lands to the west of New England all the way to the Pacific. Clinton distrusted the federal government, which he felt would probably bend towards pleasing more populous New England. New York's Indian Commission had been set up in 1783 with the express intent of effecting a deal with the Oneidas and Tuscaroras to give up their land and move west. But they also did not want to let the cat out of the bag too early. They agreed to take precautions with the Oneidas so as not to alarm them "with apprehensions that there is the most remote Intention to deprive them of the enjoyment of the District belonging to them."[43]

The Oneidas and Tuscaroras were warned that the state was hopeful of getting their lands and resettling them further west. Kirkland himself was reported to have told them of the state's design, much to the annoyance of Clinton.[44] The state commissioners agreed, "For Reasons which are obvious . . . not to mention any thing to [the Oneidas and Tuscaroras] at present with Respect to the Purchase or Exchange of their Lands" at the conference.[45] Instead, he tried to persuade them that they wanted to know the boundaries of their lands so that the state could protect them. Clinton was unable to achieve very much but did begin to establish a relationship with the Haudenosaunee which he would later turn to his advantage. He also left behind vast supplies of rum to help frustrate the proceedings at the next conference.[46]

The second congress, in October, was with the commissioners of the United States. A delegation of elites from the Continental Congress came to Fort Stanwix, including the future president James Madison and the Marquis de Lafayette. They were met by 613 Indians who camped outside the fort. The majority were Oneidas or their dependents; only twenty-seven were representatives from the Seneca, Cayuga, and Onondaga nations. The Haudenosaunee were forced to recognize United States primacy in Indian affairs, to return all prisoners held at Niagara, and to renounce any claim over the Ohio country to the west. Forts Niagara and Oswego were signed over to federal control. The US stated that under these conditions, the Haudenosaunee could return to their homelands to rebuild their villages. Many Senecas, Cayugas, and Onondagas did so, but the Mohawks opted to remain in Canada.[47] Whereas the other Haudenosaunee were treated as defeated enemies, the Oneidas and Tuscaroras were treated as friends and allies. They were promised money to rebuild their church. Article II of the treaty granted that "the Oneida and Tuscarora nations shall be secured in the possession of the lands on which they are settled." The commissioners explained that the other "four nations" should be satisfied for getting "more than, from their conduct in the war, they can expect."[48]

However, while the Oneidas had none of their land taken from them and procured some promises to help rebuild, neither had they gained anything by supporting the American side in the war. Their population had declined from twelve hundred in 1775 to one thousand in 1783, with thirty-six warriors killed in combat. Some Oneidas never returned to their homeland, instead joining Brant and other Haudenosaunee who decided to settle permanently in Canada. Some had died of disease during the exile in Schenectady. Those who did return to Oneida in 1784 tried to rebuild their lives there, but factionalism within the tribe, poverty, and alcoholism prevented any form of unity from reemerging. Instead of one village, there were five. The houses put up were makeshift structures. Kirkland lamented that the Oneidas had "depreciated" and now seemed "filthy, dirty, Nasty creatures a few families excepted." They nominally had command over some six million acres but also knew that with their tiny population they would be unable to stop settlers squatting on their lands without the assistance of the state.[49] Clinton was sure to use this to his advantage and would lose no time while the Oneidas were in a position of weakness, division, and hunger.

The period 1763 to 1784 is framed by two conferences with the Haudenosaunee at Fort Stanwix. The first was a British attempt to preserve Haudenosaunee land, or at least to spare themselves the problem of policing too rapid an expansion into Indian territory. The 1784 conference (or conferences, rather)—one with the state of New York and one with the United States—were altogether different. The state clearly had designs on Oneida lands, and although they did not achieve their aim of procuring it at Stanwix, they would in the years to come. The United States dealt with the Haudenosaunee as defeated enemies, apart from the Oneidas and Tuscaroras. It exercised restraint in a bid to induce some of the Haudenosaunee at Niagara back into the US and rob the British of the loyalty of their warriors, but there was certainly no renewal of the protections the British had offered in 1763. Within a generation, almost all of what had once been Iroquoia would be in the hands of white Americans in the state of New York. It was, at least for some of the revolution's leaders and soldiers, what they felt they had fought for.

Chapter 4

Removal, 1784–1835

The first "sale" of Oneida land after the revolution was transacted in a treaty at Fort Herkimer, signed on June 28, 1785. It was the first success in the state of New York's strategy to dispossess the Oneidas of their homeland. In time, it turned into an overt attempt to force them off it altogether. The so-called treaties in which the state purchased millions of acres of Oneida land were brought about using tactics ranging from ostensible paternalism to outright deception. The state used alcohol, stoked division, preyed on the hungry, paid off interpreters, and broke federal law in order to obtain Oneida land for scandalously low prices. It was a dark period of suffering for the Oneida people. They were among the first, but far from the last, Native people to suffer the depredations of the now-independent states of America. The purchase and removal tactics New York used on the Oneidas and other Haudenosaunee nations set the tone for America's exploitative behavior during its decades of rapid westward expansion and beyond.

In the 1785 treaty, the Oneidas turned over to the state of New York some three hundred thousand acres in the southern part of their domains near the Pennsylvania border at a price of $11,500. The story began nearly two decades earlier, in 1767. A settler at Cherry Valley, John Harper, had attempted to buy the land around the confluence of the Unadilla and Susquehanna Rivers near Oquaga from the Oneidas, but it was refused. In 1782, when the Oneidas were refugees in Schenectady, Harper tried again but was again unsuccessful. In 1784, plying some Oneida men with drink, he managed to obtain their marks on a deed agreeing a sale price of £126. One of the signers was the English-speaking and literate Oneida Jacob Reed.[1]

In May 1785, the Indian commissioners in Albany prepared a letter to the Oneida and Tuscarora nations saying that some of their number had been in contact to protest the validity of the sale. Patronizingly, the commissioners said that the state had warned the Indians that they could not sell to private individuals, and "yet We find that some of You have notwithstanding [. . .] suffered yourselves to be again imposed upon by Harper." They confirmed that the "the Sale and Writing are void and good for nothing," adding, "We hope You will be more cautious in the future." However, nearly in the same stroke of the pen, the commissioners wrote, "[As] we understand that You are disposed to sell some of your Lands, We now inform You that You have an Opportunity to do it to the Governor and Commissioners." The letter told the Oneidas that their presence was requested at German Flats "as soon as possible," adding that Onondagas, Cayugas, and Senecas would not be welcome.[2]

When Clinton met the Oneidas at Fort Herkimer, he pushed hard for a sale. Good Peter later recounted that after being told bluntly twice that the Oneidas would not sell, the Governor "produced a heap of money. . . . He then grasped a few handfuls . . . and said, all this shall be yours, on condition that you follow my advice." When that didn't work, Clinton invited "several Chiefs and Warriors" to a private evening conference, where he almost certainly offered personal payoffs and other inducements as he did on numerous other occasions. The next day, the Indians agreed to sell an even larger tract than the one Harper had tried to procure. Good Peter said that the governor promised them that the state would not seek any further purchases but threatened that "if we did not consent to his present proposed purchase, we must never thereafter tell him of our being cheated out of any of our lands; for he would not hear our complaints."[3]

The 1785 tract was far to the south of the core Oneida homeland. There was a clear justification for selling it given the hunger and the need for supplies that were ever-present among the Oneidas in the 1780s, notwithstanding Clinton's threats. Nearer home, the Oneidas wanted to reward a few individuals by granting them small portions of land, which would keep friendly faces nearby and act as a buffer from further incursions into their heartland. James Dean, the Oneidas' trusted interpreter, and Abraham Wemple, a Schenectady man who had helped feed the Oneidas during their period there, were given tracts of two by two and one by one miles, respectively, along the Line of Property. Samuel Kirkland, too, was given a square mile in 1786, half of which was for him and half as a glebe to support any future minister to the Oneidas.[4]

With these friends (as they saw them) installed, the Oneidas planned to chart a new course, leasing lands to white settlers for annual rents while retaining ownership, rather than selling outright. Knowing that they would not have the manpower or the experience to deal with hundreds of separate tenants, they became interested in a proposal from a well-connected speculator called John Livingston. He proposed leasing most of the Oneida lands (as it was only *buying* from Indians that was prohibited by state law) and managing the subletting of small parcels to settlers. The Oneidas would retain a large reservation of their own and receive an annual rent of between $1000 and $1500. They would also retain legal ownership of the land. Kirkland and Dean advocated that this was a good deal, and the Oneidas agreed to it, even though Good Peter and others were distressed at the thought of giving so much land over to settlement. Millions of acres were at stake and the term of the lease was 999 years.

Governor Clinton found out about the lease and asked the Oneidas to discuss it with him in 1788. Good Peter initially thought it would be to help prevent the Oneidas losing control over so much of their land. In fact, it was the opposite.[5] The Indian commissioners and the Oneidas met again in September 1788, this time at Fort Stanwix. By this point, the state had already declared the Livingston lease invalid. It was, after all, essentially a sale of an area larger than the state of Connecticut to private individuals thinly disguised as a lease, and the state saw it as such. But the governor knew that the Oneidas desperately needed the money that they would have received from Livingston. He offered to "help" by giving the Oneidas the opportunity to transfer the same land to the state.

The Oneidas nominated two prominent members of their nation to handle the negotiations with Clinton and the commissioners, including the private evening meetings. Peter Otsiquette was a young Oneida who had just returned from three years in Paris with the Marquis de Lafayette. He was the best educated Oneida, fluent in English as well as French. Colonel Louis Cook, a mixed-race Kahnawake Mohawk who had married John Shenandoah's daughter, was well versed in matters of land and leasing from earlier experience in Canada.[6] Cook proposed a lease of the land to the state, but Clinton would only accept a sale.

When the negotiations finished, it was agreed that the Oneidas would sell the area that had been part of the Livingston lease—that is, their entire six-million-acre homeland bar a 250,000-acre reservation south of Oneida Lake (see Figure 4.1)—to the state, in return for an immediate payment of $2000 in cash, $2000 in clothing and other goods, $1000 in provisions,

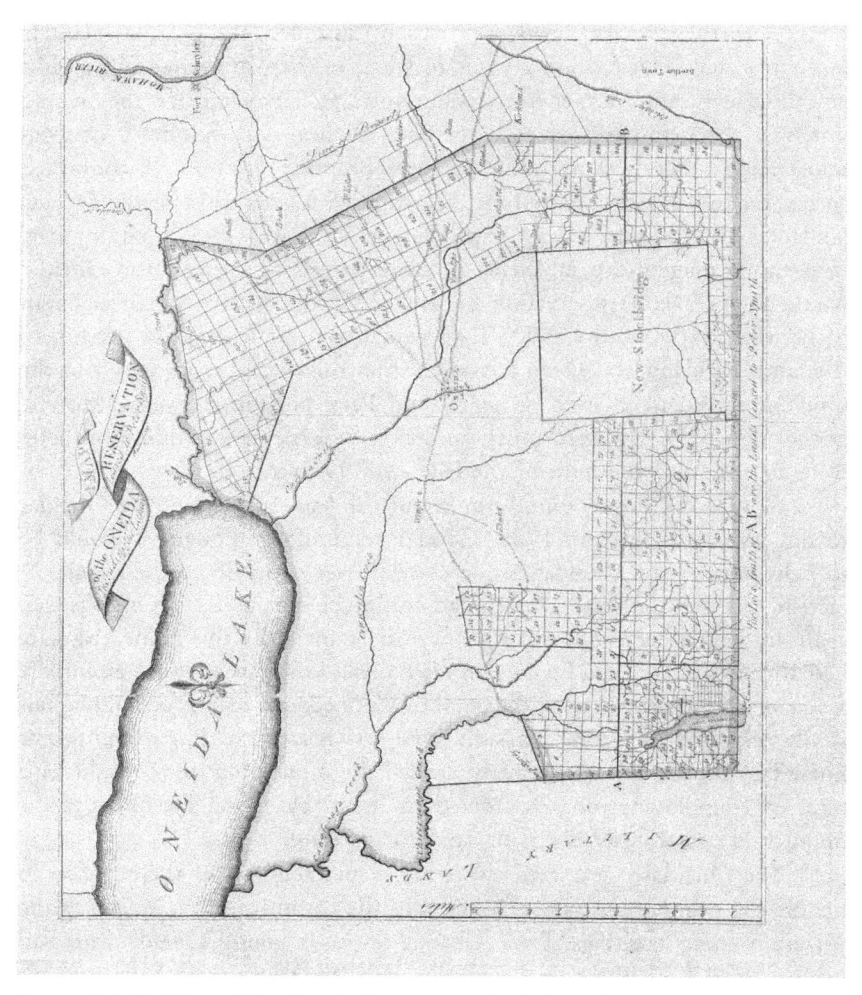

Figure 4.1. "A Map of the Oneida Reservation Including the Lands Leased to Peter Smith, ca. 1810."

and a further $500 to build a gristmill and a sawmill at Oneida. There would also be an annual payment of $600 in silver.[7] The vast hunting lands stretching from Pennsylvania to Canada were forfeited forever.

Arguably, it was not a much worse outcome than the Livingston lease would have been. The annual payment that the Oneidas would receive was lower, but the down payment was higher. The treaty gave over perpetual

84 | Land of the Oneidas

ownership to the state in the form of a permanent sale, but the term of the Livingston lease would have been 999 years, meaning no one alive then (or now) would see the day that the land would return outright to the Oneidas. There was a clause allowing the Oneidas to lease the southernmost four miles of their reservation. Fishing and trading rights on Fish Creek, which flows into Oneida Lake from the northeast, were preserved.[8]

However, there is no question that it was an exploitative treaty. Many of the Oneidas still believed it was a lease at the time of signing. Good Peter recalled, "The Governor of New-York said to us; You have now leased to me all your territory, exclusive of the reservation, as long as the grass shall grow & rivers run. He did not say 'I buy your country. . . .' Nor did we say 'We sell it to you. . . .' hence we have been deceived." He and other chiefs who came to terms with what was written in the treaty later complained to the state in 1790. They had been told in negotiations that their six-hundred-dollar annuity would have a periodic inflationary rise over time, but they discovered in the written treaty that it was, in fact, fixed at that amount forever. They also complained that the surveys showed the reservation land area to be far smaller than what they thought had been agreed.[9]

Recent historians have argued that the translators and negotiators whom the Oneidas trusted during the negotiations were in on the fraud. Colonel Cook has been portrayed as a corrupt double-dealer. He had been involved in the earlier Livingston lease negotiations for which he was promised a personal payment of two hundred British pounds by the lessees. In the run-up to the 1788 treaty, he was accepting payments from Peter Penet, a French businessman in Schenectady, to whom some of the ceded land was given. After the treaty, the state helped him to get sole ownership over a square mile of land in St. Regis. Otsiquette, it has been argued, was naïve and flighty, a friend of Governor Clinton. An image of him from Elkanah Watson's memoirs as someone who presented as a "well-informed gentleman" one day and reverted to "splashing through the mud . . . with a young squaw behind him, both considerably drunk" the next, serves as evidence of the Oneidas' misplaced faith. Samuel Kirkland was awarded two square miles, one for each of his children, for having "rendered meritorious service to the State." The translator James Dean was also a recipient of Oneida land and helped orchestrate bribe payments to some Oneidas in exchange for their signatures. Privately, he had come to despise the Indians.[10]

Many of these criticisms of the Oneidas' negotiators are justifiable. But would another team have procured a radically different agreement? The state and its governor were clearly only prepared to accept one outcome.

If the Oneidas had refused to sell, with a tiny population of around one thousand, they could not possibly have policed their six million acres against squatters and speculators. For that they would require state or federal protection, and neither were on offer. Before the treaty, they had already come to terms with the fact that settlers would be coming to their lands. Their acceptance of the Livingston lease, reluctant as it was, shows that. Kirkland probably genuinely felt that this was the best deal that the Oneidas were going to get. Although his priorities were beginning to change as he became a landholder himself, he had shown in 1784—when he frustrated Clinton's designs and warned the Oneidas to be wary of him—that he was not simply a pawn of the state.

But the taste left in the Oneidas' mouths after 1788 must have been bitter indeed. To the east, north, and south of their reservation, the land they sold to the state was rapidly broken into patents for wealthy speculators and then divided into lots for settlers, who began pouring in. To their west, the Onondaga lands were undergoing a similar transformation. Just before the 1788 conference with the Oneidas, New York negotiated the purchase of the entire Onondaga homeland in New York apart from a 64,000-acre reservation. A similar treaty with the Cayugas followed in 1789. Within a few years, the land of the Oneidas went from being the eastern end of unbroken Haudenosaunee territory upon which no white settlers lived to being completely surrounded by white settlements. Even the land within their reservation would soon start to disappear.

Before the ink was dry on the 1788 treaty, the process of chipping away at the Oneida Reservation had already begun. Peter Penet, a French exile, was hopeful to lease reservation land that he could sublet to settlers for a profit. He endeared himself to Colonel Cook by sending gifts and positioned himself as an advisor to the Oneidas during the treaty negotiations. He pretended to be an agent of the king of France on a mission to help the Indians in their relations in the new American republic. There were reasons why he was believed. He was an eloquent speaker and had earlier been involved in the import of armaments from France to the United States during the war. He had even worked closely with the founding fathers, including Benjamin Franklin and George Washington.

Penet obtained an informal agreement with some of the Oneidas to lease a piece of land within the reservation at Canaseraga and began a white settlement there, despite strong opposition within the tribe. Although the state declared the lease illegal and forced them to move, Penet still was held in high regard by some Oneidas. He was granted a ten-by-ten-mile tract of land in the northern part of the 1788 cession known as Penet's Square.

Penet tried to portray himself as the man responsible for procuring the clause that enabled the Oneidas to lease the southern four miles of their reservation and secure rental income for the future. In 1791, Penet attempted to lease the four-mile tract himself—again with the intention of subletting it to settlers. He succeeded in getting a deal signed by nine chiefs who were still loyal to him. He failed to pay, however, and fled to Haiti, never to be seen in Oneida again.[11] He died in France in 1801. In both the Canaseraga case and the four-mile-tract case, anti-Penet Oneidas petitioned the state for help in invalidating the transactions.

Clinton saw an opening that he could turn to the state's advantage once again to procure more Oneida land. He cited the problems caused by Penet's failed lease attempts to argue that without the state's help, the Oneidas would continue to be victimized by such greedy charlatans and interlopers. At the same time, he took the apparent willingness of the Oneidas to part with their reservation lands in long-term leases as evidence that a sale to the state was in line with their wishes. He knew well that it was only part of the tribe that had supported the Penet leases, but armed with these arguments, he went in for more.

§

The 1788 treaty staked out property lines for two non-Oneida groups within the Oneida Reservation. The Stockbridge Indians were secured on a four-thousand-acre, six-by-six-mile plot south of Kanonwalohale. The Brothertown Indians were provided their own reservation of roughly the same size to the southeast along the old Line of Property. Both the Brothertowns and the Stockbridges were groups of Indians from New England. Before the revolution, the Oneidas had offered them territory to come and live on, in a similar way (and with similar motivations) that they had invited the Tuscaroras earlier in the century. Supplementing Indian numbers on the land would increase their security and provide a buffer around the key Oneida settlements. As the Oneidas were beginning to turn to European styles of agriculture, the New England Indians who were far more experienced in it would also bring beneficial knowledge.

The Brothertowns were led by the Mohegan Presbyterian preacher Samson Occom. He had visited Oneida as a missionary in the 1760s and had not forgotten the place. In the 1770s he became the leading Christian voice among the Native Americans in Connecticut, Rhode Island, and Long Island. Occom's aim was to bring Christian Indians together in an independent township, free of white intervention. Occom returned to Kanonwalohale in 1774 and shared his vision. The Oneidas agreed to give the Brothertowns land to live to live on and to "adopt" them, saying, in a speech, "We receive you into our Body . . . now we may say we have one head, one heart, and one Blood." The first group of Brothertowns arrived in 1775, just as the Revolutionary War was about to begin. When British troops menaced the area in 1777, the Brothertowns left their tiny new settlement and fled mainly to Stockbridge, Massachusetts, where they lived as refugees until the end of the war. As soon as there was peace, Occom led a large number—two hundred by one account, though the actual number may have been smaller—of Brothertowns to their lands in New York in May 1784. They sailed up the Hudson to Albany and then went west, reaching their new home in time to plant for a successful autumn harvest. There were some thirty families living on the Brothertown tract by 1786. Occom was amazed to find in 1787 that some Oneidas still dressed "compleat in Indian way," referring to four men who attended a chapel service "shined with Silver, [with] large Clasps about their arms, one had two Jewels in his Nose, and had a large Silver half moon on his Breast; and Bells about their Legs, & their heads were powder'd up quite stiff with red paint."[12]

In 1786, tensions grew. Occom was called to Kanonwalohale and forced to lodge in the council house, where he could not sleep: "They have too many Vermine for me," he wrote. Some Oneidas had decided to have their land back and to reduce the Brothertown holding to a square mile. When Occom refused to concede, they proposed to let the Brothertowns live "at large" on the reservation, like the Tuscaroras without property bounds, which he also rejected. The issue arose again in October 1787. Occom recounted that on October 24 "we were call'd suddenly to appear before the chiefs of the Onoyd . . . about our Lands." Some Brothertowns had apparently tried to arrange a land transaction without consulting the "Headmen of the Place." He was given a warning. Occom came away depressed and confused by the meeting, lamenting that some of the chiefs were intoxicated and they "drove on the Business with all fury in no order, it was like a Whirlwind."

The bounds of the Brothertown lands were confirmed in the 1788 treaty with New York State, but tensions continued. The heated transaction with the Oneidas in 1787 may have been an early sign of the decision of some Brothertown Indians to lease parcels of their land to white settlers. In May

1792, Occom had to apply to the general assembly of New York to have the whites forcibly removed, since the leases did not have the appropriate approval. This pitted him against the faction of Brothertowns who were in favor of the arrangement. The result of the state's intervention was that the white lessees were allowed to stay but had to buy the land, a compromise that brought in some money but reduced the amount of land held by the Brothertowns. The factionalism drove Occom to distance himself from the Brothertowns. He died suddenly at age sixty-nine in 1792.[13]

The Stockbridge Indians were mainly Christian Mohicans from New England. They came from the "praying" town of Stockbridge, which was founded in western Massachusetts as a home for missionaries and Indians in 1732. The area surrounding the town was set aside for Indians to live on and farm. They took education and agriculture seriously, building a school for their own youths which was also attended by some Mohawks and Oneidas. Like other tribes east of the Line of Property, their land was sold and patented off by the Crown before the revolution. Their original thirty-six square miles of reserved land had shrunk to a mere twelve hundred acres by 1774. They were looking for land, just as the Oneidas were looking to bolster the number of Indians on their territory as a means of holding onto theirs. There is no formal record of the event, but it seems that the Oneidas granted a tract of land—six by six miles, the same as their original reservation in Massachusetts—to the Stockbridges in 1774, just before the outbreak of the war.[14]

During the war, the Stockbridge-Oneida connection became stronger. The Stockbridges fought alongside the Americans, sacrificing more than forty out of a total population of just three hundred. The Stockbridges sheltered and provided for forty-four refugee Brothertowns and some Oneidas while the war raged. Their emigration to the Oneida lands began in 1783 and carried on over several years. Their six-mile tract was confirmed in the 1788 treaty to the south of Kanonwalohale, where Oneida Creek runs northward through a valley with steep hills on either side upon which the Oneidas had located their main villages in previous centuries. Kirkland estimated there were about 280 Stockbridge Indians living there in 1792. Their lead minister was Rev. John Sargeant, who was later (in 1798) granted a square mile on the northeast corner of the six-by-six-mile tract. The Oneidas sold their title rights over the gifted land to the Brothertown and Stockbridge Indians in 1811 for $1200.[15] A chapel that held five hundred was built in Stockbridge. Occom often came from Brothertown to preach in what is now a tiny crossroads known as Valley Mills, in the Madison County town that still bears the name Stockbridge. The chapel, the mill, and the Stockbridges and Brothertowns themselves, however, are all long gone from today's landscape.[16]

Despite the increase in Indian numbers effected by the Brothertown and Stockbridge influx, the number of Indians on the Oneida Reservation was still tiny. Around 1790 there were six hundred Oneidas living there, plus two hundred eighty Stockbridges and perhaps two hundred Brothertowns. They would be up against 340,000 in the state of New York and just over a million in the states of New England.[17] The lands to which the Stockbridges and Brothertowns came to escape living in small enclaves surrounded by whites, was itself about to be overrun. Within three decades of arriving, they saw no alternative but to migrate again, leaving their names on the map of today's Oneida and Madison Counties, but almost no other visible trace.

§

By 1790, the Oneida Reservation was surrounded with land that had been sold to the state of New York and then rapidly sold on to white land speculators and settlers. The land immediately to the east had been ceded but not settled before the revolution. Coxe's Patent, Cosby's Manor, and the Oriskany Patent were subdivided into lots and sold. Those who came were mainly from New England. In 1787, the first farming settlement to the west of German Flats was set up by Judge Hugh White in present-day Whitestown. The development of Utica on Cosby's Manor began with three log huts in the same year. Other crude settlements started between 1787 and 1789 on Coxe's Patent, in what are now Clinton and New Hartford.[18] Baron von Steuben, a Prussian general who helped Washington lead the Continental Army during its darkest days, was awarded a sixteen-thousand-acre tract of land north of the Oriskany Patent. He died there in the town in Oneida County that still bears his name.

The Holland Land Company, a conglomerate of Dutch investors with agents on the ground in America, purchased Servis's Patent and surrounding areas. Two of their agents, John Lincklaen and Gerrit Boon, trekked north into New York from Pennsylvania in 1792 to scout out the lands, carrying bear skins to sleep in. Hearty explorers, they were nonetheless awed by the vast wilderness of the Oneida lands. They camped one night near Kanonwalohale but, unable to build a fire, they "resolved not to sleep, & to keep ourselves awake by telling stories, fearing the approach of bears & wolves." In 1793 they established a settlement at Barneveld in what is now Oneida County. Gerrit Boon hoped to make a fortune by harvesting maple sugar

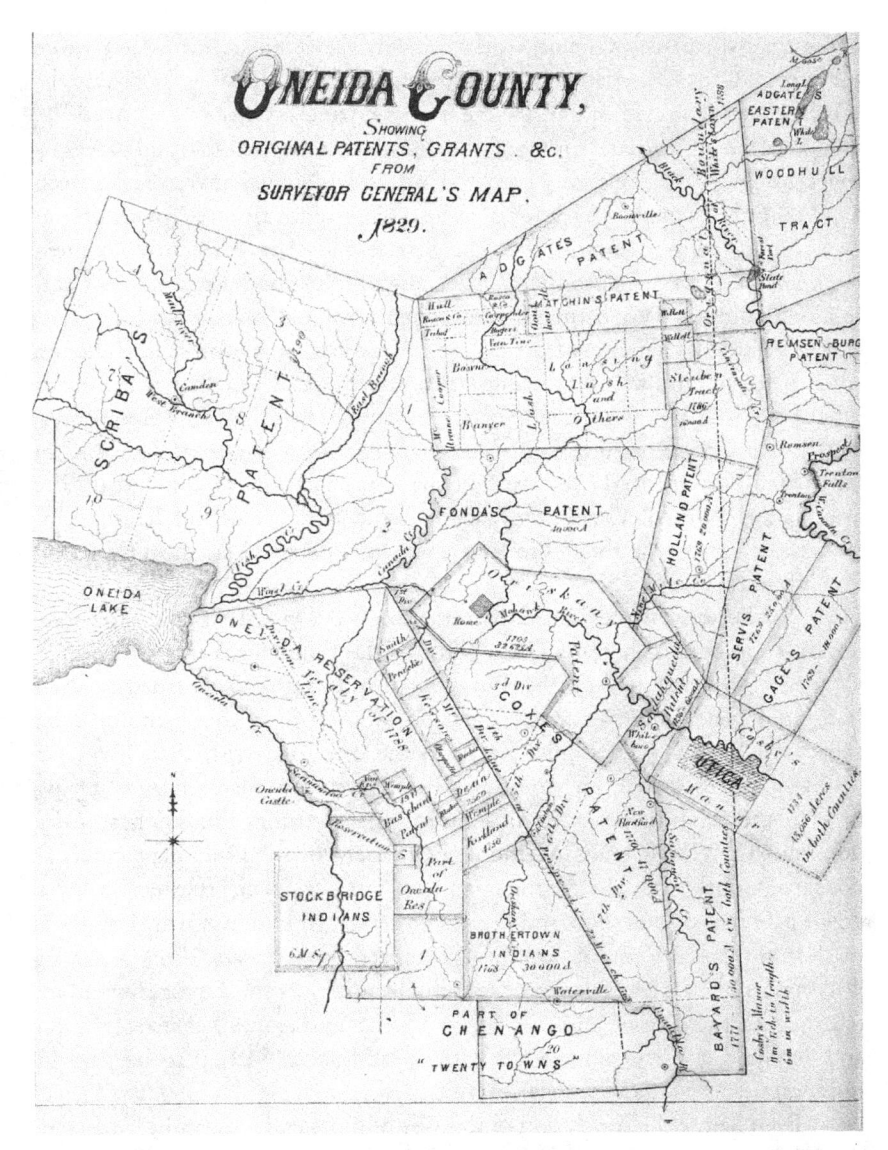

Figure 4.2. "Oneida County, Showing Original Patents, Grants, &c. from Surveyor General's Map, 1829," from Samuel Durant's *History of Oneida County*.

(at a time when the French Revolutionary Wars were making Caribbean sugar imports pricey). Although his plan failed, he did succeed in developing Utica as a depot on the Mohawk River for his hoped-for sugar empire. His name lives on in the Oneida County town of Boonville. Lincklaen wrote that from Old Fort Schuyler (Utica) east, "all this country begins to be inhabited, everywhere one hears the axe, everyone is busy felling trees!"[19]

To the immediate south of the reservation were lands purchased by the state in 1788. This was patented off to individual investors between 1792 and 1794 in blocks known as the Chenango Twenty Townships. It was common for squatters to be the first to move onto recently acquired land on the New York frontier. Often, they began the hard work of clearing and tilling it. When the rightful owner appeared, they would, in some cases, reward the squatters for the "improvements" made by selling them a small piece of land at a reasonable price, thereby also avoiding the difficult job of forcibly removing them from the land. In the Twenty Townships, squatters built the first log cabins in what are now Norwich and Oxford in Chenango County in 1788, years before the patents were concluded. The area to the south of Cazenovia Lake was sold to the Holland Land Company and named for their directing agent in Philadelphia, the Dutchman Theophilius Cazenove.[20]

To the west of the Oneida Reservation was Onondaga land. The state began its landgrabs there in 1788. Most of the Onondagas were still in the vicinity of Niagara at the time, but a small minority had returned to their homeland near Onondaga Lake after the war, led by a young minor chief called Black Cap. In a similar move to the one used with the Oneidas a few weeks later, the state commissioners portrayed themselves as trying to help the Onondagas evade unscrupulous speculators like Livingston by offering to buy their lands. Without the consent of the Onondaga chiefs at Niagara, Clinton bought all their land bar a 64,000-acre reservation for a down payment of one thousand French crowns, two hundred British pounds in clothing, and an annuity of $500 in silver.[21] In February 1789, a similar deal was reached with representatives of a minority of the Cayugas who had returned to their homelands. They too agreed to a 64,000-acre reservation and accepted a payment of $500 with an additional $1,650 to be paid in June, and a five-hundred-dollar annuity.[22]

Even before the conclusion of the War of Independence, and years before the 1788 treaty, the state had earmarked Onondaga and Cayuga territory as bounty land that would be given to Revolutionary War soldiers in return for their service. The prevailing view in Albany was that the Onondagas were on the British side during the war and that their lands would be up for grabs at its conclusion. The state promised soldiers six-hundred-acre bounties during the war. In 1782 (before the war officially ended), the state legislature approved a plan to divide up the lands to the west of Oneida territory. After the 1788–89 treaties with the Onondaga and Cayuga factions, settlement of the "New Military Tract" officially opened. The towns were named mainly for martial figures and statesmen of the ancient world like Pompey, Hannibal, and Cicero, with some poets (ancient and modern) thrown in such as Homer, Dryden, and Virgil.[23] The main land route into the two-million-acre military tract was the ancient trail that went directly through Kanonwalohale. The Onondaga Reservation itself was sold off in pieces in treaties with the state, reducing its size from 64,000 acres in 1789 to 16,000 in 1793.[24]

The lands to the north of the Oneida Reservation, stretching from Oneida Lake up to the St. Lawrence, were sold by the state in enormous patents. The biggest of all was Macomb's "Great Purchase" of 1792. The initial purchase of 1.9 million acres at a sale price of eight pence per acre was added to with further purchases bringing the total held by Macomb to well over three million acres. Alexander Macomb was an Albany fur trader who had made a fortune on ventures in Detroit during the revolution before settling in New York City after the war. The patent stipulated that at least one family must be settled on every square mile within seven years, so Macomb needed to entice buyers quickly. The tracts were subdivided into smaller, but still vast, chunks that were advertised for sale in European as well as American cities. Buyers developed schemes to settle the area quickly. Tracts V and VI were sold to Peter Chassanis of Paris, an agent for an association of French investors. An attempt was made to settle hundreds of Frenchmen in the New York wilderness in a colony named Castorland. It failed. The village name of Castorland on the Black River in Lewis County between Lowville and Watertown is all that remains.[25]

Other major subdivisions of Macomb's Purchase were sold to Thomas Boylston of Boston, who bought 800,000 acres and John Angerstein of London who bought 210,000 acres that he sold on to Governor John Brown of Rhode Island. Before the Erie Canal, the main lines of trade in the northern tracts were with Montreal. Agricultural produce, timber, furs, cattle, and potash (made from ashes of burned timber and stumps) were loaded into boats on Lake Ontario or the St. Lawrence and sold in British Canada, a problematic circumstance when Britain and America were hurtling towards a second war with each other in 1812.[26]

The area directly bordering the Oneida Reservation to the north was sold in one vast 500,000-acre patent in 1791 to Nicholas Roosevelt, who quickly resold it to a German merchant in New York, Georg Scriba. Unlike many of the great land purchasers, Scriba settled on the land himself and took a personal role in developing it. Scriba's patent included the entire north shore of Oneida Lake and extended to the shores of Lake Ontario from Oswego to Port Ontario at the mouth of the Salmon River. Before Scriba's purchase, there was already at least one squatter on his land. An island in the western half of Oneida Lake (previously used as a camp during Van Schaick's expedition from Fort Schuyler to destroy Onondaga Castle during the revolution) had been inhabited by a Frenchman called Desvatines, his young wife, and their children since 1791. There is much mythology about the family of what is still known as Frenchman Island. In one version of the story, he was a count from Lille. In another the family wintered with the Oneida Indians and joined them in their annual salmon trapping at the east end of the Lake. In one, his wife was in fact a nun and the reason for their fleeing France was to elope. In another, his cabin contained a full library of literature.[27] The existence of the French family on the island is attested to in a narrative by the German author Joachim Heinrich Campe, who visited Oneida Lake in 1796 accompanied by a guide called Vandek. He wrote:

> Across from us there was an island in the lake, abundant with trees and bushes, which was very pleasing to the eye. Suddenly, from the side where the trees were closer together, I saw a stately, tall, fine young man with a beautiful, completely European, and very elegantly dressed young woman who had a lovely three-year-old child on the sand coming towards us. Vandek could see by my face the amazement and curiosity that this sight excited in me, and said, while introducing the newcomers to me with a smile: Mr. and Mrs. von Wattines from Flanders; now our fellow citizens at Oneida Lake!
>
> The French origin of these people could not have been clearer. Their language, their clothes, their behavior—everything testified to it. The most natural assumption, which was later confirmed, was that I saw before me a pair of those unfortunate French émigrés, hurled from their fatherland by the storms of the French Revolution, that ended up here. Deep traces of the worries they had borne could be seen on both noble faces.[28]

Another early resident on Scriba's land was Francis Adrian van der Kemp, a Dutch exile and intellectual who bought a thousand-acre estate and lived on the north shore of Oneida Lake from 1794 with at least one family of enslaved people. Scriba himself settled a few miles to the west at what he called Nieuw Rotterdam (now Constantia in Oswego County).[29]

There were even some white men who had settled on the Oneida Reservation itself by the mid-1790s. Among them was a group of squatters who came from the Palatine settlements of the Mohawk valley. These were almost certainly the families that Penet had tried to settle on his illegally leased lands at Canaseraga. According to the first substantial history of the area, they came to settle at a point along Chittenango Creek that some of the men remembered traversing during a sortie from Fort Schuyler (Stanwix) during the revolution. An army captain named John Seber led a group of families there after the war. Anti-Penet Oneidas protested to the state about them, causing the county sheriff to come to force them to remove, burning their houses. However, the Oneidas allowed them to resettle on the western edge of their reservation near present-day Chittenango. John Lincklaen found them there during his travels in 1792: "We came to the Caneseroga [sic] Creek, there are 5 German families settled on the Creek, they are poor." In Kanonwalohale, Kirkland told Lincklaen that the Oneidas "allow Americans to settle on & work their lands, provided they give them 1/3 or half the yield, even their grist mill is managed on this footing by an American."[30]

Some of these now-tolerated squatters led by Conrad Clock then moved into the interior of the reservation, to what is now the hamlet of Clockville in Madison County, in 1792 in exchange for a modest rent.[31] Other whites were allowed to settle on reservation land due to their usefulness to the Oneidas. Abraham Van Eps had made an informal lease of some Oneida land in what is now Vernon in Oneida County prior to 1795 for $695 per year. He was a storekeeper who allowed Indians to buy on credit. A Mohawk valley veteran, Myndert Wemple, was allowed to live in the interior of the reservation from 1791 in what is now Wampsville (a corruption of his name), due to his skill as a blacksmith and horseshoer. In exchange for lending his highly sought skills to the Oneidas, he was allowed to run a tavern on the main trail across the reservation. Wemple's tavern later became the scene of a murder of a white settler by an Oneida named Saucy Nick.[32]

While there was an inexorable crush of settlers on every border and even within the reservation, the Oneida lands were also being crisscrossed constantly by travelers and settlers heading west. Before the 1790s, it was possible to travel by road from Albany to Old Fort Schuyler (Utica), but from there the only way further west by land was along the Indian trail that went through Kanonwalohale and on to the Onondaga, Cayuga, and Seneca homelands. That pathway became crucially significant with the opening of the Military Tract and lands further west after 1788. In 1794 the state legislature ordered the Great Genesee Road to be built roughly following the path of the trail, and in 1800 it was transferred to the Seneca Turnpike Company, which maintained it and collected tolls for its use. John Shenandoah used his home as an inn for visitors traveling along the turnpike in the 1790s and the early 1800s. Two other inns on reservation land opened, one at Wemple's and another at Canaseraga.[33]

Part of the reason the state of New York had been so successful in gaining Oneida land was that its dealings with the Indians were completely unchecked by the US government. In the period between 1777 and 1788, the string of colonies-turned-states were bound together only by the Articles of Confederation, which gave individual states near-complete control within their own borders. A weak central government existed but only to manage common interests such as foreign affairs. Federalists argued that a stronger central government was needed and after years of heated debate, a new US Constitution was ratified and federal elections held in the winter of 1788–89. George Washington was elected president and John Adams, a Federalist, became vice president. Anti-Federalists, Governor George Clinton chief among them, were dealt a heavy blow.

One of the first acts by the new Congress was to stop future agreements like Clinton's 1788 purchase, in which individual states could increase their wealth by preying on Native people who had no other protector. The Indian Nonintercourse Act of 1790 prohibited states from buying land from Indians without federal oversight. Washington himself remembered the Oneidas with whom he fought during the Revolution and did not want to see them defrauded of their lands. Washington's agent, Timothy Pickering, advised the Oneidas to be wary of future approaches from the state of New York. In 1794, Pickering offered the Six Nations a promise to protect their lands from future encroachments at the Treaty of Canandaigua. Article IV states: "The United States having thus described and acknowledged what lands belong to the Oneidas, Onondagas, Cayugas, and Senekas [sic], [engage] never to claim the same, nor to disturb them, or any of the Six Nations, or their Indian friends residing thereon and united with them, in the free use and enjoyment thereof."[34]

The Oneidas had written to the president personally in 1793 to say that they received no compensation for their services in the war, despite several requests. They told Washington, "We fear that evil disposed persons, have imposed upon You and us, or our calls would have been heard before now and Justice done to us."[35] In December 1794, after leaving Canandaigua, Pickering went to Kanonwalohale and presented the Oneidas with a treaty offering $5000 to distribute to individuals in recognition of their contribution to the American war effort. The United States also promised to pay for the building of a gristmill, a sawmill, and $1000 towards the construction of a new church to replace the one that was burned down in 1780. The Oneidas, in exchange, agreed to "relinquish all other claims of compensation and rewards for their losses and services in the late war."[36]

While settlers were flooding in, the Oneidas subsisted on their reservation. Lincklaen and Boon visited Kanonwalohale during their 1792 expedition. They attended a service at the meeting house there, heard Kirkland preaching in the Oneida language, and noted the "attention with which all the congregation assisted at the sermon, singing as well & in as perfect tune as could be in any church." Kirkland told them that the Oneidas' numbers had "diminished by half" over his twenty-six years of working with them. He reported that in the last four or five years "they began to be civilized, to live in houses & raise grain" but lamented that they "still lack the spirit of work, & [have] a taste for sedentary life—tilling the earth is burdensome to them."[37] Alcoholism and violence were serious problems. A string of fights and murders occurred in the 1790s. Jeremy Belknap reported after a few days interviewing Oneidas and their interpreters in 1796 that only thirty-six Oneida women and three or four men were "of a sober character" and that only one, John Shenandoah, always attended communion and never drank to excess.[38]

Divisions were rifer than ever among the six to eight hundred Oneidas in New York, the most serious among them between what can be described loosely as the "sachem" and the "warrior" parties.[39] It was an inversion of the division before the war between the warrior-dominated group at Kanonwalohale that was friendlier to Euro-Americans and receptive of Christianity, and the sachem-dominated traditionalist group at Old Oneida. In post-war Oneida, the sachems, in general, were more interested in leasing their lands, or selling them if necessary, and latched on to the promises of Peter Penet and other potential buyers and lessees. The warriors were opposed to leasing and, in some cases, also turned their backs on Christianity and embraced traditional religion (though some remained loyal to Kirkland). Colonel Hanyery, one of the warriors and a hero of Oriskany, was among those who petitioned to nullify the Penet lease and evict his tenants at Canaseraga in 1791. Captain Peter, Good Peter's son, was another leader of the warriors who repeatedly told the state that Oneida lands were off limits. But sachems like Good Peter himself (until his death in 1793), John Shenandoah, Beech Tree, and most of the clan mothers saw the futility of fighting the tide, knowing that settlers could and would come to the Oneida lands eventually. They may not have wanted it, but if it were going to happen, they wanted to accrue the best benefits possible for their people.

In the 1780s and '90s, the Oneidas again separated into different settlements. The majority returned to Kanonwalohale, sometimes called Oneida Castle. The site of Old Oneida was given over to the Stockbridge Indians, but a "new" Old Oneida existed a few miles from Kanonwalohale and again became the locus of the traditionalist segment of the nation. The village of Oriska was abandoned and the Oneidas who lived there moved to Canaseraga, where a Tuscarora settlement had existed before the war. A new Tuscarora settlement also existed along the six-mile path between Kanonwalohale and the Stockbridge Reservation. Unfortunately, no maps exist showing the exact locations of the villages. Both Lincklaen in his 1792 travels and Belknap in 1796 passed through Old Oneida traveling between the main Oneida and Stockbridge villages and Whitestown. Belknap describes a hill in Old Oneida from which Oneida Lake could be seen in the distance. Like its predecessor, it was probably a group of scattered homes rather than a compact village. It seems likely that the site was in what is now Sherrill, New York, with some houses on the high ground known as Marble Hill (which later became the site of the Oneidas' Orchard Reservation) and others further north and closer to the east-west trail that became Seneca Turnpike. An elderly Oneida man called Silversmith lived near the Tuscarora settlement, quite possibly on or near the place along Route 46 where the Shako:wi Cultural Center of the Oneida Indian Nation stands today. In front of his house was the Oneida Stone.[40]

Silversmith identified himself as pagan when he met Jeremy Belknap, who visited the reservation in 1796. Belknap wrote that the "objects of his devotion were the rocks and mountains, which he believed were animated by some invisible Power, which had a superintendency over human affairs." Other pagan Oneidas, he said, "address their devotions to the wind—others to the clouds and thunder." Belknap wrote that there were only eight adults who were professedly "pagan," but that their star was on the rise. Good Peter's murderous but eloquent son, a leading pagan, was said to be the most influential Oneida, while Shenandoah, a devoted Christian, was said to have "little influence in the nation, tho' one of the chiefs."[41]

The pagan group continued to drift away from the predominantly Christian Oneidas at Kanonwalohale. Some sought to reinstate traditional religious practices, including the "white dog" ceremony in 1799, in which a beloved pet was sacrificed for the purification of sins. In 1805 three women accused of witchcraft were murdered in the pagan settlement, probably in a log house where the Sherrill school building was constructed later. Luke Hitchcock, a non-Native who grew up in the area, claimed to have witnessed the execution as a boy. He said the women were killed by Han Yost, a prominent pagan and Revolutionary War veteran, and that they were "dispatched unawares, by the tomahawk." The executions prompted a formal divide between the groups known as the Christian Party and the Pagan Party and a division of the reservation lands between them.[42] Some Oneidas became interested in the teachings of the Seneca prophet Handsome Lake, whose religious code combined ancient Haudenosaunee beliefs with temperance and moral teachings, but he had less impact in Oneida than with the Senecas, Cayugas, and Onondagas further west. Others took notice of the Shawnee chief Tecumseh whose brother Tenskwatawa was known as a prophet promoting the revival of Native spirituality.[43]

Hunger was pervasive on the Oneida Reservation in the 1790s. Increasing white settlement on all sides disrupted hunting, and Oneida Lake no longer teemed with salmon. Agricultural work was still practiced by only a tiny minority of Oneida men. Even in 1796, Jeremy Belknap noted that most Oneida men refused to engage in it, saying that "scratch[ing] the ground" was for "squaws and hedgehogs." He wrote that the men had replaced their long hunting trips with "roving" among the white men—particularly the "intemperate, knavish, and profane" minority in the white settlements along the eastern edge of the reservation.[44] Collecting ginseng roots from the forest floor to sell down the Mohawk River for growing markets in distant China was one way Oneidas earned money.[45] But with food scarce and prices high, it is unsurprising that many Oneidas argued that the money that would come with land leases or sales would be better than starvation.

As soon as Penet's lease of the southern four miles of the reservation was annulled, Peter Smith, a local trader living in the nascent settlement of Utica, lost no time in trying to get hold of it himself. Smith was born in the Hudson Valley. When he moved to the old Cosby Manor patent, he got to know the Oneidas and gained their trust by giving them generous terms and even learning some of their language. With Penet gone, he offered $400 in 1793 as an initial payment, a further $200 to be paid in 1794 and 1795, and a two-hundred-fifty-dollar annuity for the duration of a twenty-one-year lease on the land. Unlike Penet, Smith was a local man with a prospering business. Those who favored leasing the land felt that Smith would be as good a manager of it as any. He promised to settle peaceable people there and appeared to be on good terms with James Dean, Samuel Kirkland, and other "friends" of the Oneidas, to whom he also offered sweeteners in exchange for the use of their influence to bring about the lease.

The pro-lease Oneidas approved Smith's bid in January 1793. He was permitted to initiate a survey of the plot. Here, however, there was trouble. The anti-lease faction of the tribe attempted to disrupt the survey, even smashing the surveyors' equipment on one occasion. There were further appeals to the state of New York—one from the anti-lease faction asking to annul the lease and another from the pro-lease faction asking for legal assistance in managing the lease (the state had promised to provide such assistance to them at Fort Stanwix).[46]

Yet again, Governor Clinton saw an opening to try to buy the land. The state advised the Oneidas that leasing the four-mile strip would be worse for them, given the unreliability of private individuals compared to the guaranteed price and annuity that the state would offer and abide by. What made this attempt different, though, was the fact that the state could not legally buy land without federal approval due to the 1790 Indian Nonintercourse Act. Furthermore, the US government had only just signed a treaty at Canandaigua promising to protect Haudenosaunee land. However, the state was determined to use the opportunity, for the stakes were higher than ever before.

With the opening of the Military Tract, the trail that went across the reservation was now the main artery for land travel between the new settlements to the west and Albany to the east. There was also the private interest of Philip Schuyler (now back in public life as a state official), who wished to get control over the land bordering Wood Creek with a view to creating a canal alongside it connecting the Mohawk River to Oneida Lake. Although Wood Creek was on the opposite side of the reservation to Smith's lease, it was hoped that deft negotiation could bring about the transfer not only of the Petersburg Tract (as the four-mile strip Smith was leasing became known) but also of some land along the Genesee Road and all areas bordering Wood Creek.

It was a decisive moment. If the state didn't act quickly and allowed the Nonintercourse law to bed in, they might never get hold of the lands they wanted along the key east-west corridor across the state. If they succeeded, however, the settlement of the western part of the state and the enrichment of the east would be the result. The state chose to exclude federal agents from the negotiations in full knowledge that any treaty they induced the Oneidas to sign would be illegal.[47]

The Oneidas sent the state representatives, including Philip Schuyler himself, back to Albany without a deal when they came to Kanonwalohale in August 1795. The annuity Schuyler offered was six times higher than that being paid by Smith, and there was more money on the table for the additional cessions running up to Wood Creek that Schuyler hoped to attain. The clan mothers continued to consider the offer, helped by the translator James Dean, who successfully persuaded them to sell the land to the state.

A delegation of twelve Oneidas went to Albany in September 1795 to sell the full 132,000 acres (of which the Smith tract represented only 45,793) in return for $2,952 as a down payment and an equal sum to be paid annually. Several Indians were given substantial individual cash rewards, some as high as $250, in exchange for their cooperation.[48] Smith, for his part, had already been given a preemption right by the state to buy the land he had previously been leasing. When the transaction between the Oneidas and the state was complete, Smith bought 22,300 of the 45,793 acres of the Petersburg Tract for $3.53 per acre. He built a house on it for himself, but sold most of it at an immense profit, quickly becoming the wealthiest man in the region and one of the wealthiest in the state.[49]

The rifts between pro- and anti-lease groups, sachems and warriors, Christians and pagans, those who fought on the American side during the Revolutionary War and those who chose to join the British or were compelled to, were profound prohibitors of any kind of consensus among the Oneidas. The state used these conflicts to assist in the procurement of their reservation lands. The federal government did nothing to hinder or punish the state for breaking the terms of the 1790 Nonintercourse Act. The "post-1790" Oneida land claim that was fought bitterly in federal courts in recent decades was for lands within the 1788 Oneida Reservation that were illegally obtained by the state of New York, beginning with the 1795 treaty. Over subsequent decades, piece after piece of the remaining Oneida lands would be purchased by state until virtually nothing remained.

§

In 1805, Samuel Kirkland suffered for over eight months with "violent and almost unceasing pain." A physician finally discovered the cause. He pulled out "a large black insect with glazed wings, nearly half an inch long" from deep inside Kirkland's ear. The missionary immediately knew it had come from sleeping on the floor at Oneida, where he had "observed great numbers of them in the ceiling & on the walls."[50] It was the latest in a long line of misfortunes. In Kirkland's final years, he looked back at a life of what he felt was service to the Oneidas, in which he endured unbelievable hardships, but for which he was repaid with ingratitude and betrayal by whites and Indians alike.

Kirkland—a landowner since his grant in the treaty of 1788—had been pulled in multiple directions in the 1780s and 90s. He remained a missionary to the Oneidas, trying, in his mind, to steer them toward religion, morality, agriculture, and civilization. He also continued to do work for the government. In 1792 he was commissioned by the War Department to lead the chiefs of the Six Nations to Philadelphia, to stop them joining the Indians in the Ohio country in their war against the United States. He began building a house on his land and brought his family there from Massachusetts to live with him. In late 1792, he received a serious injury to his eye when he brushed into a tree branch while riding. It caused such severe pain that he needed to seek medical treatment in New York and Philadelphia.[51]

While he was there, he procured support for the establishment of a school which he had been contemplating building for some time. He envisioned an academy in which Euro-American and Indian youths would study alongside each other. This would be a place of higher education for Indians who finished learning to read and write in English and their own language at local schoolhouses financed by Society for the Propagation of Christian Knowledge in Scotland, like the ones that already existed at Old Oneida and Kanonwalohale. The plan was supported by white settlers in the vicinity, whose children also lacked access to any but the most rudimentary education. In New York, Kirkland received subscriptions from wealthy donors and initial approval from the governor and regents of the state university. In Philadelphia, he saw President Washington, Pickering, and Alexander Hamilton, each of whom signaled their support. Hamilton offered to be a founding trustee. The Hamilton-Oneida Academy, as it was called until 1810, was built on the missionary's land.[52] Today it is called Hamilton College.

In 1794, a group of Oneidas complained about Kirkland in a letter to the Boston Board of Correspondents, saying that he was neglecting his duties as their missionary. For Kirkland, that was a kick in the teeth. He had indeed spent long periods away from Oneida, first on government business, then for medical treatment and to seek support for the Academy. He was still in severe pain with his eye, which affected his overall health profoundly.[53] Adding fuel to the complaint against Kirkland, an Albany clergyman, Rev. John McDonald, had also written to the Society for the Propagation of Christian Knowledge in Scotland about the deplorable state of Christianity among the Oneidas. The board sent a committee of two prominent churchmen, Jeremy Belknap and Jedediah Morse, to understand what was happening at Oneida and Stockbridge. In effect, it was an inspection. They departed from Boston in June 1796.

The pair traveled by stagecoach from Boston to Albany over four days. In Albany, they dined with Philip Schuyler, who, hot on the heels of the 1795 land purchase, was preparing for his journey to the Oneida Carry to oversee the building of the canal that would connect the Mohawk River to Wood Creek. From Albany to Schenectady (still Dutch-speaking, Belknap noted), they travelled with Schuyler in his own carriage. Belknap saw the place where the Oneidas lived as refugees during the last years of the revolution. They then boarded another stagecoach west, staying at inns along the way. One near Canajoharie, called Ruffs, Belknap described as "a dirty, noisy Dutch tavern, where we were obliged to lodge." Up to eleven passengers were packed into the stagecoach for parts of the journey, "very closely stowed, — four segars smoking a great part of the time."[54]

The public stagecoach route ended at Old Fort Schuyler (Utica). They then took a private carriage for four miles to Whitestown and rode the rest of the way to Kanonwalohale on horseback. On the way, they visited Kirkland, who was gravely ill. His new home was nearly complete, but the academy building was just a frame. From there they went to Old Oneida. They arrived in the wake of two murders there, one by an Indian called Cornelius who shot a rival called Jacob; the second by Jacob's father, who killed Cornelius in revenge. In his report, Belknap said that this sort of murder had become commonplace: "no further notice was taken of the matter." Their interpreter, James Dean, made no secret to Belknap of the "disgust" he felt "against the aboriginals."

From Old Oneida, Belknap and Morse went to Stockbridge. They took notes on what appeared to be a flourishing settlement of three hundred Indians living in good order, with well cultivated fields. Deer and birds abounded and there were pike and trout in Oneida Creek. On the six-mile journey from Stockbridge to Kanonwalohale, they passed through a Tuscarora settlement which still had one traditional longhouse. The meeting house in Kanonwalohale, where they interviewed Oneida villagers, was built of logs, as were some of the residences, though some were framed houses built in the "Dutch style." They stayed in the Euro-American style home of John Shenandoah. They were fed "Indian cakes" (corn dumplings), fried eggs, and strawberries, with tea and milk to drink. They also met with the non-Christian Oneidas, including Good Peter's pagan son, whom they described as a rowdy murderer and simply "bad."[55]

Belknap and Morse reported favorably about Kirkland when they returned to Boston. Kirkland too wrote a letter saying that the pagans and his enemies in the Penet party had penned the complaint that prompted the inspection, with the assistance of Rev. Sargeant in Stockbridge, who was jealous of the lands given to Kirkland. Although Kirkland was cleared by the board in Boston, he was cut off by the Society for the Propagation of Christian Knowledge in Scotland and lost his salary. This may have been due to his having accepted a vast property from those he served, or possibly due to the dearth of reports from him as his ability to write diminished while he suffered with his eye injury and the associated pain. The most likely reason was that the society was rethinking their policy of providing financial aid to missions in America. They stopped sending money to the United States altogether a few years later.[56]

Kirkland was never the same. Another riding accident caused lasting infirmity. The Oneida-Hamilton Academy did not live up to the vision he had for it. The school was educating fifty-two students in 1799 when Timothy Dwight visited from Yale. It struggled financially. Because Indian places needed funding, very few Oneidas attended. In 1798 Kirkland took on three at his own expense.[57] The following year, he lamented, "But one Indian boy is in the School; many have applied, and repeatedly, but the provision for their support which was calculated upon has not been made." In 1803, the Corporation of Harvard College provided a grant of one hundred dollars—enough to cover one year's tuition and board—for an Indian boy called Isaac Solegwaston.[58] But this was hardly what Kirkland had dreamed of.

Meanwhile, Kirkland lost most of his own land due to the business failures of one of his sons. Two of his children died in 1805 and 1806. His grandson and biographer wrote that he fed a hundred meals per week to Indians in his later years, implying that he was being taken advantage of: "When they came to him, they expected to be entertained. . . . This was the custom, and he could not break it up."[59] He died in February 1808.

After Kirkland's death, the academy was given a grant by the state to keep it alive. In 1812 it was renamed Hamilton College.[60] The dropping of

"Oneida" from the institution's name was intentional. Kirkland's grandson wrote that by 1812, "the Indians, though still numerous, became insignificant and unimportant amid the rapid increase of the white population; and the wants of the latter seemed to demand that the Academy should be elevated to the rank of a college."[61]

Belknap and Morse's journey showed the importance of what was going on in Oneida to the elites in the east in the 1790s. The Oneidas were seen as significant enough to warrant an expensive and lengthy trip from high-ranking religious personnel in Boston. Their land was on the most crucial route to the future of the nation, on the very frontier between white and Indian realms. They were known to President Washington, and they were at the center of a major project endorsed by some of the nation's founding fathers. But two decades later, the United States government saw little use for them. There are two reasons for this. One is that their most desirable land was sold off by 1815, meaning there was little left to get from them. The other is that the eyes of the nation shifted further west after 1815 as the result of a second war with Britain, one which the Oneidas helped the United States to fight.

§

The Oneida Reservation contained roughly 112,000 acres of land after the 1795 sale. Three years later, more was transferred to the state of New York. A delegation from the pro-sale faction of the Oneidas trekked to Albany in the winter of 1798. They signaled a willingness to sell more of their communally held lands. The state bought the northwestern part of the reservation, including several miles of Oneida Lake shoreline, plus two disconnected tracts along the Genesee Road on the eastern half of the reservation, leaving only a short stretch of the road on reservation land. This time the final treaty was signed at Kanonwalohale in June 1798. Unlike in 1795, the state of New York assured that a federal commissioner attended the signing of the treaty. Much of the ceded acreage between Chittenango and Oneida Lake was swampy, but the state split it into lots of one or two hundred acres each and found willing purchasers. The Oneidas were paid $500 and promised an annuity of $700 per year.[62]

Quakers among the Oneidas, who were trying to help them convert to an agricultural lifestyle in the 1790s, recorded that there were divisions over the transaction but also noted that pervasive hunger made additional income necessary. Recent historians have argued that the sale may have

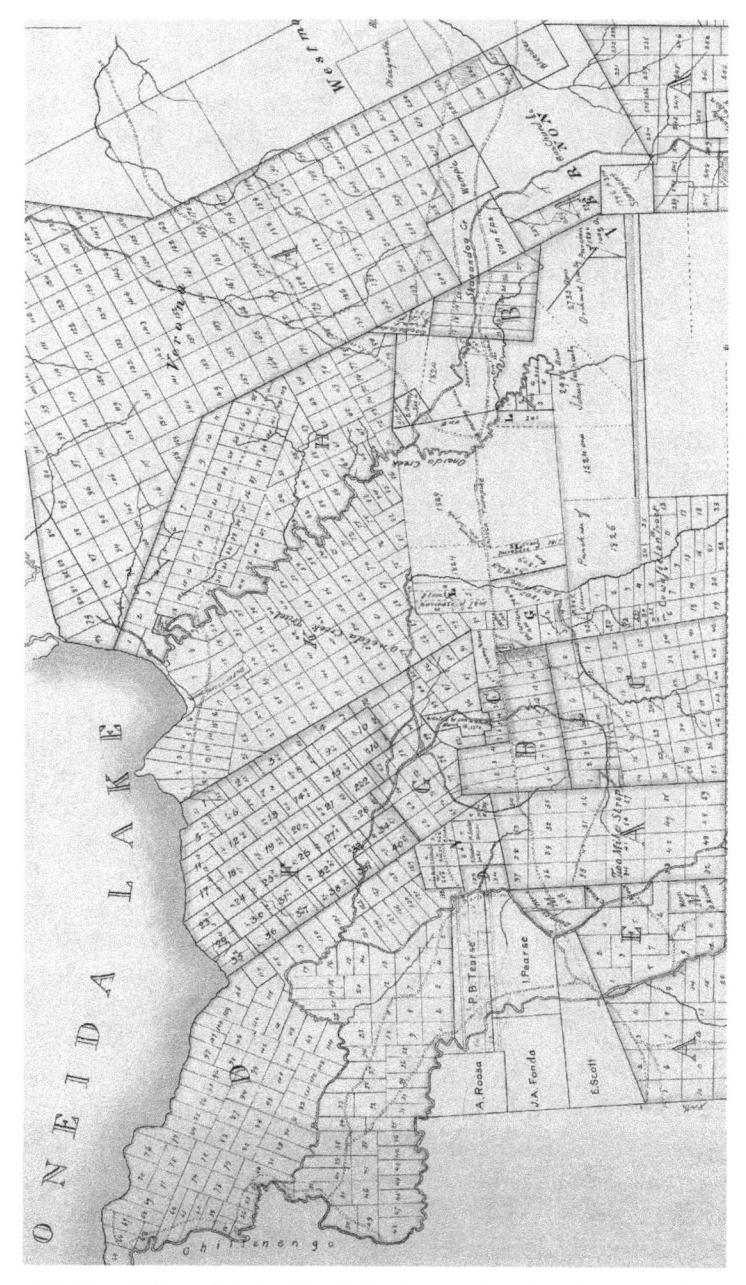

Figure 4.3. Detail from "Map of lands bordering Oneida Lake with references to Indian purchases, 1798–1817."

also been partly due to the pro-sale faction's hostility towards the Oneida people in the village of Canaseraga, which was included in the sale, and towards the pagan Oneidas settled around present-day Sherrill. The families at Canaseraga (two of which were mixed race due to marriages between Oneidas and whites) had become more adept at agriculture and hosted through-travelers on the Genesee Road in a tavern called Indian John's. The land sold along the Genesee Road came nearly to the doorstep of the new pagan settlement. The Oneidas in the main village of Kanonwalohale, who became known as the Christian Party, were the readiest to cooperate with state officials.[63]

In 1802, the whole scene replayed once more. A delegation went to Albany to offer further land for sale. Anti-sale Oneidas petitioned the state not to proceed. The state went ahead anyway with those who were willing to work with them, even paying cash to those who were able to persuade others to sign. The "purchase of 1802" was smaller than the previous two, and the payout from the state was higher. It was already home to white settlers with whom the Indians had made informal deals a decade before, after they were expelled from Canaseraga. Some, like Conrad Clock, after whom the village of Clockville was named, immediately bought the land they lived on from the state.[64]

In 1805, Christian and pagan parties agreed to split the remaining reservation between them. This would allow each to manage its own land affairs and prevent one party from selling land to the state that was felt to belong to the other. The rift between the parties had grown heated. The pagans accused the Christians of corruption in the dispensation of annuity payments and had become resentful of the Christians' adoption by the tribe of a French exile, Angel de Ferrière, who married an Oneida woman, Polly Denny. Denny herself was half Oneida and half French. Polly's father, Louis Denny, had been taken captive by the Haudenosaunee as a young man during the French and Indian War. He assimilated and identified as an Indian despite his purely European ancestry and became prominent among the Oneidas at Canaseraga. De Ferrière was a Frenchman who fled the revolution via Holland. There he met members of the Holland Land Company, who sent him to Cazenovia where he stayed with Lincklaen. He met his future wife while visiting Louis Denny, the only other French speaker in the area. He was given land and management authority of the Oneidas' mill.[65]

The split allowed each party to sell lands without seeking agreement from the other. In 1807, the Christian Party sold the "Canastota Tract."

This included further Oneida Lake frontage and a large area of swampland. Land along the Genesee Road was given to De Ferrière "in consideration of the services done" and a further four hundred acres north of the "Turnpike Road" was also granted to him.[66] A section of 329 acres where several Indian families lived in log houses was reserved (known as the "Canastota Reservation"), though that too was sold in 1810 to Captain Reuben Perkins, a Revolutionary War veteran from Connecticut who had resided near the Oneidas since 1805.[67] In 1809, the Oneidas sold their last remaining land along Fish Creek, other pieces having already been ceded in 1795 and 1802.[68] Again, the state paid bounties of up to eighty dollars each to influential Oneidas who helped see the deal through. The Pagan Party sold a large section of land in 1809 known as the "First Pagan Purchase," comprising the twelve thousand acres of land between the east side of Oneida Creek and the area in the town of Verona that was transferred in the 1795 sale, with influential treaty signers again accepting cash payments from the state.[69]

On this land was Kanonwalohale. It was surveyed in 1813. There were hopes among state officials at the time that Oneida Castle could become a new great depot on an alternative watercourse across the state, which would relieve the narrow and twisted Wood Creek of two-way boat traffic. If Oneida Creek could be made navigable from Oneida Lake to Oneida Castle, then boats coming from the west could travel there, unload onto wagons to Utica, and then continue down the Mohawk River. The 1813 surveyor plotted a grid system of streets and outlined a path for a canal alongside Oneida Creek (see Figure 4.4). It is drawn directly over the top of a pencil drawing of the Indian enclosures in situ at the time.[70] It may even have been considered a place for a new state capital; local lore holds this to be the case, and with moves in many states to locate (or relocate) their state capitals near their geographic centers around this time, there is reason to think it, though nothing is noted in the legislative documents of the time. When the first set of village lots went on sale in 1817, they sold for sky-high prices. The state later admitted some guilt in generating "extravagant anticipations" in the purchasers and awarded them some compensation.[71] The Indians still residing in Kanonwalohale moved to other locations on the reservation.

Finally, the "Oneida Creek Tract" was sold over two treaties in 1810 and 1811, once again by a delegation from the Christian Party that went to Albany for the deal. This included all the remaining shoreline of Oneida Lake, lands between the Canastota Tract and Oneida Creek, and

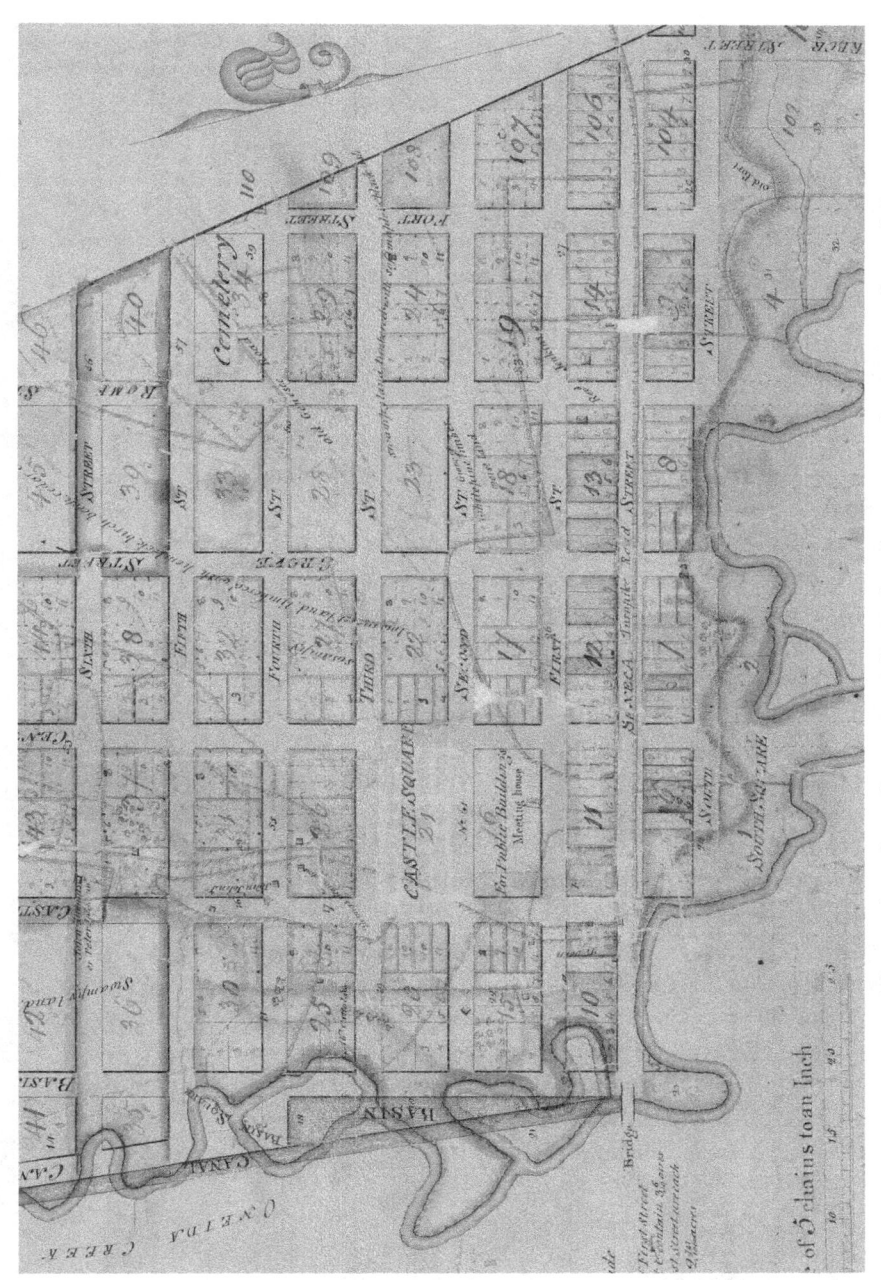

Figure 4.4. Detail from "Plan of a Village at Oneida Castle, in Vernon in the County of Oneida," 1813.

a disconnected "gore" of disputed land south of Oneida Creek. The Pagan Party had previously expressed their concern that this would be sold by the Christian Party.[72] It lay immediately across Oneida Creek from the Pagan Party homes in present-day Sherrill. An 1811 survey map also shows that there were some Indian houses there on Lots 4 and 5.[73] The gore was later returned to the Pagan Party in 1816 but sold again to the state when a large group of Oneidas opted to emigrate to Canada in 1840. Angel de Ferrière was given a two-hundred-acre plot fronting on Oneida Lake to add to his lands along Seneca Turnpike.[74]

By 1812, only about 21,000 acres of the 250,000 reserved in 1788 remained in Oneida hands. The reservation was eight and a half miles across from east to west and six and a half miles north to south at their widest points. Most of the lands along Seneca Turnpike (now Route 5) had been sold, and all lands bordering the key east-west water corridor along the Mohawk River, Wood Creek, and Oneida Lake were gone, too. Settlers rapidly bought up the new parcels and the process of creating America on Indian land began. Madison County was established in 1806. The town of Lenox made entirely of reservation land bought by the state after 1795 was created in 1809. The first town meeting was held in 1810, with a focus on ridding the area of wolves. It was agreed that a bounty of twenty-five dollars would be paid to any inhabitant who killed a wolf in the town and that five dollars would be paid to any Indian for the same.[75]

These were frontier priorities and frontier attitudes. Contempt for Indians, all Indians, was more widespread than ever in America by 1800. It had been stoked by stories of atrocities against white settlers during the revolution and the Indian wars that followed, and it was strongest on the frontier. Some American writers went far beyond arguing that Indians were inferior to whites. Newspapers carried articles propounding that Indians were a subhuman species, that they had no more right to own land than animals did, and that "extirpation of them would be useful to the world, and honorable to those who can effect it."[76] Whether the new settlers knew what the Oneidas had done for the colonists in the revolution or not, paying them a fifth of what a white man would get for the same job would not have shocked many in the town of Lenox.

§

The canal to Oneida Castle that caused a brief property boom there was never to be, but the desperation to find an alternative to the recently improved but still dismally tortuous water route across the state was widely felt by 1810. Philip Schuyler's Western Inland Lock and Navigation Company had done all it could. After leaving Belknap and Morse in 1796, Schuyler oversaw the digging of a canal across the Oneida Carry, connecting the Mohawk River to Wood Creek. The canal did cut down the time needed to move a boatload of cargo over the former carry route from a day to an hour, and the price of transport from Albany to Niagara was cut in half by 1798. But Wood Creek was still an intensely troublesome part of the journey despite the thirteen "neck cuts" that had been dug through in 1793. When water was low, stranded boats often needed to be unloaded, moved, and repacked. Between 1802 and 1803, the company tried to improve the navigation by constructing four covered wooden locks, but problems persisted. Schuyler's company was teetering on bankruptcy.[77]

Without a quick and cost-effective trade route through American territory, the settlers in western New York and beyond would find it easiest to trade via Lake Ontario and the St. Lawrence with the British at Montreal. In the longer term, it was feared, they could even transfer their allegiances. In 1810 New York's legislature was alarmed that the "commerce of the country was diverted in a great degree to Canada."[78] The state decided to intervene. DeWitt Clinton—forty years old and already a political star, having served as a US senator and a two-term mayor of New York City—was sent out with other commissioners on an expedition to explore the best route for a new canal. A single, straight cut across the state was envisioned, one that would avoid the vicissitudes of river and lake travel—the winds, floods, and low water that delayed or ruined voyages. The state wanted a reliable water route to connect the Great Lakes (and all its future trade) to the Hudson River and New York City.

Clinton and his team set out by boat from Schenectady on July 4, 1810. They reached Utica, now a flourishing town of 1,650 inhabitants where plots were selling for $3,600 per acre, on July 9. On its outskirts, Clinton found the Oneida Manufacturing Society, a cotton mill with 384 spindles that employed "forty hands, chiefly young girls, who have an unhealthy appearance." At the confluence of Wood Creek and Fish Creek, Clinton saw Oneida Indians in canoes and spearing salmon. He walked on Oneida Lake's eastern shore on what is now called Sylvan Beach, "composed of the finest sand," and encountered there "an Indian canoe, filled with eels, salmon, and monstrous cat-fish." Further along he saw a "native of the woods cooking his fish and eating his meal on the beach." The remnants of the eighteenth-century British blockhouse were still there. Clinton noted that coming out onto the lake from Wood Creek, there were sandbars where the water was only two or three feet deep. The lake traversal had to be powered by oar.

West of Oneida Lake, Clinton encountered the nascent salt trade growing up around Onondaga Lake. Thousands of barrels of salt were being produced and the saltmakers, Clinton noted, were angrily resisting the recent embargo laws that prohibited selling it via Oswego to the British in Canada. The United States was desperately trying to maintain neutrality in a war that was raging between Britain and France at the time by restricting trade with both countries and their empires. But the anger at Onondaga captured the essence of the problem. Settlers there wanted access to British markets that were far easier to reach by boat than American ones, and they were losing patience with the United States.

From Onondaga Lake, they proceeded by boat to Geneva and from there on went over land, mainly along the future route of the canal, to the Niagara River. Western New York was teeming with recent frontier settlements, most less than ten years old. Finally, on August 5 they reached Buffalo—a village of thirty to forty houses—on the shore of Lake Erie.[79]

On the return route, Clinton travelled by land on the Seneca Turnpike across the Oneida Reservation. He met Louis Denny, "a perfect Indian in dress, manners, and behavior," though his skin was "somewhat whiter." Crossing the bridge over Oneida Creek, he was taken by "a beautiful Indian girl, offering apples for sale to the persons that passed." He saw the meeting house, which he called "the Missionary church, in which Mr. Kirkland formerly preached." There were "Indians plowing with oxen, and at the same time their heads ornamented with white feathers; some driving a wagon, and the women milking and churning;—all the indications of incipient civilization." The commissioners stayed at Shenandoah's house, a "small frame building, painted red" a hundred yards from the road. He was one hundred years old, blind, and could hardly walk, but his face appeared "good and benevolent, and not much wrinkled." He smoked and conversed with his limited English.

Clinton wrote that the missionary societies that had sent Kirkland and Sergeant had failed to have any real impact on civilizing the Oneidas. The morals of the pagans, he said, "are better than those of the Christians," notwithstanding their practice of "ancient superstitions." Only the Quakers, he thought, had had any impact in teaching "agriculture and the arts of civilized life." Overall, Clinton paints a bleak picture of poverty, hunger, and disease on the reservation. He recorded that "some of the Indians are very squalid and filthy. I saw several take lice from their heads." He also noted the influence of Angel de Ferrière. He gathered a lot of information about him, some positive from his father-in-law, Louis Denny, but some negative, perhaps from Shenandoah, perhaps from his reputation in Albany. He wrote that De Ferrière, despite "symptoms of mental derangement," had prevailed upon the Indians to "confer on him donations of valuable land—which have been sanctioned by the State," including "1700 acres of the best land—a great deal of it on the turnpike," as well as a tavern on the edge of the reservation, a gristmill, sawmill, and distillery. De Ferrière possessed a fortune of around $50,000 but, Clinton noted, "he lives in a log-house and . . . is always involved in law suits."[80]

Six months later, in March 1811, the commissioners completed their report, recommending a 363-mile artificial waterway across the state. The state approved and authorized $15,000 to start work towards the building of the Erie Canal.[81] But long before spades would be put to the earth, there was a great deal of planning, financing, and legal work to be done. The outbreak of war in 1812 meant it would be six more years before the project would be launched.

§

America's second war against Great Britain and its imperial provinces in Canada had been brewing for the better part of a decade, but it was in 1807 that tensions began to be felt in the Oneida lands—where most residents were now white settlers. Britain had been at war in Europe with Napoleonic France since 1803, and during that time both Britain and France each did all they could to prevent the other from obtaining valuable trade from the United States. That including stopping American ships and, in Britain's case, forcing captured American sailors to serve in the British Navy.

Congress passed the Embargo Act during Thomas Jefferson's second administration in 1807. It outlawed shipping exports in an attempt to avoid being brought into the conflict. In upstate New York, this meant stopping all trade with British Canada. New York settlers from beyond the Hudson and Mohawk Valleys, like the saltmakers at Onondaga Lake, found themselves cut off from their closest major markets. European manufactured goods such as cloth and textiles became nearly impossible to procure after 1807. This spurred the first step in the industrialization of upstate New York when cotton works were set up at New York Mills near Utica, where De Witt Clinton encountered the unhealthy-looking workers in 1810.[82]

Removal, 1784–1835 | 113

Smuggling became a serious issue on Lake Ontario just as it did on the Atlantic seaboard. The United States retained its military base at Oswego, where they launched a naval shipbuilding program in 1808. They also began building up a fortified naval yard at Sackets Harbor at the mouth of the Black River, directly opposite the British stronghold at Kingston, Ontario. The supplies needed to build it were too unwieldy to carry over land, so they went via the water route from Albany up the Mohawk, through the Inland Lock Company's canal (across the former Oneida Carry) to Wood Creek, across Oneida Lake, downriver to Oswego, and then finally across eastern Lake Ontario. The first warship built was the sixteen-gun brig USS *Oneida*, appropriately named as it was built with materials drawn from and carried across the Oneida homelands. Its first commanding officer, Melanchton Taylor Woolsey, wrote that he "named her the Oneida after the county in which she was built . . . & a nation of Indians that inhabit the borders of it."[83] It was to be the first of five ships to bear the name in the history of the US Navy—later versions fought in the Civil War, World War I, and World War II.

When war broke out, the Oneidas declared neutrality. However, as in the American Revolution, the official stance of neutrality did not deter Oneida warriors from participating in the fighting. Up to two hundred Oneidas enlisted in 1813, and some served as officers in the Indian Volunteers Regiment. Over one hundred of them participated in the invasion of Upper Canada that year, and eighty saw action in the crucial events around their homeland in 1814.[84] The British fleet on Lake Ontario successfully attacked Oswego in May of that year and then laid siege to the main US naval base at Sackets Harbor. At the same time, a major delivery, including twenty-one big guns and a five-ton anchor cable, was being transported across Oneida Lake heading for Oswego for delivery to Sackets Harbor. With the British in command of the Lake, the delivery—now even more crucial to staving off total defeat on Ontario—had to be made with the constant threat of British interception.

A strategy was devised in which the supplies would be carried in small boats traveling close to the US shore of the lake and brought up as close as possible to Sackets Harbor while avoiding British detection. A land force (130 Oneidas) would meet them at the mouth of the Big Sandy Creek then shadow the boats, unload them, and carry the supplies over land to Sackets Harbor from there. The nineteen boats left Oswego on the 28th of May. The next day they entered Big Sandy Creek and the Oneidas arrived on time. However, the British had discovered the plot and blocked the outlet onto the lake with four boats. A British force marched inland to attack the supply ships but were ambushed by the Oneidas and American riflemen. The British attack was repelled, and the supplies were successfully carried over land the twenty miles to Sackets Harbor. One of the cables was too big to fit in any wagon and needed to be carried by a line of a hundred men across their shoulders in a two-day march. As a result, the Americans were able to fit out the USS *Superior* and repel the siege, winning dominance on the lake by the summer. The year 1814 was also decisive in the west. In the Battle of Chippewa, Oneidas faced the Haudenosaunee of the Grand River in large numbers in brutal hand-to-hand combat.[85]

The war ended in 1815. The Oneidas had—for the second time—helped the United States to prevail (technically it was a draw, but for the US, maintaining its independence was a victory in itself) in a war against Great Britain. But just as after the revolution, the years following the war would be marked with further exploitative purchases of their territory and eventually the movement of the main body of the Oneida people away from their ancestral homeland. The British ended their interference in the wars between the United States and Indians in the Ohio country. As a result, the American frontier pushed far beyond Iroquoia.

In the mid-1790s, Utica was the westernmost white area of settlement in the state, but after 1815, settlers poured into western New York, Ohio, Michigan, Indiana, and Illinois. With westward expansion came even more incentive for developing a canal and road across central New York. Oneida's frontier period was over, but its prominence as the United States' crucial arterial from east to west—foreseen by George Washington as he looked upon the muddy water of Wood Creek in 1783—was about to take shape.

§

When the building of the Erie Canal was authorized by the state legislature in 1816, its exact route was still not laid out precisely. The initial bill gave the go-ahead to start building a seventy-two-mile section from Rome (the town that had grown up over the ruins of Fort Stanwix and along the Inland Lock Company's canal across the former Oneida Carry) west to the Seneca River. Digging began on July 4, 1817. In the first two years of the project, the route west was dug mainly by local people; the large work parties of Irish immigrants on the canal came later. There were no trained civil engineers in the United States at the time. Many of the feats of ingenuity along the canal were devised on the spot. An axe man, John Jervis, became the chief supervisor of the construction of the middle section of the canal. He credited a Chittenango carpenter, Asa Waterman

Cady, with devising a plan for timber-supported aqueducts. The project was greatly aided by the discovery of a type of limestone in Chittenango that produced watertight cement, which was used to line the channel. An agent called Andrew Bartow first presented it to the canal's chief engineers at Elisha Carey's Chittenango barroom in 1818.[86]

The route went through more than twenty miles of the 1788 Oneida Reservation, on parts which had already been sold to the state. From Rome it went through Verona, on the 1795 purchase, then through the First Pagan Purchase of 1809 to what later became Durhamville, where the canal crossed Oneida Creek. The Oneida Creek Tract of 1810–11 and the Canastota Reservation lands carried it west across Madison County, and finally it traversed the northwestern part of the reservation sale of 1789 to its crossing of Chittenango Creek. The closest remaining Oneida lands were in what are now the city of Oneida, a few miles south of Durhamville. It is unsurprising that these, too, would be bought by the state and sold to developers by the end of the 1820s. In 1819, the middle section was nearly complete, and water was let into the four-foot-deep channel between Rome and Utica. By 1822, 220 miles of canal had opened.[87] In 1825 the Erie Canal was complete. Boats could travel from Buffalo to Albany. When the final stretch opened, grand scale celebrations were held throughout the state. In October 1825, Governor DeWitt Clinton arrived in Utica on a Sunday following a departure from Buffalo on Wednesday, a trip that formerly would have taken weeks.[88] He was travelling east to Albany and then to New York City, where he would ceremoniously pour a keg of water from Lake Erie into the Harbor, signifying the "wedding of the waters."

Towns like Utica, already beginning to flourish before the canal was complete, grew to become major centers of industry and culture in the 1820s and '30s. A Scottish traveler in the 1830s wrote that "the Americans call Utica the imperial city of the west."[89] Villages in the former reservation grew up along the canal at Durhamville, Canastota, and Chittenango. The canal also enabled the growth of the large cities of upstate New York. Syracuse had nearly seven thousand and Rochester over ten thousand residents by the end of the 1820s; both grew into major urban centers during the ensuing decades due to their location on the canal.[90] The cities of the Great Lakes—Cleveland, Detroit, Chicago, and Milwaukee—and the millions of acres of land converted to farming in the old northwest, were supplied with passengers from the east and a route to market for their products. New York City also grew tremendously as a result, becoming America's preeminent metropolis in the nineteenth century.

In Rome, where the first stretch was dug in 1817, some residents were aggrieved that the bustling trade through the town center on the Inland Lock Company's canal between the Mohawk and Wood Creek was lost. Wood Creek itself went from main artery to disused backwater overnight. The Seneca Turnpike too lost prominence.[91] But the numbers benefitting from the canal far surpassed those who lost out. In the 1790s, Washington's nightmare had been that settlers west of the Appalachians would break away from the states of the seaboard, or even join the British, Spanish, or French spheres to the north and west if their trade interests there were stronger. The Erie Canal meant that the territories to the west and the settlers thereon, linked indissolubly by trade through New York, would be thoroughly American, tied economically and spiritually to the original thirteen states.

The Erie Canal's success prompted further canal building across the country. A side cut canal was dug that connected the Erie Canal at Higginsville in the town of Verona to Oneida Lake. To fill it with water, a feeder canal had to be dug from Oneida Creek through the present-day city of Oneida (the water from the feeder entered the Erie Canal itself rather than the side cut), prompting the purchase of that area from the Oneida Indians in 1829.[92] The side cut, completed in 1835, enabled timber and farm produce from north of Oneida Lake to reach American markets via the Erie Canal rather than British ones via the St. Lawrence and Canada.

Far larger in scope, the Chenango Canal was built between 1833 and 1837, over ninety-seven miles from Utica to Binghamton on the Susquehanna, connecting the farming communities of southern Madison and Chenango Counties to markets in New York's cities. The Black River Canal, constructed between 1837 and 1856, extended north from Rome to Boonville through 109 locks, again drawing products down from northern New York onto the Erie Canal and the Hudson, rather than out via the Black River onto Lake Ontario and on to Canada.[93] As New York City boomed, Montreal declined. Canal building carried on well into the railroad era. Long after trains became the primary means of travel for passengers, the canals still carried most of the cargo freight; they were the nation's main economic arteries throughout the century in which America became a major world power.

§

John Shenandoah died in 1816. He was said to be 106 years old. In accordance with his wish to be buried next to Samuel Kirkland, his tattooed body was interred in Clinton in a funeral attended by the students at Hamilton College and by the Oneidas. The president of the college, Rev. Dr. Azel Bakus, gave an address that was translated for the Indians by James Dean. Bakus relayed the words that Shenandoah said shortly before his death: "I am an aged hemlock. The winds of a hundred winters have whistled through my branches; I am dead at the top. The generation to which I belonged have run away and left me: why I live, the Great Good Spirit only knows. Pray to my Jesus that I may have patience to wait for my appointed time to die."[94]

For a man whose name is so widely known, it is surprising that no biography of Shenandoah has ever been written. He was born a Susquehannock in the early eighteenth century but adopted by the Oneidas, presumably as a captive. In his funeral oration, Bakus recounted that in his early days he was "very savage and addicted to drunkenness," but after a trip to Albany in 1755 in which he woke up on the streets stripped of all his clothing following a night of hard drinking, he turned his back on alcohol forever. Bakus credited him with being the messenger to German Flats who tried to save the village from a massacre in the French and Indian War. His conversion to Christianity was genuine. In the American Revolution, he met with Washington but was later taken prisoner by the British and (probably forcibly) assisted in the burning of Kanonwalohale. His opponents among the Oneidas never forgot the help he gave the British side. Even thirty years after his death, Abraham Denny told Henry Schoolcraft that Shenandoah was a "tory in the war, notwithstanding his high name."[95]

DeWitt Clinton noted in 1810 that Shenandoah had once been the most prominent chief among the Oneidas before the split into Christian and pagan factions. He was a leading treaty-signer after the war and a friend of the speculator Peter Smith (who named his first son after him). This makes his epitaph on the memorial near his home, erected by the Daughters of the American Revolution in 1912—"The White Man's Friend"—rather uncomfortable. Some Oneidas called him that during his own lifetime and resented him for being too happy to cooperate with the people who were swindling them out of their land.[96]

Shenandoah was, however, a representative of the last generation of Oneidas that could reasonably have shared in Kirkland's dream of a strong, Christianized Oneida nation in its ancestral homeland that could gain most by working in partnership with the United States, whom he believed would honor their promises. He is the central figure in one of America's most iconic folksongs, "Oh Shenandoah," in which he epitomizes Indian pride and integrity—the chief who "disdained the trader's dollars" but who

118 | Land of the Oneidas

ends up being duped by an unscrupulous Yankee, who steals his daughter.[97] With his death, so, too, died his dream. The generation to which he belonged truly had departed, replaced with the harsh reality of life on an ever-dwindling reservation.

Eleazar Williams became the missionary at Oneida in 1816. He was twenty-eight. Unlike his predecessors, he was an Episcopalian rather than a Presbyterian. He moved into Shenandoah's house and immediately impressed the Oneidas with his energy and eloquence. He was an Indian himself. A Kahnawake Mohawk (with some white ancestry—his great-grandmother was an unredeemed captive from the raid on Deerfield in 1704), he grew up in Canada, was educated in Massachusetts, and was adept in Iroquoian languages as well as English. He revitalized Christianity at Oneida. The Pagan Party chose, under his leadership, to convert fully to Christianity and renamed themselves the Second Christian Party. A church was conceived and later built in the heart of the pagan settlement in what is now Sherrill.[98]

Purchases of Oneida land had resumed no sooner than the war had ended in 1815, with the state first buying four relatively small tracts on or near the Seneca Turnpike, including a ten-acre plot around a toll gate within the remaining reservation and one hundred acres on its eastern edge.[99] Late 1816 and early 1817 was a year of famine for the Oneidas due to the failure of their crop. Desperately in need of money, the Second Christian Party made another land sale to the state that Williams helped to orchestrate. They ceded the 4,126-acre Cowasselon Tract (about a fifth of their remaining land) to the west of Stockbridge, filling in a gap between the 1795 tract to the south and De Ferrière's Seneca Turnpike plots to the north. Members of the Denny family were accorded some of the plots, as was Eleazar Williams himself. The Second Christian Party regained the title to the disputed "gore" that the Christian Party (now known as the First Christian Party), had sold in 1810.[100]

Williams became a major exponent of removal. The concept of moving away from tribal homelands to new territories further west, where the harmful influence of whites would be reduced, had been behind the Tuscaroras', Stockbridges', and Brothertowns' decisions to relocate to Oneida lands in the eighteenth century. Now, with the Oneida Reservation constantly shrinking, surrounded by whites on all sides, the Oneidas began to consider moving west themselves. The Tuscaroras had already relocated to a new reservation in Niagara County before Clinton's visit in 1810. A quarter of the Stockbridges decided to relocate to Indiana in 1818.[101] Williams went to Washington in 1820 and procured some support for a mission to Green Bay, Wisconsin, to investigate buying land from the Menominee Indians there. He made two trips, in 1820 and 1821. Several Oneidas accompanied him on both trips, but the majority in New York were strongly against removal. Despite this, and without any real authority to do so, Williams negotiated a land sale with the Menominees and Winnebagos in 1821 and 1822 of 860,000 acres for $2000. In 1822, he persuaded them to expand the sale to cover close to seven million acres in exchange for an additional $3000, though the legality of both transactions was disputed for years afterwards. In 1832 the size of the purchased lands was settled at five hundred thousand acres.[102]

Although most of the Oneidas initially came out strongly against the emigration plan, the prospect of starting new lives on abundant lands in Wisconsin was not without appeal. Their reservation at this point was 16,000 acres and their number 1,096, not including the 273 Stockbridges and 360 Brothertowns in New York.[103] Pro-emigration leaders like Daniel Bread argued that at 160 acres per head in New York, the Oneidas were in a position comparable to the poorer among their neighbors. The population of New York State west of Albany had risen from 23,416 in 1810 to 108,891 in 1820, and the growth was only beginning. Hunger, constant battles against squatters and trespassers, and the pervasive presence of alcohol, which was now readily available at white-owned taverns in and around the reservation, were features of life that seemed impossible to controvert if they remained in New York. The Oneidas had around "300 families of white people, besides Negroes and mulattos" squatting or residing on their remaining lands in 1820. A hundred Oneidas left for Green Bay in 1823 and 1824—the beginning of an exodus that continued in fits and starts for over a decade.[104]

The wave of departures coincided with the opening of the Erie Canal. In the summer of 1824, General Lafayette returned from France for a tour of the United States, forty years after fighting to help it achieve its independence. In June he rode on the canal through what was the wilderness of Iroquoia during his participation in the American Revolution. Traveling through Oneida County, he saw bustling settlements, but no Indians. In Utica he was greeted with immense fanfare. The chiefs of the Oneidas were summoned to join the celebrations "at the particular request of Lafayette," who remembered some of them and knew more than most the extent of their contribution to the American victory.[105] At the time of Lafayette's visit, most of the Oneidas were still in New York State. But in the fifteen years following the opening of the canal, hundreds of them would ride it west to Buffalo and carry on westward from there, never to return.

In 1824, the Oneidas sold more land to pay for the costs of moving to Wisconsin. State officials were glad for them to go and began a practice of buying sections of land each time a new group emigrated. When a group proposed to leave, the state would calculate the percentage of the tribe's population departing, then work out the number of acres held in common by the Oneidas in New York and pay for a proportionally sized tract. The larger the group departing, the larger the number of acres bought. The First Christian Party, which was in general more in favor of emigrating, sold off two tracts, 1,192 acres in total, in 1824—one for $350 and an annuity of $240, the other for $800 and an annuity of $60. The state sold the land in thirty-one lots for a total of $25,367.30. Both sections were along the Seneca Turnpike. The first was on the west side of the reservation. In its extreme northwest corner was a small section of the Erie Canal. The other section was on the east end of the reservation and included the land where Shenandoah's house stood. The Indians living there were named in the treaty and given five years (six for one) to "to remain in peaceful enjoyment of the improvements in their possession at their respective places of residence" before they would need to get out. Angel de Ferrière bought two of the lots that touched on the canal route (Lots 2 and 3). The buyer of Lot 22 of 65 ¾ acres was Sands Higinbotham, a young merchant from Vernon who later founded the city of Oneida.[106]

There had been plans among the Stockbridges (and Brothertowns) to migrate further west since the 1790s. In 1809 Stockbridge chief Hendrik Aupaumut visited a tract intended for settlement on the White River in Indiana and went to Washington to gain approval for the move from President Jefferson. In 1818, a party sold some of their New York reservation to the state to finance the emigration, but the entire plan fell through at the last moment.[107] They were, nonetheless, determined to move out of New York. They were one of the tribes involved in the 1821 and the disputed 1822 agreement with the Menominees and Winnebagos to buy new lands for emigration in Wisconsin.

The Stockbridges sold nearly all the land on their six-by-six-mile reservation to the state in thirteen treaties between 1818 and 1830.[108] One of the more controversial of these was the so-called "New Guinea" plot, south of present-day Munnsville, sold in 1825. This 362-acre tract was later thought to be a place where fugitive slaves lived on lands provided by the Stockbridges. In fact, the occupants were mixed African-Native families who had been taken in by the tribe but who did not wish to remove with them to Wisconsin. A handful stayed and one, Nathan Pendleton, Jr., classified as mulatto in census reports, was called "the last of the Stockbridge Indians residing here" in 1847.[109] Between 1822 and 1829, all other Stockbridges emigrated to Wisconsin. The Brothertowns, too, all emigrated out of Oneida County starting in 1822.[110] The Oneidas had originally invited the Stockbridges and the Brothertowns to live among them to bolster their numbers and to "buffer" the Oneidas' core lands from the encroachment of whites. By 1830, hope of stopping whites overrunning even the core Oneida Reservation itself had gone.

In 1826, another group of Oneidas—this time members of the Second Christian Party—sold a further tract to finance emigration. The land sold included another area along Cowaselon Creek, south of De Ferrière's Turnpike plots, at a price of three dollars per acre, again with the stipulation that the final payment would only be made when "the Governor shall be satisfied that the said Indians are about to move to Green Bay." Before the ink was dry, other members of the predominantly anti-emigration Second Christian Party protested to the state that they had not given their consent to the transaction and that half the signers of the treaty were actually among the First Christian Party. But the treaty was upheld.[111] Those in the Second Christian Party who agreed with the sale split off and were officially recognized by the state as the Orchard Party. In 1827 the Orchard Party sold 264 acres on either side of Oneida Creek south of the Smithfield Turnpike, the present Peterboro Road.[112]

Thus, just as the Oneida population in New York was beginning to decline rapidly due to emigration, those who remained were divided into three camps, each with their own lands and ability to negotiate treaties with the state: First Christians (mainly pro-emigration Episcopalian since Williams's arrival), Second Christians (mainly anti-emigration, converts to Christianity since Williams's arrival and led by Han Yost's son Moses Schuyler—and therefore sometimes called the Schuyler Party), and now Orchards (mainly pro-emigration former Second Christians). To add further complexity, the Orchards welcomed Methodist missionaries and were sometimes called the Methodist Party. Some First Christian Party defectors were invited to live among the Second Christian Party after reneging on their agreement to emigrate but never officially joined them.[113]

In February 1829, all remaining land north of the Seneca Turnpike and west of Oneida Creek was sold by the First Christian Party to the state for $1500. This area later became the city of Oneida. The treaty stipulated that some funds were reserved to help pay for a schoolteacher in Green Bay. Timothy Jenkins, attorney to the Oneida Indians and a future Democratic congressman, received a plot along Oneida Creek running north from where it is crossed by the Seneca Turnpike—where modern-day Main Street, Oneida, connects to Route 5.[114] A second sale in the same month disposed of the last remaining lands along the Seneca Turnpike on its south side, six hundred acres for $1000.[115] It was stipulated that payment would be withheld until the Indians living on the land signaled that they would definitely move to Wisconsin, which they did with a petition in October, reserving only the right to burn firewood and harvest the crops they had grown on the land before they left.[116] The reservation that remained amounted to about eight thousand acres. One thousand more acres were sold by the Orchards for $1200 in 1834.[117]

Those who emigrated went along the Erie Canal to Buffalo, where they boarded ships to carry them across Lake Erie and on to Green Bay. The pace of Oneida emigration picked up after the settlement of the land disputes in Wisconsin in 1830. By 1838 there were 624 Oneidas in Wisconsin, more than half the tribe. In 1840 the collectively held land remaining to the Oneidas in New York amounted to 4,509.85 acres, just under 2 percent of the 250,000 acres reserved to them in the 1788 treaty, and most of that land was about to disappear, too.[118]

Historians have tended to lump the post-War of 1812 treaties together. After all, the state was just continuing the process started in the 1780s, chipping away at the remaining holdings of a divided and demoralized tribe. There was nothing in these comparatively nickel-and-dime transactions to match the multi-thousand- (or even million-) acre tracts of the first decades after the revolution.[119] But looking at them in detail brings two important issues to light. First, they show the origin of the Orchard Party in the disputes over the 1826 land sale. Although they were mainly pro-emigration, some members of the Orchard Party never left New York State and became known as the Marble Hill Oneidas. In recent years, their quest for recognition as a tribal group separate from the main body of Oneidas in New York has become a heated issue with serious ramifications. Second, these small-scale treaties show that the motivations of the state of New York in their dealings with the Oneidas had changed dramatically. George Clinton and his contemporaries' main aims had been to get hold of Oneida land to raise revenue for a cash-strapped state, preempt a rival claim from Massachusetts, and secure key land and water routes to the west. By the 1820s, all that had been achieved. The state's purchases of Oneida lands after that were less about the land itself than about moving the Oneidas off it. The 1820s sales effectively offered a per capita rate for each Indian who agreed to emigrate permanently. "Indian removal" is remembered as a federal policy of the post-1830 Jacksonian era. But New York had already written the book.

§

During the Presidency of Andrew Jackson (1828–37), Indian removal became US government policy. It was an expansion of the practices used in several previous administrations. For its advocates, removing eastern Indians to places west of the Mississippi River offered a solution that was best for whites, and—some thought—could be best for Indians, too. New, larger reservations would be created, far from the problems that white settlers had imposed upon the Indians in the east. But for many of its supporters, Indian removal was simply a way to solve the problem of having islands of sovereign Indian lands surrounded by white settlements. Anti-Indian racism and the possibility of obtaining the remaining Indian lands in the east at cheap prices were motivating factors as well.

The Indian Removal Act was signed in 1830. Indian nations, particularly in the southern states, were forced to remove to "Indian territory" in Oklahoma. One of the architects of the policy was Indian Commissioner John Schermerhorn, a minister from the Mohawk Valley. The policy bothered some people's consciences, especially in the northeast, where there was heated opposition. The removal of the Cherokee Indians from their homelands in the South provoked a particularly strong reaction from Boston intellectuals like Ralph Waldo Emerson. The 1835 Treaty of New Echota between the United States and the Cherokees, which preceded their removal, was signed only by one faction of the tribe. Forced marches from Georgia and North Carolina killed thousands, while whites piled into their lands searching for gold which had recently been discovered there. Jacksonian Democrats accused New England opponents of the policy of hypocrisy, given that most of the Indian nations of the northeast had already been exterminated or pushed westward.

Many of the Oneidas still in New York felt that their future in the United States was doomed. Schermerhorn and others were putting pressure on the Wisconsin Oneidas and the New York Haudenosaunee to move to Kansas. The Green Bay reservation was reduced in size to one hundred thousand acres, to discourage further emigration there and push Indians to resettle west of the Mississippi. The First and Second Christian parties eventually also agreed to emigrate, but not to Wisconsin or Kansas. Deeply distrustful of the US administration, Moses Schuyler—the leader of the Second Christian Party—and others decided to seek British support for emigration to Canada. They purchased a 5,400-acre tract on the Thames River in Ontario in 1840.[120] As in previous treaties with New York, it was agreed that a proportionate number of acres per capita would be bought by the state and that the Indians who remained would be left with a proportionately sized reservation "in a single parcel or tract in a form as compact and convenient as may be found practicable."

Four local men—Timothy Jenkins, Sands Higinbotham, Nathan Burchard, and Salmon Case (not to be confused with the Ohioan Chief Justice Salmon Chase)—compiled lists of which Indians intended to stay and which wished to go. Those who opted to remain in New York numbered 178, while 578 declared their intention to emigrate. The reservation for those 178 Oneidas who remained was agreed to be roughly fifteen hundred acres. The remaining three thousand would be sold to the state. The land sold included the "Gore"—later the home of the group known as the Oneida Community (see chapter 5)—and the lands where Sherrill would later grow over the former pagan settlement. Higinbotham was charged with organizing the remaining Indians onto a rectangular plot (the final dimension was 1388.75 acres) that became known as the "Oneida Reservation of 1840" or "Windfall" (See Figure 4.5). The treaty had a new aspect: it allowed Indian families on the reservation to gain private ownership of their portion of it by applying with Burchard, Case, and Jenkins.[121]

In 1841, ninety-eight Indians of the Orchard Party remained on 484 acres in Oneida County a few miles to the east of the Windfall (which was in Madison County). Forty-four of them decided to emigrate to Canada. In 1841 and 1842, the Orchard Party sold two more small plots along Peterboro Road. The Orchard Reservation was cut down to 266.88 acres. Sixteen more announced they would go in the first treaty of 1842, lobbing another seventy-five acres off the remaining lands. After 1842, only forty Orchard Indians remained on a plot of about 191 acres.[122] The Green Bay and Ontario Oneidas were thereafter treated as separate legal entities from the Oneidas in New York. The Windfall Reservation and Orchard plots were in the hills, miles away from the thoroughfares of the Erie Canal, Seneca Turnpike and, later, the railroads that spurred rapid growth of towns and cities on land that had recently belonged to the Oneidas.

For the most part, the remaining Oneidas lived impoverished lives. Indians and whites who had not been intricately involved in the treaties would have struggled to understand in any detail exactly how the reservation

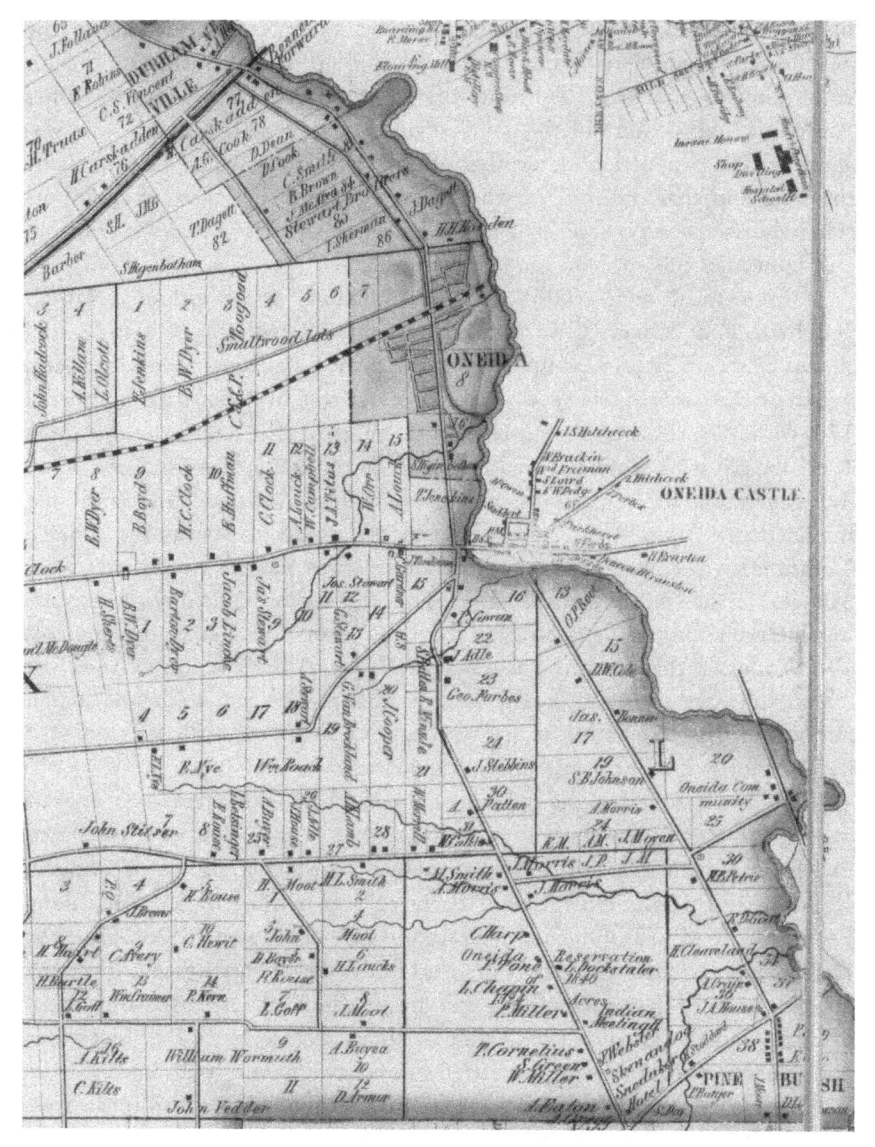

Figure 4.5. Detail from Gurdon Evans, A. D. Byles, and Robert Pearsall Smith, "Topographical Map of Madison County, New York" (1853).

had been chipped down so rapidly, almost to nothing, while the Indians remained so poor. One would be forgiven for thinking that the Oneidas' land had simply been taken from them. Map makers could not keep up. Various maps of Oneida County and the Town of Vernon even up to the 1870s show the Orchard Reservation as far bigger than it was; the various sales of the 1830s and '40s of a hundred acres here, seventy-five there, were perhaps too complex (or seen as too unimportant) to sort through.[123]

In the 1880s a committee was formed by the state of New York to examine what it called the "Indian problem." They sought to understand how things had got as bad as they had on the reservations that remained within the state and determine the causes. One motive was to try to set the record straight, proving that every acre of Indian land had been purchased, not stolen. The report asserted that "in dealing with its Indians the State of New York has been often generous and always just."[124] It printed the texts of all treaties between the state and the Haudenosaunee, including all the purchases of Oneida lands between 1788 and 1842. Yet, reading them, it is difficult to accept that treaties involving such an imbalance of power could be deemed fair, even by the standards of the time. In the 1840s, most Indians were still signing treaties with an *x*, and their consent was confirmed only by noting that the terms of the treaty were explained to them verbally. And of course, the state's post-1790s treaties with the Oneidas were nearly all in violation of the Indian Nonintercourse Act.

Within a generation, the Oneidas in New York had gone from the predominant entity on a vast borderland between Indian and white realms in America to being a tiny minority clinging to their few remaining acres of ancestral land. In 1842, the Oneida population in New York numbered about 40 Orchards on their 191 remaining acres in Oneida County, and about 180 on the 1,388-acre Windfall Reservation in Madison County.[125] Most of the Oneida people had left and were building new lives and communities in Wisconsin or Canada. But the history of the Oneidas in New York was far from over. It would get worse before it would get better.

Chapter 5

Reckoning, 1835–1865

During DeWitt Clinton's 1810 journey into the then wilderness of central and western New York, he came upon a religious "revival" meeting in a clearing a mile outside Lyons. Two hundred people gathered, "called together by a trumpet," to hear four fiery preachers, one of whom argued the importance of conjuring up the "fires of hell" in sermons to focus the mind. The crowd broke into emphatic spiritual "groans." One man looked into the tear-soaked eyes of another, "admonishing him of the necessity of repentance." Clinton's associate visited Jemima Wilkinson, a self-proclaimed prophetess residing with a band of followers in the Finger Lakes.[1] These were early signs of developments to come—a spiritual tremor that spread quickly eastward into central New York, where it would reach its powerful climax.

Central New York was the breeding ground of a religious awakening that bled into a new social radicalism in the northern states during the years leading to the Civil War. What began as a wave of emotional evangelization metamorphosed into a crusade against social evils and sin in society at large, above all African slavery. The Civil War arguably had its origins as much in the ancestral land of the Oneidas (upon which the remaining Indians were now a tiny minority) as in the plantations of the South. The spiritual atmosphere also led to the foundation of America's most successful—and notorious—utopian community in the very cabins left by the departing Indians.

So powerful were the fires of religious emotion in central and western New York during the 1820s and '30s that it came to be known as the "burned-over district." The impulse came partly from a reawakening of the New England religious experience. Founded and largely populated by Puritans,

New England had itself experienced waves of intense religious revival—most notably the Great Awakening of the 1730s and '40s, which had so shaped the likes of Samuel Kirkland. A century on, most people living in upstate New York were original or second-generation settlers from New England. In their first decade of rough pioneer life, setting up homes and establishing farms took up most of a settler's energy, but once communities were established, the religious spirit came back out to the fore. Frontier revival meetings led by Congregationalist, Presbyterian, Methodist, and Baptist preachers stirred overwhelming reactions. In the first years of the nineteenth century, evangelists like Lorenzo Dow visited Oneida County, holding camp meetings that were attended by hundreds of settlers. They left behind a religious charge that brought new congregations to life on the frontier.[2]

However, it was the Erie Canal that converted the isolated flare-ups of evangelical enthusiasm into an intense spiritual blaze in central and western New York. It sped up the conversion of large areas from unsettled frontier to stable communities ready to put greater focus on religion. The Erie Canal and its arterials also gave revivalists something to rail against. The insobriety of transient canal boat crews and twenty-four-hour-a-day traffic (including on the Sabbath) made easy targets for preachers in the burgeoning towns along its route.[3]

The most famous of all the itinerant evangelists of the 1820s and '30s was Charles Grandison Finney. Born in Connecticut and brought up in Jefferson County, New York, he was ordained in 1824 and began touring the region immediately. He was a charismatic preacher who was larger-than-life in the revival format. His language was passionate and emotional. After cutting his teeth leading small-scale revivals in northern New York, he came to Oneida County in 1825. His revivals in Rome and Utica brought him success and notoriety, but most of all infused the region with a religious fervor that changed spiritual as well as political life for generations. He came to Rome on the invitation of the local reverend Moses Gillet. Finney's revivals started with preaching, door-to-door visits, and invitations to large meetings. Finney recalled that when he started speaking in Rome, he instantly connected to listeners, whose heads "were bowed down with deep conviction for sin." The meetings started, first in private homes "crowded to . . . utmost capacity," then in larger venues: a hotel dining room, Rome's courthouse building, and a school.[4]

Finney stayed in Rome for twenty days. Ministers flocked there from the surrounding area to see what was going on. The religious spirit led to outbursts of emotion, fainting, and writhing in seats, even by the "stoutest

130 | Land of the Oneidas

men" of Rome. Finney found people so overcome that they would lay "prostrate on the carpet" while others "bath[ed] the temples of their friends with camphor . . . rubbing them to keep them from fainting." Each evening, Finney would ask that anyone who had been "converted" over the course of the day step forward and report themselves. Gillet recorded five hundred "conversions" in Rome. When Finney left, Gillet told him, "So far as my congregation is concerned, the Millennium is come already. My people are all converted."[5]

Finney then moved on to Utica for the spring of 1826, where the experience was similar. Three thousand were counted as converts—nearly the same as the number of residents living in Utica, though many of the attendees came from the surrounding towns and villages. There was opposition. A group of local ministers called the Oneida Association printed pamphlets denouncing Finney's methods. One meeting was interrupted by an "aged clergyman" who was "was very much annoyed by the heat and fervor of the revival" and made a "violent speech" against it in the middle of the proceedings.[6] But Finney went on to hold revival after revival through the 1830s and '40s, drawing enormous crowds across upstate New York.

Finney and other evangelical revivalists emphasized the importance of making a conscious and personal choice to turn away from sin, not only for salvation in the afterlife but also to attain a better life on earth. In striving for perfection in the eyes of the Lord, true believers could create a society based on Christian principles. He and his followers advocated for temperance and for the abolition of slavery in the United States. They denounced institutions that, in their view, emphasized elitism such as Freemasonry and branches of Christianity that emphasized hierarchy, formality, and ritual—especially Roman Catholicism.[7] The revivals' main impact was on middle-class people, most of all women, who often charged themselves with instilling evangelical values into the generation of children born in the 1820s, '30s, and '40s, some of whom took those values with them to the battlefields of the Civil War.[8] Great divisions were already starting to emerge on race and slavery in central New York in the 1830s. The antislavery agitation that took root in the region, which made it home to some of the nation's most important abolitionists and thousands of others who supported slavery's destruction, was closely linked to the evangelical movement that shaped its middle class.

§

Religion and antislavery politics were united at the Oneida Institute, the first school in the United States that was open to Black and white students on terms of full equality. Its president, Beriah Green, was an antislavery evangelical preacher who wanted to make the Oneida Institute an abolitionist school. Green was a controversial figure with a national profile. He was later targeted by pro-slavery mobs in Utica, and his school eventually failed. But his actions set into motion the rise of an even more influential abolitionist who threw his immense fortune into the campaign to end slavery. Gerrit Smith, the son of the Indian trader Peter Smith—raised on his father's land, which he had leased from the Oneidas and then bought from the state in 1795—became a firebrand after witnessing well-heeled rioters attempting to disrupt the first meeting of the New York Anti-Slavery Society, which Green had called together in Utica in 1835. From that day, from his home in Peterboro in Madison County, Smith's influence grew locally and nationally. It played a part in John Brown's raid on Harper's Ferry. It was constant fuel to the sectional conflict that culminated in civil war.

The Oneida Institute's main building when it opened was the farmhouse of Hugh White, the first permanent settler in the region. It sat on 115 acres of land on the outskirts of the village of Whitesboro, a few miles from Utica, along the Mohawk River and Erie Canal. Its original purpose was to be a "manual labor and literary academy" for students over sixteen, providing an education not only in the traditional, academic sense but also one in which manual work—farming, carpentry, and blacksmithing, for example—was a core part of the curriculum. Students worked in the fields alongside their demanding academic studies and imbibed evangelical Christianity. The institute's founder, the Presbyterian minister George Washington Gale, had been running a similar but smaller manual labor school on his farm before moving to Whitesboro. Charles Grandison Finney was converted to evangelicalism by Gale in 1821. When Gale looked to pass on the reigns to a new president in the early 1830s, both he and the trustees attempted to persuade Finney to take over, but in the end the job was given to the Connecticut-born Congregationalist minister Beriah Green.[9]

From his inauguration onward, he was clear to all who listened to his weekly sermons and public speeches about his abolitionist vision for the Oneida Institute. He was the first president of the American Anti-Slavery Society, founded in Philadelphia in 1833. His no-compromise stance led to the resignation of conservative trustees and brought Green into the spotlight, nationally and locally. "Immediatists" like Green who wanted the complete, immediate abolition of slavery with no compensation to slaveowners were seen as dangerous and irresponsible, even by many people who were opposed

132 | Land of the Oneidas

to slavery and wanted to see it end. Britain ended slavery in its empire in 1833, but on a gradual timescale with compensation payments given to slaveholders for the loss of their "property."

Green believed in equality between Blacks and whites and wished to see them working alongside each other at the Oneida Institute, as well as in all parts of American life. This put him into conflict with the American Colonization Society, a group that proposed "returning" free Blacks to Africa. Behind the society's efforts was a feeling held by a large portion of its members that Blacks were inferior, or at the very least would not be able to fit in with American society and culture once released from bondage. In Utica, Green attacked the society in a debate with one of its leaders, Rev. Joshua Danforth. Mobs disrupted the proceedings and Green was hanged in effigy.[10]

Despite nagging debts which eventually led to the institute's closure in 1843, Green enrolled as many future Black leaders as he could. Some of them, like Samuel Ringgold Ward and Jermain Wesley Loguen (both of whom had escaped bondage in the South) later became prominent central New York abolitionists. Green's opponents derided Oneida as a "nigger school."[11]

In 1835, Green initiated the creation the New York Anti-Slavery Society, calling its first meeting on October 21 at Bleecker Street Presbyterian Church in Utica. It was attended by nearly six hundred delegates. As the meeting was starting, a mob of about eighty men broke into the church shouting, "Open the way! Break down the doors! Damn the fanatics! Stop your damn stuff!" The rioters were far from being local rabble; they included prominent (and wealthy) lawyers, bankers, and merchants. Oneida County's US Congressman, Samuel Beardsley, was among them. He considered the abolitionists to be "right down idiots." Some of the rioters' motivations may have been as much political as they were antiabolitionist. Beardsley and others were Democrats who were working to calm southern fears that the New York politician Martin Van Buren, poised to take on the party's nomination to succeed President Andrew Jackson, might be soft on abolitionists. There were kickbacks in store for them from the party machine in Albany if they succeeded in this task.[12]

No one was hurt in the riot, but the well-dressed mob set to ringing the church bell, yelling, and stomping on the balcony, mimicking recent antiabolition riots in New York City. Around the same time, similar mob actions against abolitionist meetings were happening in other northern cities as well, including Boston, where William Lloyd Garrison was dragged through the streets with a noose round his neck.[13] Amidst the scene in

Reckoning, 1835–1865 | 133

Utica, a man from Madison County rose up, appalled by the behavior of the mob, and suggested reconvening the meeting in his village, Peterboro, the next day. Unlike the other delegates there, he was not an abolitionist, but neither could he stand to see principled discussion be silenced. And he had the means to make sure it wasn't.

Gerrit Smith was born in Utica in 1797, two years after his father acquired his vast tract of Oneida lands. Although his father was already wealthy and became ever richer during his childhood, Gerrit grew up doing manual work. He later called his father "cold and repulsive." Peter Smith held slaves, possibly seven. The family moved to Peterboro in 1806. Peter Smith chose it for its hardwood trees that would be useful fuel for a glass factory; the Peterboro village green was cleared in 1795. Peter was on intimate terms with the Oneidas since his days as a fur trader in Utica, and Gerrit grew up with Indians (almost certainly Oneidas) as frequent visitors, who sometimes stayed the night, sleeping on the floor.[14] His older brother was given the middle name Skenandoah after the Oneida chief. He was called "Peter Sken" for short.

Gerrit studied at Hamilton College between 1814 and 1818, where he was a good scholar (he finished first in a class of ten students and even married the college president's daughter) but fond of gambling. His mother died in 1818 and his wife the year after. He took over his father's land business in partnership with his uncle Daniel Cady—the father of Elizabeth Cady Stanton, who later became the most prominent voice in the women's rights movement. His father moved to Schenectady in 1825. Peter Smith—once known as the "saw mill" by the Oneidas, a man of wealth and a judge in Madison County—became morose after leaving his business to his son, brooding on sin. In his later life, he was obsessed with the distribution of religious tracts and pamphlets.[15]

With Peter Smith went the strong Indian connection. Although Gerrit did on at least one occasion have an Indian guest and at various times criticized the US government for current or past treatment of Indians in other parts of the country, the Oneidas—from whose land his fortune was established—did not figure prominently in his life, work, or philanthropy.[16] He would undoubtedly have known of their poverty. The turnpike road from Peterboro to Vernon (and thence to Utica and Albany) passed by the remaining plots of Oneida land. There may have been some reluctance to engage too closely with the Oneidas. His father's purchase from the state in 1795 had been on the back of an illegal treaty and the fortune Gerrit was handed had come from the sale of tracts at vastly higher prices per acre

134 | Land of the Oneidas

than what the Indians had received for the same land. The Indians' land holdings had plummeted from millions of acres down to virtually nothing in his lifetime, while his own land empire grew to gargantuan size.

Smith was extremely vigorous in his business affairs. In 1818, he bought eighteen thousand acres of land near Florence, New York, on the edge of Tug Hill. In 1827, he bought land on the east side of the Oswego River upon which the city of Oswego was built, hugely increasing the value of his holdings. He also bought up 91 percent of shares in the Oswego Canal Company. During the 1840s, he bought vast tracts all over New York State at extremely low prices that had been put on the market due to owners owing back taxes. In 1843, for example, he bought forty-eight thousand acres spread across fifteen counties for a total of $17,468, roughly thirty-six cents per acre. He was then able to sell the land on at much higher prices. He recorded his land transactions meticulously.

Although he did suffer difficulty in the economic crisis known as the Panic of 1837 and its aftermath, he was, from the mid-1840s onward, a man of extreme wealth who could afford to distribute philanthropy on a life-changing scale. Smith's relationship with land, the source of his ability to be a benefactor, was complicated. There was no small degree of guilt involved in it. Although he owned upwards of eight hundred thousand acres, he also argued that laws should be passed to stop the wealthiest citizens from being able to buy up all the land, which would leave the poor with nothing. In the 1840s, he gave away thousands of acres of land to families who were "virtuous, landless, and poor."[17]

Influenced in part by his second wife, Ann Carrol Fitzhugh, Gerrit Smith underwent his own religious conversion in 1826. He became a friend and correspondent of Charles Grandison Finney. Although he was initially connected to the Presbyterian church, he eventually came to oppose doctrinal separations between Protestant Christians and helped found the interdenominational "Church of Peterboro" in 1843, with a chapel set up (at his expense) in 1847.[18] Like Finney, he saw Christianity as a command to do good on Earth. The quest for salvation was a personal choice. It required Christians to attempt to live as perfectly as possible, avoiding sin and evangelizing by promoting moral rectitude both in one's own life and in society at large. Like other Christians whose religious experience was shaped in the burned-over district, there was a millennial streak in his thinking, a belief that the end of the world and the day of judgment could be close at hand. Salvation could be hoped for by those whose actions conformed with God's law, which in some cases differed from man's.

In the late 1820s, he began petitioning Congress to ban post-office traffic on the Sabbath. He became an outspoken advocate of temperance. In an 1833 pamphlet arguing for stricter licensing laws, he wrote that when he returned to Peterboro after college, "more than every other man in it was a drunkard."[19] He described thirty-eight men of the village, telling the story of each individually, and showing that since the religious reawakening and the growth of temperance societies within the churches began in the late 1820s, most had turned their back on drink and lifted themselves from the poverty to which it had reduced them.

In Smith's letter, one of the men—"number 12"—is described as "a colored man, about 30 years of age, with a family . . . [who] was a very great drunkard, and very poor."[20] This man may have been a son of one of the slaves owned by his father. New York State abolished slavery in a gradual process beginning in 1817 and ending in 1827. The 1820 census showed that New York had 10,088 slaves and 29,279 free people of color, but the majority lived in the southern part of the state. The number of Blacks in upstate New York was relatively small. Madison County had ten slaves and 182 free Blacks in 1820; Oneida County nine and 368. Lewis and Oswego Counties had no slaves at all.[21] Since his religious conversion, Smith had taken an interest in the plight of Black Americans. His wife was raised in Maryland and developed a bond with a slave of the family who was sold when they moved to New York. Later the Smiths found her, paid for her release, and cared for her in Peterboro.[22]

In the early republic, many expected that slavery would eventually disappear, just as was happening in the northern states. However, the religious revivalism that both Smith and his wife imbibed, with its emphasis on social reform, coincided with a resurgence in slavery in the South. Cotton grown on southern plantations was becoming extremely profitable, and westward expansion meant that the practice of slavery was also taking hold in new territories, destabilizing the balance of power in Washington.

The evangelized Smith felt that slavery was wrong, but prior to 1835 he shared a commonly held belief that Blacks were inferior to whites. The best possible solution, therefore, was for Blacks to "return" to Africa. In so doing, they would bring the arts, sciences, and—most importantly—Christian religion of the more advanced Americans to help the people of that continent rise from barbarism to civilization. In 1831, Smith wrote that Blacks are "incapable of freedom on our soil," that they should go to "the land of their origin, which is their appropriate, their only home," and that "we should hasten to clear our land of our black population."

He began in 1828 making large donations to the American Colonization Society. He established a manual labor school for Black men in Peterboro, which opened in May 1834 with fifteen students. It was like the Oneida Institute in terms of mixing classical education with manual work in its curriculum, but very different in philosophy, particularly after Beriah Green took over the academy in Whitesboro. Whereas Green wanted to educate Blacks and whites together on terms of full equality, Smith's school's hope was to teach Blacks to live prosperously but separately from whites, to "go to Africa with a sound education of head and heart." The school was paid for by Smith himself.²³

When the 1835 New York Anti-Slavery Society meeting reconvened in Peterboro, Smith opened it by saying that he was "not a member of the American Anti-Slavery Society, and not yet prepared to become such" for reasons, he said, that already "were before the public." He was alluding to his known support of the American Colonization Society.²⁴ However, even before 1835, he was having doubts about the colonization project. He had already established a friendship with Beriah Green. He accepted the invitation to attend the anti-slavery convention in Utica as an observer.

The vehemence of the antiabolitionist mob awakened him. It wasn't the first time he'd seen supporters of slavery in central New York bear their teeth. He had been pelted with rotten eggs on his way in to a "Friends of the Slave" meeting in Syracuse in 1831.²⁵ But this riot was far more sinister. In addition to breaking up the meeting, the Utica mob chased delegates back to their hotels and even pursued some of the wagons heading to Peterboro, throwing stones. In his 1851 *Annals of Oneida County*, Pomroy Jones wrote, "As might have been anticipated, hundreds became abolitionists, merely from sympathy." The mob also broke into the offices of the *Utica Standard and Democrat*, which advocated abolitionism while still printing Van Buren's name on its header. Delegates traveled through the night, some overland by wagon, others by canal boat to Canastota, where they arrived at three a.m., and thence by land to Peterboro. Smith raced home and set his house staff to work preparing food for the three hundred who arrived and assembled at the Presbyterian church across the village green from Smith's mansion.²⁶

Beginning that day, and continuing throughout the months following the meeting, Smith underwent a second "conversion," this time into an ardent proponent of immediate abolition. He resigned from the American Colonization Society. The following year, he was elected president of the New York Anti-Slavery Society. In 1837 he resigned as a trustee at Hamilton College over its refusal to adopt a public antislavery position. In 1838 he argued for abolition in a debate with the celebrated author James Fenimore Cooper.²⁷ He cofounded the Liberty Party, the first national political party devoted to abolition, which stood candidates for president in 1840, 1844, and 1848 (the 1848 candidate was Smith himself). He made large donations to the Oneida Institute and even named his son after its abolitionist president. He began travelling to churches in central New York to "preach politics" on Sundays. In Madison County villages like Bridgeport and De Ruyter, he spoke sometimes from the pulpit, sometimes in the open air, recalling the revival atmosphere of the 1820s. He called Liberty Party politics "Bible politics," sometimes to small congregations, sometimes to crowds of four thousand or more.²⁸

In his preaching, he pleaded, even demanded that local congregations act to end slavery immediately. He purposefully sowed division. He wrote that a chief duty of an abolitionist is to refuse to "countenance the preacher, who refuses to plead and pray for the slave."²⁹ When some local ministers attacked Smith, he replied in an excoriating circular letter "To the Pro-Slavery Ministers of the County of Madison" (1843): "My declaration, that I am willing to spend my Sabbaths in pleading for God's enslaved poor, has proved an occasion for a new and rich display of your proslavery [sympathy] and pharisaism. You are warning the people in your respective cages not to hear me 'preach politics' on the Sabbath—that is, not to hear me explain how wicked and how murderous is your own proslavery voting." He called out individuals, including the author of a "stupid" article in the *Madison County Eagle* about him and a minister who had made a speech against him the previous year in Morrisville, whom he charged with "disgusting and abhorrent wickedness." He called them "betrayers of Jesus Christ; no more with the friends, but with the enemies of God."³⁰

By the mid-1840s, Smith had fierce enemies and ardent supporters locally. Divisions in church congregations over the issue of slavery erupted, pitting neighbors in small towns and villages throughout central New York against each other. In Whitesboro, the Oneida Presbytery distanced itself from Beriah Green. After the riots in Utica, infighting in the congregation led to a schism. The anti-Green faction invited a new minister, David Ogden, to take over in 1836 despite knowing that he opposed immediate abolition and supported colonization. In 1837 Ogden began denouncing "fanatical abolitionists" from the pulpit. Green retaliated by denouncing Ogden vehemently in his own newspaper, *Friend of Man*. The dispute became so bitter that seventy-one congregants left the church in support of Green.

138 | Land of the Oneidas

Pomroy Jones recorded of the Presbyterian church of Whitesboro, "Abolitionism has more troubled this Presbyterian church and society than any other in the county," but similar divisions occurred in the years that followed across central New York. In the tiny hamlet of Vernon Center, soon after the completion of a beautiful new church building, the congregation split along similar lines. Jones recorded that in 1842, "a difficulty arose in the church, which, anon, became so sharp, that the two parties, like Paul and Barnabas, separated." Antislavery congregants formed a new association of "Independent Congregationalists," taking "a much more decided and strong ground as a church on the slavery question, than the body from which they dissented believed it their duty to assume." In small, close-knit communities, the consequences of such division, which separated neighbors and even families, were severe. Student bodies split as well. At the Hamilton Literary and Theological Institution (now Colgate University) in Madison County, outspoken abolitionist students were expelled.[31]

A similar division in local politics added to the unsettled atmosphere. In 1843, Smith called the two dominant parties—Whigs and Democrats—"our two giant proslavery foes." Like the churches, the national political parties were trying to retain support across the country, in both the North and the South. In upstate New York, objection to pro-slavery policies in both parties, however, led to heated division in the mid-1840s. Democrats who opposed slavery became known as "barnburners," while those who supported it, or at least opposed antagonizing southern slaveholders, were "hunkers." A leading hunker voice was Samuel Beardsley, the Utica congressman who had helped organize the 1835 antiabolitionist riot. He represented New York's 20th district in Washington until 1844. Opposing him within the party was his former student and the attorney to the Oneida Indians, Timothy Jenkins. Jenkins resided in Oneida Castle, near the site of Samuel Kirkland's home in Kanonwalohale. He won the 20th district seat in 1844 and became a leading voice in Washington against the expansion of slavery into new territories gained through annexations and purchases west of the Mississippi. Whigs were also internally divided. "Conscience Whigs" opposed slavery while "Cotton Whigs" were pro-South in outlook.[32]

Although it remained controversial, antislavery activity in central New York continued to grow in the 1840s. Newspapers like *The Abolitionist* and the *Madison and Onondaga Abolitionist* were published in Cazenovia during that decade.[33] From the late 1830s, the Underground Railroad ran through central New York. Fugitive slaves, who had escaped from the South, came north seeking passage to British Canada. The most traveled route on the Underground Railroad came up from New York City to Albany, west along the Erie Canal through Utica and Syracuse, and then on to Oswego, Rochester, or Buffalo, where fugitive slaves could board a ship or a ferry to traverse the border. In 1838 Smith wrote that fugitive slaves were staying in his home, on their way to "the monarchical land whither republican slaves escape for the enjoyment of liberty." They exposed to Smith and to his neighbors their "whip-scarred backs."[34] For those who encountered fugitive slaves, the Southern institution was no longer an abstract, far-away issue. It had come to their town.

§

Before the 1840s, the name "Oneida" was used for the lands of the Oneida Indians and sometimes for their main village. It was then the name of an Indian reservation, a frontier zone called by settlers the "Oneida Woods," and, from 1798, a county of the state of New York. After 1840, the name was also given to a village, originally called "Oneida Depot," that later became the city of Oneida—the last major settlement to be established in central New York State. It was also used by a group of "Bible Communists" nearby called the Oneida Community, whose meteoric rise, fall, and metamorphosis into the twentieth-century company Oneida Limited was as much intertwined with the "Oneidas" that surrounded it as it was a singular and spectacularly bizarre part of the American story all its own.

When a young merchant from Vernon bought two large parcels of land, recently ceded to the state by the Oneida Indians to finance their removal to Wisconsin, he could not have foreseen that an industrial center would grow up there within his lifetime. Sands Higinbotham was born in 1790 in Rensselaer County, of a New England family that had come there from Rhode Island. They moved further west. He grew up in Utica, working in the shop of his half-brother. He set up his own shop in Vernon, even further west in Oneida County along the Seneca Turnpike. He began buying plots of land in the 1820s and listed his profession as farmer on census returns throughout his life.[35] The two large purchases he made in 1829 and 1830 included land where the new feeder for the side cut from the Erie Canal to Oneida Lake would run. He built a home there into which he relocated in 1834.

It was a quiet island of wilderness that, due to its retention by the Indians, had escaped the conversion to agriculture that most of the surrounding areas experienced two decades earlier. The canal villages of Durhamville and Canastota were several miles away, and the small hamlet of Oneida Castle was nearby, but it was thirty miles to Utica and thirty-five to Syracuse. Workmen came to dig the feeder canal in 1835, and Higinbotham induced a few of them to stay by parceling off small plots on generous terms. It is likely that some of these were Irish immigrants as, unlike nearly all other towns and villages in the region, a Catholic church was established in the village almost contemporaneously with the first Protestant churches, including the Presbyterian church, which Higinbotham himself set to organize.[36]

What changed everything for Higinbotham was the advent of the locomotive. The first rail line in the United States built for steam trains began service in 1831 between Albany and Schenectady. It was a means for passengers (much more than cargo) to bypass the time-consuming system of locks around Cohoes Falls. In 1833 another stretch was built between Schenectady and Utica, carrying its first passengers in 1836. That year another railway was chartered, this time between Utica and Syracuse via Rome, running parallel to the Erie Canal. It would need to cut directly across Higinbotham's farm. Higinbotham presented a deal which would allow the railroad right of way across his land on the condition that each passenger train stop there for ten minutes to take refreshments. The deal was accepted. He built a railroad house for the passengers with a hotel and a post office in the bar room. He attracted residents with affordable plots to build up a village around the train station, which became known as Oneida Depot.[37]

On July 4, 1839, the first train steamed across his land. An early historian who may have witnessed the event at first hand described the "wild scene" of celebration as the railway coaches moved "slowly and carefully" across the recently broken land littered with freshly dug-up stumps. She describes "a few—a very few—of the remnant of red men remaining here, of the once numerous and powerful Oneida Nation" among the crowd as curious "mourners upon the scene," watching another "inroad . . . upon the domain of their ancestors and their own homes." The village was developed in "blocks" and grew rapidly from its core around the railway depot with stores, hotels, a bank, gristmill, and several churches appearing within the first few years of the railway opening. In 1848 the settlement changed its name from Oneida Depot to Oneida Village, or simply Oneida.[38]

Higinbotham himself was a good patron for the village. He was known as a political man—a strong Whig and later a Republican—but he refused to hold office himself. He served as a trustee at Hamilton College.[39] He acted as an advisor to the Oneida Indians in their complex 1840 land sale and creation of the Windfall Reservation, seemingly with no personal gain. His son, Niles, donated parcels of land that became parks. The village grew in a very short time to be the most important commercial center between Syracuse and Utica, far outstripping the older villages in the surrounding area in population. The railroad continued to grow in significance. Although it didn't supplant the Erie Canal, it did begin to carry freight as well as passengers, leading the old Seneca Turnpike—once the main artery across the state and a major motivating factor in New York's treaties with the Oneidas—into further decline. Within a few years of the opening of the Syracuse and Utica Railroad, train lines carried on west, making it possible to traverse the state from New York City to Albany to Buffalo. The independent companies merged into the New York Central Railroad in 1853 (see Figure 5.1).

In the early winter of 1848, sleighs turned up at Oneida Depot to collect some travel-weary refugees and carry them to a collection of Indian cabins four miles away on Oneida Creek. These were the humble beginnings of the most successful utopian community in the United States. The story began sixteen years earlier in Vermont. John Humphrey Noyes, a twenty-year-old man with worldly aspirations, was attending a four-day revival in the village of Putney. He was a religious skeptic, practically dragged there by his mother.[40] When he returned to his parents' house, he was suddenly struck ill. On his sick bed he decided that he would devote the rest of his life to God. Within a few months he left his job as a clerk and enrolled at Andover Theological Seminary in Massachusetts. There, he experienced a period of intense spiritual turmoil made worse by a cycle of eating and drinking binges and harsh self-loathing. Seeking direction from the Lord, Noyes opened a Bible to a random verse, Matthew 28:6, which read, "He [Jesus] is not here," and promptly decided to leave Andover and go to Yale.[41]

While at Yale, Noyes encountered ideas promulgated by James Latourette, a Methodist minister in New York City. Working from John Wesley's *Christian Perfection*, Latourette focused on the notion that separation from God was the source of sin. He argued that if one were in perfect unity with God, one could be sinless and therefore perfect. Unlike Wesley, Latourette believed that perfection was an attainable goal for Christians and was therefore labeled a "Perfectionist."[42] Followers soon began believing that they had reached the state of sinlessness and started dispersing into upstate New York and east into Connecticut, just as John Humphrey Noyes arrived at New Haven around his twenty-second birthday. Yale's theologians viewed perfectionism as heretical, but Noyes was captivated by it (though he later

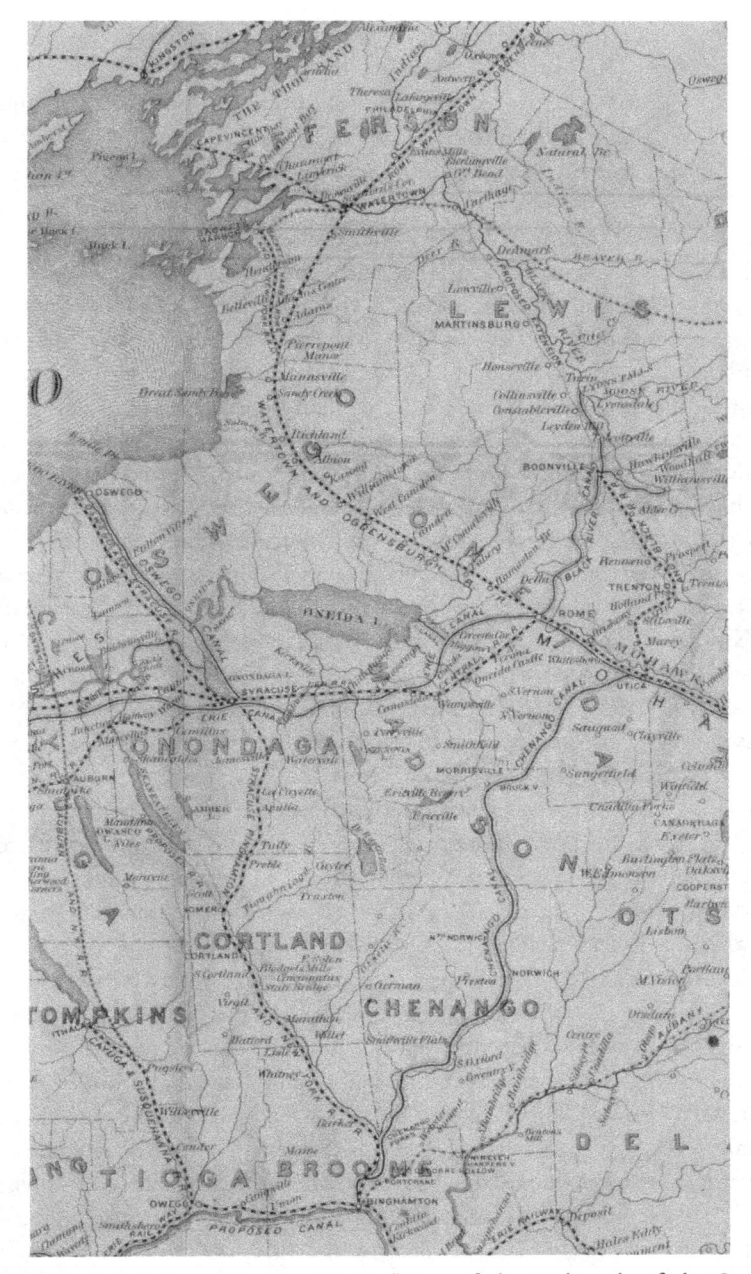

Figure 5.1. Detail from Sylvanus Sweet, "Map of the Rail-roads of the State of New York" (1863).

fell out with Latourette). He spent hour upon hour reading and interpreting the Bible. On February 20, 1834, he publicly declared himself to be "sinless." He wrote that when he came to this conclusion, "joy unspeakable and full of glory filled my soul."[43]

Noyes's recently attained license to preach was quickly revoked. In New Haven, Noyes and his allies were banned from churches and ostracized from the Yale community. Noyes called everyone who didn't believe in his perfection "non-Christian" and became fond of quoting John 3:8: "He that commiteth sin is of the devil."[44] The New Haven perfectionists were moderate compared to the extremists who lived mostly in New York State. Members of an Albany group of perfectionists were tarred and feathered for flaunting the fact that two men and a woman slept in the same bed without fear of God's wrath.[45] The New Haven perfectionists ran several periodical publications, including Noyes's *Perfectionist* (1834–86) and *Witness* (1837), which discontinued when money ran out. Within a few years the perfectionist "movement" was in shambles and had split into small antagonistic factions.

As Noyes traipsed around New England trying to generate interest in and capital for his newspapers, he became deeply embittered by the perfectionists' dissolution into "broken and corrupted regiments."[46] He continued to develop his own perfectionist theology. The idea that man could attain holiness on Earth was maintained, but unlike many perfectionists, Noyes believed that once one reached that exalted state, he could never sin again and yet remain a Christian. Indeed, he felt that sin was a repudiation of Christianity and therefore a sinner could not be a true Christian.

The basis for Noyes's argument was his belief that "the second coming of the Son of Man was coincident with, or immediately subsequent to the destruction of Jerusalem," or in other words, that Jesus had returned to Earth, as he had promised, around AD 70.[47] In the large, blotchy type of Noyes's second-hand printing press, which he used to publish his first book, *The Way of Holiness* (1838), he explained that "the simple declaration of Christ, that within the generation of his contemporaries he would come . . . is sufficient basis for our faith." But for those who were more skeptical, Noyes explained how this grand event failed to be recorded historically: "History takes cognizance only of events . . . which come with outward show." Therefore, the Second Coming belonged to an "invisible world" not recorded by historians. Only a small group of people, the desert fathers, knew of his return and became the first to live in a state of holy perfection. However, "since the fathers fell asleep [died]," humanity had forgotten this event of the "invisible world" and was only awaiting a messenger from God to reawaken mankind.⁴⁸ By 1838, when Noyes published this argument, he saw himself as God's messenger.

As he watched the perfectionist movement crumbling all around him, Noyes became convinced that his unquestioned, dictatorial leadership was essential. He violently criticized rival perfectionist groups and their leaders. Noyes also began developing ideas about marriage and social structure. These ideas were in embryonic stages during the 1830s and weren't fully instituted until Noyes's followers moved to Oneida in 1848. In August 1837, a perfectionist periodical in Philadelphia called the *Battle-Axe* ran a letter that Noyes had written to a friend which had not been intended for publication. In this letter he wrote, "When the will of God is done on earth, as it is in heaven, there will be no marriage. The marriage supper of the Lamb, is a feast at which every dish is free to every guest. . . . In a holy community there is no more reason why sexual intercourse should be restrained by law, than why eating and drinking should be—and there is as little occasion for shame in the one case as the other."⁴⁹

Its publication placed Noyes in an extremely uncomfortable situation, leaving him open to attack for advocating adultery even before he'd had the opportunity to try it (that opportunity did come, later). In 1838, he married Harriet Holton, one of his Vermont followers. She sent Noyes money after the disastrous *Battle-Axe* letter and proposed to him. Noyes's motives for his acceptance of Harriet (who was by all accounts very plain, especially in comparison to Abigail Merwin, whom Noyes had been pursuing for some time without success) are questionable. Yaacov Oved suggested that for Noyes, "marriage would save him from the accusations of promiscuity, prompted by the publication of his letter."⁵⁰ Harriet's wealthy family may have been alluring to the bankrupt young man. She knew of John Humphrey's recently published views on marriage.

The young Noyes also developed a strong, lifelong interest in socialism. Robert Owen was the first to develop a socialistic community in America at New Harmony, Indiana, in 1825. Despite its failure, several new communities called "phalanxes," some based on the theories of the French writer Charles Fourier, sprang up in America. Brook Farm, a transcendentalist commune, was founded in Massachusetts in 1842. Noyes later wrote that he and his early followers "received a great impulse from Brook Farm" and were inspired by its newspaper, *The Harbinger*.⁵¹

Noyes began to believe that to achieve unity with God, it was necessary to attain unity with fellow humans. Only on a basis of absolute material equality would the worldly walls of jealousy and hostility be broken down.

Reckoning, 1835–1865 | 145

Among "saints"—that is, those who achieved Christian perfection—everything should be shared, from material goods to labor to spouses. This would later become an inseparable part of the religion practiced at Oneida, a marriage between perfectionism and socialism that Noyes called "Bible Communism." But in Vermont only a few timid experiments took place.

The "Putney Community" began as a Bible School set up by Noyes in 1839 with a small nucleus of his family and a few neighbors. In 1846, Noyes felt that it was time to bring some of his theories into real execution. He convinced a large portion of his congregation (about thirty-five persons) to sign a "Statement of Principles" in which each member surrendered all material possessions to form a communistic society in which all work and property would be shared equally. Noyes made it clear that he was to be the unquestioned leader of this community. Provision #3 of the statement reads: "John H. Noyes is the father and overseer whom the Holy Ghost has set over the family thus constituted. To John H. Noyes as such we submit ourselves in all things spiritual and temporal, appealing from his decision only to the spirit of God, and that without disputing."[52] The community placed Noyes's authority above any other worldly force. Noyes said to his followers during the signing of the statement, "Our association is established on principles opposed at every point to the institutions of the world. . . . *The Kingdom of Heaven Has Come.*"[53]

Meanwhile, Noyes developed a method by which complex marriage could become a reality. He called it "Male Continence." To allow "the elevated spiritual pleasures of sexual connection," Noyes later wrote, men must restrict "the more sensual part [ejaculation] to its proper occasions."[54] Noyes felt that in his form of communism, sex would be a regular and fundamental part of social interaction. His first extramarital experience was with a married follower, Mary Cragin, in 1846. Throughout 1847, a few other community members began experimenting, though Noyes was the director of all these affairs and permission had to be granted through him. The community continued to grow throughout this period, and a revived newspaper called the *Spiritual Magazine* attracted interest in Noyes and his followers.

Despite Noyes's obvious fondness for the press, these early sexual experiments were performed furtively. What really generated curiosity in Noyes was news of his "miracles." In 1847 he placed his hands on the forehead of a bedridden young woman named Harriet Hall who was unconnected to his community. She attested that she was "unable to move or be moved" and was "nearly blind," but after Noyes's visit, she was miraculously cured: "My

146 | Land of the Oneidas

eyes were perfectly well," she wrote. She was able to walk again and work without impediment.[55] Noyes, however, made a grave mistake. In inviting Mrs. Hall's husband to join the community, he divulged the recent sexual experiments, which were secret even to some of the inner circle at Putney. Instead of joining Noyes, Mr. Hall told the state attorney what he had heard. Noyes was arrested for adultery. After being released on a two-thousand-dollar bail, he fled the state.[56] The time had come to relocate his utopia.

Before his arrest, Noyes attended a convention of perfectionists in Lairsdsville, Oneida County, and another in Genoa, further west in Cayuga County. Converts there resolved to form a "heavenly Association in Central New York," and in January 1848 they invited Noyes to lead it.[57] Jonathan Burt was the part-owner of a sawmill on Oneida Creek (his partner was his brother Horace, who experienced recurring bouts of insanity).[58] Born in Massachusetts, Burt had converted to perfectionism years before, in 1834, after hearing a New Haven perfectionist preach in Chittenango, where he lived at the time. The sawmill and forty-acre lot he purchased in 1845 were on the old disputed "gore" which had caused tension between the Christian and Pagan parties of Oneidas, and which had finally been sold to the state in 1840. The mill itself was called the "Indian sawmill" and was probably left by the Oneidas of the Second Christian Party when the majority emigrated to Canada in the early 1840s.[59]

Burt was forty years old when he invited Noyes, three years younger, to relocate onto his land. He had already allowed three families of perfectionists to settle there (against his wife's wishes). Noyes had large amounts of money with him, which he used to recompense the Burt family, and set to negotiating the purchase of adjoining plots, gaining control of 160 acres, including a group of log homes left by the Oneidas. Noyes's followers from Putney arrived by train in 1848 to start the Oneida Community "in the log huts of the Indians." They arrived in Oneida Depot, were met by delegations from the sawmill and carried by sleigh the four miles back. Other families came west from Vermont by the Erie Canal, bringing the total up to fifty-one, half of whom were minors. They set to work immediately on building a communal home for themselves called the Mansion House. By the end of the second year, there were 172. By the third year, 205.[60]

The arrival of the Community in Oneida caused mixed reactions in the surrounding area, and inevitably some hostility. Adultery was considered as great a sin there as it was in Vermont. In 1842, for example, villagers dragged a Peterboro man named Henry Devan who had been accused of "fornication" through the streets.[61] In 1850 a complaint about the Community was filed with Madison County. This led to a hearing in county court, but witnesses from the Community were not called and the complaint resulted in no bill of indictment against them. Oneida County was next to act. Community members were summoned to Utica and made to answer detailed questions about their practices. The Community wrote a circular letter to their immediate neighbors in the towns of Vernon (Oneida County) and Lenox (Madison County), which resulted in a petition to the district attorney supporting the Community's right to stay in the area. "We the undersigned . . . are willing to testify that we regard them as honorable businessmen, as good neighbors, and quiet, peaceable citizens," it read. Timothy Jenkins of Oneida Castle, the local congressman, gave a personal endorsement.[62]

Why were the Community's closest neighbors willing to come to their aid? Upstate New York was still strongly marked by the religious enthusiasm of the Second Great Awakening. The energies associated with evangelical religion which fed into temperance, abolitionism, and a quest for a higher and better society might have led to greater open-mindedness towards Noyes and his followers, who were similarly seeking to live out reformist ideals. They avoided hostility by not attempting to recruit new members in the immediate vicinity.[63] They may also have seemed less threatening than other new arrivals in the area. Thousands of penniless immigrants from famine-stricken Ireland appeared in central New York and other parts of the northeastern United States in the late 1840s, bringing Roman Catholicism, which many Americas saw as a grave danger to their way of life. The anti-immigrant Know Nothing Party swept the 1854 elections in Massachusetts and did nearly as well in New York, winning several US congressional seats and coming a strong second in the state gubernatorial election.[64] The Community members, by contrast, like nearly all the residents in Vernon and Lenox at the time, were of old New England Protestant stock, with the only substantial difference being their views on marriage and shared property within their own walls.

These explanations may have played a role, but they do not tell the whole story. Even in upstate New York, aberrant religious groups like the Mormons (founded by Joseph Smith further west in Palmyra, near Rochester) were pushed out. Gerrit Smith, the best example of an upstate reformer, was no friend of Noyes's Oneida Community and referred to their sexual practices as "disgraceful."[65] However, in Oneida Depot, Sands Higinbotham and others were trying to build up the population to justify the continued existence of a train stop there.[66] The value of land in the

148 | Land of the Oneidas

immediate vicinity would be much higher if there was a flourishing train station nearby. Jenkins, too, owned a large tract between the rail station and Seneca Turnpike. Trade from Burt's sawmill and the Community's farming output would also increase the volume of trade at the station. Members of the Community were repeatedly referred to as "industrious." Most had been successful farmers or tradesmen, and they came with money that they had saved. The key reason for the support the Oneida Community received from the people of Vernon and Lenox, therefore, is almost certainly that their presence in the area was good for business.

§

The year 1850 marked a turning point on the issue of slavery that brought central New York abolitionism into the national spotlight. The United States had gained possession of the western parts of the continent following its 1846–48 war with Mexico. The most heated debate of the year was whether the government should allow slavery to expand into the new territories acquired in the Mexican Cession of 1848. While the issue was raging in Congress in the summer of 1850, Gerrit Smith's friend William Chaplin was caught in Maryland transporting two fugitive slaves (both of whom were the "property" of southern congressmen) on August 9. Chaplin and the fugitives fired on the Maryland militia.[67]

The outrage that Chaplin's actions provoked in slaveholding states, and even in many parts of the North, contributed to the approval of the Fugitive Slave Act of 1850 by Congress, which had been fiercely debated throughout the summer. The new law introduced draconian punishments on anyone in any part of the United States involved in helping enslaved people to attain their freedom. Even bystanders could be required to help capture fugitive slaves so they could be returned to their "masters." Anyone who would "willingly obstruct" the capture of a person fleeing from slavery or who attempted to "aid, abet, or assist . . . harbor or conceal such [a] fugitive" could be fined up to $1,000 and face six months in jail. They could also be made to pay an additional $1,000 in civil damages for each fugitive helped to the "party injured by such illegal conduct," that is, the slaveowner.[68]

Between Chaplin's arrest and the passage of the new Fugitive Slave Act, Smith and other New York abolitionists organized the Great Fugitive Slave Law Convention, a massive two-day meeting at Cazenovia on August 21 and 22, 1850. Two thousand abolitionists and fifty fugitive slaves attended.

Frederick Douglass, a former slave who escaped bondage in 1838 and had since become a famous writer and orator, presided. He had recently started the *North Star*, an abolitionist newspaper in Rochester, New York. Another formerly enslaved person in attendance was Jermain Loguen, who had been educated at Beriah Green's Oneida Institute after escaping from his slave master in Tennessee. He had become a Methodist preacher and ran one of the most active stops on the Underground Railroad from his home in Syracuse. The convention's pronouncements were militant, in the vein of Chaplin's action. It called upon slaves in the south to run away armed, kill their pursuing masters, and even to stage an insurrection if necessary to obtain their freedom. Chaplin's bail was set at an eye-wateringly high $19,000. Smith paid $12,000 himself and enough subscriptions were obtained to free him and enable him to flee and avoid trial.[69]

After the Fugitive Slave Law's passage on August 26, further meetings were held in Canastota, Hamilton, and Peterboro. The broadsides advertising them read: "5,000 Men & Women Wanted. . . . We want such men and women to attend these Meetings as would rather suffer imprisonment and death than tolerate the execution of this man-stealing law."[70] The dissolution of the Whig coalition in upstate New York was now inevitable. The national Whig Party voted in favor of the compromise that brought about the Fugitive Slave Law. A Whig newspaper in Buffalo criticized five New York Whigs who broke party ranks and voted to reject the law. Whig newspapers in Albany and Watertown rebuked the Buffalo report and praised the five who, it said, showed themselves capable of "discriminating between truth and trash."[71] Antislavery Whigs, or those who did not want to see slavery expand into new territories, began deserting the party. So did those with similar views from the Democratic Party, gravitating mainly to the Free Soil Party (a competitor to Smith's Liberty Party but with the focus being on preventing slavery's expansion rather than immediate abolition). The 1850 meetings in Madison County lambasted those that stuck with the "Devil-prompted parties" of Whigs and Democrats that were equally to blame for passing "the accursed law, under which oppressors and kidnappers are now chasing down the poor among us, to make slaves of them."[72]

Despite the support offered at these conventions, the new Fugitive Slave Law prompted hundreds of Black people living in upstate New York to flee immediately to Canada. To protect those who stayed, as well as future refugees, abolitionists set up "vigilance committees," like the one in Syracuse that was put to the test in 1851. A fugitive slave called William "Jerry" Henry was at work making barrels. On October 4, a group of federal marshals burst in, shackled him, and carried him to the office of the US commissioner in Syracuse, Joseph Sabine. The leader of the vigilance committee, Charles Wheaton, was tipped off by Sabine's wife of the arrest. It was probably not a coincidence that the arrest was made during the Liberty Party's convention, which was being held in Syracuse's Congregational Church. Daniel Webster, a prominent senator from Massachusetts who supported the Fugitive Slave Law, said in a speech in Syracuse the previous summer that "the law will be executed in its spirit and to the letter . . . in all the great cities; here in Syracuse in the midst of the next Anti-Slavery convention, if the occasion shall arise." The editors of the *Northern Journal* in Lowville picked this up in their weekly edition after the arrest. The arrest of Jerry Henry, they concluded, "looks very like a determination to fulfil [Webster's] prophesy."[73]

Wheaton ran to the church and alerted the Liberty Party delegates, who went en masse to Sabine's office. In the chaos, Henry managed to escape and ran through the city with his hands still in shackles, until he was tackled by two constables and carted off, screaming in despair, to the police office at Clinton Square. Abolitionists and sympathetic onlookers—between twenty-five hundred and three thousand—flooded the square, some chanting, "Let him go." The local militia was mustered. A street battle may have ensued if Wheaton had not successfully pleaded with the commander of the National Guard regiment, Origen Vandenburgh, to stand down the troops. A group of rescuers, organized by Smith, Loguen, and Wheaton, smashed through doors and windows bearing clubs and axes. Henry was captured and, still in shackles, hurried to a safe house that helped him into hiding. Eventually he was smuggled onto a ship from Oswego to Kingston, Ontario. Loguen, who, if arrested, would also have been returned to slavery himself, also fled.[74]

The 1852 presidential election was the last to be fought primarily between Democrats and Whigs. The victor, Franklin Pierce, a Democrat from New Hampshire, strongly opposed the abolitionists, seeing them as a major threat to the Union. Gerrit Smith ran for a seat in Congress for the first time in New York's 22nd district (Madison and Oswego Counties) and won, becoming one of four Free Soil members of the House of Representatives. Democrats triumphed nationally, but that was in a large part due to the division of the Whigs. In Oneida County, for example, voters in the 20th congressional district voted overwhelmingly Whig, but the votes were divided between Orasmus B. Matteson on the official Whig ticket and Joshua A. Spencer, the former mayor of Utica, who ran as an

"Independent Whig," opposed to the national party's line on slavery.[75] Some northern Democrats too separated from the national party over the same issue. In Oneida, the sole weekly newspaper, *The Oneida Telegraph*, endorsed a mix of Free Democrat and Free Soil Candidates in the 1852 elections. In the same issue, it also marked (with approval) the one-year anniversary of the Jerry Rescue and defended Harriet Beecher Stowe's *Uncle Tom's Cabin* against criticism, upholding its depiction of slavery in the South as one of "fidelity and truthfulness."[76]

Uncle Tom's Cabin had been published in book format in March and depicted vividly the inhumanity of slavery in the South. It became a major sensation. The *Oneida Telegraph* stated in June 1852 that "at the present day, the public mind is more deeply interested in the question of slavery than in any other one subject. The sale of *Uncle Tom's Cabin* shows it."[77] Across the center of the state that year, newspapers began commenting on the story of Solomon Northrup, a Free Black from Saratoga who had been kidnapped and enslaved in the South. His ordeal was revealed in the *New York Times* and later in the book *Twelve Years a Slave*. The *Northern New York Journal* of Watertown called his treatment "extremely revolting to humanity."[78] In Chenango County, the *Oxford Times* reran the *New York Times* account, referring to the South a "land of heathenism."[79] *Uncle Tom's Cabin* equated slavery with the persecution of Christians, which struck a chord in the burned-over district.

After Pierce's election and the passage of the Kansas-Nebraska Act that opened the possibility of those territories becoming slave states, Democrats who opposed the extension of slavery looked for a permanent alternative political home. In Oneida, even Gerrit Smith was attacked for not taking a strong enough stand in Congress to prevent its passage. The *Oneida Sachem*, successor to the *Telegraph*, wrote in its pilot issue in 1854: "Hitherto, we had labored under the idea that Gerrit Smith was the most open, avowed and fearless enemy of the Slave Power to be found anywhere. We are sorry to say our opinion has changed. . . . For our part, we would have fasted . . . and sat up nights till we had to prop our eyelids open, if there was even the remotest possibility of defeating such flagrant wrong, outrage and fraud as was perpetuated by the passage of the Nebraska Bill."[80]

The Republican Party formed in 1854 and became the main opposition party to the Democrats in time for the 1856 election. In Oneida County, former Whigs like Matteson and former Democrats like Timothy Jenkins of Oneida Castle abandoned their old parties and joined the Republicans.[81] In 1856, the whole of upstate New York, apart from Albany and Buffalo, selected Republicans for the House of Representatives, and every county in central New York went in favor of the Republican candidate John C. Frémont for president.

Despite winning New York and New England, Frémont was defeated by the Democratic candidate James Buchanan. On his inauguration in 1857, the *Oneida Sachem* called Buchanan the "servant" of the South, predicting, "The policy of the next four years should be high-handed and damnable."[82] In the same issue, the news of the Dred Scott decision, which denied citizenship to all "men of the African race," is conveyed with no impartiality: "The entire sensibility of the moral world is shocked by the depth of infamy which this nation is made to encompass. [The United States] is changed from a land of freedom to one of oppression and darkness." In a moral call to arms, it says, "The star of Liberty has set, never again to rise until an indignant people in their wrath dispel the clouds of wickedness and corruption with which they are surrounded."[83]

However, to suggest that central New York constituted a great antislavery bloc in the run-up to the Civil War would be misleading. The Republican Party platform advocated stopping the further expansion of slavery but did not call for its abolition in places where it currently existed. And not all central New Yorkers were Republican. Oneida County's vote for congressional representation in the 1856 election was still 43.8% Democrat. The Democratic *Utica Observer* was read in the town and countryside. Some young men who later fought in the Civil War, like Hermon Clarke of Waterville in southern Oneida County, had no interest in abolitionism or Republicanism; their reason for fighting was to preserve the Union.[84] There were large mills that were totally dependent on southern cotton. The Utica Cotton Mills in New Hartford employed 156 operatives, using 1,150 four-hundred-pound bales of cotton per year. In Utica, the Steam Cotton Mills Company on State Street employed 165 millhands, with capacity for 300. Huge investment had been poured into the works in the late 1840s: "The buildings, engine and machinery are all of the best kind, neither money nor time having been spared." Largest of all was New York Mills in Whitestown, which employed 325 and went through forty bales of cotton per week. Other large mills were located at Clark's Mills in Kirkland and in the town of Paris in Oneida County.[85]

Pomroy Jones, in his *Annals of Oneida County* (1851), criticized local newspapers like the *Oneida Standard* which, he said, "became obnoxious for its advocacy of abolitionism, or doctrines and measures akin to it."[86] Jones's attitude towards slavery came through in his relation of the settlement of the town of Western in Oneida County. General William Floyd, one of the signers of the Declaration of Independence, moved there from Long Island, bringing his slaves with him. Jones related several stories of Floyd's dealings with his slaves, including two called Bill and Long Tom. The former slaves stayed in the town after emancipation. Jones related that one of them told people that "she was very sorry she had her freedom given her," for when she "lived with massa Floyd," he provided well and always treated her kindly, but now "she did not know how to take care of herself, and [. . .] suffered for the necessities of life."[87]

In 1860, New York held a statewide referendum asking voters whether full suffrage rights should be extended to Blacks. The proposal was defeated heavily with only 36.4% voting in favor. Even in the Republican heartland upstate there was mixed support: Madison, Oswego, Onondaga, Tompkins, and Chenango Counties voted in favor, but most votes cast in Oneida, Lewis, Jefferson, and Broome Counties rejected the proposal.[88]

The storm clouds grew darker as the 1850s wore on. Fugitive slaves on the Underground Railroad continued to come through central New York. Gerrit Smith's mansion in Peterboro was a main "station," as was Jermain Loguen's house in Syracuse. Loguen himself (see Figure 5.2) is said to have sheltered fifteen hundred fugitive slaves at his home at 293 East Genesee Street during the years of the Underground Railroad. He openly wrote about his aid to runaways in local newspapers. Many others also sheltered fugitives secretly; it was, after all, a crime according to the Fugitive Slave Act. Harriet Tubman, an escaped slave herself, went on secret missions into Southern territory to persuade enslaved people to follow her north to Canada. She often brought them to Peterboro. Smith clothed fugitive slaves and gave them use of the third floor of his mansion. He helped them on their way west to Syracuse, Rochester, and Niagara Falls, or to Oswego to board ships to Ontario. During the years of violence between pro- and antislavery settlers, in what became known as "Bleeding Kansas" in the mid-1850s, Smith and others organized aid for antislavery militants.[89]

One of the key leaders in Kansas was John Brown, an Ohio-born abolitionist whom Smith had known since 1848. Before going to Kansas, Smith had given land in the Adirondacks to Brown at one dollar an acre. There Brown set up a farm among the members of a Black colony in Essex County to whom Smith had also gifted land. Brown also visited Peterboro frequently. He plotted to launch a violent raid into the South, which he hoped would spark a slave rebellion. Smith gave him money and support. He even hosted a conference of the inner circle of Brown's patrons called the "Secret Six" (though only four were present) at Peterboro in February 1858. Brown launched his

154 | Land of the Oneidas

Figure 5.2. Portrait of Rev. Jermain W. Loguen, 1859.

fateful raid on the US arsenal at Harper's Ferry, Virginia, on October 16, 1859. Brown was captured and hanged, and his body returned and buried at his Adirondack farm. Smith tried desperately to hide evidence of the part he played, knowing he would almost certainly be sent to the gallows for it.[90]

John Brown became a hero and a martyr to some in the North and a demon to most southerners. They were outraged not only at the raid itself but by the fact that many in the North publicly mourned his death and refused to condemn his actions.[91] The 1860 elections took place in the maelstrom. Abraham Lincoln ran as a Republican against two Democrats, fellow Illinoisan Stephen Douglas and John Breckenridge as a breakaway Southern Democrat. Central New York backed Lincoln resoundingly. Lincoln won the election, but with a popular vote of only 40 percent and nearly no votes in any states south of Pennsylvania, his prospects for holding the Union together were slim. Shortly after his inauguration in 1861, southern states announced their secession. When the federal government refused to abandon its military post at Fort Sumter, off the coast of Charleston, South Carolina troops opened fire. Civil war had begun.

Reckoning, 1835–1865 | 155

§

During the 1840s and '50s, a process of historical reckoning began in the Oneida lands. In those years, the first ethnographic studies of Haudenosaunee traditions, culture, and customs began appearing, and historians and novelists turned their attention to the area's past. With the Oneida Indians all but gone from the landscape, writers began to consider what was lost. Critical voices questioned whether what was done had been right and whether the destruction of the past equated to progress. Though steeped in the attitudes of their times, the works of James Fenimore Cooper, in particular, captured the imaginations of readers in America and internationally, in his own generation and in all subsequent ones. He portrayed the world of the New York frontier, preserved it, dramatized it, and brought it to life just as it was fading forever from existence.

Earlier works had attempted to trace out the history of the Haudenosaunee, with some attention given to the Oneidas. Cadwallader Colden's *History of the Five Indian Nations* was originally published in 1727 and revised in 1747. Colden treats the manners and customs of the Five Nations as one. Where he describes the Oneidas (Oneydoes, in his spelling), it is with reference to actions they took in their relations with the English, Dutch, or French. Reference to precontact history is limited. The Haudenosaunee Confederacy, he says, "has continued so long, that the Christians know nothing of the Original of it."[92] He supposed, wrongly, that the Five Nations' original home was in the area around Montreal. He describes a war between the Five Nations and the "Adirondacks" (Algonquins) predating the French settlement of Quebec, referring most likely to the fighting in the early stages of the Beaver Wars. Colden was the surveyor general in the colony of New York when he began his work and later a governor of the colony. He saw the Haudenosaunee as "barbarous People, bred under the darkest Ignorance," but also saw in them a "bright and noble Genius" that he attempts to display through a range of anecdotes from their interaction with the early colonial powers.[93]

The next significant attempt at a history of the Haudenosaunee did not appear until most of them were gone from their native lands. In 1826, David Cusik's *Sketches of the Ancient History of the Six Nations* was published on the Tuscarora Reservation in Lewiston. Cusik describes the Haudenosaunee as having originated near Oswego Falls. Tarenyawagon, the Holder of the Heavens, directed them to go east. Near the Hudson, one family broke off and became the Mohawks. The whole group then headed west. Tarenyawagon ordered the next family to split off and live by Oneida Creek; they became the Oneidas, and so on. Cusik's work is fascinating, but much of it is unreliable. Many of its stories appear to be the work of Cusik's own rich imagination, highly influenced by the Old Testament, with no correspondence to wider Haudenosaunee oral history or to any known archaeological evidence.[94]

Henry Schoolcraft's *Notes on the Iroquois* was the first attempt to write the history of the Haudenosaunee using all sources available at the time, from prehistory to the 1840s. It grew out of the New York Indian census of 1845 in which Schoolcraft was a lead organizer. He refers to the work as a set of revised notes taken during that project, with a few further "historical notices and researches" included.[95] For Schoolcraft, his work with the Oneidas had personal resonance. His father, Lawrence, had been a colonel in the Revolutionary War. He moved from eastern New York to Vernon in Oneida County in 1809 to set up the Oneida Glass Factory. Lawrence succumbed to alcoholism and died in 1840. He was buried in Vernon Village Cemetery. During his visit to Oneida, Schoolcraft visited his father's grave "on the banks of the Scando," the creek named for John Shenandoah, who until his death lived a few miles downstream. In Schoolcraft's notes, he recorded that his father was given the Oneida name *Sachan*, meaning "a strong wind." In the 1840s, the glass factory was still there, managed by Henry's brother-in-law, Willett Sherman, who resided in a porticoed house that still stands on Peterboro Road, a short distance from the Orchard Reservation. Most of the Indians who knew his father, however, were gone, either to Wisconsin or to Canada.[96]

In Schoolcraft's meetings with the Indians, he asked them to tell their stories and recorded what they said. At the top of Prime's Hill in Madison County was the Oneida stone, from which, Schoolcraft wrote, "they represent themselves, by a figure of speech, to have sprung." Schoolcraft visited it, on a farm belonging to Job Francis. He was guided by two Oneidas called Tshejoana and Skanawadi. From the hilltop, they could see for miles across the valley and to Oneida Lake beyond. Schoolcraft took an interest in archaeological findings. Farmers in Onondaga County showed him relics from the Jesuit mission found while ploughing their fields—a brass crucifix, a compass, and dial. One non-Native resident kept a "collection of antiquarian aboriginal articles" in his home which had been discovered in the vicinity, some of which had been dug up from Indian graves. He was also interested in "Ante-Columbian" artifacts such as stone hatchets, arrowheads and spears, bone needles, pipes, and pottery.[97]

Within a few years of Schoolcraft's work, Lewis Henry Morgan's *League of the Ho-de-no-sau-nee, or Iroquois* took the scholarly study of Haudenosaunee tradition and culture still further. Lavishly illustrated, it was the first attempt to show readers the world of the Haudenosaunee. Unlike Schoolcraft, Morgan had a profound interest in Iroquoian languages, albeit with a much greater knowledge of Seneca than of the others. He provides the names of the hereditary sachem titles (in the original language, with a translation in English) in each of the nations, including nine of the Oneidas. He provides a long list of place names, using the language of the region to record each. The Oneida language names and their meanings for settlements from Watertown (*Kä-hu-ah'-go*, or "Wide River") to Binghamton (*O-che-nang*, or "Bull Thistles"), as well as the significant rivers and lakes, are provided. Oneida Depot, only in its second decade of existence, is named "*De-ōse-la-tá'-gaat*, Where the [train] Cars go fast."[98]

Morgan's work added an antiquarian appeal to the romanticization of the Oneidas and their country that had been building up in fictional literature for some time. The French writer John Hector St. John de Crèvecoeur's three-volume *Voyage dans la haute Pensylvanie et dans l'état de New York* was published in 1801. It was written from the point of view of "an adopted member of the Oneida Nation." Taking the form of a travelogue, it was a fictionalized account of the American frontier around 1790. Crèvecoeur was a one-time immigrant to the colony of Pennsylvania who had returned to France during the American Revolution. He visited the mixed Oneida village at Oquaga in 1775. The episodes in the book that take place at Fort Stanwix, Whitestown, Oneida Lake, and other parts of central New York were imagined, though probably tinged with impressions related to him by his friend Barbé-Marbois, who was present at treaty negotiations at Fort Stanwix in 1784.[99]

Another three-tome novel set on the New York frontier published even earlier, in 1798, was Sophie von la Roche's *Erscheinung am See Oneida* (Visitors to Oneida Lake). The plot was based loosely on the story of the Devastines (or Des Wattines) of Frenchman's Island, which she probably heard about through letters from her son living in America. Although von la Roche was a well-known author in Germany and a pioneering woman in literature, her Oneida novel was never translated into English.[100] Similarly, Crèvecoeur's writings were well-known during his lifetime and he is still widely remembered for his earlier book *Letters from an American Farmer*, but his fictionalized travelogue was hardly read even in France and was not translated into English until 1961.

The novels of James Fenimore Cooper, on the other hand, particularly his *Leatherstocking Tales*, a series of five books set in upstate New York, were

158 | Land of the Oneidas

celebrated and widely read during his own lifetime and have been regarded as classics of American literature ever since. Cooper was raised in Cooperstown, Otsego County, in what had once been the border area between Mohawk and Oneida lands. Cooperstown was named for James Fenimore's father, William Cooper, who settled there in the 1780s. The elder Cooper's life shared much in common with Peter Smith's. From humble origins, he had made a fortune in land speculation, built a village (which, like Peterboro, he named for himself), and became a judge and the preeminent citizen of a new upstate county. A Mohawk settlement had existed there prior to the American Revolution. After the revolution, with the Mohawks gone, Otsego Lake was visited by roaming Haudenosaunee (presumably Oneidas) and Mohicans who sold baskets and moccasins, and occasionally begged for food. The novelist viewed all New York Indians as a "stunted, dirty and degraded race" but was fascinated with tales of adventure on the old frontier in which they played a central part. Like many others, Cooper saw the Indians as a once-great people who had been ruined over years of interaction with whites.[101]

Cooper depicts the Oneidas and describes their territory in several of the books. *The Pioneers* (1823) was set in the 1790s, but one of its principal characters, an old frontiersman named Natty Bumppo, recollects events from a much earlier time. Bumppo was based on settler-squatters like David Shipman who, "dressed in tanned deerskin," was already residing on William Cooper's land when the latter arrived. The setting of the book is Templeton, a fictionalized version of Cooperstown. Cooper cast his father as Judge Marmaduke Temple. Bumppo's companion in *The Pioneers* is Chingachgook, an aged Mohican, who symbolizes the decline and coming extinction, as Cooper saw it, of the once-heroic Indians of New York.[102]

Judge Temple and Natty Bumppo recollect crossing Oneida Lake and "the Ontary" in Indian-style bark canoes in their younger days. Lamenting the death of Chingachgook at the end of the novel, Bumppo remembers him as a young warrior and mourns not only his friend but the entire Indian race. Looking across the landscape, he says, "It raises mournful thoughts, to think that not a red-skin is left . . . unless it be a drunken vagabond from the Oneidas, or them Yankee Indians"—referring to the Brothertowns and possibly the Stockbridges who had adopted non-Native styles of agriculture and relocated to the Oneida Reservation in the 1790s—"who belong to none of God's creatures . . . neither white man nor savage."[103]

In *The Last of the Mohicans* (1826), we see Chingachgook and Natty Bumppo in their prime. It is a prequel to *The Pioneers*, set in 1757 during the French and Indian War. The Oneidas are involved in the adventurous plot. In one scene, Chingachgook's son reveals the scalp of an Oneida that he killed,

Reckoning, 1835–1865 | 159

either in a case of mistaken identity or in an instance of side-swapping by Indians in their alliances with the British and the French.[104] Another prequel, *The Pathfinder* (1840), takes place in the mid-eighteenth century, mainly on Lake Ontario and the Thousand Islands. It opens with Mabel Dunham on a journey westward with her Uncle Cap across Oneida lands from Albany to Oswego, where the young girl's father is stationed, accompanied by a Tuscarora guide called Arrowhead. When they see fire, the whites assume it is from an Oneida or Tuscarora camp, but Arrowhead can tell by the smoke that it is a "pale-face fire."[105] There they discover Natty Bumppo, Chingachgook, and Jasper Warren, a young sailor. Together they carry on to Lake Ontario, evading a band of French-allied Indians on the warpath on their way.

Cooper opened *The Last of the Mohicans* with a short introduction, explaining that all the Indian peoples described in the story have "disappeared" from the landscape, apart from "a few half-civilized beings of the Oneidas, on the reservations of their people in New York."[106] Although Cooper held the Indians of his own day in contempt, he also gloried in their part in central New York's past, at once celebrating and mourning the lost days of Indian greatness, unbridled wilderness, and frontier adventure. His depictions of the American wilderness and the Indians and frontiersmen who inhabited it inspired the landscape painters of the Hudson River School as well as poets and novelists in America and Europe in the nineteenth century and beyond. His influence was central to the creation of an American romanticism in art and literature.

Cooper's works were also emblematic of the nation's, and New York's own, troubled relationship with its history. Central New York was the glorious setting of the events of the American Revolution and of frontier adventure, but the Indians, once the "noble savages" of white imaginations, had either died, fled, or were living in poverty on what had once been their unspoiled homelands. While Cooper saw this as sad but inevitable, Schoolcraft and Morgan laid the groundwork for a more respectful approach to understanding Native American history and culture. Their work began a process of reassessing America's relationship with its Native people that went far beyond romanticizing the former greatness of the "Indian race." They began a more truthful, if uncomfortable, process of reckoning that continues into the twenty-first century.

§

President-elect Abraham Lincoln's train carried him through central New York from his home in Illinois to Washington, DC, for his inauguration.

On February 18, 1861, he traversed the state in a single day from Buffalo to Albany on the New York Central line. The train stopped only a handful of times for short speeches. Five hundred people in Oneida went to the tracks just to see his train pass. In Utica, the train stopped for a few minutes and Lincoln made a light-hearted speech from the carriage: "I have appeared here simply to thank you for this noble reception, to see you and to allow you to see me. I am not sure but, at least as regards the ladies, I have the best of the bargain. In conclusion, I have only to say farewell."[107] The humorous speech belied the grave crisis that the nation was in. The next time Lincoln would pass by these places, he was in a casket.

The outbreak of war at Fort Sumter was conveyed in heated and emotional terms in *The Oneida Sachem*: "The traitors of the 'Confederate States' have chosen war. The gauntlet has been thrown, and we must pick it up. To hesitate is but to be a traitor with them. . . . For eighty years we have enjoyed the blessing of a free and constitutional Government. We are now called upon to lay a sacrifice upon its altar."[108] Recruitment began immediately. Five infantry regiments were raised in Oneida County over the course of the war, nicknamed the First through Fifth Oneida. The first two—the 14th New York State Volunteers (First Oneida) and the 26th (Second Oneida)—sprang to life in May 1861. Both regiments were composed of ten companies with nine to eleven officers and fifty to sixty enlisted men. The companies were recruited in different locations: eight at Utica and one each at Boonville, Lowville, Rome, Whitestown, and Oriskany. Some companies in the Oneida regiments were recruited in other parts of the state—companies from Syracuse and Hudson were included in the First Oneida, while two companies from Rochester joined the Second Oneida. Individuals and companies from central New York also joined other New York State regiments during the war. But the fact that most of the men in the Oneida regiments were from the area meant that they were closely followed by local newspapers, which ran regular reports from correspondent soldiers.

Most infantry volunteers joined for either a two- or three-year period of service. Few had any prior military experience and entered service at the rank of private. Some of the officers in the First and Second Oneida, including the commanders of both regiments, had been members of the Utica Citizens' Corps, the local militia, prior to the war. The First Oneida was commanded by Colonel James McQuade, a bookkeeper and bank clerk in Utica. The Second's commander was Colonel William H. Christian, Utica's chief surveyor and a veteran of the Mexican War.[109]

Despite similar composition and an almost identical start to the war, the contrast between the experiences of the first two Oneida regiments was stark. Both were initially posted at Washington, DC, after several weeks of drilling. They were spared in the major battles of 1861 and suffered no casualties until the second year of the war. Both served exclusively in Virginia and Maryland. The First Oneida's most significant casualties occurred in the Seven Days' Battle from June 35 to July 1, 1862. In total they lost 61 men to enemy fire and 43 to disease before their return home in 1863.

The Second Oneida fared far worse, with 150 killed in the same period. They fought in some of the bloodiest battles of the first half of the war: Second Bull Run in August, Antietam in September and—deadliest of all, for them—Fredericksburg in December 1862. Numbers of wounded were higher still—113 from the Second Oneida were cut down at Fredericksburg alone. When they returned, the regimental flag had 38 bullet holes and was smeared with the blood of one of the five men who had fallen while carrying it in battle. The regiment was also battered by a dispute with the state over the length of their service agreement.[110]

The leaders of the two regiments also faced very different fates. James McQuade of the First Oneida returned to Utica a hero and was later elected mayor. William Christian of the Second, however, suffered from "shellshock" and found himself unable to lead in two battles. He was forced to resign his command. He spent the rest of the war trying without success to regain a position in the Army. The dishonor was humiliating for him. Although he was treated with respect by some of the men in Utica after the war, he never recovered. Unable to resume his old employment, his depression turned to dementia, and he was committed to the Utica Insane Asylum in 1886.[111]

The 97th Regiment (Third Oneida) was formed in February 1862 at Boonville, composed of men from Oneida, Lewis, and Herkimer Counties. The "three years men" of the Second Oneida joined it when their regiment was mustered out in 1863.[112] They took their nickname, "Conkling Rifles," from Roscoe Conkling, the Republican representative from Oneida County. They fought in numerous battles in Virginia and at Antietam and Gettysburg. By 1865, they had an aggregate total of 891 casualties, 339 of whom were dead and the rest gravely wounded.[113] The 117th (Fourth Oneida), formed in August 1862, before the heavy fatalities of the post-Antietam phase of the war were known. The 146th (Fifth Oneida), however, came into being in October, by which point there would have been no doubts about what was in store.

In Oneida, women of the First Presbyterian Church made their own US flag the day after the war began, "for none could be bought," and kept it flying from the steeple throughout the war "until whipped into shreds." Despite there being members in the congregation who held vastly different opinions about the war, "even to the most opposite extremes," the church sent supplies to the army and prayed for the sons, fathers, and brothers who had gone to war. "Two brave boys from the Sunday School," its semi-centennial history recorded, "did not return."[114]

Among those that survived, thousands came back with life-changing injuries. Parker B. Wilkinson, a landless young farm laborer living in Wampsville, Madison County, in 1860 joined the 78th Regiment in 1862 and remained in the South with the Army until 1865. When he returned to central New York, he continued to work on farms, but injuries to his feet and a double inguinal hernia he suffered in June 1863 caused problems for the rest of his life. By 1880 the pain in his feet made it impossible for him to carry on with farm work. He moved to Peterboro and drove stagecoaches while continuing to suffer from damage to his kidney and liver dating to the war. In 1900 one of his feet became so swollen and gangrenous it had to be amputated. Three years later he died of septicemia—blood poisoning. The *Oneida Dispatch* recorded on June 9, 1903, "Thursday night at about 6 o'clock occurred the death of Park [sic] Wilkinson, one of our oldest residents. He was an old soldier, the disease from which he died having been contracted in the war."

There is no way of calculating the total number of men from central New York who served or died in the Civil War. The five Oneida Regiments were far from being the only ones in which men from central New York served. Hundreds joined other New York volunteer regiments, cavalry units, or the Navy throughout the war. Erie Canal boatmen joined the 50th New York Regiment. Men from Oswego and Jefferson Counties served in large numbers in the New York 24th. The New York 149th, which played a prominent role in the Union victory at Gettysburg, was composed of men who mainly hailed from Syracuse and Onondaga County. The Oneida Independent Company Cavalry, formed in the village of Oneida, served the commanding generals of the Union Army throughout the war.[115]

Black volunteers were excluded from white regiments and had to serve in "colored regiments" commanded by white officers. Alberto Robbins of Peterboro joined the 55th Regiment of the Massachusetts Colored Infantry in 1863. John Stevenson, a formerly enslaved person residing in the town of Fenner in Madison County, joined the 29th Connecticut Colored Volunteers. Although they were segregated in service, they both joined the local Cazenovia chapter of the Grand Army of the Republic (a veterans' organization set up after the war) alongside white veterans from the area.[116] At least sixty Black residents of Oneida County served in the military, including a washerwoman attached to the 2nd New York Heavy Artillery and a man named William Henry, who was rejected from the army due to his weight (397 pounds), so instead joined the Navy and served on board the USS *Hornet*.[117]

The tiny band of roughly 160 Oneida Indians left in New York had few who were of the age and fitness to serve, but many of the Oneidas in Wisconsin (some of whom were part of the original migration) joined up, making up a large part of Company F in the 14th Wisconsin Volunteers. They were decimated by the war. Company D of the 132nd New York was organized by Cornelius Cusic, a Tuscarora, and was a mixture of German immigrants from Brooklyn and New York Haudenosaunee, including Oneidas.[118] One New York Oneida, Abraham Elm, left the reservation to find work as a lumberman in Vermont. When war broke out, he joined the 5th Vermont Infantry Regiment. He returned to Oneida following his years of service and later fought a court case after being arrested for attempting to vote in 1876 (Indians were barred from voting in federal elections).[119]

Politically, central New York was so solidly Republican that few antiwar Democrats bothered campaigning there during the war.[120] However, Democrats from the region were prominent in state politics, none more so than Horatio Seymour. Born in Onondaga County and brought up in Utica, he studied law under the antiabolitionist participant in the 1835 riot, Samuel Beardsley. Seymour had already served one term as governor of New York State between 1853 and 1854 and was mayor of Utica in the 1840s. In 1862 he was elected governor again—an office with enormous national import in the most populous state in the Union. Seymour was a vocal critic of the president. When Lincoln announced a military draft in 1863, large-scale riots broke out in New York City, Buffalo, and elsewhere, which also included violence against African Americans.

Seymour, rather than condemn the rioters, appeared to approve of their actions. When he addressed a crowd of New York rioters, he was greeted with "vehement and prolonged cheers." He asked them to refrain from "destruction of property" but also called them "my friends" and said he would ensure that "no injustice . . . be done in the matter of conscription." US soldiers standing on guard were booed and jeered by the same crowd who cheered for Seymour.[121] Seymour's actions as governor did not endear him to soldiers serving in the Army. Even soldiers from Democratic families like Hermon Clarke became sharply critical of the party's moves to undermine the war effort.[122]

Seymour did have numerous supporters, however, in central New York and throughout the state. From the outset, Democrats across the North blamed abolitionists for the war. Seymour had been a prominent advocate of the Crittenden Compromise, a proposal to avoid war by guaranteeing the future of slavery in the United States, in 1860. Many northerners held racist views. Even in Syracuse, the city where the Jerry Rescue had occurred in 1851, a racist placard was put up in 1861 to intimidate Frederick Douglass when he came to lecture, saying "Nigger Fred is Coming" and calling on citizens to "rally" to bring down the "traitor."[123] Seymour spoke about what he called the "negro problem," which he said was rooted in the "unchangeable distinctions of race."[124] In October 1863, the *Syracuse Courier and Union* announced with excitement that Seymour, the "popular Chief Magistrate of the Empire State, foremost as he is always found in matters pertaining to the welfare of the country and her people," would be holding a mass rally. Remembering a speech from Seymour in the city the year before, in which "multitudes swarmed within the sound of his voice," it concluded, "Let the people turn out in their might, and deal another staggering blow on the head of the Abolition foe to the Constitution."[125]

After the war, Seymour ran as the Democratic candidate for president in the 1868 election against Ulysses S. Grant. His campaign railed against what he called the "military and negro policy" by which slavery was dismantled while the post-war South was occupied by the US Army.[126] A campaign badge for his 1868 campaign read: "Our Motto: This is a white man's country; Let white men rule."[127]

Republican newspapers in central New York, however, rejoiced in the moves the Lincoln administration made to end slavery. In the Emancipation Proclamation, issued in September 1862, the president announced that slaves in the Confederate States would be forever freed from bondage beginning on January 1, 1863. In 1864, with the tide of the war turned distinctly in favor of the North, the *Cazenovia Republican* gleefully pointed out that General George McClellan's prediction that any changes to slavery by the president would cause the disintegration of the Union Army proved to be false: "On the contrary, at no time since the war commenced has victory so signally attended our arms as since the issuing of the emancipation proclamation."[128]

The Thirteenth Amendment, passed on January 1, 1865, declared a permanent end to slavery in the United States. In Watertown, the "Death Knell of Slavery" was announced in the February 2 issue of its *Daily Reformer* newspaper. "This finishes the work of our fathers when they laid deep and broad the foundation of the Republic. But it had one rotten pillar in it; when that is taken out and replaced by a granite one of universal freedom our temple will be strong and enduring as time."[129]

Even the Oneida Community came to support the war as its aims shifted from simply preserving the Union to ending the blight of slavery. Noyes had earlier declared himself and his followers to be "independent" from the United States. In an 1837 letter to William Lloyd Garrison, he stated he had "subscribed [his] name to an instrument similar to the Declaration of '76, renouncing allegiance to the government of the United

States," which he saw as a "bloated, swaggering libertine, trampling on the Bible . . . with one hand whipping a Negro tied to a liberty-pole, and the other dashing an emaciated Indian to the ground."[130] In 1860 the Oneida Community gave the air of being little concerned with the events leading to war. On November 8, 1860, only three lines in their paper *The Circular* indicate that Abraham Lincoln had been elected president. No commentary is given, and the statistics of Russia's population census seem a much more important actuality; it is given five times as much space. The same indifference to the American political situation is shown in a November 22 article on the threatened secession of South Carolina from the United States. The reporter states simply, "Personally, we shall be satisfied with either result."[131]

By the spring of 1861, however, a change had taken place. A few days after the first bullets flew at Fort Sumter, *The Circular* reported that "the American Government, as it has hitherto been known among the nations—the base, reprobate system of outrage, which has so long upheld Slavery, crushed the Indian, and patronized and fostered robbery and corruption—*has come to an end*." The author elaborated, stating that the antihuman government was entirely controlled by the South and that the new government in Washington, headed by Abraham Lincoln, is an "essentially different" one, run by the Northern spirit and worthy of the Community's support.[132] Another article in the same issue stated that "there is no middle ground for honest or earnest men to stand on. With the North are truth, justice, liberty, and human rights; with the South are falsehood, injustice, oppression, and outrage."[133]

As the war dragged on, the Community continued its support, though it returned to a more critical outlook on American life in the North. In response to the draft riots, *The Circular* blamed "the wretched material condition of the poorer masses and the ignorance, stupidity, brutality, and degradation accompanying these, together with the apathy of the rich."[134] In 1864, the publication's editor wrote that "Abolishing Slavery by War is like curing fever by calomel. The remedy, though effectual, remains in the system as a cause of disease."[135] They did, however, regard the end of slavery as a "triumph of Right over Wrong . . . of God over the Devil."[136]

When the news of Abraham Lincoln's death at the hands of an assassin reached Oneida, he was given the warmest elegy of a political figure ever to appear in the pages of *The Circular*. The April 17, 1865, edition reads: "Lincoln, the plain, the genial, the compassionate, the mirth-loving and God-fearing President, the 'Father Abraham' of the people—[was] cut off from life in his moment of felicity . . . by the sting of a dying serpent."[137] The president who was barely deigned three lines upon his election was now remembered by the Community as the closest thing America ever had to a spiritual leader. From that point on, the Community's interest in improving the "sinful" world through political processes waned.

The Community sent none of its men to participate in the war. They explained in their newspaper that they were "already enlisted in another army, which, under the command of Jesus Christ, was engaged in the general battle with the hosts of evil." But they boasted that they did pay war taxes of more than $10,000.[138] Perhaps they felt it a good way to justify their actions to their neighbors who might have looked with scorn on the unscathed and prospering Community as the dead were counted and the wounded returned home. Only one member of the Community, in its outpost at Wallingford, Connecticut, was drafted, and they were able to take advantage of the clause that allowed draftees to avoid service by paying $300. Males at Oneida avoided the draft, apparently due to their location on a bend in the creek which caused the draft officer in Madison County (where they resided) to think the Community location was in Oneida County. Not unreasonably, perhaps, there were suspicions that a bribe had been paid.[139]

§

Lincoln's dead body passed through Oneida on the evening of April 26, 1865. Official gatherings were held in Albany and Buffalo. The train did not stop in between, but in every village and town crowds came to witness the train passing. The *New York Tribune* recorded that "a funeral in each house in central New York would hardly have added solemnity to the day."[140]

With the end of the Civil War came the end of the many other things as well. The economy and ethnic composition of central New York would change dramatically in the half-century after the war. Indeed, that transformation was already underway with recent German and Irish immigrants who arrived before and during the war years challenging the demographic predominance of New England Protestants with family roots running deep in the colonial past. Thousands more would come. Before the Civil War, most people lived in the countryside and farmed for a living. In the decades after, cities grew, industrial centers expanded, and farming became a harder way to make a living.

Perhaps most importantly, the moral world changed as well. The spiritual fires in the burned-over district would never regain their previous intensity, nor would moral crusades in central New York like the one against slavery ever find as many enthusiastic followers. The rough and ready world of the canallers, farmers, and country preachers would give way to a more urbane and cosmopolitan one, where cities like Syracuse and Utica became the centers of progress and rural towns and villages stopped growing. A new era dawned.

Figure 6.1. Albert Bierstadt, *Evening on Oneida Lake*.

Chapter 6

Consummation, 1865–1917

Oneida Lake was an unusual subject for Albert Bierstadt, the most famous American painter of his day. Several years after the Civil War ended, he stood on the lakeshore at sundown. The painting that resulted was one of several Oneida landscapes that he made in his lifetime, though he had made his fame (and fortune) as a painter of the American West. Bierstadt was born in Germany, grew up in Massachusetts, and returned to Europe as a young man to study art in Düsseldorf. On voyages west during the 1860s and '70s, he made sketches for grandiose paintings that he completed after returning to his 10th Street, New York, studio. Like other painters of the loose conglomeration of New York–based artists known as the Hudson River School, Bierstadt celebrated and romanticized the American landscape. His personal specialism was depicting the drama of mountain storms, the majestic peaks, and the sublime vistas of the Rockies and California.

Bierstadt was internationally renowned—he was awarded honors and medals from France, Bavaria, Austria, Russia, Turkey, and Belgium.[1] Around the time he visited Oneida Lake, some of his canvasses were selling for $25,000 (roughly $500,000 in today's money). He may have stopped at the lake on a journey to Niagara Falls that he took with his wife in 1869, following their two-year honeymoon in Europe. A new train line, the Oswego and New York Midland, began service that year. From New York City and around the southern Catskills, it wove up through the rural hills and villages of Chenango and Madison Counties, crossing the New York Central line at Oneida. From there it went to the northeast corner of Oneida Lake and westward to the port of Oswego where goods or passengers could continue by boat north to Canada or west to Niagara. A station was built at Fish Creek and, later, another at Sylvan Beach which allowed passengers to access the lake and the newly built hotels along its shore.[2]

Bierstadt's *Evening on Oneida Lake* depicts tall trees on either side of the vista, framing the sinking sun that silhouettes them, casting shadows that foretell the coming night. A majestic buck stands alert in the foreground, gazing out at the viewer. A doe and fawn cross a shallow inlet behind him. The sky is bathed in somewhat implausible hues of red and orange. It is difficult to work out where on the lake he stood. It was most likely at the outlet of Fish Creek, where hotels were being built and which was walkable from Fish Creek station. The creek there would not be as shallow as the painting suggests. The trees in the middle ground frame the composition nicely but did not actually exist. Bierstadt was never one to let the truth stand in the way of a good picture. Although he may have worked from some sketches he made on the spot, this was a studio production. Bierstadt was immensely popular in the decades after the Civil War, but his reputation as an artist came under attack as critics pointed out that his paintings, grand as they were, were often exaggerated, dramatized versions of nature. The mountains were disproportionately high, the skies overly dramatic, the colors artificially enhanced for theatrical effect. In the later decades of the nineteenth century, the "real thing" came into vogue. Agents and investors wanted impressionistic paintings, done in *plein air*, out in nature. Intimate, even ordinary, landscapes were in, and grandiose, majestic panoramas out. Bierstadt's star began to fade.[3]

What brought the famous painter to central New York was his wife, Rosalie Osborn. She was a divorcée from Waterville, Oneida County. Her grandfather, Amos Osborn, had been one of the Yankee pioneers in the town of Sangerfield, not far from where the Brothertown Indians lived. Rosalie's father, also called Amos, was a man with high cultural aspirations. Educated at Hamilton and Yale, he was a farmer, lawyer, politician, bank director, church patron, and a lifelong "student of literature and the sciences." He circumnavigated the globe in 1855–56, collected fossils, and was also a serious historian.[4] Rosalie was known as a beauty with a flirtatious air. Her first husband was the New York City author Fitz Hugh Ludlow, a friend of Bierstadt's. Ludlow became famous for his book *The Hasheesh Eater* (1857) about his own drug use. Their marriage failed and Ludlow struggled with addiction and ill health for the rest of his life, staying for some time with his father, who had moved to pastor a church in Oswego.[5]

After obtaining a divorce, Rosalie married Bierstadt in the Grace Church at Waterville in 1866. The couple based themselves in the Hudson Valley, traveled extensively, and spent lavishly. In later years, they lived primarily in the Bahamas, but they did visit Oneida County from time to time, even wintering there while Bierstadt worked in a studio built by Amos Osborne in 1873–74. He completed several other paintings of the scenery around Waterville.[6]

The life Rosalie lived was a far cry from the one of humdrum routine and farm work that most of her childhood neighbors in Waterville knew. While Bierstadt and Rosalie toured the world, hobnobbing with the rich and famous of both Europe and America, the town of Sangerfield—in which Waterville was the largest settlement—was wrangling with a powerful gang of horse thieves. The Loomis family, like the Osbornes, were the second and third generation descendants of the original New England pioneers on Oneida land. They were not destitute. On the contrary, they were noted for genteel dress and polished manners. But stealing became a way of life for the family, led by its kleptomaniac matriarch Rhoda Mallett. Her husband, George Washington Loomis, died in 1852, but they had several children and a web of relations in the area. The head of the family, named after his father and usually called "Wash," was bright, articulate, handsome, and, like his father, extremely personable. He was the leader of the notorious "Loomis Gang."

During the Civil War, they stole horses from all parts of central New York and hid them in the nearby Nine Mile Swamp, a thick cedar-filled gully on the northern reaches of the Chenango River. They would smuggle them via a relative in Durhamville to the Erie Canal, to be moved on to other parts of the state. Horse theft was particularly lucrative during the Civil War, when the US Army needed all the horses it could get and would pay $150 and upwards for each animal. With plenty of money, the Loomis Gang was able to buy support, or silence, where it was needed. They also peddled in counterfeit money, committed numerous robberies, and were implicated in several murders. In 1864, they were almost certainly behind the burning of the Madison County Courthouse in Morrisville, where they believed indictment notices against them were filed. "Wash" Loomis was present at the blaze, feigning outrage and offering his help at the water pump. The pump didn't work; the arsonist had got to it earlier and cut the hose. When it was discovered that the indictments hadn't been in the courthouse, but in the county clerk's office next door, gang members broke into it, stole the papers, and burned them.

John L. Filkins was the Loomis's nemesis. As deputy sheriff in Oneida County, he spent years trying to bring the gang down legally, but with little success. In October 1865, he went rogue. With several other men—some of them veterans recently returned from the Civil War—he went to the Loomis farm at one in the morning, called Wash out, and beat him to death. An angry posse of one hundred fifty men hanged Wash's brother "Plumb" Loomis and burned down the farm the following year in an act of vigilante justice.[7]

The rise and fall of the Loomis Gang was certainly exciting, but this drama was the exception, not the rule, in rural upstate New York. The focus of most families outside the main cities was on farm work. Despite easier access to markets due to the development of water routes and railways over the nineteenth century, earning a living in agriculture became harder as the century wore on. Competition from the west and the cost of new machinery cut into profits. Seed drills and planters, mechanical reaping machines, mowers and threshers came into common use during and after the Civil War. Corn, potatoes, oats, barley, buckwheat, rye, hops, peas, and beans were important crops in central New York. Many farmers shifted from wheat production to dairy in the nineteenth century, unable to compete with the larger wheat-producing farms further west. Silos to hold fodder for dairy cows became common from the 1880s onwards.

The reduced need for human labor contributed to the movement from the countryside to the cities for work. Some farms were unable to keep up and were abandoned or sold, a trend that continued over the century to come. The number of farms in Oneida County gradually decreased from 8,390 in 1880 to 4,420 in 1945. Urban areas in New York State grew exponentially during the same period, fueled in large part by immigration. Statewide, the percentage of people living in the countryside compared to urban areas also decreased steadily from mid-century onward. By 1900, nearly three-quarters of New Yorkers lived in urban areas. Multiethnic, teeming cities like Syracuse and Utica became increasingly different—politically, demographically, and economically—from the countryside that surrounded them.[8]

In the 1830s, the number of immigrants coming to the United States averaged about 57,000 per year. In the 1840s it shot up to nearly 150,000 per year and in the 1850s to 271,000. Even while the Civil War raged, between 90,000 and 200,000 immigrants arrived each year. In the fifteen years from the war's end to 1880, an average of roughly 285,000 immigrated annually. In the 1880s, numbers per year sometimes topped a half million.[9] New York was the biggest port of entry. Many stayed in the city, but hundreds of thousands moved into central and western New York. Most came from Ireland and Germany. An earlier wave of Welsh immigrants assimilated quickly in the Oneida County countryside, but the great waves of Irish, German—and later Italian, Polish, and Jewish—immigrants that came to central New York settled largely in immigrant sections of the cities of Utica, Syracuse, Rome, and Oneida. Differences in language and religion from the US-born population generated tension. These immigrants turned upstate cities into industrial powerhouses and transformed them in ways that remain relevant in the twenty-first century.

The Welsh were the first major group of immigrants in the nineteenth century to settle in large numbers in central New York. The first Welsh immigrants arrived in 1795 and established a community in Steuben, Oneida County. The Baron von Steuben's land grant had been passed to his aide, Benjamin Walker, to manage after his death in 1794. Walker encouraged Welsh immigrants without the means to buy property to take up leaseholds there. By 1812, there were roughly seven hundred Welsh people in Steuben, with another major area of Welsh settlement growing a few miles to the east in Remsen. By mid-century, three quarters of the population in those towns was of Welsh origin. The 1855 New York census showed four thousand Welsh-born residents in Oneida County, including 860 in Utica. There were also settlements of over a hundred and fifty in Eaton and Nelson in Madison County, where Welshmen bought farms from previous Yankee settlers who moved further west.

The Welsh were unlike the Yankees—those whose ancestors had come from New England—of central New York in many ways. Welsh, not English, was their native language in most cases. Welsh churches in Oneida County such as the Moriah Church and Bethesda Church in Utica and Capel Cerrig in Remsen continued to hold Welsh-language services well into the twentieth century. Welsh language newspapers were printed in Utica. *Y Cyfaill* (The Friend), a Welsh Presbyterian newspaper, ran from 1838 to 1933. *Y Drych* (The Mirror) was published in Utica for nearly seven decades starting in 1851 and was the main Welsh-language newspaper throughout the United States.

However, their Protestantism helped the Welsh to integrate. Welsh denominations tended to mirror the Congregational-Presbyterian style of worship of the New England settlers.[10] Politically, the Welsh in central New York were strongly Republican, unlike Irish immigrants who tended to be

Democrats. Within two to three generations, few Welsh families had not joined with other American families (of New England origin or otherwise) through marriage. Protestants of Yankee descent who were horrified by the Catholic influx during the peak years of Irish immigration saw the Welsh as reliable allies. As Pomroy Jones (of Welsh descent himself) put it in his *Annals of Oneida County* (1851), "A Welsh Catholic would be an anomaly, and they are peculiar in their hatred of all that appertains to Popery."[11]

Immigration from Ireland was a far tenser issue in the middle decades of the nineteenth century, in central New York and nationally. Irish immigrants came to America in several great waves. Ireland was ruled by Britain throughout the nineteenth century. The elite there were mainly Protestant, but most Irish people were Roman Catholic. Thousands eked out an agricultural living as tenant farmers, but when major crop failures hit the country in the notorious "potato famine" starting in 1845, starvation and eviction led to mass emigration. In 1847, the numbers of Irish immigrants to America more than doubled from around 50,000 in 1846 to 105,000 and remained as high over each of the eight ensuing years, peaking at 221,000 in 1851.[12]

Unskilled, hungry, and traumatized Irish immigrants poured into Boston and New York, desperate for work and food. The established populations reacted with alarm, seeing the huge Irish influx as a threat not only to stability and public resources, but to their very way of life. Roman Catholics represented a tiny minority in the US before large-scale Irish immigration. Anti-immigrant and anti-Catholic groups coalesced in the Know Nothing Party in the 1850s. The *Oneida Sachem* noted on April 19, 1856, that Irish Catholics in Albany "burned in effigy the editor of the *Transcript*, a K.N. paper."

With hostility and poverty facing them in the major port cities, many Irish immigrants ventured inland to wherever there were better prospects for employment. Many came north via the Hudson and west via the Erie Canal on their way to the Midwest. Thousands stayed in cities and towns along the way. Utica and Rome both had large Irish-born populations by the 1850s. St. John's in Utica was the first Catholic church in the central or western part of New York State. Jones noted in 1851 that it was "full to overflowing" on Sundays. St. Patrick's (Irish) Catholic Church came into existence in 1850. In 1872, it had 1,500 communicants and 275 pupils in the Sunday school, mainly living on the then-west side of Utica.[13] In Syracuse, the far westside neighborhood of Tipperary Hill became an almost exclusively Irish enclave. Onondaga County's first Catholic church (since the seventeenth-century Jesuit mission) was St. Mary's, organized in 1842. It quickly became too small and another, St. John the Evangelist, was started in 1852. By the mid-1850s, there were four in Syracuse.[14]

St. Patrick's Day was celebrated in Utica by Irish immigrants from 1821 onward. The *Oneida Weekly Herald*'s coverage of the 1855 St. Patrick's Day Festival paid particular attention to the toasts at the dinner held at Concert Hall. Some showed loyalty to the United States: to the president, the army, and the "Union of the United States—Let it be perpetual." Others to the "Catholic Monarchy of the United States," the "Irish Republicans of 1798 and 1848," and the "Catholic Monarchy of Ireland" would have raised the eyebrows of anti-Catholic readers around Utica.[15] There were plenty of those. The state's first so-called "nativist" political convention was held in the city in 1844. In 1854, a group of Know-Nothings in Utica, including the prominent lawyer Alexander Coburn, broke away from the party over an internal dispute but still resolved to oppose "persons of foreign birth or Catholic faith." In the 1854 New York gubernatorial election, the Know-Nothing candidate won 1,068 votes in Oneida County (6 percent of those cast) and over 3,000 in Onondaga County (24 percent of the total).[16]

To the old Protestants of the burned-over district, Roman Catholicism was regarded with suspicion well into the twentieth century. Anti-Catholicism ran deep in the evangelical message of Finney and others. The Utica-born author Harold Frederic used the juxtaposition of "native" Protestantism and "foreign" Catholicism in the upstate town of Ocatvius—a fictionalized version of Utica—to drive the plot of his most celebrated novel, *The Damnation of Theron Ware* (1896). The title character is a Methodist minister who, having grown up in the Protestant countryside, finds himself entranced and beguiled by the Roman Catholics in Octavius. Two characters in particular, the Catholic priest Father Forbes and a young Irish organist called Celia Madden, shake his worldview and eventually cause him to abandon his ministry. Frederic began his career as a journalist for the *Utica Morning Herald*. He wrote the novel in London, where he worked as a foreign correspondent for the *New York Times*. Like Theron Ware, Frederic himself was fascinated with Irish Catholicism. Unlike him, he grew up among it, living as a boy at 324 South Street, in the heart of a city and a neighborhood teeming with Irish immigrants.[17]

However, there were some factors that helped the Irish to settle in the central part of New York with less friction than they experienced in New York City and the Hudson Valley. Local leaders like Democrat-turned-Republican Oneida County Congressman Timothy Jenkins were largely friendly towards immigration, seeing immigrants as "our natural allies" in the political rifts of the 1850s.[18] An early settler of Utica, Nicholas Devereux, was an Irish Catholic who was successful in business and a founding benefactor of St. John's and Utica's orphan asylum. He built up a good name among the early influential families of Utica, and his respected status played a role in creating a more welcoming environment for Irish immigrants there. From the 1830s onward, Father William Beecham roamed the countryside of central New York, administering Catholic rites to the poor who needed them, caring for the laborers in their camps who built the Black River Canal, and helping them to send money and messages back to Ireland. He, too, built up a good reputation and relationship with non-Catholics. Two years before his death in 1876, he managed to get the board of education in Rome to pay for and provide teachers' certificates to staff in his school "without subjecting them to an exam." According to a letter published in Durant's *History of Oneida County*, the board chose to do it out of a "profound respect for his character" and "the warmest attachment to him personally," though it may equally have been a matter of expedience, given the number of children needing a school place at the time. The urban population in central New York's cities was undergoing a massive growth spurt.[19]

Like subsequent waves of immigrants, the Irish in central New York were concentrated in large numbers mainly along the Mohawk-Erie corridor, with fewer settling in the rural areas. They contributed to huge growth in the cities while the population in the countryside stagnated or declined. In the decade between 1860 and 1870, largely rural Madison County's population decreased marginally. The population of Jefferson County, even further off the beaten path of immigration, fell by over 4,000 in the same ten years.[20] The agricultural counties of Otsego, Chenango, and Lewis all either stagnated or shrunk, partly due to deaths in the Civil War. Syracuse, by contrast, exploded from 28,119 in 1860 to 43,051 in 1870—an increase of 85 percent. Utica, too, grew by 6,500, a 30 percent rise, and Rome by 13 percent. A growing number of jobs in the towns as industry expanded during and after the war brought some American-born citizens in from the surrounding countryside. But immigration was the dominant factor by far. Both Utica and Syracuse were one-third foreign born in 1870, and Rome was a quarter.[21] Of those who weren't Irish, most were German.

Germany before 1870 was not a unified country but a conglomeration of kingdoms and principalities with mainly German-speaking populations. Some areas of Germany, notably parts of the Kingdom of Bavaria and the Rhineland were mainly Catholic, while many others were Lutheran Protestant. Germany did not suffer the same sort of cataclysmic famine that Ireland experienced in the 1840s, but there was a wave of attempted revolutions in 1848 that failed, prompting thousands of so-called Forty-Eighters to emigrate to America. Most German immigrants came seeking a better life and economic opportunity. Like the Irish, they sailed into American port cities, mainly (but not exclusively) in the North, before, during, and after the Civil War. From there many moved west or stayed in urban areas along the way that offered employment, including the rapidly growing cities of central New York. They were also perceived as a threat by the Know Nothing Party and targeted in their literature and propaganda as beer-swilling foreigners coming to take jobs from US-born Americans. German Catholics were tarred with the same brush as the Irish, as anti-American "Papists."

By 1875 Oneida County had 6,706 German-born residents, more than half of whom lived in Utica. There, the Germans lived in the densely packed, heavily immigrant 9th ward bordered by Columbia Street to the north and the Chenango Canal (now Route 12) to the east.[22] In Syracuse, more than one in ten was German-born in 1875, with most living on the north side, in the adjacent 2nd and 4th wards bounded by the Erie Canal (now Route 690) to the south and the Oswego Canal (now Route 81) to the west—including the area along North Salina Street that later became Syracuse's Little Italy district.[23]

In both cities, German-language newspapers were published, the longest-lived of which, the *Wöchentlicher Syracuse Demokrat* (renamed *Syracuse Union* in 1865) ran from 1856 to 1941. Germans in Utica read the *Utica Demokrat* (from 1853) and, after the war, the politically independent *Utica Deutsche Zeitung*, which in 1870 was named one of the three official papers of the city, alongside the *Observer* and the *Herald*.[24] Hundreds of Germans and Irish men from central New York fought in the Civil War. The 12th (Onondaga) and 101st Regiment (Second Onondaga), mustered in Syracuse in 1861 and 1862, included entire companies of Syracuse Germans (Companies B and H, respectively). In the 149th (Fourth Onondaga) Company A was Jewish, Company B was German, and Company C was Irish "with but few exceptions."[25]

German immigrants set up churches, both Catholic and Protestant, and built communities in Utica and Syracuse. St. Joseph's Catholic Church in Utica was organized in 1840 with sixty German families. By the late 1850s, two hundred families attended. St. Mary's in Utica, also German, was originally a Lutheran church and then became a Catholic church in 1870. Zion Lutheran Church was built on Cooper and Fay Streets in Utica. A German choir, the Männerchor (still in existence) was formed in Utica in 1865.[26] In Syracuse, the area around Butternut and Park Streets was known as "Schwobenland," a reference to the largely Swabian population from what is now southwestern Germany, complete with a German theatre (Wöse's) and numerous German taverns. Swiss Germans lived in the area called Schwitzer Hill around Seward and Alvord Streets.

In 1871 Germans in Utica and Syracuse held grand festivals to celebrate the Kingdom of Prussia's victory in the Franco-Prussian War, which prompted the unification of Germany under the Prussian monarchy.[27] Few could have foreseen that a generation later the United States would be at war with the German Empire. In time, many Germans (and Irish) and their first-generation children left Syracuse, Rome, and Utica, settling in other locations in central New York, like the smaller but still bustling industrial town of Oneida. Within two generations, many Germans (particularly Protestants) married into old New England families. The language and most other aspects of German identity faded away in the third and fourth decades of the twentieth century.

§

Italian immigration to the United States started to grow from a relative trickle to a steady stream in the 1880s and '90s. In the 1900s and 1910s, this turned to a flood, with 3.4 million Italian-born immigrants arriving in those two decades. Most were from the poorer, rural, southern part of Italy, which had not reaped the benefits of national unification in the 1860s and '70s under a government that acted predominantly in the interests of the industrialized north. Even more than in previous waves of immigration, New York City was the main point of entry. Italians moved to cities across the United States, but the overwhelming majority remained in New York City and State. Like the Irish and Germans before them, thousands of Italian immigrants came to central New York, enticed by the availability of work. The 1910 census showed a population of 739,000 with Italian birth or parentage living in New York State—up from 182,000 ten years earlier. Roughly half lived in New York City. Syracuse had over 7,000. Oneida County with its two urban centers of Utica and Rome had 4,240.[28] The number in Oneida County would more than double by 1920 to 11,333, including 8,500 in Utica, overtaking Syracuse in numbers of Italian immigrants despite its smaller overall size, and nearly all others in Rome. Madison County had over 1,000, mainly in the railway towns of Oneida and Canastota.

Parts of Syracuse and Utica became Italian enclaves. One in five Italians in Syracuse lived in its Little Italy neighborhood, the same area that had recently been home to thousands of German immigrants. In Utica, the majority (over 5,000 of the 8,500) were in the 8th ward in the northeastern section of the city, with Bleecker Street its main thoroughfare.[29] It became known as "the *colonia*," where Italians were the majority and where Italian American politicians came to hold significant influence that still features in the twenty-first century. Italian-born immigrants represented nearly a tenth of the city's population in 1920. They took up jobs in the same textile factories that had employed newly-arrived German and Irish immigrants a generation earlier.[30]

Large numbers of eastern European (particularly Polish) and Jewish immigrants also came to America in the decades prior to the First World War. In Utica, a synagogue called the House of Jacob was built in 1870 at 117 Whitesboro Street. Many subsequent Jewish immigrants settled in the immediate vicinity. The Keneseth Sholom (Society of Concord) was founded even earlier, in 1842, in Syracuse. Jewish immigrants came predominantly from Poland, which prior to World War I was divided between the German, Austro-Hungarian, and Russian Empires. The Russian-controlled areas of Poland were noted for repression of both Poles and Jews. Jews throughout the Russian Empire were targeted in violent, organized pogroms in the late nineteenth and early twentieth centuries that pushed many to leave. Most Jewish immigrants in Utica worked as peddlers (earning a living by selling various items, sometimes door-to-door), cigarmakers, or grocers.[31] Catholic Polish communities formed in places like the factory town of New York Mills, west of Utica, and in Syracuse's inner-city 7th ward. Some Poles also settled within the Italian *colonia* in East Utica. In 1920, there were over seven thousand Polish-born residents in Oneida County, and another five thousand in Onondaga County—the largest numbers in New York State outside New York City and Buffalo.[32]

The main factor in the rise of large immigrant communities in the cities of central New York was the availability of work. From the late 1840s on, America was being transformed by industrialization and the urbanization that accompanied it. In Syracuse, salt production was the main industry through most of the nineteenth century. The lands containing salt springs around Onondaga Lake were reserved by the state in 1784. Commercial salt production began there in 1788, but it wasn't until the opening of the Erie Canal in 1825 that the industry really took off. As the country grew, the market expanded and by the 1850s Onondaga salt was being bought and sold throughout the United States. Large cities like Buffalo and Chicago got all their salt from Syracuse. In 1860 the various companies producing the salt were combined into the Salt Company of Onondaga.

Before 1820, Syracuse did not exist. By 1850 it was a bustling town of twenty-two thousand, having just overtaken Utica in size of population. By 1880 its population had more than doubled and by 1890 it had over eighty-eight thousand residents, twice the size of Utica. The Civil War years were the most profitable (explaining the population explosion at the time) with tariffs on imports and the needs of the army making Onondaga salt a near-monopoly in the North.[33] German and other immigrants found work as salt boilers, operating kettles that boiled brine in buildings known as salt blocks. Others worked as porters carrying salt bushels or moving the tons of coal needed to boil the brine. An immigrant writing back to relatives in Germany in 1852, urging them to join him in Syracuse, wrote that the "inexhaustible salt springs around Onondaga Lake" meant that "everyone can find a job here." He added that the large German population in the city meant that "although we are in a strange land, we are among Germans, our own people."[34]

The Utica Steam Cotton Mills, founded in 1847, was still the city's biggest employer in the 1870s. Its sprawling four-story factory buildings still stand on State Street, backing on to Route 12, which follows the route of the Chenango Canal (see Figure 6.2). In the 1870s, seven hundred people worked there. Immigrants from the 9th ward walked to work where they converted five thousand bales of cotton into six million square yards of sheeting and shirting fabric per year. Two woolen mills stood in the 9th ward (both also still standing). The Globe Woolen Company in a four-story factory on Court Street and Stark Street employed four hundred in the 1870s, making "fancy cassimeres" out of Ohio-sourced wool to sell in New York City. The other was on Columbia Street, just west of St. Joseph's Catholic Church.

Numerous smaller knitting and clothes-making factories, iron foundries, a brick works, a match factory, a soap and candle works, and several tobacco-rolling plants employed hundreds of immigrant and American-born hands.[35] Francis Xavier Matt, a German immigrant, became the most prominent brewery operator in Utica after setting up the West End Brewing Company in 1888 on the site of a previous brewery owned by Charles Bierbauer. Of the major nineteenth-century factories in Utica, Matt's is the only one that has remained in continuous operation (including during Prohibition) to the present day.

Figure 6.2. Detail from D. G. Beers, "Utica, 2nd, 3rd, 6th, and 9th Wards" in D. G. Beers's *Atlas of Oneida County, New York*.

§

While Syracuse and Utica became major industrial centers, smaller towns along the canal and rail lines like Oneida and Canastota grew rapidly, too, becoming important manufacturing hubs in the decades following the Civil War. In the 1880s, Oneida had several tanneries, a cart and carriage works, a foundry and iron works, several cigar manufacturers, and a window-making plant.[36] The two titans of Oneida around the turn of the century were C. Will Chappell, the founder of the enormous casket factory that loomed over the New York Central line along North Warren Street. The other, Julius M. Goldstein, owned Powell & Goldstein Cigar Company (his original business partner, John E. Powell, had died in the early days of the company). Its rolling factory was on the corner of Main and Madison Streets.

Both resided in large mansions and employed, between them, most of the town's working-age population. Both launched their businesses in 1879. Chappell and a partner, already in the undertakers' supply trade, bought out a casket producer in Rochester, built a new factory in Oneida, and began churning out coffins. He oversaw the expansion of the factory buildings as president of Chappell, Chase, Maxwell & Company. In 1890 the company merged with National Casket Company, of which Chappell became the vice president and general manager. When President William McKinley was assassinated in 1901, the *New York Times* reported that his casket was "furnished by the National Casket Company of Oneida and is elaborate in design . . . made of solid crotched Santo Domingo mahogany."[37] Ulysses S. Grant, too, laid in state after his death in 1885 in an Oneida-made casket designed by Melvin Henry Hubbard, the architect of Oneida's Catholic and Baptist churches.[38]

In the 1890s, the Boston-based Biographical Review Company published volumes containing the life stories of the leading men of the counties of central New York. It sought to illustrate the biographies of the "great men," those who were most "useful and honored in their day and generation." Its purpose was to memorialize them as heroes to emulate, not only for success in their careers, but also for their patriotism, enthusiasm for education and social improvement, and their general "enterprise in public life."[39] In his biography in the *Leading Citizens of Madison County*, Chappell is lauded for leading his casket business "to its present enormous proportions," making it (without any sign of a pun intended) "a very successful undertaking." Chappell's story in *Leading Citizens* starts with his "lineage far back in the history of New England" and his more recent Yankee forebears who were eminent early settlers of Cazenovia. Chappell was educated at Cazenovia

Seminary. Throughout his life, while his company prospered, Chappell connected himself with "prominent and public-spirited enterprises." He was a trustee of local banks, churches, and schools, a supporter of the Oneida Water Works and fire company, and an active Democrat in politics.[40]

The other baron of Oneida industry, Goldstein (see Figure 6.3), received not so much as a mention in the *Leading Citizens*. It would have been understandable if he felt he'd been purposefully snubbed—he probably was. Goldstein's Oneida factory was producing upwards of six million of his trademark "Napoleon" cigars per year, making it one of the largest US producers.[41] Goldstein became wealthy and built a fine home at 532 Main Street to rival Chappell's on the corner of Grove and Elizabeth Streets (Goldstein's still stands, Chappell's doesn't). Whereas Chappell had an all-American pedigree, Goldstein's origins were foreign and obscure. He was born in Schneidemühl in the Kingdom of Prussia (now Piła, Poland) and immigrated in 1871 at the age of seventeen.[42] He lived in New York City and found work in a cigar factory there, eventually becoming an interpreter and a foreman in charge of one hundred men. One of his charges there was Samuel Gompers, who went on to lead the American Federation of Labor.[43]

JULIUS M. GOLDSTEIN
FIRST ELECTED MAYOR OF THE CITY OF ONEIDA, 1901. MANUFACTURER OF CIGARS.
ONEIDA, N. Y.

Figure 6.3. Portrait of Julius M. Goldstein in *Notable Men of Central New York*.

There is no information about his parents' origins or what education, if any, he received. He was a slight man, five foot five, with an oblong face and spectacles. He was almost certainly Jewish, though his religion was not mentioned in any of the many newspaper articles that were written about him. How and why he ended up in Oneida is also unclear. His obituary in the *New York Times* states that he "came up-State for his health."[44] The 1880 census captures him at the age of twenty-six, living in Oneida at 27 Madison Street in an accommodation that was shared with seven other men who were unrelated to him, three of whom were also immigrants. By 1899 he employed 175 men in his factory. Ten years later, he had 275 on his payroll.[45] In 1887, with his business prospering, he married an Oneida woman, Henrietta Nixdorf, herself the daughter of German immigrants.

Whether his omission from the *Leading Citizens of Madison County* piqued him or not, he appears to have thrown himself into public life in the 1890s, seemingly meeting or exceeding Chappell's contributions in all areas. He became active in county and village councils, and when Oneida was incorporated as a city in 1901, he became its first elected mayor. He was a philanthropist, donating large sums to local hospitals and endowing an old-ladies' home near his mansion.[46] He went on hunting trips to the Adirondacks with local notables.[47] He was on the board of trustees of Oneida's Glenwood Cemetery and donated hundreds of trees to beautify Allen Park on Oneida's south side.[48] He, too, became prominent in state political affairs, but unlike Chappell, as a Republican. He hosted Presidents Taft and Theodore Roosevelt, and several New York governors, in Oneida.

He also made a point of showing his patriotism. A statue of Napoleon stood in front of the Powell & Goldstein cigar store in Oneida with an American flag in its hand (the statue is still on display in the Madison County Historical Society in the one-time home of Niles Higinbotham). In 1898, at the height of the Spanish-American War, someone stole the flag. The *Oneida Evening Union* reported that Mr. Goldstein "is very wroth . . . not for the intrinsic value of that flag . . . but the principle of the thing is what he contends for, and his patriotism rebels against such despicable acts." Goldstein offered a reward of twenty-five dollars "for the detection, arrest, and conviction, of the perpetrator of the crime."[49]

Tragedy attended both the Chappell and Goldstein families. C. Will Chappell was killed in an automobile accident near Canastota in 1909.[50] He was buried in Glenwood Cemetery in Oneida, with a suitably grand, orb-topped monument to mark his grave. Goldstein, too, would be buried in Glenwood in an even grander family mausoleum. He was preceded by his son-in-law, Jesse L. Oberdorfer. Oberdorfer was the heir to his father's fortune and the one-time treasurer of his company, Oberdorfer Brass, in Syracuse. He was married to Goldstein's daughter, May, by a Syracuse rabbi in 1911.[51] The 1930s saw the "almost complete disappearance of his once considerable fortune," and he grew despondent. His true passion had always been the stage, but he sacrificed it for a business career which was ending in failure. In 1935, he committed suicide by drinking poison. It may not have been his first attempt. He had nearly died behind a locked door in Goldstein's mansion in Oneida in 1913 and required resuscitation. After Jewish funeral services at his home in Syracuse, his body was driven to the Goldstein mausoleum.[52] Henrietta Goldstein died and joined him there three years later and Julius three weeks to the day after his wife.

The acceptance among blue-blooded Americans in Madison County that the immigrant Goldstein appears—with his Jewish surname, frail health, slight build, and obscure origins—to have lacked in his early career had come to him at last. His photograph was included opposite Chappell's in a directory titled *The Notable Men of Central New York* in 1903.[53] Not only was he Oneida's first elected mayor, but in his later life, he was invited to join several of the fraternal orders that bound together men of rank throughout the United States. Both Chappell and Goldstein were Freemasons. Chappell was a member of the Doric Chapter, No. 193, Royal Arch Masons of Oneida (of which he was high priest), as well as the Syracuse Commandery, No. 25, K.T. and the Syracuse Consistory.[54] Goldstein was also a member of the Oneida Lodge, No. 193, when he died.[55] He was a charter member of the Oneida Country Club and a founding member of the Oneida Lodge of the Benevolent and Protective Order of the Elks.[56]

When Goldstein died, "close friends and employees" acted as bearers in his funeral. Hundreds attended, possibly thousands. He was lauded as an "outstanding citizen of Oneida." Tributes were paid by the city's "various civic and Masonic groups." The service was led by the rector of the local Episcopal church.[57] Whether Goldstein considered himself a Christian, either by conversion or convention, or a Jew—or neither—is unknown. It was not commented on in the press. To the people of Oneida, it doesn't seem to have mattered, at least not at the end of his life. He had become an accepted, respected, and celebrated person in a city where he had once been a poor, unknown immigrant. He was a pioneer of sorts, and a successful one. His story was unusual in many ways. Few immigrants in central New York became as prominent or as wealthy as he did, for one thing. But it speaks of the process of assimilation that all immigrant families went through. Their status changed—sometimes in a single generation, sometimes in two or three, from outsiders to Americans. Some families retained their languages and customs, handing them down to children and grandchildren. But inevitably, in taking on new identities, certain aspects of their original ones were lost.

Goldstein's Oneida story epitomizes the immigrant dream of America as a land of opportunity, one where the most repressive economic and political aspects of life in the Old World could be forgotten. Almost. The same newspapers carrying Goldstein's death notices in 1938 also brought news to readers of the exploits of Adolf Hitler in Germany and the storm clouds of war looming in Europe.

§

The second half of the nineteenth century was a period of architectural efflorescence. Grand new buildings and homes in the cities and villages of central New York were built to symbolize prosperity. In Syracuse, the architect Archimedes Russell designed vast stone churches, department stores, schools, hotels, courthouses, and—perhaps his most iconic building—the Crouse Memorial College at Syracuse University.[58] His Snow Building on Warren Street, built in 1887–88, was a proto-skyscraper at eight stories, 102 feet in height. The area around Clinton Square, traversed by the Erie Canal, was framed with towering Gothic structures like Joseph Lyman Silsbee's Syracuse Savings Bank building (1876). Within the lifetime of some of its inhabitants, Syracuse had gone from a miniscule frontier settlement of log houses to a city of fifty thousand, with architectural magnificence to rival any city of its size in the United States (see Figure 6.4).

Utica too underwent a transformation, particularly along Genesee Street. Its grand city library on Elizabeth Street, opened in 1878, demonstrated municipal values of education and self-help. It boasted of having 28,330 volumes, "prophetic of the dawn of a new era for our reading public," and a lecture hall. Built in the Victoria Gothic style with ornate decoration, it was esteemed to be unsurpassed "by any similar institution in the country." Ornate city block buildings advertised a thriving commercial culture.[59] Smaller cities and towns like Watertown, Rome, Lowville, Oneida, and Norwich all have their own range of impressive stone churches, schools, libraries, clubhouses, and hospitals that sprung up or replaced old wooden structures in their central streets in the decades after the Civil War.

Figure 6.4. Clinton Square, Syracuse, circa 1905.

This development of architecture carried on into the twentieth century, reaching its zenith in the years leading up to the First World War. The Savings Bank of Utica opened a pedimented, gold-domed, Greek temple-like structure on Genesee Street in 1900. At the turn of the century, Utica's showcase 1878 library building became too small for a city that had nearly doubled in population since it was built. A new, and even grander, library building on Genesee Street was completed in 1904.[60] Public buildings reflected a confidence matching central New York's economic predominance. Utica's Union Station was completed in 1914. The three-story beaux-arts colossus with a marble-columned interior echoes the grandiosity of New York's Grand Central Station, completed the year before, and was designed by some of the same team of architects. In the same year, on August 3, a bronze statue of the Baron von Steuben was unveiled on Memorial Parkway and Genesee Street. The German ambassador and President Woodrow Wilson were supposed to be present for the unveiling, but both gave last minute apologies "because of the situation in Europe."⁶¹ The First World War had broken out the week before.

Enormous, imposing stone county courthouses were constructed in Syracuse in 1907 and Utica in 1909. Even predominantly rural Madison County got its own impressive domed courthouse building in 1909 in tiny Wampsville, a short walk from where Wemp's Tavern once served alcohol to travelers and Indians on the Oneida Reservation.

Private homes from the period used the same architectural language to conjure status and culture. New mansions were built for the wealthier citizens throughout central New York, some of wood, some of stone. Even in agricultural villages, those who could afford to constructed ornate homes. Jigsaw-cut trims adorned Italianate, Gothic Revival, Second Empire, and Queen Anne style houses. Upstate New York's architecture is not unique for the period. Similar styles were used throughout the northern United States, making similar statements to viewers. But there are certainly some one-of-a-kind examples. In Georgetown in southern Madison County is Timothy Brown's "Spirit House." Known at one time as Brown's Free Hall, it was built under the influence of the wave of spiritualism that took hold in the years during and after the Civil War, characterized by seances, communication with the dead, and a genuine belief in invisible spirits. Brown built the house on his own over ten years, allegedly guided by spirits, while his wife, who did not "share his enthusiasm," earned wages working for a local cheesemaker. The upper floor of Brown's triple-facia fronted house was a spiritualist meeting hall. Its spindly layers of woodwork give it the look of a gothic tower turned upside down. Spires hang like icicles around the front and sides.⁶²

One of the most fascinating of all the architectural creations of the period—and another one that is genuinely unique—is the Mansion House, the home of the Oneida Community (see Figure 6.5). From 1859 to 1861, the grandiose stone and brick "New Mansion" replaced the earlier wooden structure that was used to house the Community in its first years. A further extension called the Children's House doubled its square footage when it was completed in 1870. It was surrounded by gardens, orchards, and tree-lined paths influenced by Frederick Law Olmstead. The Oneida Community had no aversion to temporal beauty. They cultivated it. The Mansion House featured the most fashionable architectural forms of the day. The Second Empire style is reflected in the mansard roof, while a five-story tower and a cupola, along with a dramatic silhouette, show the influence of Italianate and Gothic Revival styles. The building was designed "in house" by one of the Community's leading members, Erastus Hamilton.

Figure 6.5. The Oneida Community Mansion House, 1870.

Like the grand buildings of Utica and Syracuse and the private mansions built in central New York's prosperous Gilded Age neighborhoods, the Community's home was meant to convey status and success. Erastus Hamilton said upon the opening of the Mansion House, "Religion and education lead the people by the hand in the way of prosperity and refinement. . . . A religious people are certain to be prosperous."[63] By the 1860s, the Oneida Community was economically highly successful. Like the most well-off among their neighbors, they put to the side any qualms they had about showing it.

§

Though the Mansion House shares outward similarities with the best architecture of the surrounding area, one can gain a much better sense of its architectural agenda on the inside. Before the Community's downfall, it contained only single bedrooms, which were sparsely furnished and undecorated.

However, the communal spaces were large and pleasant. There was a large and well-stocked library, striking living and dining rooms for conversation, and a central auditorium that sat seven hundred people. The purpose was to encourage social and group life and discourage isolation or pairing off into exclusive relationships. The children slept in a separate wing, so they could be raised communally rather than by their own biological parents.[64]

During their first years in Oneida, Noyes dreamed that the Community would support itself on agriculture alone. Members canned fruits and vegetables and tilled the fields, but it did not bring in enough income. Other communities like Brook Farm died out, financially strangled while standing by this agricultural vision. Noyes accepted that that the Community would need to expand into the realm of manufacturing to support their way of life.[65] The Community began experimenting in silk production and produced handbags. They opened a branch in Wallingford, Connecticut, which served as both a retreat and a printing office. But the real breakthrough was the invention of a new type of steel animal trap by Community member Sewell Newhouse.

The Newhouse trap was enormously successful. In 1857, nine thousand traps were sold. In 1863, ninety thousand orders were coming in each year and by 1870 sales exceeded three hundred thousand annually.[66] Profits soared. Several warehouses were built where community members assembled the traps, including the large Willow Place factory, also designed by Hamilton, between Seneca Turnpike and Sconondoa Creek in what is now Sherrill. In 1862 the Community began hiring paid outside labor for their factories. Community members continued to work alongside hired men, particularly when a financial downturn in the 1870s affected profits. The expansion of the rail network led to greater speed and distribution of their products. On April 3, 1871, a batch of traps traveled to California for the first time on an all-rail route. In 1877, the Community began producing tin-plated spoons at its Wallingford branch. The silverware operation was transferred to a new plant at Niagara Falls with a workforce comprised almost entirely of hired labor at the dawn of the 1880s.[67]

In their relations with hired workers, the Community sought to be a good employer and pay fair wages. But overfamiliarization was discouraged. Community children were forbidden to speak to the hired men.[68] The Community's focus during the 1850s and '60s was on completing the realization of Bible Communism. It published a newspaper called *The Circular* and accepted new members, rejecting far more applications than it accepted, but the primary focus was always inward. Community members knew that their lives were vastly different from those around them, even their closest neighbors, and were guarded in their interactions with outsiders.

Noyes's idea of sex in God's kingdom on Earth was like a pyramid of which he was the apex. A system of "ascending fellowship" placed the most spiritually advanced members (usually the oldest) at the top and gave them the responsibility of inducting younger members into the sexual system. Entry was much more demanding for males due to the level of self-control necessary to achieve "male continence." A young man would begin learning to bring a woman to orgasm while containing his own under the direction of a spiritually wiser woman past the age of menopause. When he perfected this function, he would then be permitted to move on to younger women. For girls the initiation was different. Around the age of twelve they were compelled to enter a liaison with Noyes (except in his very last years) in which they would become familiar with the physical and spiritual aspects of intercourse.[69]

Once these initiation periods were over, a member could petition the board, ultimately under Noyes' direction, to request a sexual partner. The board kept sex regulatory, making sure no one was having too much or too little, and ensuring that younger members spent a fair amount of time with their spiritual superiors. Most importantly, it made sure that no couple paired off into an exclusive relationship in which the forbidden "special love" was present.

Noyes saw sex as having religious importance, a show of "faith that worketh by love," in glorification of God.[70] Indeed, sex, music, prayer, and work were all equally important in Noyes's view, but sexual intercourse allowed the greatest degree of intimacy between the "saints" and therefore held the greatest potential for closeness with God. As Noyes said, "What we love in [a] particular tune is *music*, and what we love in [a] particular woman is *love*—and love is God."[71] The prohibition of "special love" was essential in maintaining a communal family in which each member held an equal amount of love for all. Of course, much work was needed to undo convention. Noyes railed against what he called the "marriage spirit." Members who showed a particular fondness for each other were denied further "interviews" (as they were called) together. They were placed with a spiritually superior partner and doused with "mutual criticism," a Community practice in which members took feedback on their spiritual development from other members in a group setting.[72]

Another reason Noyes frequently gave for the implementation of this sexual system was the advancement of women. Noyes saw marriage in its normal conditions as a form of ownership in which woman was merely an object. He cited Matthew 22:30 ("in the resurrection they neither marry nor are given in marriage") to argue that "the institution of marriage, which assigns the exclusive possession of one woman to one man" is a worldly system that destroyed the natural relations between the sexes.[73] The advanced position of women at Oneida extended to nearly all areas of the social system. They were involved in all aspects of the manufacturing business from packing and shipping to management. They were entitled to an equal share of the Community's communally held assets as their male counterparts. Women held important positions in the Community's committees and many of Noyes's most valued advisors were women. They were given equal time for study and were "praised . . . for reading Malthus and Plato." The near equality of genders extended even to clothing. Community women wore short dresses that extended to the knees with "frocks or pantaloons" underneath. Hair was kept short, cut just below the ear.[74] On November 9, 1864, a woman called Emily Otis wrote a letter to her friend Beulah Hendee, who had joined the Community the month before: "I often imagine how you look in your short dresses. I see you here & there into all sorts of fun & frolic untrammeled by long skirts and hair."[75]

Women's rights became a hotly debated topic nationally in the 1840s and '50s, particularly in the North. Upstate New York was home to some of the most outspoken proponents of women's suffrage and equality. Gerrit Smith's cousin, Elizabeth Cady Stanton, was one of the leading organizers of the 1848 Seneca Falls Convention, a milestone in the women's rights movement. The "Declaration of Sentiments" published by the convention attacked all aspects of American law and social practices that constrained women in an inferior, subjugated position. One of the attendees, Amelia Bloomer, gave her name in 1851 to the "freedom dress," similar in style to the dresses worn by Oneida Community women.

The 1852 National Women's Rights Convention in Syracuse launched the speaking career of Matilda Joslyn Gage (see Figure 6.6), who, from her home in Fayetteville, became one of the most important advocates for women's suffrage. It also convinced Susan B. Anthony, who was visiting from Rochester, to join the movement. Support for women's rights in upstate New York was linked to the abolitionist, temperance, and social reform movements, all of which had common roots in the religious-reformist impulse in the burned-over district. They also had a similar cast of characters. Two of the organizers of the Jerry Rescue the year before, Gerrit Smith and Rev. Samuel J. May, were in the audience when Gage began her speech: "Let Syracuse sustain her name for radicalism."[76]

Figure 6.6. Photograph of Matilda Joslyn Gage in 1871.

Some women's rights activists looked to the Oneida Community for support, initially at least. The Community responded explaining that women's equality was not an official doctrine of theirs. They offered little support to the movement, saying they would steer clear of the "loud" women's rights activists.[77] Nevertheless, the social system at the Oneida Community abolished some of the same practices and attitudes that women's rights activists were challenging in society at large. The Community's 1867 handbook proudly proclaimed that it relieved women of "household drudgery, and . . . the curse of excessive and undesired propagation." It gave women a standing of equality "with their brothers in education and labor."[78]

But the system that freed them came with other constraints. Children were taken away from their mothers soon after birth and placed under the care of a nursery master. From then on, mothers were only allowed short weekly visits to prevent "special love" of their mother from developing in the child. Pierrepont B. Noyes, a biological son of John Humphrey, described being deprived of visits to his mother as a punishment for misbehavior as a small child. He wrote that once when this happened, "I . . . went berserk. Forgetting my Children's House training and my fear of its head, I raged; I howled, I kicked, I lay down on the sinkroom floor and exhausted my infantile vocabulary in vehement protestations and accusations." He was then punished with another week. Later in life he reflected, "The turbulence was mine, but the greater tragedy was my mother's."[79]

The aim was to raise the children in a community family in which all the adults were their mothers and fathers, and all the children their sisters and brothers. Looking back, Pierrepont B. Noyes realized that it did work to a significant extent, and there is plenty of evidence to show that both women and children were happy with their situation most of the time. In an undated private letter from Community woman Jane Bailey to her daughter about a trip she was taking to the state fair, she wrote, "I felt very thankful, among other things, that I had not left a family of little children at home with no one to take care of them, to cry because mama did not come home."[80]

There were other strains created by the family arrangements at Oneida. Despite the general acceptance of their neighbors, they knew that many people nearby despised their organization. Pierrepont B. Noyes also wrote in his memoirs about a boyhood trip to Turkey Street, the area along the Seneca Turnpike near their Willow Place factory: "Looking back, we saw a mob of Turkey Street boys running down the road toward us, their actions suggested hostile intent." They called the Community boys "bastards," and a "little boy, wearing a cap so big that it covered much of his dirty face," dared them to fight.[81] Candice Bushnell wrote "home" to the Community on March 1, 1865, relating another experience in the "outside world." While traveling, she had learned that a local preacher had given a sermon on "the divine institutions of marriage" and portrayed the Oneida Community as the "very sink of hell."[82] There was undoubtedly much outward hostility against the marriage and family systems at Oneida. Those who entered the Community on their own free will were compelled to defend their decision and those who were born into it had no choice but to accept that many people outside were horrified by their way of life.

However, there was also a surprising amount of support and respect to be found outside. In 1865, the *New York Tribune* and the *Rome Sentinel* published highly positive articles about the Community, praising their industry and noting the value placed on education, science, and culture there. Sexual practices are ignored apart from a passing acknowledgement that "they have quite peculiar views among themselves in relation to marriage."

The articles conclude that "when they first settled in their present location, some eighteen years since, they were generally shunned and more or less persecuted, but they have now lived down all persecution and have in fact become highly respected by their neighbors and business acquaintances."[83]

In 1870 the Oneida Community was reaching such heights of prosperity that its members felt that soon "hundreds and thousands" of communities on the Oneida model would appear all over the country as people saw what God had done for this band of Bible Communists. Applications for membership were flooding in. The young men at Oneida were considered trainees who would lead these future communities and thus complete the bridge between heaven and earth that already seemed so close to being attained.[84]

The Community often invited guests to visit. In 1870, Noyes flung the doors open. When the New York and Oswego Railroad (also called the Midland) was being planned in the late 1860s, Noyes took a page out of Sands Higinbotham's book. He offered the railroad right of way across Community land in exchange for an agreement that trains should stop there. He recognized that not only would the Community's manufacturing prosper with easier access to the rails, but also that his home could be made into something of a tourist attraction, bringing in revenue and providing an audience for his social theories. On October 5, 1868, he wrote in the *Circular*, "I want to wait faithfully on God. I see his footsteps in the Midland and in all our prosperity." A station and telegraph office were built on Community property. On May 16, 1870, the *Circular* stated, "The opening of the Midland RR, landing passengers at our door, has brought us visitors from all parts of the land, and there is hardly a state in the Union that is not represented in our Reception Rm. Book." The members began to grow fond of their railroad. On July 4 of the same year, they wrote, "The RR is propitious to women's independence. She can come and go . . . without waiting for a man." Between June and October 1873, 2,530 dinners were served to paying guests.[85] Sometimes up to 1,300 visitors a day descended at the station to be treated to music, home-grown strawberries, and to climb the Mansion House's North Tower and survey the beautiful grounds.[86]

Most of the guests left with highly favorable impressions, but the openness also exposed the Community to some hostile visitors. In July 1874, John W. Mears appeared for a tour. Mears was a professor at Hamilton College who had been appointed by the Presbyterian Synod to investigate the Community. He reported back that the Community was a "pestilent and organized iniquity." Mears argued that the Community ingratiated itself with its immediate neighbors by contributing to local charities and providing well-paid jobs. Unsurprisingly, he received backlash from local newspapers, some of which would defend the Community until the end.[87]

Noyes's obsessions in the 1870s were science and socialism. Far from turning away from the scientific breakthroughs of the nineteenth century that challenged traditional Christian beliefs, Noyes and other members of the Community embraced them. The Community's large reading library is still intact and catalogued. Through it, one can trace the evolution of thought both within the Community and in the world at large during its thirty-three years of existence at Oneida. The oldest books are nearly all on religious subjects: theology, interpretations of the scriptures, and religious histories, some in Latin and Greek, are mixed with the works of social theorists. Fourier (in French and English) and Owen are well represented. However, moving to the shelves dating from the 1850s and '60s, books on physics, botany, chemistry, mechanics, and titles such as *The Science of Bee-keeping* and *South American Geology* are interspersed among religious studies. Within the Mansion House, science was viewed as an exploration of the creations of God, which enlightened the spirit and strengthened the bond with the creator. By the end of the 1860s, nearly every issue of the *Circular* contained several scientific articles.

Inspired members of the Community invented corn-cutting machines, potato washers, mop-wringers, and rotating tabletops. So great was Noyes' appreciation of modern science that many of the younger generation of perfectionists, including his oldest son, were sent to Columbia, Yale, and Colgate Universities for scientific studies. Noyes read Darwin with great enthusiasm during the 1860s and began theorizing on how science and religion could be united under his rule at Oneida.

In 1869 the Community instituted Noyes's most audacious plan. He called it "stirpiculture," a eugenics experiment based on scientific theories with the aim of producing a spiritually superior race. The main idea was to systematically pair the most spiritually perfect men and women in the Community as breeding partners, in the expectation that their children would be of superior genetic makeup. Of course, as pinnacle of the spiritual pyramid, Noyes was to father the most children. It was he who chose who could and could not have babies. Sixty-two children were born under stirpiculture during the last nine years of the Community's existence. Noyes himself fathered eight of them by different women.[88]

Just as the Oneida Community reached the pinnacle of its success, the causes of its demise came clearly into view. When the first batch of Community-raised children returned to Oneida after university, they were not as they were when they left. In some cases, their religious views were fundamentally changed, if not completely eradicated. Theodore Noyes, the oldest son of John Humphrey, was expected to take over the role of "father" of the Community. He came back from Yale in 1867 with a medical degree but with profound doubts about God's existence. Theodore's inability to preach his father's religion sparked an intense leadership debate that resulted in the division of the Community into antagonistic factions in its final years. John Humphrey Noyes began attending séances with his son in a desperate attempt to wean him away from scientific unbelief, without success.[89]

The systems of "ascending fellowship" and stirpiculture also created a great deal of tension. Some couples left the Community after being denied the right to propagate by Noyes. The exclusivity inherent in Noyes's plan to create superior children by pairing up those he saw as most worthy among the perfectionists corroded community cohesiveness.[90] Financially secure and feeling comfortably tolerated by his immediate neighbors, Noyes was also exhibiting ever-riskier behavior, some of which eventually brought him into conflict with religious and secular authorities. He was becoming increasingly interested in incest. One of the stirpiculture children he had was with his niece. He actively plotted to have a child with his own daughter but did not implement the plan. He called it "consanguineous stirpiculture," writing privately in 1869 that "in overthrowing the worldly notion about incest I am conquering the devil's last stronghold." A bar against incest, he thought, was one that would need to be overcome for the purpose of "founding a new race." He also contemplated having couples perform sexual intercourse on stage.[91]

The Oneida Community finally met its end in 1881 after several years of painful events, contrasting sharply with the preceding decades of relative happiness. A relative newcomer to the community, James W. Towner, challenged Noyes's leadership and in particular his practice of initiating young girls between the ages of ten and thirteen into the Community's sexual system as "first husband."[92] An outside "crusade" against the marital and sexual practices of the Community came to life in February 1879 when John W. Mears brought ministers of the Presbyterian, Congregational, Methodist and several other denominations together at Syracuse University's Hall of Languages to discuss what to do about the Oneida Community. A Community spokesperson told reporters the 145 men and 161 women of Oneida were not worried. But with strong factionalism emerging inside, Noyes could feel his grip loosening. Mears wrote directly to the ministers of the village of Oneida to enlist their support, with some success. In June the crusaders met again. Having obtained damning information (but not saying what it was or from what source; it may well have come from dissenters within the Community) they told reporters they would push for Noyes's arrest. One newspaper printed that it was on the basis of incest.[93]

Noyes traveled to a station in far-away Holland Patent, where he could board a train inconspicuously. On June 22, 1879, he absconded to Canada, never to return, leaving his community without a real head. From Canada, he wrote in August with a proposal that the community end the system of complex marriage but retain communism. It was agreed that the sexual system would end on August 28, 1879.

During the last days of complex marriage, as one historian put it, "frenzied sexual activity took place" in the Mansion House. Some men and women who had lived for years with multiple sexual partners bade farewell to the system in their own way, now that the strict controls that governed it no longer applied. Noyes's niece Tirzah Miller, for example, "slept with James Herrick and Erastus Hamilton and mused about Homer Barron," all in a forty-eight-hour period. Without complex marriage, and with their leader in exile, the association ceased to function.

In 1881, the Oneida Community's remaining members voted to end their experiment in communal living. The downfall had come. Almost to rub salt in the wounds of the Community in its year of annihilation, a former member, Charles Guiteau, carried out the assassination of US President James Garfield on September 19, 1881. Though he had been kicked out of the Community more than fifteen years previously and retained no connection to it, Noyes's nemesis John W. Mears could not help arguing that the assassin's work was clearly connected to the moral corruption of the Community he had fought doggedly to destroy.[94]

§

Despite the hard times encountered by a few hundred members of its utopian community, the half century after 1865 was a golden age in central New York. The rugged life of the pioneers and the storm clouds of the Civil War era were distant memories by the dawn of the twentieth century. In the 1830s, the Hudson valley artist Thomas Cole created a series of five paintings called *The Course of Empire*. In it, he depicted the same piece of land at five stages of development. The first painting, *The Savage State*, shows the land as wilderness. The second, *The Arcadian or Pastoral State*, depicts the land being transformed by agriculture, with men still living close to nature. The third is entitled *The Consummation of Empire*. The same piece of land is now resplendent with grand architecture and a teeming population. An air of prosperity has replaced the savage state. The old inhabitants of the wilderness and the pastoral farmers are now out of view. The focus has shifted to urban grandeur and the symbols of power.

Cole's paintings depict an imaginary ancient city, but in the nineteenth century, central New York underwent a similar transformation at warp speed. Its cities with their bustling streets and towering, grand buildings were at the height of their power. The wealth of the west flowed through its waterways and along its tracks. New York had become the Empire State—the most populous and prosperous by far, with the now-giant nation's jugular vein running directly across it. But Cole's paintings also came with a warning. The final two paintings, *Destruction* and *Desolation*, show the once-great city being enveloped in chaos and finally depopulated and abandoned. To a certain degree, the boarded-up factories, abandoned churches, and derelict homes in central New York's once-flourishing inner cities by the end of the twentieth century would testify to a similar fate.

Chapter 7

Boom and Rust, 1917–2000

If the nineteenth century was the period of consummation, when central New York with its canals, railways, and thriving cities was a keystone in the edifice of American empire, the twentieth century was one of desolation, even destruction. It didn't all happen at once. Indeed, the area continued to be a highly attractive place with a thriving economy well into the 1960s. European immigration slowed down due to the First World War and new immigration restrictions imposed in the 1920s. But thousands of Black people from the American south moved to Syracuse and Utica to find better lives and take up jobs in what had previously been overwhelmingly white cities.

From 1970 onwards, a steep decline set in. Jobs in manufacturing disappeared by the thousands. Cities depopulated. Property prices stagnated. Factories and warehouses were closed, boarded up, and torn down or left to become derelict. Houses, too. While the descendants of European immigrants left city neighborhoods and moved to suburban areas, or to different parts of the country, Black people were largely confined to blighted sections of the urban landscape, partly by design.

By the end of the century, confidence and pride had turned to anger. Central New York's prominent position in America declined in step with its population loss and economic deterioration. And yet, its history became more important than ever as the century wore on. The Oneida Indians began fighting for two major land claims in the US Supreme Court, based on illegal treaties signed two hundred years earlier. The ramifications of their landmark victories were felt throughout a nation becoming more alive (in some places, at least) to what had befallen its Native people. At the same time, a new Indian-owned business empire emerged on Oneida land, bringing about a better life for most of its Native people, but also bitter animosities among neighbors that are still only beginning to heal.

In 1917, all that was in the future. The cities of central New York had been transformed during its golden age into urban industrial centers with teeming immigrant populations. The countryside was still dominated by the descendants of the original settlers from New England, who eyed some of those groups—particularly the Catholic Irish, Italians, and Poles—with suspicion. Central New York's immigrant populations struggled for acceptance, and many chafed under hard conditions in the industrial and agricultural jobs available to them. The cataclysmic war that broke out in Europe in 1914 added complexity to this process.

The United States attempted to remain neutral in the World War that broke out in 1914, pitting Britain, France, and the Russian Empire against Germany, Austria-Hungary, and the Ottoman Empire. It wasn't until 1917 that the US entered the war on the British side. Even during the years of neutrality, World War I upset the balance in the ethnically diverse cities of central New York. In Utica and Syracuse, German Americans initially showed strong public support for Germany, holding rallies and fundraisers. Many in the Irish community also rallied to support Germany against Ireland's British overlords. Central New Yorkers of British ancestry, however, including Oneida County's Welsh community, supported the British side. Some three hundred and fifty Uticans volunteered to join the British armed forces before America entered the war in 1917. Lebanese and Syrian immigrants also supported Britain's aim of defeating the Ottoman Empire. Italy joined the war on the British side in 1915, and the cities' Italian communities rallied to Italy's support. Italian-language papers in Utica like *La Luce* and *Il Pensiero Italiano* ran strong anti-German editorials. Three hundred Italians left Utica to join Italy's army; eight hundred more joined the US armed forces in 1917–18. The Italian-language *Gazzetta di Syracuse* told its readers in 1918: "The people who host us here expect real and solid proof from the Italian 'colonia' in Syracuse—some 25 thousand strong—of our patriotism; none of us should attempt to shirk it."[1] Utica's Polish community of about four thousand also rallied to support Britain, whose victory would offer the best hope of an independent Poland. One hundred eighteen Syracuse Poles served in World War I. Ten died. Their names are recorded on a memorial erected in 1935 by the Polish community near the Catholic Basilica of the Sacred Heart of Jesus on Park Avenue.

After America's entry into the war, German Americans in central New York and throughout the US were in an uncomfortable situation. The *Utica*

Globe published overtly anti-German cartoons, including one in which a German American saboteur is portrayed with bombs and kerosene. German language instruction was banned from Utica schools.[2] But Germans also joined to US army in large numbers after 1917, setting the scene for a return to favor in the community after the war. Some of them never returned. One of the first Oneida men to die in Europe, for example, was a twenty-two-year-old plumber and grandson of four German immigrants to Syracuse who joined up in 1917. He was killed not by a German bullet but by "lobar pneumonia" that he contracted on the troop ship that carried him across the Atlantic. It was almost certainly a case of the Influenza A virus that came to be known as "Spanish flu" in the first wave of the 1918 pandemic; it was a disease that was particularly deadly to young men (just like the war). At the same time in Syracuse, there was a flu outbreak among soldiers at the recruit training camp that was erected at the New York State Fairgrounds, which city health officers initially tried to downplay.[3]

Italian and Polish Americans were seen by many in central New York to be supportive of the right cause during World War I, but the acceptance that it brought them during the war years was temporary. Some held them responsible for fomenting dangerous labor unrest and suspected them of having connections to organized, violent crime. As central New York's cities became more industrialized in the second half of the nineteenth century, labor unions and workers' strikes evolved into a feature of life there, just as they did in other major industrial centers. The 1877 Railroad Strike that paralyzed major cities like Pittsburgh, Chicago, and St. Louis also rocked the upstate cities of Buffalo, Rochester, Syracuse, and Albany.[4] In the early twentieth century, major strikes broke out in Utica's textile factories. Strikes by predominantly Polish workers in New York Mills in 1912 and 1916 provoked company owners to turn fire hoses on workers, drive cars through picket lines, and evict tenants from company-owned housing. The *New York Times* reported in 1912 that the city of Utica was "under martial rule," with state troops "encamped in strictly wartime fashion."[5]

The biggest confrontations happened in 1919, when factories returned to competitive normality just as demand dropped at the end of World War I. In Utica, over four thousand predominantly Italian textile workers went on strike, frequently clashing with police over a ten-week period. On October 28, live rounds were fired into a crowd, seriously wounding five Italian strikers. The strikers were lashed in the local press as "aliens," anarchists, and communists, despite some of the picket lines being headed by war veterans in uniform.[6] In Rome, another four thousand workers walked out, first from the largest two mills, Rome Manufacturing and Rome Wire, and then from smaller mills, demanding reduced working hours. In July 1919, striking workers there threw stones at strikebreakers and attacked company bosses. Two hundred New York State troopers were sent to quell the violence. An estimated sixteen hundred workers left Rome permanently; many of them returned to Italy.[7] At the same time in Syracuse, Italian and Polish workers at the Globe Malleable Iron Works went on strike. The company's management tried to keep the factory running by hiring African American strike-breakers, which led to rioting and violence against Blacks in the city.[8]

The unrest in Syracuse, Rome, and Utica was part of a larger story. The "Red Summer" of 1919 was so called due to the number of strikes across the country and fear that they could portend a leftist political coup like the Communist Revolution in Russia in 1917. Recent immigrants were particularly suspect; some saw them as threat to American democracy. Republican administrations in the 1920s introduced immigration quotas, effectively ending the Italian, eastern European, and Jewish influx of the previous three decades. A rally of ten thousand upstate New York Ku Klux Klansmen was held in Jamesville, near Syracuse, in 1928. Speeches there started with a "bitter attack on the Catholic Church" and focused on the Klan's mission of upholding "real Americanism." The Klan's popularity dwindled in upstate New York after masks were banned in 1928. But the support it received in the 1920s shows the extent of hostility aimed at immigrants, non-Protestants, and Blacks.[9]

Organized crime led by Italian American "families" in US cities rose during the Prohibition era (1920–1933). In Utica, the Falcone brothers, Salvatore and Joseph, both born in Sicily, became crime bosses. Mafia-controlled gambling and prostitution operations, and frequent homicides, earned Utica the nickname of "Sin City of the East." The Falcones reigned in the area until the 1970s. When old age set in, others battled for preeminence, setting off a twenty-year spate of violence that included a mob associate being blown up in his car in South Utica in 1970 and a long list of murders that extended throughout the 1970s and 80s.[10]

Although a few Italian Americans in central New York conformed to a negative mafia stereotype, the overwhelming majority of Italian immigrants worked hard, long hours, often for low pay, both in the city and in some of the rural areas between Utica and Syracuse. Some took seasonal work harvesting fruit and vegetables for canning at the Burt Olney plant in Oneida.[11] Others established their own farms in the unforgiving "muck" of northern Madison County. A vast swamp south of Oneida Lake and north of Canastota was drained in the 1890s and early 1900s. The Childs Commission Drainage Ditch (or Childs Ditch) was begun in 1898. It converted the waterlogged swampland into extremely fertile black soil known as muck. An Italian, Michael Paterelli, started a farm there in 1902 and began attracting recent immigrants to the area. The soil was exceptionally suited to growing onions and Canastota became the second largest onion producer in the United States. Small farm plots predominated in the early years, but in the 1920s and '30s many farmers sold up to the Smith-Coulter Farm, a sprawling agribusiness that occupied over one thousand acres of the muck by 1937.[12]

The most famous son of the muckland, Carmen Basilio, became a world champion boxer in the 1950s. Joseph and Mary Basilio, Italian immigrants, set up their own onion farm and raised ten children in the muck. Carmen was born in April 1927 and worked in the fields as a child, dreaming of finding a way out. "Did you ever work on an onion farm?" he said at the height of his fame. "It's a tough life. No money in onion farming. Don't ever buy an onion farm." Carmen began boxing at Canastota High School. He joined the Marines at age seventeen during the final year of World War II and was stationed in the Pacific, then started boxing again when he returned in 1947. In 1955, he became the welterweight champion of the world after defeating Tony De Marco. His most famous fights were against Sugar Ray Robinson in 1957 and 1958, the first of which he won to take the world middleweight title at Yankee Stadium. In 1956, he was earning nearly $40,000 per fight, about nine times the median household income at the time. He was known as an honest fighter at a time when boxing was controlled by the mob. Bribes for throwing matches reached upwards of $100,000 in the 1950s. Basilio testified against prominent mob figures in boxing shortly before retiring in 1961.

In the 1950s, as his boxing career brought him wealth and international stardom, Basilio lived in Chittenango and invested in a local gas station while his father continued operating his onion farm until 1954.[13] After retiring from prizefighting, Basilio took up a quiet life teaching physical education at Le Moyne College. He later helped his nephew, Billy Backus, also born in Canastota, to enter the sport. Backus became world welterweight champion in his own right in 1970. In 1990, their hometown of Canastota became the site of the International Boxing Hall of Fame.

But there is an even more poignant monument to the world that made Basilio. Canastota's post office building, built in the 1930s, contains a large New Deal-funded mural painting called *The Onion Fields* by Ithaca artist

Alison Mason Kingsbury (see Figure 7.1).[14] Unveiled in 1942, it depicts a hard-working farming couple, with a male figure, sleeves rolled up, on his knees harvesting in the flatland muck while his wife, standing by his side in the fields, scans the distant hills of Madison County. It is a depiction of hard work and hope. The waves of Germans, Welsh, Irish, Italians, Poles, Jews, and others who settled in central New York in the century between 1820 and 1920 came to work and to build better lives. The struggle for acceptance was difficult for some groups, the Italians in particular, but by the 1930s each community had firmly established roots in the area and were in various stages of becoming fully assimilated into American life. Like in other American cities, some ethnic groups signaled that they had "made it" in America by erecting statues. In Syracuse, an enormous monument to the German writers Schiller and Goethe near the then-German enclave around Butternut Street was erected in 1911. Italian Americans contributed to statues of the Genovese explorer Christopher Columbus that were erected in 1934 in Syracuse and 1952 in Utica.

The end of mass immigration after World War I meant that that demographic changes in central New York's cities from 1918 onward revolved around internal migration rather than immigration. The largest change by far was the influx of thousands of African Americans from the southern states. Anti-Catholicism gradually faded. Second generation Italians and Poles were hard to distinguish by their looks or accents from their white American-born contemporaries. Race, rather than religion or ethnicity, became the essential criterium upon which people's place in society would be defined.

§

Figure 7.1. Alison Mason Kingsbury, "The Onion Fields" (1942).

Black people resided in central New York from the very beginning of non-Native settlement. Enslaved people were held as property in the pioneer generation, albeit by only a select few of the wealthiest men, such as Revolutionary War General Nicholas Herkimer and the trader Peter Smith. Their descendants remained long after slavery was ended in New York in 1827. Others came as fugitives from slavery during the days of the Underground Railroad. Some remained and started families in the years before the Civil War.[15] Black people were, however, a tiny minority in the area until the twentieth century. The "Great Migration," in which around six million African Americans left their homes mainly in the rural south between 1910 and 1970, would have a profound impact on nearly all major cities in the northeast, including Syracuse and Utica.

Blacks in the south left for northern cities for some of the same reasons as the European immigrants who came there before: better economic opportunities, an escape from rural poverty, and the prospect of steady work in urban factories. There was a distinct difference, however, in that they were also leaving a system of racial segregation under the south's "Jim Crow" laws, a legacy of slavery, and a rise in violence and lynching by groups like the Ku Klux Klan. Like European immigrants, Blacks arriving in northern cities normally settled in neighborhoods with others like them. Unlike European immigrants, however, there were barriers that hindered, and in some cases prevented, ever leaving their ethnic neighborhood. The results are still felt, profoundly, to this day. Whereas Germans, Italians, Irish, and Poles whose ancestors arrived ten decades ago or more tend not to live in neighborhoods surrounded by others of their own ethnicity in American cities, Black people often do. Syracuse provides a particularly striking example of why that is the case.

Black migrants from the south began to settle in Syracuse in large numbers during the First World War. Initially, many lived in the area along the Erie Canal (now Erie Boulevard) just east of the downtown manufacturing district and opposite the heavily Italian neighborhood north of the canal. Centered on the intersection of South Crouse Avenue and East Water Street, now an area of vacant urban lots, this neighborhood was labelled the "Negro" section of Syracuse by City Engineer Henry C. Allen in a 1919 map of the city.[16] Black sections of Syracuse grew as more migrants came north. The 1920 census showed a population of 1,426 Blacks in Onondaga County and 640 in Oneida County (0.6 percent and 0.4 percent of the total population, respectively).[17] By 1940 the number had grown modestly to 2,082 in Syracuse and 514 in Utica.[18] The real boom in Black migration to central New York's cities came during and after World War II in the "Second Great Migration." By 1970, the Black population in the Syracuse metropolitan area was 23,398 and 7,681 in Utica-Rome.[19]

Since 1919, efforts were made in Syracuse to keep the growing Black population within the bounds of certain neighborhoods that were already in decline. The 1934 Home Owners' Loan Corporation (HOLC) map of Syracuse describes the original "Negro" area along the Erie Canal as "a colored slum section—occupied by the lowest type of colored race," with "no favorable influences," "no sales for years," and "dwellings in a deplorable state." Blacks were also moving into the 15th ward areas west of University Hill along South Townsend and McBride Streets by the 1930s, mixing with the Jewish immigrant population there. Some of that area was razed in 1938 for the construction of the first public housing project in New York State, Pioneer Homes. In more prosperous areas of Syracuse, deeds sometimes stipulated that properties could not be sold or rented to Blacks. More often, agreements not to sell to Blacks in certain parts of the city were informal or unspoken.[20]

In the post-war era, the neighborhoods of the South Side, Brighton, and Southwest Syracuse (already marked as in decline on the 1934 map) transformed into predominantly Black sections of the city. The construction of I-81 running north-south through the heart of Syracuse in the 1960s destroyed much of the 15th ward, causing many Black people to relocate south and west of the interstate. The highway made the delineation between predominantly Black sections of the city to its west and the more well-off, predominantly white areas of University Hill and outer Comstock to the east even more apparent.[21]

The "white flight" to the suburbs was aided by the rise in affordability of automobiles and the building of highways after World War II. It led to an unofficial segregation in public schools. In 2000, the city of Syracuse was 25.3% Black, with 37,336 Black residents out of city total of 147,306. Only about 5,000 Black residents of Onondaga County lived outside the city limits. For whites, by contrast, only 94,663 lived in the city limits of Syracuse out of a total of 388,555 in Onondaga County.[22] Utica reflected the same trends. The HOLC's 1937 map of Utica marked the central area of the city west of Genesee Street as a "hazardous" neighborhood, noting that "all of Utica's small Negro population is concentrated in this area along the railroad track." The Cornhill area along James Street became a heavily African American neighborhood after World War II.[23]

Although life was hard, many who grew up in Syracuse's 15th ward later expressed that there was a close-knit community and sense of togetherness before the area was razed to build the highway. Most people were able to find work, especially during the war years and post-war boom.[24]

One Black Syracuse woman became a nationally known figure. Anna Short Herrington was born in South Carolina and, upon moving to central New York in 1927, around the age of thirty, found work as a cook at fraternity houses at Syracuse University. At the 1935 New York State Fair, she was seen cooking pancakes by the Quaker Oats Company, who hired her to portray the character of Aunt Jemima in their brand of pancake mixes and syrups. The Aunt Jemima figure was based on stereotypes with roots in blackface vaudeville performances, but it allowed Harrington to earn enough money to buy a twenty-two-room boarding house on Monroe Street underneath what is now I-81.[25]

After the war, Jim Brown rose to fame and prominence as an athlete at Syracuse University in the 1950s, before becoming one of the first Black stars in the NFL and an important civil rights activist. Alex Haley, the author who compiled *The Autobiography of Malcolm X* (1965), lived at Hamilton College (the institution founded in the late-eighteenth century by Rev. Samuel Kirkland as Hamilton-Oneida Academy) as a writer in residence and then on Dominic Street in Rome in the late 1960s. It was there that he began work on his magnum opus, *Roots* (1976), tracing his family's history back to Africa through generations of slavery in America.[26]

But there were few real opportunities for Black people to advance in central New York. As manufacturing jobs started becoming scarcer beginning in the 1960s throughout the north, Black neighborhoods in Syracuse, now hemmed in and dislocated by highway and urban renewal projects, and in Utica became poorer. Frank Wood, the director of the Syracuse's most important Black community center, stated in a 1965 pamphlet that in Syracuse, "the Negro is the 'last hired and first fired', [and] this is even more true now than it was in the past because the areas in which Negroes have usually been employed . . . are the areas in which jobs are being lost to automation at the rate of 40,000 per week on a national scale." Dwindling economic prospects was one of many factors contributing to an increasing sense of frustration in the 1960s and 70s. Riots broke out in 1967 in Syracuse in response to the beating of a Black man on Burt Street by police. Shop windows were smashed, and police cars were attacked.[27] The percentage of people living below the poverty line in Syracuse grew steadily from 14 percent in 1969 to 23 percent in 1989.[28]

These issues were not unique to central New York cities. But what makes the situation in Syracuse and Utica particularly, and bitterly, ironic is the region's nineteenth-century history as a hotbed of abolitionism. Utica's impoverished Cornhill neighborhood is adjacent to Roscoe Conkling Park. Conkling was a radical Republican from Utica who played a vital role in pushing through the legislation that ended slavery and granted voting rights to African Americans in the 1860s, despite withering criticism even from many parts of the North. Separate Black and white sections of Utica grew during the twentieth century within walking distance of where Beriah Green turned the Oneida Institute into an abolitionist training ground and pioneered complete racial integration a century before. Syracuse once rose in defiance of fugitive slave legislation and rallied to the rescue of the escaped slave Jerry Henry in 1851, long before its separate, racially based neighborhoods developed. In 1990, the city commissioned a statue to commemorate the Jerry Rescue on Clinton Square. Today, it is the rallying point for Black Lives Matter marches.[29] The problems of racial division and inequality are as vexatious as any in the history of central New York's cities, defying easy solutions. It is not hard to imagine, however, what Jermain Loguen, Gerrit Smith, and Beriah Green would feel if they were to see them today.

§

The story of upstate New York in the first six decades of the twentieth century is one of continuous growth in wealth, population, manufacturing output, and infrastructure. There was a slowdown during in the twelve years between the Wall Street Crash of 1929 and the outbreak of World War II, but even in those years, upstate New York was one of the most economically powerful parts of the nation. The foundations were laid in the nineteenth century with the growth of the industrial centers of Syracuse and Utica, and smaller factory-dominated cities like Rome and Oneida in between. Manufacturing ruled on the great east-west corridor that George Washington once saw as key to the future of the nation. Immigration prior to World War I and Black migration from the American south afterwards fed an incessant demand for labor in the factories, mills, and rapidly growing cities of central New York.

Utica had been a major center of America's textile industry since the 1830s. In 1910, nearly eight thousand Uticans were employed in the city's fifteen knitting and three cotton mills, and others specializing in worsted, cordage, and twine. In 1940 the mills and clothing factories were still the city's largest employers. Syracuse's salt industry went into decline after the Civil War, but other factories grew there, turning the "salt city" into a major manufacturing hub. In 1900 it had major employers in the Syracuse Chilled

Plow Company, making agricultural machinery; the Merrell Soule Company, which made food products like mincemeat and powdered milk; and several typewriter factories. The Solvay Process Company was founded in 1881 as a chemical plant, using the salt brine that Father Le Moyne had detected flowing into Onondaga Lake two hundred years before. Smaller firms produced candles, engines, Franklin automobiles, gears, boilers, and radiators.

Rome became a major producer of brass and copper goods after the Rome Iron Mill Company diversified its production in 1878. Other Rome-based companies also took to copper and brass manufacture, such as Rome Wire, Rome Electrical Company, and Rome Turney Radiator Company. By 1940, one tenth of copper products in the United States were manufactured in Rome.[30]

During the world wars, many companies switched to military production. Demand for industrial products was high, and it remained so after the transition back to normal conditions following World War II. The 1950s were boom years. Utica's textile industries had been declining since the 1920s, but other thriving industries took their place in what have been called the post-war "loom to boom" years. The Utica Chamber of Commerce worked to attract new producers to the city. Chicago Pneumatic Tool Company set up a major new plant in East Utica in 1948, hiring twenty-five hundred employees. Other companies followed, including General Electric and Bendix Aviation, which set up plants in Utica before 1955.[31]

Part of what attracted Chicago Pneumatic to Utica was its reputation for good labor relations.[32] There was far less unrest than there had been in the early 1920s. The last violent strike in the area—at the Remington Rand typewriter plant in Ilion, Herkimer County (and its branch plants in Syracuse, Tonawanda, Connecticut, and Ohio) in 1936–37—was countered aggressively by company president James Rand Jr. using what became known as the "Mohawk Valley Formula" for strikebreaking. Working with local police and even the courts, Rand broke the strike with a combination of tactics ranging from threatening workers to hiring thugs to impersonate strikers and stage a riot at Tonawanda, all part of a smear campaign to depict strikers as violent insurrectionists.[33] Strikes like these were distant memories during the boom years of the 1950s and 60s. General Electric opened a massive plant called Electronics Park in Liverpool, a few miles north of Syracuse on Onondaga Lake, in 1947. Employment there peaked at seventeen thousand in 1966.[34] Another GE plant in Utica employed sixty-five hundred, making it that city's leading employer as well.[35] Chrysler and General Motors set up facilities in the Syracuse area during the 1930s at DeWitt and Salina, respectively.[36] The Carrier Corporation employed seven thousand at its plant in East Syracuse.[37] Solvay Process Company continued to operate along the Erie Canal west of Syracuse producing soda ash (used in soapmaking and glassmaking) and other chemicals. It merged with Allied Chemical in 1920. It was a major producer of industrial waste, contributing greatly to the toxification of Onondaga Lake.[38] But as a major employer, it contributed to Syracuse's twentieth century economic boom.

Syracuse continued to grow rapidly, with numbers residing within the city limits peaking at 220,583 in 1950. The slowdown in growth in the city from that point to the late 1960s is attributable to thousands of mainly white families leaving urban areas for the growing suburbs, where the major new plants were located. The population of the Syracuse metropolitan area was the fastest growing in the state after the Great Depression. It continued its rapid growth until 1970 when it reached 629,190—a 55 percent growth since 1940. The Utica-Rome metropolitan population grew less rapidly than Syracuse, but still reached 335,809 in the same year, making for a combined population mass along the Erie Canal corridor in central New York of roughly a million.[39]

Employment levels were high and poverty rates were relatively low for American cities. Syracuse's Charles E. Hancock Airport (named for the district's long-serving Republican congressman) opened for passenger flights in 1949. To the already impressive array of colleges and universities at Syracuse, Hamilton, and Colgate were added several new institutions of higher education: Le Moyne College, founded in 1946 and named for the French Jesuit who once preached to the Haudenosaunee on the shores of Onondaga Lake; Utica College, also established in 1946 as a branch of Syracuse University; and several state and community colleges including Mohawk Valley in Utica (1946), Onondaga (1961), and Morrisville, formerly an agricultural college which became part of the SUNY network in 1948. Cazenovia College, with its foundations in a nineteenth-century seminary, became a bachelor's degree-granting institution in 1988. The SUNY College of Environmental Science and Forestry, originally founded as a branch of Syracuse University in 1911, also became part of the SUNY network in 1948, as did Syracuse's Upstate Medical University in 1950.

Syracuse and Utica continued to accrue cutting-edge architecture. Syracuse's twenty-three-story State Tower (1927) and Niagara-Mohawk building (1932) are two of the finest examples of grand-scale art-deco architecture outside New York City. Art museums in Syracuse and Utica with roots in nineteenth-century local collections were provided architecturally stunning new buildings by world-class designers in the 1960s. I. M. Pei's Everson Art Museum in Syracuse and Philip Johnson's Munson-Williams-Proctor Arts Institute in Utica are modernist masterworks that attract as much attention as the collections they house.

A set of 1951 promotional films titled "Your Thruway New York!" presented the case to the public for the construction of a superhighway that, it claimed, would launch New York boldly into a new era of prosperity.[40] With the rise in automobile traffic in the 1930s and 40s had come traffic jams and congestion in the towns and cities through which any east-west traversal of the state must pass. The film narrator set out the problem and the state's (already decided-upon) solution: "One glance at history tells us what must be done. The old Erie Canal . . . put many of our cities on the map. . . . Today we need a great new commercial highway, the Thruway! Linking New York City with Albany, with Schenectady, and along the canal's route to Utica, Syracuse, Rochester to Buffalo!" The film presented advantages for factories and farms, which could ship their products more quickly and cost-effectively to markets. It showed how tourism would be opened up by the thruway and a series of new "arterial" highways running north and south, perpendicular to it—similar to the branch canals that ran up the Black River and Chenango Valleys in the nineteenth century. It also presented advantages for national security and defense in the Cold War climate. The United States was at war in Korea during the first three years of the thruway's construction. No one needed to mention the importance of being able to move men and material quickly in the event of a nuclear war with the Soviet Union.

The New York State Thruway (completed in 1956) and its arterials—I-81 and Route 12, which cut (notoriously) straight through Syracuse and Utica respectively—had the most transformative impact on central New York since the Erie Canal and the railroad of the century before. Yet those modes of transport were still far from obsolete. The old Erie Canal of the 1820s was widened and deepened in western New York. A new "Barge Canal" made use of the Mohawk River between Albany and Utica—reverting to the original idea of the Inland Lock Company—but with the advantages of modern machinery that made lock-building and water-level control more manageable. From Rome, the Barge Canal cut straight through into Oneida Lake, leaving out the old canal towns of Durhamville, Canastota, and Chittenango. Syracuse, too, was bypassed on the new route. In Syracuse, the old canal was filled in; later, the Route 690 elevated highway would follow its path. In other parts between Syracuse and Utica, disused sections of the old canal that had once been called "Clinton's Ditch" began to look the part; the waterway and its old towpath remain but are now used only for recreational purposes. The Barge Canal was completed in 1918. The Mohawk was dammed north of Rome in 1908 to create a large reservoir to feed it. The site of the village of Delta now lies under the waters of the aptly named Delta Lake.[41]

The New York Central Railroad also continued to tie east to west throughout the twentieth century, and even today it is used for heavy freight and passenger trains. Many of the ancillary lines closed in the thruway era, notably the Oswego & Western in 1957. In 1965 the New York Central was rerouted to allow faster transit and to remove its lines from the center of cities and towns like Oneida and Canastota, where train derailments had caused several lethal accidents. The downside was that public transport options that had once connected the towns and cities of central New York became almost nonexistent, further entrenching the reign of the automobile and the urban sprawl that accompanied it. From the 1960s on, new strip malls and fast-food restaurants grew upon what were recently farm fields on the outskirts of towns while downtown businesses struggled.

Leisure became serious business during the post-war boom years. The Adirondack region, once the playground of the wealthy elite, was democratized by the highways. The state of New York created the Adirondack Park in 1892 as a forest preserve, partly to ensure control of a clean water supply for New York City. Passenger trains began running to the southwestern Adirondacks when the Mohawk and Malone line opened in 1892, allowing those who could afford to stay in new resorts along the route to reach their destination within a day's journey from Utica. The most notorious trip was that of a young, unmarried couple in 1906. Chester Gillette, the nephew of a Cortland, New York, skirt factory owner, and Grace Brown boarded a train from Utica to Big Moose Lake. While canoeing, Gillette murdered Brown, possibly to try to hide her pregnancy. Gillette was arrested in Inlet and executed by electric chair in 1908, following a highly publicized trial in which the couple's love letters became a national sensation. Theodore Dreiser's novel *An American Tragedy* (1925) and two films were based on the murder in the Adirondacks.

But it was the building of Route 28 in the 1920s and the new four-lane Route 12 running north from Utica in the post-war era that brought everyday people from central New York into the Adirondacks in large numbers. Some came in family cars and as tourists and campers; others bought plots of non-state-owned land within the park and built cabins. Old Forge and Inlet along the Fulton Chain of Lakes became tourist hubs. The New York State Department of Commerce's 1959 edition of its travel guide, *New York State Vacationlands*, listed dozens of new hotels, motels, and rental cottages along Route 28. There were golf and tennis facilities, boat cruises, seaplane rides, a museum, a fairy-tale themed park called Enchanted Forest, plus hiking, fishing, and canoeing galore. State campgrounds in the Adirondacks offered inexpensive vacation destinations for working-class families from central New York at Eighth Lake and Golden Beach on Raquette Lake (both developed by Civilian Conservation Corps workers during the Depression), and later at Limekiln Lake (opened in 1964) and Nicks Lake (1966).[42]

Other tourist destinations with roots as late nineteenth-century resorts, but now easily accessible and affordable to enjoy, included Alexandria Bay in the Thousand Islands region and Sylvan Beach on the eastern shore of Oneida Lake. As in the Adirondacks, the grand hotels and sanitoriums of the railroad era largely disappeared, but far greater numbers of people were able to visit for a day or weekend trip by car. A few miles to the south of Sylvan Beach, the state purchased the last undeveloped areas on the lakefront and opened them to campers as Verona Beach State Park in the 1940s. Earlier, it purchased areas of natural beauty around Chittenango Falls, Green Lakes near Fayetteville, and Selkirk Shores on Lake Ontario, all of which were opened to the public as state parks during the 1920s. It was part of a wider strategy by the state of New York to establish a network of natural spaces through its conservation department's parks division (established in 1926) that city dwellers could use for outdoor recreation in the age of the automobile.[43]

The economy of central New York in its boom years was further bolstered by military bases that housed thousands of soldiers, scientists, and military personnel. The largest of these was Fort Drum, near Watertown. Fort Drum's origins were in the fortress at Sackets Harbor that had played a vital role in the War of 1812. The armed forces maintained their presence at the mouth of the Black River, with troops quartered in the limestone Madison Barracks (on and off) throughout the nineteenth and early twentieth centuries. In 1898, the Army purchased 868 acres of land for a target range further inland. By 1910, the Army owned seventeen thousand acres and used it as a training ground called Pine Plains. Further land purchases and a grand-scale construction program took place on the base during World War II. Italian and German prisoners of war were housed there. After the war, it was renamed Camp Drum (and later, Fort Drum) after the First Army commander Hugh A. Drum. The base was expanded significantly in the late 1980s, when it became the headquarters of the Army's 10th Mountain Division, causing per capita income in Jefferson County to jump by 30 percent almost overnight.[44]

Further to the south, in 1941 the War Department purchased land in Rome, Oneida County, for the construction of what became known as the Rome Air Depot and, after 1948, Griffiss Air Force Base. Its laboratories and test sites scattered around Oneida and Madison Counties (including one atop a hill in Stockbridge, a few miles from the ancient Oneida village sites) were important centers of aviation research. In 1965, Griffiss was the biggest employer in Rome, far eclipsing its old copper manufacturing industry in economic importance. It employed 8,400 people (three quarters of whom were civilians) and made Rome one of the fastest-growing areas in the state after World War II. The military-industrial complex of the Cold War was working well for Rome. Presciently, though, as John Thompson warned in his landmark *Geography of New York State* (1966), "the favorable trend associated with the air base is in danger of being reversed, if the base should curtail its operation or be closed."[45]

§

Close to the site of Kanonwalohale, in the heart of what had once been the Oneida Reservation, a new entity rose from the ashes of the Oneida Community. The Community itself, originally housed in the log cabins left by the Indians before the construction of its grand Mansion House, met its demise in 1881. John Humphrey Noyes fled to Canada. Complex marriage was demolished. The bold experiment in "stirpiculture" created a generation of Community children with no experience of traditional family life who would need to find their way in the world. When the Community as a social experiment collapsed in 1881, it still had a profitable business and a factory. The Community's main product was the one upon which its prosperity was built: the Newhouse trap. But its future (unbeknownst at the time) lay in the silverware operation it had recently relocated from Wallingford, Connecticut, to Niagara Falls, New York.

A "plan of division" was drawn up to distribute assets by assigning shares in a joint-stock company to each former member. Those who wished to leave the Community could. Many in the "Townerite" faction started new lives in California.[46] Those who wished to stay could continue to live in the Mansion House, pay rent, and earn wages working for the company. The majority did. The single dormitory rooms were converted into family apartments. The new company—Oneida Community, Limited—stayed afloat under the direction of old Community men. In 1894, a twenty-four-year-old Pierrepont B. Noyes, a stirpicult son of the Community's founder, joined the board of directors. He became the company's general manager in 1899.

Noyes used aggressive advertising to push the silverware side of the business, which began to eclipse trap-making as the company's focus in the first decade of the twentieth century. In 1905, he laid out plans for a town where workers could live between the Mansion House and the factory buildings. Streets were named for prominent Community men, and a central Noyes Park would be the hub of the town's life. Factory employees could buy generous 88-by-165-foot lots from the company and were given financial incentives to build their own homes.

In 1913, the silverware plant moved from Niagara Falls to Oneida. Three hundred fifty Niagara Falls workers were invited on a chartered train to visit the new location, and many chose to follow their jobs there. The company paid for a clubhouse, sports facilities, churches, and a school for the new town. It was on the site of an Oneida Indian settlement, but—as at Oneida Castle—there was nothing left to remind residents of its Native past. (Even the wooden church where Eleazar Williams once preached to the Oneidas was removed.)[47] In 1916, it was chartered as the City of Sherrill. The trap-making business was finally sold off in 1924, but by this point Oneida was a major silverware producer. The company continued to prosper even during the Depression. In the 1930s, it employed between two thousand and twenty-five hundred workers. It changed its name to Oneida Limited in 1935.[48]

P. B. Noyes continued to exert predominant influence on all aspects of the company's activities and ethos until 1950, though he handed most of the day-to-day management to his son-in-law, Miles Robertson, in the 1930s. Noyes's vision for Oneida Limited was one that echoed the communitarian impulse of his father's generation, but with more room for individuality and without the theology. There was an emphasis on treating workers well and paying them fairly. Managers would be paid more but modestly compared to other companies, and they were expected to share the pain by accepting wage cuts in tougher times. Noyes felt part of his company's mission was "the amelioration of the working class." His vision extended far beyond Oneida to society at large. Even at the end of his career in 1950, he spoke of the need to go farther "into the socialist field, meaning the creation of a more even spread of well-being among all classes of our population."[49]

Many of the company's managers came from within the "family" of descendants of the Oneida Community. In the early 1900s, attractive family homes were built in the area surrounding the Mansion House known as Kenwood, separated from the workers' homes of Sherrill by Oneida Creek. Some married "outsiders" but even in 1935, fifty-five years after the Community's dissolution, nearly two-thirds of the 167 people residing in Kenwood were descendants.[50]

Intellectual and artistic pursuits were celebrated. Noyes himself authored a science fiction novel and a book on international affairs in the 1920s. Jessie Catherine Kinsley, who was twenty-two at the time of the dissolution, created woven tapestries from her home in Kenwood that continue to beguile art historians. Kenneth Hayes Miller, born in the Community during the stirpiculture years, left Kenwood and became a renowned modernist painter in New York City but returned "home" to conduct summer painting lessons.[51] Hope Emily Allen, born in Kenwood in 1883, became an important medieval historian but also studied Oneida Indian folklore and mythology. Her sources were two Oneida women who lived on Marble Hill (the Orchard), Anna Johnson and Lydia Doxtater, who worked as her cleaners in Kenwood. She developed close relationships with them and recorded their stories between 1918 and 1926, helping to preserve vital aspects of Oneida culture.[52]

Despite its success, there was always an enigmatic air about Kenwood and its history to outsiders. P. B. Noyes knew that there was a lot of explaining to do regarding Oneida Limited's origins, and he was happy to do it, on his own terms. He wrote two memoirs, one of which—*My Father's House*—focused on his unusual boyhood at Oneida. He commissioned the celebrated author Walter D. Edmonds to write a history of the company. Edmonds's *The First Hundred Years* (1948) illustrates the company's origins in the nineteenth-century commune, but leaves its sexual practices, communal marriage, and stirpiculture out entirely. P. B. Noyes's cousin, George Wallingford ("G.W.") Noyes, would have written a very different history. An obsessive annalist, he withdrew from his company duties in 1920 to focus on researching the Community into which he had been born. He built a fireproof room-sized vault in his Kenwood home that housed the sauciest of the Community's records.

Some of the documents, journals, letters, and diaries that G.W. possessed were the ones that had been removed from the Mansion House and sent to John Humphrey Noyes in Canada at a time when he feared prosecution, to ensure they could not be used as evidence of statutory rape or incest if seized by authorities in the United States. After Noyes's death, the papers were repatriated and given to his favored nephew.[53] G.W. typed up thousands of pages of them, but his efforts to preserve aspects of Community history that others thought were better forgotten were not universally appreciated. He was given a legal warning that Oneida Limited would stop any attempt to publish work that "places undue emphasis upon certain social practices of the Community" that could "destroy or impair the good will connected with its business."

In 1947, the leading men of Oneida Limited decided the time had come to subvert further interest in the gritty details of their parents' and grandparents' sexual lives by emptying G.W.'s vault and burning its entire contents. Sexual researchers were still turning up, asking questions about the Community's past. At a time of post-war paranoia about spies, communists, and sexual deviants, this was not the sort of interest that was welcomed at Oneida. It is impossible to say how much was lost, but at least some was saved. G.W. had died in 1941. Before he did, he deposited multiple copies of 2,200 pages of typed transcriptions of journal and diary excerpts in safety deposit vaults in the U.S. and Canada. The company found most of them and burned them too, but two copies survived.[54] The past is difficult to escape in Oneida.

Oneida Limited continued to thrive under P. B. Noyes's son, Pierrepont Trowbridge ("P.T."), who led the company between 1960 and 1981. In 1965, Oneida Limited had twenty-three hundred employees, growing to three thousand by the end of the decade, making it one of the largest employers in central New York.[55] It began to resemble other large corporations, particularly after stock in the company went for sale on the New York Stock Exchange in 1966. Wage differentials between workers and senior managers widened. The days of advancing into the "socialist field" were long gone.

After P.T.'s retirement in 1981, the company was led by nondescendants. It went through ups and downs in the 1980s and 90s, but at the end of the millennium, it seemed to have survived the wave of factory closures that plagued the growing "rust belt." When Peter Kallet became chief executive in 1998, the company had a market capitalization of $518.8 million and was America's largest producer of stainless-steel tableware. Stock was selling for over thirty dollars per share and the company employed over five thousand people. In 1999, it survived a $625 million takeover bid by Libbey, Inc., by simply ignoring it. Commentators were impressed at the chutzpah. One columnist wrote, "Oneida's stubbornness is based on a belief, not unfounded, that it knows what it's doing," but also wondered how long Oneida could continue to buck the trend and keep manufacturing profitably: "Just as the Oneida Community was ultimately consumed by 'the World,' the world economy could become an issue for Oneida Ltd."[56] In 2001, it did.

§

The thirty-year period between 1970 and 2000 was almost a mirror image of the thirty years that preceded it in central New York. The 1940s, '50s, and most of the '60s brought growth, opportunity, and security. The 1970s, '80s, and '90s saw their exact opposites: decline, job loss, and uncertainty. It was the longest period of sustained decline since the first settlers arrived from New England. Though it was not alone—other cities across the Northeast and Midwest went through a similar conversion from manufacturing heartland to "rust belt"—the turmoil and sense of disorientation as change after painful change pommeled Utica, Syracuse, and other parts of central New York in this thirty-year stretch was profound. It opened with a revolution and ended with a riot.

The decisive moment that led to America's full-scale involvement in the Vietnam War occurred while President Lyndon Johnson was in Syracuse. He was in the city in August 1964 to dedicate the new I. M. Pei-designed Newhouse Communications Center building at Syracuse University. He was also garnering support in a traditionally Republican county that would swing Democrat in the November 1964 presidential election for the first since 1852. Johnson used the speech to declare that North Vietnam had deliberately fired at the USS *Maddox* in the Gulf of Tonkin.[57] It was the incident of aggression that was used to justify America's official entry into an already-raging war between South and North Vietnam. A half million US soldiers were in Vietnam by 1968. Over one hundred fifty men from Onondaga, Madison, and Oneida Counties died there.[58]

The year 1970 should have been a year of celebration at Syracuse University, marking a century since it received its charter. Instead, it made national headlines for racial tensions and student insurrections on campus. A group of Black football players known as the Syracuse 8 boycotted the team from the start of spring training in April 1970 and throughout the 1970 football season over mistreatment by the university and its coaching staff. The debate drew in former SU stars Floyd Little and Jim Brown and resulted in a complaint to the New York State Division of Human Rights.[59] Meanwhile, antiwar students at Syracuse led by Student Government President David Ifshin were making national headlines by occupying the university administration building in February, in an attempt to force a student poll on the future of ROTC (Reserve Officers Training Corps) on campus.[60]

On April 30, President Nixon announced that he was expanding the war into Cambodia. Mass protests were organized at university campuses across America. At Kent State in Ohio, four student protestors were shot by the Ohio National Guard. The following day, students at Syracuse built barricades blocking all entrances to campus. Some smashed windows and firebombed buildings. During the student strike that ensued, students marched through downtown Syracuse, burned President Nixon in effigy on campus, and demanded the university pay $100,000 to help release the Black Panther Bobby Seale from prison. University Chancellor John Corbally worked closely with Thomas Sardino, Syracuse's chief of police, to avoid any violent confrontations, but Corbally threatened to shut campus himself for the rest of term if the disruption continued.[61] This helped kill the movement's momentum. The barricades came down and normality resumed.

The student revolution was over, but a period of tension and anxiety in the center of the Empire State was only beginning. Although the economy was strong in the 1960s, the number of manufacturing jobs was already beginning to decline. In Utica-Rome, there were forty-three thousand employed in manufacturing in 1954; in 1963, the number had dropped to thirty-eight thousand, even while the overall value of manufactured goods produced increased. The urban core of Utica was already experiencing a process of dereliction. The old nineteenth-century mill buildings stood empty; the closely packed urban neighborhoods around them became undesirable. The large manufacturing plants in the early 1900s tended to be locally owned and invested in the communities in which they were located, but by the 1960s, companies like General Electric that ran the largest plants in Utica were headed by national corporations with head offices outside the area.

Urban blight was already a feature in Syracuse, too, by the mid-1960s. With the flight to the suburbs came new shopping malls in DeWitt (Shoppingtown), North Syracuse (Northern Lights), and Fairmont (Fairmont Fair), but once-thriving shopping districts and residential areas in the central city became places of empty storefronts, sharply declining property values, and a shrinking tax base.[62] Employment at General Electric and Carrier plants in the suburbs had been growing, but smaller factories in the center were failing. As in many American cities, the workers who lost out first when the smaller, urban factories laid off workers were predominantly Black. With the suburban factories still prospering (initially, at least), the economic gap between white families on the outskirts of the city and Black families in central-city neighborhoods became more pronounced. It contributed to an already well-established separation, with fewer natural places for Black and white people to mix in their day-to-day lives.

In 1966, the geographer John H. Thompson predicted that, notwithstanding some of the urban problems emerging in the city center, the Syracuse metropolitan would continue to grow to hit one million by 1980 and edge towards two million around the millennium.[63] Those decades turned out very differently. Nearly all the manufacturing jobs that made Syracuse and Utica-Rome prosperous in the 1960s were gone by the mid-1980s. General Electric's television sales began to decline, causing several rounds of layoffs in Syracuse. December 1966 brought 1,350 lost jobs, followed by a further 1,075 in February 1967, and 1,500 in March. The whole plant was shut down for a week to cut inventories. The company was facing competition from abroad, particularly Japan. It petitioned the government to raise tariffs on imported television tubes by 150 percent.[64] Syracuse workers at GE went on strike in 1969 but layoffs continued as the company's market share decreased in the 1970s and 80s. By 1977, only twelve hundred workers remained at GE in Syracuse, down from twelve thousand ten years earlier.[65] The *New York Times* told the story of workers racing their cars across thousands of once-full parking places in the huge lots surrounding the plant before starting their jobs in "cavernous, mostly empty" buildings on the two-hundred-acre Electronics Park complex. Citing high labor costs that made it impossible to compete, GE moved most of the production that used to take place in Syracuse to new plants in Ireland, Taiwan, Singapore, and Yugoslavia.[66]

Nearly every other manufacturing concern in Syracuse and Utica went through a similar process. Carrier, Syracuse's second largest employer in 1965, had only sixteen hundred employees left in 2003 where it had once employed seven thousand.[67] Allied Chemical dismissed its last fourteen hundred workers in 1986 and left Syracuse completely—a victim (ironically, given its legacy of toxic waste around Onondaga Lake) of recycling. Its main product, soda ash, was used for glass making. When bottle recycling became widespread, demand plummeted. Forty-six million dollars in annual salaries and $3.4 million in local taxes dried up nearly overnight.[68] In Utica, Chicago Pneumatic dwindled from nearly two thousand employees in the mid-60s to 430 in the mid-90s, before it finally shut down the plant completely and moved its operations to Charlotte, North Carolina, in 1996.[69]

With the hemorrhage in manufacturing jobs in the 1970s, 80s, and 90s, population levels and house prices stagnated or declined. Growth within the Syracuse and Utica city limits had already stalled due to suburbanization in the 1960s. The city of Utica's population dropped from 100,000 in 1960 to 60,000 in 2000. Syracuse's city population dropped from 216,000 to 146,000 in the same four decades. Its metropolitan area effectively stopped growing in 1970. It had 662,577 in 2000, the year in which Thompson had predicted it would be approaching 2 million. Utica-Rome's metropolitan population shrunk from 335,809 in 1970 to 299,896 in 2000.[70] A major contributor to the negative growth was the closure of Griffiss Air Force Base in September 1995.

The catastrophic decline in the fortunes of central New York's metropolitan areas was part of a larger shift that forced the once-prosperous manufacturing belt across upstate New York and the upper Midwest to convert to a post-industrial economy. The viability of manufacturing was challenged by rising globalization, which made the relatively high cost of labor a major drawback in competing with international producers. Other cities in upstate New York fared equally badly, if not worse. GE's troubles in the 1970s affected its base city, Schenectady, just as profoundly. It abandoned its company headquarters there in 1974.[71] Rochester's economy was rocked when Eastman-Kodak began slashing manufacturing jobs. In 1982, the company employed sixty-two thousand people. Undercut by foreign manufacturers starting with Fujifilm in the 1980s, 80 percent of those jobs had been cut by 2000, and by 2012 the company was bankrupt.[72]

New York, long the most populous and powerful state, lost its dominant position in the nation. Its population was surpassed first by California in the 1960s, then by Texas in the 1990s, and then by Florida in the 2010s. The south-to-north migration of the post–World War II decades reversed completely in a new rustbelt-to-sunbelt migration. Upstate New York's urban areas, already suffering blight and depopulation due to suburbanization in the 1960s, were riddled with boarded up homes and buildings by the millennium—reminders of its more populous, and prosperous, not-too-distant past, and symbols of its overwhelming decline.

As the twentieth century drew to a close, a group of concert organizers made plans to use the decommissioned Griffiss Air Force Base as a venue for a major music festival called Woodstock '99. It was intended to commemorate (and capitalize on) the thirtieth anniversary of the legendary 1969 music festival held on a leased alfalfa farm in Bethel, in the Hudson Valley, that had become symbolic of the peace-and-love idealism of the hippie era. The original Woodstock festival had been a financial failure. The organizers of Woodstock '99 were determined to avoid a repeat. They ensured ticket prices would be high enough to cover the $38 million in costs and still turn a profit. A perimeter fence would keep out interlopers.

The festival should have been a boon for the local economy, and Oneida County officials were supportive of the event. But serious cracks started showing up well before the first fans set out for Rome. County health officials tried to fine organizers $1.5 million for failing to submit key plans on time.[73] The festival opened on July 22. An estimated four hundred thousand attended. It was searingly hot, and the sun reflected off the runways. There were hardly any trees to shelter under, and the prices for food and water were extortionately high. The crowd became angrier and on the final day, riots erupted. The perimeter fence was pulled down. Fans smashed and looted ATM machines and set vendor vehicles on fire. Woodstock '99 was in many ways the antithesis to the 1969 celebration of peace, love, and music. There were five reported rapes, four deaths, 123 hospitalizations, and thirty-nine arrests.[74] It left so toxic a legacy that twenty years later plans for a Woodstock fiftieth anniversary concert hardly got beyond the proposal stage. Needless to say, any hope that Griffiss Air Force Base could be used as a major festival venue again faded to oblivion.

However, there were some positive developments in the last three decades of the twentieth century, amidst the decline. It would be an exaggeration to equate these years too closely to the "destruction" that followed "consummation" in Cole's *Course of Empire* cycle. Affluent suburban lifestyles predominated in places like New Hartford to the west of Utica, and Fayetteville-Manlius to the east of Syracuse, where white-collar professionals in sectors unaffected by manufacturing's decline made their homes. Large new shopping malls like Sangertown Square in New Hartford (1980) and the Carousel Center (now called Destiny USA) on the south shore of Onondaga Lake (1990) made up, to some extent, for the loss of buzzing business districts in the urban areas, while at the same time exacerbating the demise of downtown by drawing more spending dollars to the outskirts.

There was, however, some success in reinvigorating downtown Syracuse. The run-down, industrial, nearly empty Armory Square area was given a new lease on life in the early 1990s through the work of the Downtown Committee of Syracuse. At its heart, the imposing 1850s brick armory building reopened as the Milton J. Rubenstein Museum of Science and Technology in 1992. Syracuse University opened the 49,250-seat Carrier Dome stadium in 1980, drawing enormous crowds into the city for sports and other events. It was small consolation, though, to thousands in the city and elsewhere in central New York who found themselves out of work or struggling to pay for food, housing, and health care with the jobs they were able to get.[75]

Both the 1970 and the 1999 unrest were to a large extent perpetrated by out-of-towners on local soil. Syracuse students came from all over the country, as did many of the fans that attended Woodstock '99. To describe central New York State as a hotbed of popular protest in 1970 or as a cauldron of pent-up anger in 1999 based on these events would be misrepresentative. In the former case, many people in the area would have agreed with President Nixon's well-publicized statement that the college radicals were in fact over-privileged "bums." The president won most of the votes in nearly every upstate county in both 1968 and 1972. Likewise, the rioters in Rome in 1999 were a small minority of the four hundred thousand concert-goers. But there is something oddly appropriate that these two events bookended a thirty-year period of decline and demoralization in an area that had for generations been a land of hope and promise. The "pointless white-guy anger" (to use a *Rolling Stone* columnist's phrase) that reared its head at Griffiss Air Force Base was part of a larger story. It had not appeared out of nowhere. Anger was, in a sense, a natural response to the decline in jobs and opportunities caused by globalization in a place where a more stable, prosperous way of life had recently prevailed. It would exert a powerful influence on local and national politics into the twenty-first century.[76]

§

Economic pain and population stagnation were unfamiliar phenomena in central New York's metropolitan areas in the 1970s after decades of growth. But in the rural areas of central New York, they had been realities for far longer. Rural Oneida County towns like Ava and Florence in the north, and Augusta in the south, have hardly changed in population since their first decades of settlement. The town of Western, where Charles Grandison Finney held one of his early revivals, had a population of about twenty-five hundred in the days of the Second Great Awakening. It shrunk to roughly two thousand by 1880 and has not fluctuated by more than a few dozen in each of the decennial censuses since then. The town of Marshall, on land that the state could hardly wait to buy from the Brothertown Indians to make room for white settlement, now has 2,131 residents—a hundred fewer than in 1840. Pomroy Jones, the author of the *Annals of Oneida County* (1851), would easily recognize most of these places in the present day. The roads, churches, farms, and homes are, for the most part, still just where they were.

The entirety of Lewis County, bordering Oneida County to the north, with its tiny seat at Lowville and the Tug Hill plateau in the southwest, had fewer residents in 2000 (26,944) than it had in 1860 (28,580). Southern Madison County has hardly changed demographically since the era of Yankee settlement. The rural towns of Brookfield and Georgetown have fewer residents now than they did in 1830. Surnames are overwhelmingly English, church buildings are overwhelmingly Protestant, and many people still make their living from the land. Peterboro looks much the same as it did in Gerrit Smith's day, apart from the absence of his mansion, which burned down in 1936. While urban centers grew, swelled, and expanded, these areas stayed—to a certain degree, at least—frozen in time. Large swathes of Chenango, Oswego, and Jefferson Counties tell the same tale.

Trends in the countryside that began in the decades after the Civil War pervaded through the twentieth and into the twenty-first century. Improvements in technology and machinery were beneficial to those who could afford them. Labor needs on farms reduced. Those that couldn't keep up struggled and eventually fell by the wayside. The number of farms reduced as small farmers sold up or even abandoned their holdings; more prosperous farms increased their acreage. Land—once the key to fortune—declined in value after 1880.[77] Throughout the US farms struggled, even during the Roaring Twenties. When the Depression hit, milk prices plummeted. Upstate dairy farmers dumped thousands of gallons of it to try to pressure officials and dealers into raising milk prices. In 1939, the Dairy Farmers' Union met in Utica to organize a strike. The supply of milk to New York City dried up. In response, Mayor Fiorello La Guardia forced dealers to raise the price of milk.[78] Conditions improved during World War II. In the 1950s, Oneida County was the top milk-producing county in New York and New Jersey, with eighteen hundred dairy farmers and an income of $21 million from milk alone. In 1959, at the height of the Cold War, the Russian dairy region Krasnaya, northwest of Moscow, challenged Oneida County to a friendly competition to produce a record milk yield.[79]

In general, though, the farmers of central New York were, to most of America, out of sight and out of mind during the great boom and bust years from the 1960s onwards. Depressed land prices did entice some new life in the 1980s, when thousands of Mennonite and Amish farmers moved to upstate New York from other, more expensive parts of the Northeast and Midwest. The trend continued into the twenty-first century. The horse-and-buggy-driving population in New York State is currently over seventeen thousand, with large settlements in the Mohawk Valley and central New York.[80] Large farms have taken to hiring migrant laborers from Guatemala and Mexico as temporary guest workers on programs like the H2-A agricultural visa since the 1990s.[81]

But farming communities have remained staid. The number of farms inches slowly downward, average acreage per farm slowly upward. Most farm fields are used to grow hay. Corn and soybeans take most of the remainder. Farm owners are overwhelmingly—almost exclusively—white, many with deep family roots in their communities going back multiple generations. Ninety-five percent of farms are family operated. Only a quarter of them use hired labor. Dairy still predominates. Rural communities' fortunes are still pegged to a large degree to the rise and fall of milk prices. Since the 1960s, consumers in cities and even small towns buy nearly all their food in supermarkets, limiting any day-to-day interaction between farmers and nonfarmers.[82]

An event that brought rural life in central New York to national attention was the murder trial of Delbert Ward, who was accused of killing his brother William (Bill) on a Madison County farm in 1990. William had been ill for some time, but when his body was inspected, there were signs that he may have been asphyxiated. Delbert was brought in for questioning and confessed to smothering his brother out of mercy to stop his suffering. Later, he retracted his confession, saying he had given it under pressure and in hopes he would be released from questioning more quickly. What really caught the attention of the public was the window that the case opened on life in a small rural community, one that had been invisible and largely unknown to people in the nearby city of Oneida, let alone to people in New York City and beyond who watched the story unfold on national news.

The four Ward brothers—Bill, Lyman, Roscoe, and Delbert—were in their sixties at the time. They grew up together on their grandparents' farm. Their parents died when they were young, and they left school before the legal leaving age to fend for themselves on their thirty-cow farm. They lived their entire lives on a dead-end rural road with no indoor plumbing or central heating, earning about $7,000 a year between them, selling products from their farm. Celebrity journalist Connie Chung interviewed the brothers on *A Current Affair* for national television. *Brother's Keeper*, a documentary film covering Delbert's trial, exposed the gulf between the Wards' impoverished homestead and the world of the lawyers, district attorneys, and courtrooms they found themselves in. It also told the story of the Munnsville community that rallied to the Wards' support, holding potluck dinners and dances to fundraise for Delbert's defense costs. Roscoe's assessment that "Delbert couldn't kill an old dog half dead" rang true. He was acquitted and released. The Wards came across to audiences as charming in their way, if rough around the edges.[83] The crews left, the news moved on to other stories, and all the film's stars returned to their lives of rural obscurity.

§

Sometimes, it is the realization that a way of life is about to disappear forever that spurs an interest in trying to preserve it through literature and art. Just as writers like James Fenimore Cooper filled pages with stories of the old New York frontier for readers in the middle of the nineteenth century, Water D. Edmonds brought central New York's canal age back to life for thousands of readers in the 1920s and '30s, just as it was coming to an end. By that time, old-fashioned canal boats pulled by mules along the tow paths were a thing of the past. The digging of the modern Barge Canal for large, motorized freight transport and the filling-in of the old arterial canals (and some disused sections of the old Erie Canal itself) in the first two decades of the twentieth century were nails in the coffin. The popular Tin Pan Alley song "Low Bridge, Everybody Down," first recorded in 1912, with its folky lyrics (mined from much earlier canal songs) about an old Erie Canal–boat driver and his mule Sal, who knew "every inch of the way from Albany to Buffalo," was an early hint of the twentieth-century appetite for canal nostalgia.[84]

Walter D. Edmonds was born near Boonville in 1903 at his grandfather's farmhouse, called Northlands. He grew up spending summers there, while traffic still bustled along the Black River Canal, but his upbringing was not typical of rural Oneida County. Edmonds's father was a patent lawyer in New York City. Edmonds attended a private boarding school in Connecticut and then went to Harvard, where he began publishing fiction in the 1920s.

Throughout a highly successful literary career that spanned seventy years, rural Oneida County with its characters, folklore, and history was his constant muse. His early novels like *Rome Haul* (1929) and short stories collected in *Mostly Canallers* (1934) were a welcome distraction from the Depression during the 1930s. Edmonds's storytelling is exciting and entertaining. For Americans from Ohio to California, many of whose grandparents or great-grandparents came west via the canal, Edmonds's true-to-life tales awoke a nostalgia for a bygone era. He became one of America's best-selling and most widely admired writers.[85]

Edmonds's most successful novel was *Drums along the Mohawk* (1936), a fictionalized account of the American Revolution on the New York frontier. Like Cooper's *Leatherstocking Tales*, it tells a gripping story of white men and Indians in a reimagined eighteenth-century setting. Indians appear as hostile enemies or as useful allies to the white protagonists. An

Oneida Indian called Blue Back is portrayed as trustworthy to the Americans but distressed at what was happening to other Haudenosaunee. After witnessing the burning of Onondaga Castle "with cold-blooded calculation that overlooked no ear of corn," by Morgan's Rangers, he felt that he "no longer comprehended white men."[86] The book was made into a film by John Ford in 1939, featuring two of Hollywood's biggest stars, Henry Fonda and Claudette Colbert, with the famous Seneca actor John Big Tree as Blue Back. Edmonds's next novel, *Chad Hanna*, about a boy from Canastota who joins a circus, was also adapted as a star-studded film (with Fonda in the lead role again) in 1940.

The success of Edmonds's *Drums along the Mohawk* was part of a wider twentieth-century fascination with the Revolutionary War–era on the New York frontier. In 1912, fourteen bronze tablets were placed along a forty-mile stretch between Herkimer and the site of Fort Stanwix, which at that time was only marked by a cannon in the center of Rome. It was a group effort by several benevolent societies including the German-American Alliance (Herkimer was a Palatine German community), the Utica Chamber of Commerce, and the Sons and Daughters of the American Revolution.[87] The Daughters of the American Revolution prepared another monument to mark the place of Chief Shenandoah's home along Route 5 between Oneida Castle and Sherrill, also unveiled in 1912.[88] A few years later, it was blocked by a beer advertisement. The DAR petitioned for its removal but nothing was done. Then, a local newspaper reported, on "Hallowe'en night, the objectionable sign mysteriously disappeared."[89]

The siege of Fort Stanwix, restaged in Utah for the silver screen in Ford's 1939 adaptation of *Drums along the Mohawk*, had never been completely forgotten in Rome, even though the site of the fort itself was buried under the city's urban core for over a century. It was granted national park status in 1935, but it wasn't until the 1960s, in a wave of urban renewal, that plans for its reconstruction gained traction. Rome's mayor, William Valentine, and *Rome Sentinel* editor Fritz Updike saw an opportunity to gain urban renewal funding to clear a deteriorating urban neighborhood by persuading the Parks Service to build a full-scale reconstruction of the fort that would bring tourism to the city. They were helped by New York Senator Robert F. Kennedy, who was looking to bolster support upstate.[90]

The plan involved demolishing sixty-nine buildings, including some of Rome's most historic structures, and rehousing 136 families. But of those buildings, 90 percent were identified as having minor to major deficiencies, nineteen were "deficient warranting clearance," and only six were listed as being structurally sound. One objective was to safeguard against economic devastation if Griffiss Air Force base were ever to close by creating a "flourishing tourist industry" for the area. Other projects around Rome, including an Erie Canal village and a restoration of Fort Bull, were also envisioned.[91] The $50 million urban renewal project was approved, and digging began in 1970. After clearances and archaeological surveys, the Interior Department offered a $4.3 million contract in 1974 to the B. S. McCarey Company of Rome to rebuild the fort in time for the bicentennial of the 1777 siege.[92]

In 1976, a floating museum of New York Revolutionary War–era history called the "bicentennial barge" made its way across New York State from New York City to Buffalo and back. It drew huge crowds, particularly along the Barge Canal west of Albany. When it stopped in Rome, so many thronged to it that a gangway collapsed.[93] Rome timed other historical celebrations to coincide with the barge's arrival to commemorate the city's history, including an Italian day with "history's biggest spaghetti dinner."[94] It all took place in the shadow of the nearly-complete reconstruction of Fort Stanwix. Wooden cladding gave it an authentic frontier fortress look (hiding a reinforced concrete structure) that brought the eighteenth century into the daily life of twentieth century Romans.

This and other encounters with the old New York frontier that revived it in the imaginations of new generations were causes for celebration and even pride. At the time of the battle's bicentennial, Rome made a (controversial) claim that the "stars and stripes" flag of the United States first flew in battle over Fort Stanwix.[95] Thousands of visitors came to the fort, where they saw an interpretive film and interacted with a specialist troupe in Revolutionary War–era costumes, speaking and acting as if they were in 1777. There was something quaint and comforting about delving into the glorious events in the Mohawk Valley that brought America its independence. But the eighteenth-century was complex. The Indians who add interest to *Drums along the Mohawk* and who fought at Oriskany had not been consigned neatly to history. There was a less comfortable reckoning ahead.

§

Since the 1840s, the remaining Oneida Indians in New York lived on two small plots of land—one in Oneida County, south of the present-day city of Sherrill and known as the Orchard, the other a few miles away along what is now Route 46 in Madison County, known as the Windfall. In 1842, there were forty "Orchards," as the residents were known, living on 191 acres of land. The Windfall Reservation had about 178 residents on 1,388 acres. During the 1840s and '50s, they witnessed the growth of a non-Native village that bore their name and the birth of the Oneida Community, as Noyes and his Putney followers moved into their old cabins along Oneida Creek.

At first, most tried to eke out an existence farming their small plots, but as already noted, economic conditions were becoming harder and harder in the decades after the Civil War for small farmers who could not keep up with buying the latest machinery. Once behind on that front, there was little hope of ever catching up. Oneida men began looking for work in factories or taking other jobs for subsistence. Some found work in factories in Syracuse. Many went to live on the Onondaga Reservation. By 1916, nearly half of the 255 Oneidas in New York had relocated there.

The 1843 treaty that created the reservations allowed Indians to hold their plots on it individually rather than collectively if they wished. Many took up the offer; some went on to sell their plots to non-Native buyers. Court rulings and state reports in the 1870s, '80s, and '90s argued that the Oneidas were no longer a distinct nation, as many lived and worked in the same way as their white neighbors. Yet some of the same reports bemoaned the fact that the Oneidas still spoke their Native language and noted that they still received cloth each year from the federal government to uphold its eighteenth-century treaty obligations to them.[96]

Both the Windfall and the Orchard had a church and (until the late 1880s) a state-run school. But attendance at school was low, conditions were poor, and the education received there was minimal. Some New York Oneidas who wished to pursue education beyond a rudimentary level went to Virginia to study at the Hampton Normal and Agricultural Institute or to the Carlisle Indian Industrial School in Pennsylvania. Hampton (now known as Hampton University) was a school built for Black students in 1868. It began accepting Native Americans in 1877. Members of sixty-five tribes attended Hampton between 1877 and 1923. At least twelve New York Oneidas and many Wisconsin Oneidas attended. Chapman Scanandoah, a Windfall Oneida, studied mechanics there between 1887 and 1894, starting at age seventeen. He paid his tuition by working full days in the machine shop and attending night school after supper. He worked at General Electric's Schenectady plant after finishing his education, and then joined the US Navy in 1897, serving as a machinist on the USS *Marietta* during the Spanish-American War.[97]

One thirty-two-acre farm was still held in common by a group of Oneidas. It was known as the Hanyoust residence after the family that lived on it, but it was in fact the only vestige of the reservation that had not been allotted off into privately owned plots. In the 1880s, the Hanyoust residence was held in common by Mary Scanandoah (née Hanyoust); her sister Margaret; two brothers, Isaac and William Hanyoust; and their families. It was used for meetings and ceremonies and was the place that returnees from Onondaga or elsewhere would visit when they came back to their homeland. It therefore had an odd status—it was a family farm, but it was in fact not "owned" by the Hanyousts, as, unlike other properties, it had never been formally allotted to an Indian family.

It did, however, require upkeep and maintenance, which the Hanyousts struggled to pay for. Trouble began in 1888, when Mary Scanandoah transferred the administration of the land to her brother Isaac. Isaac "leased" the land and secured a mortgage loan of $1,250 from a local lender called Philander Spaulding. Later Spaulding transferred his ownership of the debt to another local man, Patrick Boylan, which passed to his wife Julia upon his death in 1897. The lease should never have been approved, as the thirty-two-acre plot was not, in fact, a private property. But it was approved, and there were payments due on it. Isaac was unable to keep up with them. He transferred the lease back to Mary in 1897, and she transferred it to her son Chapman, who was serving in the Navy. No one was able to pay the $1,250 loan back to Julia Boylan, and so her lawyer moved to foreclose on the property and evict the residents.[98]

In 1907, it was ruled that the Hanyoust residence should be sold at auction. Mrs. Boylan bought the property for $725. The Hanyousts protested to the governor, Charles Evans Hughes. A legal analysis by the New York State deputy attorney general, George Decker, concluded that the sale at auction and the original mortgage on the farm were unlawful and therefore void. The New York State Supreme Court ruled against Boylan in the Oneidas' favor, but that decision was overturned in an appeal by Boylan's lawyers. In *Boylan vs. George et al.* (1909), the court ruled that the Oneidas in New York had no tribal government and lived among whites, so therefore should not be treated as a sovereign Indian tribe.

On November 29, 1909, officers from Madison County and the city of Oneida forcibly evicted Mary and William Scanandoah from their home. They were physically removed and placed in the road (now Route 46), along with all their belongings. Five times they tried to walk back into their residence, only to be removed again. According to her nephew, William Hanyoust Rockwell, the fifth time, Mary was "picked up bodily and dropped so heavily into the roadway, she was not able to walk back to the house again that was her home." William's horse was turned out of its barn. The Hanyoust farm's residents went to live at Onondaga. There were still a small number of Native people living near the Windfall and at the Orchard, but there was no longer an Oneida Reservation in their ancestral homelands, or so it seemed.

The Oneidas appealed to the U.S. Supreme Court, helped by George Decker. After years of wrangling, the Supreme Court found in *United States v. Boylan* (1920) that Decker's argument had been correct. It overturned the *Boylan v. George et al.* decision, concluding that the Oneidas in New York were a "distinct tribe or nation" under the jurisdiction of the federal government and that the mortgage and sale of their thirty-two acres—being federal treaty lands—had been unlawful. The court ruled that the Hanyoust plot was an Oneida Indian Reservation.

After the Supreme Court returned the thirty-two acres at Windfall to the Oneidas, William Hanyoust Rockwell came back to live on the land, but most of the Oneidas at Onondaga—including Chapman Scanandoah, who had left the Navy and taken up farming and patenting inventions in his spare time—remained where they were. There were more jobs in the Syracuse area. The Windfall-born Scanandoah brothers, Chapman and Albert ("Doc"), worked at Crouse-Hinds Company and Solvay Process, respectively, while living at Onondaga.[99]

What began as a local dispute over a tiny parcel of land in Madison County became part of a much larger process of reckoning with what had been done to the Haudenosaunee since the Revolutionary War. The New York State Legislature appointed a commission led by Assemblyman Edward A. Everett to investigate the legal dividing line between state and federal authority in relation to the Haudenosaunee nations. They met with Oneidas and Onondagas on the Onondaga Reservation in August 1920.

The Everett commission concluded in 1922 that nearly all New York State's treaties with the Haudenosaunee since the 1784 Treaty of Fort Stanwix had been illegal. The state legislature did not act upon this finding. In the late 1920s, Minnie Kellogg, a controversial Wisconsin Oneida, began campaigning for the recognition of Haudenosaunee land claims, but her methods divided Indian communities. A Canadian-born Oneida who later moved to New York, Wilson Cornelius, also continually pressed government officials for recognition that the land taken by the state in its illegal treaties still rightfully belonged to the Oneida people, usually receiving no reply.[100]

The land claim movement revived in the 1940s. In 1946, the federal government established the Indian Claims Commission, giving tribes a chance to seek redress for any past failings by the United States to honor its treaty obligations. The government's seeming willingness to address historic wrongs was a cause for hope. The ICC could not return land but could award monetary compensation to Native people with land claims by comparing the money paid for their land in treaties to its actual value at the time.[101]

An Oneida woman, Mary Winder (née Cornelius, Wilson's daughter), and her sister, Delia (Dolly) Waterman, took leading roles in pushing for an Oneida land claim. Oneidas from Wisconsin, Ontario, and New York met in 1948 to discuss the matter, and a land claim petition was officially filed by the three Oneida communities in 1951 with the Indian Claims Commission for the six million acres acquired by the State of New York after the American Revolution. It took until 1969 before a decision was handed down, agreeing that the federal government had failed to live up to its promise to protect Oneida land. It then took another nine years for the Court of Claims to confirm United States liability on the basis that it had neglected its obligations.

The ICC agreed to award the Oneidas $3.3 million. It would have worked out to around $250 each if divided among them, a paltry sum for six million acres of land. Some Oneidas feared that accepting it could compromise their position in higher-stakes litigation that was underway in the early 1980s. The Oneidas withdrew their complaint in 1982.[102]

It wasn't until 1970 that the Oneidas were allowed to launch a challenge to have their land claim recognized in federal court. By that point, the baton of leadership had passed to a new generation. Chapman Scanandoah, Mary Winder, and William Hanyoust Rockwell died in 1953, 1954, and 1960, respectively. Dolly Waterman's son-in-law, Jacob Thompson, a Mohawk, took the lead in petitioning government officials and discussed the issues with George Shattuck, an attorney in Syracuse. Shattuck saw merit in the case that the Oneidas presented. The federal government was still fulfilling its promise from the Treaty of Canandaigua (1794) to deliver cloth to the Oneidas every year and yet was ignoring the other promise that it made in the treaty: that they would protect the Oneidas' land.

Shattuck agreed in 1965 to help the Oneidas to get a real settlement for their land claim that would go beyond the relatively small-scale, one-time payments that the ICC could offer, ideally one that would offer the Oneidas not just cash that could quickly be used up but land that would be made inalienable, providing a home in central New York for future generations. If that failed, he would devise a legal strategy to get the case heard in court. The lawyer was up-front. His firm would take up the case not out of a desire to "do good" for the Indians, but because they thought there was a chance of earning a hefty contingent fee if they were successful. The transparency was well-received.[103]

At the time Shattuck took on the case, there were about five hundred Oneidas in New York, ten thousand in Wisconsin, and twenty-five hundred in Ontario. Shattuck began by petitioning state and federal authorities, including Governor Nelson Rockefeller and Presidents Johnson and Nixon, over a three-year period starting in 1967, requesting a settlement out of court for the exploitative and illegal land treaties to which the Oneidas had been subjected. When that failed, he initiated legal action. There was a major roadblock that had always prevented the case being heard. Federal courts would not hear a case that was fundamentally about rights over land, because such cases were the domain of the state courts. However, the Oneida case could not be heard by state courts either, because Native American cases were a federal matter.

Shattuck nonetheless filed a lawsuit in federal district court in 1970 focusing on the 1795 New York-Oneida treaty. It was a test case, and Shattuck carefully constructed it as a challenge to see if he could get it around the legal roadblocks and establish a precedent for bringing Indian land claims to federal court. Rather than suing for "ejectment," which would force a decision on legal ownership of land, Shattuck decided to sue for two years' worth of rent on county-owned land "on the premise that the Oneidas still owned the land and were entitled to rent from the current occupants." The reason for choosing the 1795 treaty was that it was the one that most clearly violated the 1790 Nonintercourse Act, as no federal agent was present in the negotiations.

The 1795 treaty covered about one hundred thousand acres of land in Madison and Oneida Counties. The Eleventh Amendment restricts federal courts' ability to hear cases against state governments, so the defendants in the case were the two counties rather than the state of New York. When the courts refused to hear the cases, Shattuck petitioned the US Supreme Court. The Supreme Court heard Shattuck's arguments, as well as the counterarguments by Oneida and Madison Counties, in Washington on November 6 and 7, 1973. It published its decision on *Oneida Indian Nation of New York v. County of Oneida, New York, et al.* on January 21, 1974. It was a major victory for the Oneidas, ruling that federal courts can hear Native American land claim suits.[104]

The 1974 Supreme Court decision was a landmark for Native American land claim cases. It opened the door for federal court hearings, setting a precedent for high-profile cases by other eastern Indian tribes, some of which relied on a more aggressive "mass-ejectment strategy," that is, seeking to reclaim not just rent, but the land itself. The Passamaquoddy and Penobscot Indians, for instance, demanded the return of over five million acres in Maine. They were granted an out-of-court settlement of 350,000 acres of land and $81 million in monetary compensation.[105]

For the Oneidas, it meant their case against the counties could go to trial. The hearing took place at federal district court in Auburn, beginning November 12, 1975. The key witness for the prosecution was Jack Campisi, an ethno-historian, who proved that New York State deliberately violated the Nonintercourse Act with the 1795 treaty, in full knowledge that the transaction was illegal. The court's decision was published on July 12, 1977. Judge Edmund Port concluded that the treaty transaction was indeed illegal and that the Oneidas were therefore still the rightful owners of the land. The counties were ordered to pay rent on the land for 1968 and 1969, though the monetary value of the rent was not set—that, it said, would be "determined in a subsequent trial."[106] Judge Port later ruled that any money the counties should have to pay would need to be reimbursed by the state of New York, since it was the state that had been the actual wrongdoer.

The amount of money at stake was small—the two years' rent only applied to lands owned by the counties, a tiny fraction of the claim area. It was assessed in 1982 at $16,694.[107] But the case was never about the county rent money. Now that it had been established that rent was chargeable on land that had been in non-Indian hands for nearly two hundred years, the Oneidas would have greater leverage to push the state to settle out of court. Otherwise, there would be clear basis to sue for far more than two years of county rent money.

While Judge Port was writing his decision, Shattuck formulated his next move on behalf of the Oneidas. He wanted to press for a settlement of the so-called "pre-1790 claim" of around six million acres—essentially the full extent of Oneida lands from Canada to Pennsylvania as they were outlined in the 1784 Treaty of Fort Stanwix. He sent a petition to President Carter on March 21, 1977. This claim rested on the fact that the 1788 treaty, in which the Oneidas ceded all their land apart from a 250,000-acre reservation, was understood to be a lease and not a sale. Shattuck believed that because this land was the "gateway to the American west," the Oneidas "could have grown to be a wealthy nation had not possession of this land been illegally taken from them by the state in the 1785–1840 era."

Shattuck's Syracuse law firm, Bond, Schoeneck & King, decided it could not continue to advise the Oneidas, however, because of a conflict of interest. With ejectment strategies now on the table, a local commercial law firm that also represented non-Native clients in the land claim area (indeed, some of the firm's lawyers, including Shattuck himself, owned houses on it) could no longer offer impartial advice. The Native American Rights Fund (NARF) took over the case. Two suits on the pre-1790 claim were filed in 1978 and 1979. These were finally rejected by the Circuit Court of Appeals in 1988, and the US Supreme Court decided it would not hear the case.[108] The court decided it couldn't rule on events that happened before the Constitution came into effect in 1789.

Simultaneously, the NARF represented the Oneidas in its "post-1790" claims for roughly 250,000 acres in the 1788 Reservation in Oneida and Madison Counties. It proceeded on an "ejectment" basis, causing uncertainty over property values and tension with homeowners in the area. The Oneidas' opponents portrayed the case in a way that stoked fear and resentment. The attorney for the counties, Allan van Gestel, wrote that the Oneidas were claiming "exclusive right to possession of . . . the portion of central New York State that runs from the Pennsylvania border in the south to Canada in the north."[109]

What the Oneidas' lawyers were really seeking was a negotiated settlement. An Oneida spokesperson said, "It is not the desire of the Indians to evict any non-Indians from their home."[110] But many residents in the area were worried. Some were angry. The emotive words of van Gestel and others, which purposefully depicted the land claims in the worst possible light, struck a powerful chord. The counties determined to fight back.

Oneida and Madison Counties petitioned the Supreme Court to review the 1974 Oneida decision. In 1984, it did. The court considered the case important enough to be heard again, given its relevance to other land claims. The argument hinged on whether redress for wrongs could justifiably be sought 175 years after they occurred.[111] The court published its decision on March 5, 1985. In *Oneida County v. Oneida Indian Nation of New York State* 470 U.S. 226 (1985), called *Oneida II* for short, the court upheld the *Oneida I* judgment of 1974 and stated that there was no time limit that should apply to such cases. Four of the nine justices dissented, arguing that the court should apply laches, or, in other words, that too much time had passed. Again, there were major ramifications.

The decision upheld the right of Native American tribes to pursue land claims cases in the nation's courts. It set the scene for further settlements of such cases by the Wampanoags ($4.5 million in 1987), Senecas ($60 million in 1990), and the Cherokee, Choctaw, and Chickasaw Nations ($40 million in 2002), among others. Critics of the court's decision, however, argued that it would result in years of "protracted litigation" and have a "devastating effect on property values, local businesses, and local economies" in land claim areas.[112] Later, groups like Upstate Citizens for Equality, which opposed the Oneidas' land claims in central New York, rallied around this view. Ironically, the Oneidas—whose breakthroughs in court helped pave the way for some Native American tribes to achieve settlements for their land claims—were very far from any settlement with the counties or the state of New York for its own in 1985; not years but decades of fighting and frustration lay ahead.

§

Despite their stunning legal successes in the *Oneida I* and *Oneida II* cases, Oneida people in New York often lived in poverty. Many of the Oneidas who lived at the Onondaga Reservation had gone there because of better work opportunities in the Syracuse area than they would have in rural Madison County. The decline of manufacturing in Syracuse and spiraling job loss across central New York from the 1960s onward hit its Native people hard. Negotiations for a settlement of their land claim had no end in sight. Apart from the token $16,694 they had been awarded in rent money, there was nothing to show for years of struggle in the courts at the end of the 1980s.

When William H. Rockwell died in 1960, some Oneidas living in Onondaga returned to the thirty-two-acre plot in Madison County and set up residence on it, partly to ensure that it did not pass out of Oneida ownership again. It was called the Oneida Indian Territory. Those who lived on it were mainly in secondhand mobile homes along a dirt path with no access to running water. In the early 1990s, nearly half of those living on the territory were unemployed. Two-thirds of households were living on less than $15,000 per year.[113]

In the late 1970s, Arthur Raymond "Ray" Halbritter (b. 1951) became a prominent leader on the territory. He was appointed as a representative of the Wolf Clan, with the approval of the clan mother, Maisie Shenandoah, in 1977. Halbritter's vision was to build businesses that would put Oneida people to work and lift the nation up out of poverty. In 1979, the Oneidas began hosting bingo games in doublewide trailers on the territory.

Indian bingo was not an Oneida invention. A Supreme Court decision in 1976, *Bryan v. Itasca County*, ruled that states cannot regulate gaming activities on Indian reservations, meaning that jackpot limits and opening hours could not be restricted in the same way they were on non-Native land.

In 1985, the Oneidas built a bingo hall with capacity for eight hundred, which Halbritter told reporters earned over $7 million in its first year of operation. Jackpots exceeded $50,000.

Halbritter became the federally recognized representative of the Oneida Indian Nation of New York in July 1987. It was a time of major setbacks in the Oneidas' land claims cases. As previously noted, the pre-1790 land claims filed in 1978 and 1979 were shot down in court in 1988, and appeal to the Supreme Court was denied. The Oneida Indian Nation's main money-earner, its bingo hall, burned down in February 1988. Local and national media presented the tribe as divided into warring factions.[114]

But the Oneidas were also making positive impacts and gaining attention at a national level in the late 1980s in unprecedented ways. A Wisconsin Oneida, Charlie Hill, rose to prominence as a stand-up comedian and writer. He was the first Native American comedian to perform on the *Tonight Show with Johnny Carson*.[115] In 1989, an Oneida woman who grew up on the territory, Joanne Shenandoah, released her self-titled debut album. *Joanne Shenandoah* was a landmark in Native American music and launched the career of one of the most beloved and widely acclaimed Native vocalists of all time. She performed at five US presidential inaugurations. Both Hill and Shenandoah drew inspiration and the core material for their art from their Oneida experience.

While Shenandoah was recording her first albums, Ray Halbritter, her cousin, was completing a JD degree at Harvard Law School. When Halbritter returned to Oneida, another page had turned in Indian gaming. In 1988, the US government passed the Indian Gaming Regulatory Act, which allowed Native American tribes and state governments to sign compacts to allow Native people to build Las Vegas–style gambling casinos on their land. Halbritter set to work with Governor Mario Cuomo on a gaming compact, which was agreed in April 1993. The Oneidas bought large tracts of farmland adjacent to thruway exit 33 in the town of Verona, Oneida County, seven miles north of the territory. It was land that was part of the original 1788 Oneida Reservation, taken by the state in its illegal 1795 treaty. Like other tribes, the Oneidas also took advantage of tax rules that enabled them to sell gas and cigarettes more cheaply than competitors and began setting up a chain of gas stations under the brand name SavOn.

The Turning Stone Casino opened its doors in July 1993. It proved a major success, due in large part to its ease of access from the thruway. A hotel was added in 1997, and a second hotel in a twenty-story tower complex was completed in 2004. Restaurants, shops, three golf courses, concert venues, and bars were added on in a process of growth and expansion that has carried on over nearly three decades. In 1996, the casino's estimated annual profits were $60 million, rising to over $80 million in 2001.[116] By 2000, the Oneida Indian Nation had over three thousand employees, 90 percent of whom were non-Native. It was the largest employer in Oneida and Madison Counties. In 1999, according to the Oneidas' annual report, Turning Stone drew almost four million visitors. Twenty years later, it employed 4,750 people with a payroll of $161 million.[117]

Halbritter proved to be a versatile business leader. When New York State changed its tax laws in a way that would cut their profit margin from selling name-brand cigarettes, Oneida Nation Enterprises bought out a cigarette-making plant for $6.6 million. They moved the rolling machines, installed them in the old bingo hall on the territory, and began producing their own.[118]

Profits brought benefits to Oneidas in New York that went beyond job creation. Within a year of the casino's opening, Halbritter announced that it was enabling the nation to fund seventy members to access further education in 1994, compared with seven in 1990.[119] The Shako:wi Cultural Center opened on the territory in 1993 as a museum to preserve Oneida artifacts with an outreach program providing education about Oneida culture and traditions. Casino earnings were reinvested rather than distributed to members, but enrolled Oneidas did get a share of non-casino revenues. In 1996 they were receiving $600 a month, and in 2001 they received $1,100 quarterly. In 2013, each enrolled Oneida received about $16,000 annually, according to the *Washington Post*.[120] A housing program delivered fifty homes for nation members in an area near the territory, helping Oneidas into better and safer accommodation. The nation established its own medical facilities and police force, easing long-standing tensions with local services. Distribution payments to members, whilst generous, are far lower than they could be. Halbritter has often said that he does not want payouts to members to be so large that they would encourage or enable people not to work. Subsidized housing for members comes with a requirement of matching funds or taking on employment.[121]

With their earnings, the Oneida Indian Nation set to buying land within the post-1790 land claim area on the open market. Some of it was for the establishment of new gas stations or other businesses, but it also included farmland far from main roads. By 1996, they owned thirty-five hundred acres. Ten years later, that figure stood at over seventeen thousand.[122] The Oneidas maintained that because the land they were purchasing was part of their 1788 reservation—and because it was clearly established that the process by which those lands were purchased by the state was illegal—it should be exempt from taxation.

Halbritter saw the choice to exploit all taxation exemptions available and to profit from gaming as "the quickest way to build an economic base" that would enable the nation to break the cycle of intergenerational poverty. He viewed the casino and cigarette profits as means to an end—a temporary measure. "We have tried poverty for 200 years," he explained, "so we decided to try something else."[123]

Some Oneida people were critical of Halbritter's leadership. Melvin Phillips, a descendant of the Orchard Party living on ancestral land at Marble Hill, near Sherrill, fought for recognition of the "Marble Hill Oneidas" as a separate entity from the Oneida Indian Nation of New York. Negotiations between New York and Wisconsin Oneidas became strained over land and casino rights in the reservation area, as well as negotiation strategy with the state. Some Haudenosaunee people at Oneida and elsewhere strongly disagreed with profiting from gambling. Others accused Halbritter of drifting from traditional forms of Oneida government, of silencing dissent, and of embracing capitalism too firmly.[124]

Storms broke out when land claim litigation restarted in 1998. Since the Supreme Court decision in 1985 in *County of Oneida v. Oneida Indian Nation of New York State*, the nation had been in talks with New York State officials, seeking a settlement in the hundreds of millions of dollars for their post-1790 claims. A stay was placed on the land claim case in 1987 to enable the settlement negotiations. Eleven years later, no agreement had been reached and the stay was lifted. To increase the pressure, in December 1998 the Oneidas amended their complaint by adding all twenty thousand private landowners who had homes or property on their post-1790 lands to the list of defendants.[125]

As in other cases, this was legal maneuvering to try to induce the state to concede with an out-of-court settlement. But it caused alarm and a backlash. Some people whose homes lay on the reservation felt unfairly targeted and were concerned about how property values would be affected. In January 1999, the Oneida county executive sought to clarify the situation in a Q&A statement for homeowners who suddenly found themselves being sued for ejection: "Are landholders in jeopardy of losing their homes? We don't think so. We feel that the proposed inclusion of these 20,000 innocent landowners and a request for ejectment are intended to force the parties to the negotiating table after years of inactivity in these actions."[126]

But for some residents, "we don't think so" did not provide sufficient certainty, while others bristled at being used as part of a tactic to force a settlement. A pressure group called Upstate Citizens for Equality (UCE) formed to protest the land claim and the expansion of nation businesses. It received a surge of support. In January 1999, they organized a motorcade protest encircling Turning Stone. Over the course of 1999 and 2000, the reputation of UCE was severely damaged by some of its supporters' use of bigoted language and imagery. A New York State assemblyman joked at one UCE meeting in January 1999 about being "scalped," a remark for which he refused to apologize.

Some extreme Oneida opponents posted billboards and signs intimating violence, for example, an image of a shotgun pointed at Halbritter with the caption, "Come get your rent." In November 1999, the *Utica Observer-Dispatch* received a letter purporting to be from a group called the United States Freedom Fighters promising to execute Indians and white patrons of Oneida Indian Nation businesses.[127] The FBI investigated, but the authors were never found.

UCE leaders denied accusations of racism and denounced the threats. Some members tried to portray themselves as patriots who, like the colonial rebels of 1776, were fighting an unfair and arbitrary tax system. In the motorcade protest, activists dressed in Revolutionary War–era costumes and paraded a replica of Fort Stanwix.[128] An irony, of course, was that the casino was on the very route that Oneida warriors took from Kanonwalohale to that fortress in 1777. When they got there, they provided colonial forces with vital support that changed the course of the Revolutionary War.

Another major point of contention was the tax status of land bought by the nation within the land claim area. The nation's view was that the land they bought was their own reservation land, and that as such it should not be subjected to local property taxes. For the towns and counties, however, it meant substantial decreases in tax revenues that would impact their ability to deliver services, including to Indian-owned land. The casino needed to be supplied with water, for instance, which came from the town of Verona in Oneida County. The nation tried to offset this by making large donations to support local amenities. A *New York Times* article noted that one UCE protest set off from Verona's town hall, which had just been refurbished using a grant from the Oneida Indian Nation.[129] By 2000, the Oneidas contributed $2 million to local school systems.[130] But the principle behind the dispute was that the guaranteed tax base was being indelibly cut down with each land purchase.

The UCE and others were determined to force Oneida Nation Enterprises to pay tax on the repurchased land on which their businesses were built. They argued that it was wrong that present-day counties and communities could be denied more of their tax income with each additional acre that was bought by the Oneida Indian Nation, even if the land was once part of their reservation. Robert Witmer Jr., who represented the counties in the land claim case, said, "Our founding fathers would be rolling over in their graves if they ever thought it would come to this."[131] Another Supreme Court showdown was in the offing.

For the Oneidas, saving tax money was not the issue (their generous donations to the local community show that). It was about sovereignty. They argued that the land they bought was not only their ancestral home, but it was also part of an Indian reservation that only left Oneida possession because it was taken from them in illegal treaties. Now that it was back in their hands, it should be exempt from taxation like the rest of their reservation holdings. Witmer's appeal to the founders is another irony in this story; the "founders" he thought would be rolling in their graves were presumably the same that signed the 1790 Indian Nonintercourse Act to prevent states taking advantage of Native American people in exploitative treaties. That the Oneidas were having to buy back their reservation lands at all was because the state of New York willfully and repeatedly disobeyed the law the founders wrote.

§

The story of the twentieth century in central New York is, in one sense, quite simple: it is like a roller coaster train that goes up a lift hill to a great height, then plummets downward in a free fall, taking its passengers with it, willing or not. Economically, it is difficult not to see it in those terms. Its manufacturing boom and bust are its most salient details. But culturally, the story is far more complex. The last waves of newcomers from the era of unrestricted immigration found work and, eventually, acceptance in central New York's cities. Men like Carmen Basilio from the Canastota muck gave the old Yankee burned-over district a new image. The descendants of the Oneida Community forged a third way between the social idealism of John Humphrey Noyes and the capitalism he railed against.

It was a time of increasing division. Rural and town life became more divergent than ever with few connections remaining between the two by the end of the century. Black migration from the south reshaped central New

York's cities. But the combined effects of redlining, highway planning, and the decline in manufacturing led to an urban landscape characterized by racial division, dereliction, and concentrated poverty.

Nostalgia for the area's past came to the fore, fulfilled by the likes of *Drums along the Mohawk* and the reconstruction of Fort Stanwix. But just as central New York celebrated its past, new battles raged about events that coincided closely with the nation's founding. The Oneida land claim cases that reached the US Supreme Court in the 1970s and '80s were based on the fact that their lands were taken by the state of New York in treaties that were illegal by federal law.

The Oneida Indian Nation of New York was able to benefit from new legislation that allowed gaming on their lands. The revenue raised helped many Oneida people in New York to escape poverty, but it did not come without problems. Some opponents in central New York argued that the Oneida Indian Nation, with its casino and its lawyers (who were now suing to eject them from their land, or so it seemed), was going up while everyone else was going down. Some of the Oneidas' opponents used language and tactics that were intended to intimidate or to demean; some even threatened to kill Indians and their supporters. The year 2000 ended with a range of new lawsuits challenging the Oneida Indian Nation's tax status and business enterprises in the works, including one which would end up in US Supreme Court in 2005.

All this occurred against the backdrop of increasing anxiety and uncertainty across central New York, and more widely across the nation, in the final decades of the twentieth century. Woodstock '99, with its violence, arson, and vandalism, seemed to encapsulate the spirit of the time. The major forces impacting most Americans' lives during this period were the rise of the global economy, the end of the Cold War, and—particularly in the "rust belt"—the disappearance of secure jobs and the stable way of life they supported. This is what lay behind some of the anger. As a new millennium dawned, there seemed to be no end of trouble in sight. The twentieth century cast a long shadow that remains very much with us more than two decades into the twenty-first.

Epilogue: 2000–2023

Tensions around the Oneida land claim and the Oneida Indian Nation's business enterprises were high in central New York in 2000. But in 2023, very little of that remains. There are several reasons for this. One is that residents in the area around the Turning Stone Casino, once the nexus of protest, now have a great deal to lose and little to gain if Oneida Nation Enterprises were to falter. It is by far the biggest employer in the region, with some 4,500 jobs dependent on its success. Another is that the land claim case is no longer active in the courts. Compromises to the most divisive issues around taxation and land ownership have been found.

The process by which this was achieved was complex and often difficult. There are some in the area—including its recent congresswoman, Claudia Tenney—who continue to attack Oneida Nation Enterprises and its CEO, Ray Halbritter. But the picture now is largely one of peace and stability, certainly compared to the way things were around the millennium.

An initial step in this process occurred in September 2000 when a US District Court judge ruled that landowners of Madison and Oneida Counties should be removed from the list of defendants in the post-1790 land claim case.[1] This eliminated the most emotive aspect of the case for non-Native people in Madison and Oneida counties. It was not enough, however, to prevent a seemingly endless series of lawsuits aimed at the Oneida Indian Nation of New York or at Oneida Nation Enterprises in the early 2000s. Upstate Citizens for Equality filed suit against New York State Governor George Pataki for supporting the Oneidas' right to trade at Turning Stone, arguing that the 1993 gaming compact had not been approved by the state legislature. That case, *Peterman v. Pataki*, resulted in a finding in 2004 that the gaming compact had indeed not received the correct legislative approval at the time of signing, but the Department of the Interior upheld its legality in a 2007 review.[2]

In 2000, the city of Sherrill sued the Oneida Indian Nation for property taxes on the SavOn gas station it established a short walk away from the old Willow Place factory on Route 5. *City of Sherrill v. Oneida Indian Nation of New York* wound its way through the legal system for five years. A US District Court ruled that Sherrill should not seek to collect tax on the land bought by the Oneida Indian Nation. Sherrill appealed, and the case was granted certiorari, meaning that it would be heard by the Supreme Court. In a majority decision authored by Justice Ruth Bader Ginsburg in 2005, the court decided that the Oneida Indian Nation could not reclaim regulatory authority by purchasing lands that had been in non-Indian hands for generations. In her words, the Oneidas could not rekindle "embers of sovereignty that long ago grew cold."[3] They were entitled to own land purchased on the free market, but that land would not automatically be removed from the tax roll and become part of their reservation.

It was a victory for Sherrill, though celebrations were muted in a city that saw its main factory and employer, Oneida Limited, melt down in 2002–4 after one hundred twenty successful years. Some Native American activists condemned the decision as racist. It coincided with a lower federal court's dismissal of the Cayuga Nation's land claim in western New York. Critics attacked the court for rolling back on earlier decisions that benefitted Native Americans, "creating a new jurisprudence that benefits states, local governments, and private property owners that come into contact with tribal interests."[4] Ginsburg later said that she regretted the decision.[5]

The ruling did clarify that there was an alternative avenue to make Oneida-purchased land exempt from taxation. It could be transferred to the federal government, which would hold it in trust for the Oneida Indian Nation.[6] The nation almost immediately applied to transfer all 17,370 acres of land it owned within the land claim area into federal trust. The Bureau of Indian Affairs held public hearings and consultations over nearly three years before announcing, on May 20, 2008, that it would accept 13,004 acres, permanently removing them from local control and taxation.[7] The Department of the Interior reasoned that the trust would enable the Oneida Indian Nation to "protect it for future generations," and to "promote the health, welfare, and social needs of its members."

The trust area was created of three contiguous patches of Oneida-owned property in Oneida and Madison Counties. It included the Turning Stone Casino, its golf courses and RV parks, 3,076 acres to be used for hunting and fishing, 2,274 acres of wetlands, and burial grounds and historic sites purchased by the nation. Oneida-owned land not included in the trust included nine gas stations, marinas on Oneida Lake, and other plots that were not contiguous with the three main trust areas. The Oneidas were ordered to pay back taxes but would henceforth pay no tax on the lands held in trust. Opponents argued that what they thought they had gained in the 2005 ruling, an agreement that the Oneidas could not take land off the tax rolls simply by buying it, had been rendered meaningless.[8]

This set off another flurry of litigation. On the day of the 2008 announcement, various politicians promised to fight the DOI's decision. Seven more lawsuits were filed between May and August by the State of New York, Madison and Oneida Counties, the towns of Vernon and Verona, and the City of Oneida. Private citizens' groups, including Upstate Citizens for Equality, also filed suit. New York's governor, David Paterson, called the land-into-trust decision "arbitrary and capricious." He challenged a policy that he said would give rise to "super-rich tribal nation states, fed by tax-exempt gaming revenues, that can remove endless amounts of land from local and state regulation and taxation."[9] Several of these complaints were dismissed by Judge Lawrence Kahn in federal district court in September 2009.[10]

Alongside the land-into-trust debate that kicked off in 2008, the land claim litigation—started in the 1970s and reopened in 1998—continued to frustrate, divide, and bubble up in the courts. In 2002, Governor Pataki was close to sealing a settlement agreement that would have given $225 million to the Oneidas in New York, $25 million to the Oneidas in Ontario, and $250 million to the Oneidas in Wisconsin, but negotiations broke down.[11] In 2007, Judge Kahn absolved Madison and Oneida Counties of blame in the case and ruled against ejectment in the land claim area, but agreed with the Oneidas that they had the "right to seek redress for long-suffered wrongs" done by the state of New York.[12]

Three years later, the land claim suffered a major blow when the case came before the US Circuit Court of Appeals. In a 2-1 decision, it ruled that the Oneidas were not entitled to any land or money for their claim due to the length of time that elapsed since New York's treaty violations. The counties and UCE considered it a great victory.[13] The Oneidas appealed the decision, but the Supreme Court refused to grant certiorari, though Justices Ginsburg and Sotomayor wanted to hear the appeal. The Wisconsin Oneidas' longtime attorney, Arlinda Locklear, called it a "gross miscarriage of justice."[14]

Governor Andrew Cuomo, who assumed office in 2011, set out to solve what he called "one of the truly lingering, festering, negative situations in the state" by negotiating a final settlement with the Oneida Indian Nation of New York.[15] He started by phoning Halbritter, adopting a more conciliatory tone than had been the case with previous governors (Halbritter said that by contrast Eliot Spitzer, who held office briefly between 2007 and 2008, told him he could send one hundred troopers to shut him down in five minutes). Cuomo then brought in Oneida and Madison County officials. Cuomo was keen to allow other casinos to open in New York State, but to entice Halbritter to settle, he offered to ensure that no competing casinos could open in a ten-county area surrounding Turning Stone. In exchange, Halbritter agreed to pay 25 percent of slot-machine revenues annually to New York State (estimated at $50 million in 2013). A quarter of that money would be distributed to Oneida County and 7 percent of it to Madison County.

A further inducement for the counties to sign was a promise by the Oneidas to limit the amount of land they would ever take into trust to twenty-five thousand acres. Each county would also be paid millions in back property taxes. Finally, the nation agreed to terms that would stop them undercutting local competition in gas and cigarette sales by imposing a nation sales tax equal to state and county tax on sales to non-Indians.[16]

The state and counties agreed to drop their lawsuits. The signing of the deal in 2013 was momentous. It put an end to forty-three years of litigation between the Oneidas of New York and the counties of Oneida and Madison. It was a remarkable feat of diplomacy, but, predictably, yet another round of backlash came in its wake.

The towns of Vernon and Verona initially refused to drop their lawsuits, though agreements within Oneida County about distribution of money to the towns over the course of 2014 were met with approval. The UCE redoubled its efforts to fight the 2008 land-into-trust decision, arguing that the federal government's action was unconstitutional.[17] Their case, *Upstate Citizens for Equality, Inc. v. United States*, was dismissed in the 2nd Circuit Court of Appeals in 2016. UCE's application for certiorari was denied in 2017, though Supreme Court Justice Clarence Thomas publicly dissented from the decision and argued that the court should have heard UCE's case.[18]

An article in the *New York Post* denounced the 2013 settlement as a "rotten deal" in which the counties would get only a fraction of the back taxes they were owed. It described Halbritter as the leader of the "casino Oneidas," one who "claims to have some Oneida blood" and uses casino revenues to pay politicians while the Oneidas themselves are "mostly dirt-poor."[19] The author was Claudia Tenney, a lawyer from New Hartford and New York state assemblywoman. Tenney became one of Halbritter's most outspoken opponents. She repeatedly claimed he is not an Oneida, referred to him as a "fraud," "someone who cheats and lies for a living," and, in a 2015 tweet, called him "spray tan Ray." The latter prompted a statement from the nation saying, "It is a sad day when anyone attacks another person's skin color. . . . There is no place in our political discourse for this type of hate speech."[20]

Despite Tenney's attacks, most of the major legal challenges that characterized the post-2000 period are now settled. The relative peace has allowed Halbritter to focus on his twin passions: economic expansion and cultural impact. The Oneida Indian Nation opened a $20 million new casino in Chittenango in 2015 called the Yellow Brick Road and a third called Point Place in 2018, both in easier reach of Syracuse than Turning Stone. The former's name is a nod to its location in the hometown of L. Frank Baum, the author of *The Wonderful Wizard of Oz*. This provoked some hostile reactions due to Baum's vehemently racist, anti-Indian writings in the 1890s while he was editor of a South Dakota newspaper. Halbritter explained that members of Baum's family apologized and that the casino's name represents forgiveness.[21]

Simultaneously, Halbritter spearheaded a campaign to persuade sports teams to stop using Indians as mascots. His challenge of the Washington Redskins in particular, whose name derived from a slur term for Native Americans, brought national recognition. He paid for advertisements and funded studies showing how Indian caricatures affected Native Americans' sense of self-worth. More than thirty Native American organizations backed the campaign, but Redskins owner Dan Snyder stated emphatically that he would never change the team's name.[22] The franchise finally did drop the Redskins name and mascot in 2020 in a wave of reviews of institutional racism following the death of George Floyd and ensuing protests. Halbritter said the team "finally made the right call."[23]

While Halbritter was in the national spotlight, Claudia Tenney and others continued making ad hominem attacks. In 2013, Tenney told the *Daily Caller*, "There is not a drop of Oneida in him," citing a census of the Oneida Reservation from his great-grandmother's time that lists her as "not belong[ing] to the Six Nations." Some articles in the national press detailed controversies in Halbritter's route to power. Others called Halbritter an "Obama crony" and questioned why Oneidas only received $16,000 per year compared to Seminoles who received $84,000 despite a lower earnings-to-membership ratio. Nation spokesperson Joel Barkin hit back, calling the attacks on Halbritter "bigotry at its worst."[24]

The "Change the Mascot" campaign was preceded by other cultural projects bankrolled by the Oneida Indian Nation. In 2004, the nation presented a 2,200-pound bronze sculpture to the National Museum of the American Indian in Washington, DC, titled *Allies in War, Partners in Peace*. It depicts Chief Shenandoah, Polly Cooper (an Oneida woman who is said to have fed the continental soldiers at Valley Forge), and George Washington, along with the icons of the three Oneida clans—a wolf, a bear, and a turtle—under the tree of peace.[25] In 2012, it made a $10 million contribution to the new Museum of the American Revolution in Philadelphia.[26] It later bankrolled a twenty-seven-minute film narrated by Kevin Costner called *People of the Standing Stone: The Oneida Nation, the War of Independence, and the Making of America* (2017).

Closer to home, the nation sponsored efforts to revive the Oneida language. Few Oneidas who grew up in New York State after World War II were fluent, and the language was in danger of extinction. Margaret Splain spent her childhood on Marble Hill. She described how her mother could understand Oneida, and her grandmother spoke it with people of her own age, but said, "They didn't teach [our generation] the language."[27] By 2000, there was virtually no one left in New York who had grown up speaking Oneida as their first language. The nation in New York began a language revitalization program. They commissioned Ray George, a member of the Oneida Nation of the Thames who did grow up speaking Oneida at home, and the Berlitz company to create a learning curriculum. They then supported eight New York Oneidas to learn the language full-time so that they could instruct young learners.[28]

The Oneida Indian Nation's businesses are currently thriving. Even the COVID-19 pandemic, which closed operations temporarily during 2020, has not dented Halbritter's business and cultural ambitions. He launched Standing Arrow Productions in 2021, a company promoting Native American representation on screen. He announced in February 2021 that he would produce a film adaptation of Sally Jenkins's book, *The Real All-Americans*, the story of the Carlisle Indian School's football team.

Oneida Nation Enterprises also launched a $25-million project to build seventy vacation cottages at Sylvan Beach, yards from the place where the eighteenth-century British blockhouse guarded against French and Indian raids, where De Witt Clinton saw Oneida Indians spearfishing in canoes in 1810, and where Albert Bierstadt sketched studies for his *Sunset on Oneida Lake*. The nation's 2021 annual report carries details of its charitable donations, language program, scholarships, historical commemorations, investments in the local community, and its unveiling of a new monument at the site of the Oneida Carry in Rome. All this was possible due to the success of the nation's businesses and their policy of reinvesting 100 percent its gaming revenues into local operations.[29]

§

Oneida Limited, the descendant company of the nineteenth-century utopian Oneida Community, started 2000 bullishly. Sales had been growing year-on-year since 1996. They invested over $100 million in acquiring companies internationally and in the United States to add products to their tableware range. But Oneida began unravelling after the terrorist attacks on the World Trade Center on September 11, 2001. Airlines banned the use of stainless-steel knives on board, instantly cutting off $25 million in annual sales. Other orders dried up in the market downturn of 2002. Shares in Oneida sold for $12.95 in October 2002, less than half what they had been in 1999. A year later they were $3.05 and finally $0.84 in 2004. The company began laying off workers at its main plant in Sherrill in 2003. Due to its large outlays before 2001, the company's debt hovered around $233 million.[30] Quarterly losses continued and by September 2004, the company had no choice but to announce it would close its main plant in early 2005. Oneida Limited survived in name, pared down to a small group of importers, but for all intents and purposes, the company that Noyes built had reached an inglorious end.

The last of the great industries that made central New York State a manufacturing powerhouse in the twentieth century was gone. In a sense, the only surprising thing about Oneida Limited's demise is that it was staved off for so long. When he announced the closure of the Sherrill plant in 2004, CEO Peter Kallet stated what had been a constant refrain for thirty years in central New York and across the rust belt: "We tried everything. . . . Manufacturing is not economically viable."[31]

Yet this particular closure was uniquely bitter. Oneida Limited had been founded and survived for decades with an idealism about what a fairer, socially oriented company could do. Though that idealism faded away in its later years, there was a sad irony in that while workers were left without jobs and saw their pension plans (heavily built on Oneida Limited stock) evaporate, company executives were able to retire with guaranteed payouts of $300,000 per year.[32] Workers had to file a class action lawsuit to recover some of their lost pensions in a process that took until 2010 to settle.[33]

§

There are two ways to view the first two decades of the twenty-first century in upstate New York. From a negative point of view, there is a lot to look upon. Economically, the overall decline or, at best, stagnation that has beset the region for the last forty years shows no sign of radically changing. The largest industry sectors in central New York by far are government, health care, and social assistance. More dynamic production sectors such as finance, scientific and technical services, construction, and enterprise account for a tiny minority of jobs. Population statistics continue to show zero or negative growth in most areas, particularly the cities. Property values are far below the state average, and vacant, dilapidated properties are a significant problem for local governments.[34]

A drugs epidemic has gripped central New York in the last decade, bringing addiction and death in its wake. Oneida County had the highest rate of heroin overdose deaths per capita in New York State in 2016, and Onondaga County was second in opioid overdose deaths in the same year.[35] This is part of a drugs crisis that is gripping smaller cities throughout the eastern United States, but as Senator Chuck Schumer wrote in a bid to support Oneida County's application for HIDTA (High-Intensity Drug Trafficking Area) status, the heroin scourge has been "particularly pervasive" in upstate New York.[36]

The cities of Syracuse and Utica remain racially divided, and in a sense, at war with their history. In 2017, Syracuse was named one of the ten "worst cities for Black Americans" based on analysis of income, poverty levels, incarceration rates, and other indicators. Forty percent of Blacks live below the poverty line, compared to 11 percent of whites. Syracuse also has one of the highest rates of extreme poverty in Black neighborhoods, which tend to be separated from predominantly white neighborhoods by highways, most significantly I-81. Syracuse's overall poverty rate, 32.1 percent in 2017, was higher than ever, and is the ninth worst in the United States. Syracuse's Hispanic population, which has grown significantly since 2000 to nearly thirteen thousand, is nationally significant for its poverty rate of 58 percent.[37]

The Black Lives Matter movement staged protests in both Syracuse and Utica starting in 2016, citing institutional racism at national and local levels. In 2020, a small but vociferous march from Oneida Square in Utica was held to protest incidents of alleged police brutality against minority groups in the city. A group called the Utica Abolitionists—for its aim to abolish the police rather than any overt nod to the abolitionists of Utica's past—led the march.[38] Sadly, the land that was once known throughout the nation as a hotbed of abolitionism and a place where African Americans escaping slavery could find refuge and support, had no more success in dealing with racial issues in the final decades of the twentieth and first decades of the twenty-first centuries than any other part of the United States.

Currently, debates are raging about the statutes of Christopher Columbus in both Utica and Syracuse. In both cities, statues of the Italian explorer were put up in the twentieth century (1934 in Syracuse and 1952 in Utica) with financial support from their Italian American communities. Protestors say Columbus launched a genocidal conquest and should no longer be a celebrated figure. In Utica, repeated acts of vandalism against the statue in October 2020 culminated in a protestor draping a Ku Klux Klan outfit over Columbus's body.[39] In the same month, Syracuse mayor Ben Walsh announced the statue in Syracuse would be moved in response to longstanding opposition to it, prompting a lawsuit from the Columbus Monument Corporation which seeks to preserve the statue.[40]

Politically, central New York is also deeply divided. The region voted virtually en bloc for Republicans for nearly one hundred years between the Civil War and the 1960s. The seismic shift in American politics during the Kennedy and Johnson administrations, hinging largely on civil rights legislation, lost the Democratic Party substantial support in the South but turned traditionally Republican areas, including some parts of central New York, into battlegrounds where either party can prevail. The 2018 and 2020 elections in the 22nd Congressional District, which included all of Oneida, Madison, Chenango, and Cortland Counties, and parts of several others, were among the most hotly contested in the United States.

Until 2016, the seat was held by moderate Republican Richard Hanna from Utica. Claudia Tenney, who previously challenged Hanna from the right, won the 2016 Republican primary and went on to win the district. In 2018, a Tenney campaign memo accused her Italian American opponent Anthony Brindisi's family of mob-style "violence and intimidation," calling them "thuggish" and "criminal." Italian American groups and Brindisi's campaign team called the allegations baseless, part of a pattern of "blatant and false attacks on Italian-Americans." Tenney's attacks on Ray Halbritter also ensured the enmity of the Oneida Indian Nation. Even the Haudenosaunee writer Doug George-Kanentiio, a vocal critic of Halbritter, came out strongly against her.[41] Despite strong endorsement from President Trump, who visited Utica to fundraise for her, she was narrowly defeated by the Utica Democrat in 2018.[42]

In a 2020 rematch, the result was even narrower. The district was the last in the nation to declare a winner in February 2021. Tenney prevailed by a margin of 109 votes out of 326,555 cast. Donald Trump won more votes in the 2020 presidential election in most of the counties of central New York than his opponent, Joe Biden, with particularly strong support in rural areas. A drive through northern Oneida and Lewis Counties in the summer of 2021 was as good an indicator as any of the resentment over Trump's defeat. Hundreds of houses along country roads fly flags with pro-Trump or anti-Biden slogans—some as blunt as "Fuck Biden." A small but noticeable number of Confederate flags also fly on homes here, a supreme irony in rural central New York towns that were once some of the most solidly pro-Lincoln areas in the United States. Young men who lived on these roads fought and died to put down the rebellion that this flag represents.

But there are positive signs as well. The annual gross domestic product in the Syracuse area is beginning to grow again. There are efforts underway to build the population base by promoting the area to workers in larger east coast cities.[43] Some of the employers who left during the steep decline at the end of the twentieth century are coming back in modified guises. In 2015, General Electric announced it would return to Utica, pledging one thousand new jobs at the SUNY Polytechnic Institute Campus.[44] Oneida Limited's factory buildings in Sherrill were bought by some former employees who have found a new niche in the silverware market. Their company, Sherrill Manufacturing, struggled initially, but is now selling flatware called Liberty Tabletop to consumers who are willing to pay a bit more for a "made in the USA" product. Numbers employed there are far below what they were in the days of Oneida Limited's prime, but sales topped $1 million for the first time in 2015.[45] Starting in 2016, the Utica-area economy saw its first substantial growth in decades. Poverty rates in Oneida County decreased from 16.1 percent in 2017 to 14.8 percent in 2019, and child poverty is at 19.6 percent, down from 26 percent in 2014.[46]

Syracuse is attempting to grapple with the racial divisions in the city exacerbated by I-81. In 2021, $800 million was awarded in the state budget to begin an estimated $2 billion project to reroute the highway that has divided the inner city into affluent and poor sections since the 1960s. There is substantial opposition from the suburbs. There are even concerns among groups that the project is designed to help that it could lead to gentrification that would price them out of their neighborhood in the future. But others see it as a move towards restorative justice, one that will help Black neighborhoods and businesses that were destroyed by the highway to return to life. Supporters acknowledge that moving a highway will not correct all of Syracuse's urban problems but see it as a necessary step towards dismantling the status quo of division and concentrated poverty.[47]

Immigration was the key to the rise of the cities of central New York in the nineteenth and early twentieth centuries. Now, it is back. Utica began welcoming refugees in the late 1970s when its urban population was in freefall. The Mohawk Valley Resource Center for Refugees opened in 1979 and took charge of resettling wave after wave of new arrivals. During the 1980s, individuals and families from Vietnam, Laos, Cambodia, and the USSR settled in Utica. Larger numbers came during the 1990s—particularly refugees from the war that raged in the former Yugoslavia, mainly from Bosnia. Between 1997 and 2006, about forty-five hundred Bosnians started new lives in Utica. By 1999, sixty-five hundred refugees lived in the city, making up about 10 percent of its population. Bosnians settled in the Italian neighborhoods along Bleecker and Elizabeth Streets. In 2008 they bought a crumbling historic Methodist Church on Court Street for $1000 and converted it into a thriving mosque. They bought land in Deerfield for an Islamic Cemetery. Bosnian-owned small businesses started up in Utica—hair salons, discos, restaurants, a karate club. Refugees took jobs as janitors, nursing home aides, dishwashers, and housekeepers. Some work for the Oneida Indian Nation at the Turning Stone resort. Some go five in a car from Utica to work in yogurt factories and dairy farms in the countryside.

In 2003–4, a new wave of refugees began settling, mainly Karen people who escaped persecution in Myanmar and Somali Bantus who fled civil war. By 2017, over sixteen thousand refugees had come to Utica. There has been some, but relatively little opposition to the resettlement program. Utica is nicknamed "the town that loves refugees." Local leaders are mainly highly supportive, seeing the new refugees as the latest in a long line of immigrants that shaped the city since the nineteenth century.[48]

Syracuse has also been welcoming refugees and helping them resettle in some of its run-down, substantially vacated urban neighborhoods. Over ten thousand refugees, primarily from Burma, Bhutan, and Somalia, resettled there between 2000 and 2016, predominantly on the north side of the city. In 2014 alone, Onondaga County took 1,112 refugees—more than a quarter of the New York State total.[49]

Finally, the rise of the Oneida Indian Nation of New York out of poverty in the last thirty years stands out as a positive sign. Oneida Nation Enterprises is now a vital employer. The 2013 landmark agreement with the state settled legal struggles extending back over four decades and allowed the Oneida Indian Nation, the state, and the counties and people in the land claim area to look forward to a more harmonious future. For the Oneidas in New York, there is now room to reclaim traditions, language, and culture. The nation is endeavoring to diversify their business further beyond gambling into providing resort and tourism opportunities.

The Oneidas' business enterprises have allowed people whose ancestors inhabited this land long before Europeans nearly wrought their destruction to change their destiny. They can now work for Indian-owned businesses, access health care, and live in adequate housing without needing to move away from their homes. There has been criticism of how this was accomplished, some of it understandable, some less so. Yet it was a sad fact that before the 1990s, many of the Native people of this central part of the state of New York lived in obscurity and poverty around the lands that bear their name. That that is no longer the case is an indicator of progress.

The history of the United States—its economic growth, its spread from east to west, its wars, its morality, and its political crises—has been continually shaped by what happened in central New York State, the land of the Oneidas, for centuries. Two decades in, it too early to say if the twenty-first century will tell a tale of success or of failure for this part of the United States. But there are grounds for hope.

Conclusion

Central New York State—the land of the Oneidas—has had great significance to the wider history of the United States since the nation's foundation. At times, its importance was strategic, at others, symbolic. Often it was both. During the War of Independence, it was the site of a crucial battle and siege that undermined Britain's attempt to divide the American colonies. That the battle happened here was no accident. The fighting that took place around Fort Stanwix was at the key portage along the most crucial overland corridor from the settlements of the eastern seaboard to the Great Lakes and the interior of the continent. Militarily, the significance of that corridor only increased after independence, particularly during the years of hostility between the United States and Britain, which controlled Canada and the St. Lawrence River. Economically, it has been important to all generations of Americans—particularly in the canal and rail era, but also in the age of the superhighway.

The contribution of the Oneida Haudenosaunee people to the colonists' victory in their Revolutionary War was crucial, but the United States did precious little to reward them for it. The state of New York bought up their land in so-called treaties that flagrantly violated federal law. For the Oneidas and other Haudenosaunee people, dispossession was only the latest in a long line of tragic events extending back to the dawn of the seventeenth century. Their land had a strategic significance in European eyes long before the creation of the United States of America. French and Dutch (and later English) colonizers vied for trade and influence there for decades. Violence, disease, guns, alcohol, and Christianity impacted the Oneidas on their ancestral land, just as they did other Native peoples in the eastern half of North America in the early colonial era. Because the Oneidas' lands were in a place where imperial ambitions overlapped, they were able to benefit at times when European entities competed for their favor. But they also repeatedly found themselves caught between warring entities that demanded their allegiance and attempted to destroy them when it was refused.

Over the course of the nineteenth century, central New York's significance to America grew. The Erie Canal that ran across it was the key route for goods and passengers from the nation's largest city to the ever-expanding west. It was a key battleground in the struggle for the nation's soul in the antebellum years. The spiritual fires there that gave it the nickname "the burned-over district" also gave rise to a moral impulse to purify American society. Central New York reformers railed against intemperance, irreverence, and—most of all—the brutal system of slavery. It was home to one of the most audacious experiments in American religion, the Oneida Community, and to leaders in the struggle for women's rights.

Central New York's canal towns grew large and prosperous. Their manufacturing output and large immigrant workforces symbolized a new, modern America in the Civil War era and into the twentieth century. But the energies that made it one of the safest sections on the Underground Railroad slowly faded in the Gilded Age. Alongside the growing wealth and prosperity still visible in fine buildings and mansions that remain from the period, tensions emerged over immigration and labor conditions. The contrast between the declining rural areas and the expanding cities increased year on year.

In twentieth-century America, central New York's symbolic importance to the nation lay in its dramatic economic boom and bust. The region was vital to the making of America as an industrial superpower. But the era of globalization from the 1960s onward delivered America's manufacturing heartland a devastating blow. The boarded-up factories, depopulated neighborhoods, and dilapidated housing in central New York's cities and towns at the dawn of the millennium looked like those in scores of others across the rust belt. Yet there was a particular irony in that this region, once noted for its spiritual zeal and social idealism, seemed so divided and depressed. It is now a crucial political battleground in the shifting sands of Trump-era party politics.

America has a complex relationship with its past. In 2023, battles continue to rage about what the founding fathers wanted and what their words should mean to us after two and a half centuries of bewildering change. Here, too, central New York's complex relationship with its own history is symbolic of a larger process of national reckoning. In the post–World War II era, some Americans were willing to acknowledge that earlier generations of their countrymen had not only done immeasurable harm to certain groups in the past, but that many of those harms continued to have ramifications in the present. Some argued that action should be taken to correct these harms, but the realities of doing so proved complex.

That historic wrongs happened here is clear and well established. As in most other parts of America, the Native people of central New York were deprived of their land by an overpowering force, one that used a wide variety of tactics, from ostensible negotiation to outright lies and intimidation, to get what it wanted. Much of the land the state of New York acquired here was gained via treaties that violated federal law. The Oneidas pointed out this wrong for decades, but it was only in the 1970s that their arguments really began to be heard. This is also a land where slavery was practiced, where immigrants faced discrimination, and where racial division remains a striking feature, particularly in the cities of Utica and Syracuse. Central New York is grappling with problems that have long roots decades or even centuries into its history.

The past is therefore very much—and, I would suggest, exceptionally—present in the land of the Oneidas. It is now, and it was in previous generations. Much of this book focuses on the way people in this region constantly grappled with history and how that process changed from one generation to the next. In the 1830s and '40s, James Fenimore Cooper idealized it. Lewis Henry Morgan and Henry Schoolcraft studied the history and traditions of the Oneidas and other Haudenosaunee people in the mid-nineteenth century, while local historians compiled annals on the region's pioneer era, just as the generation who lived it faded away. Nostalgia for the Revolutionary War and canal eras in central New York's history was more than a local phenomenon in the twentieth century; it inspired bestselling books, songs from Tin Pan Alley, and Hollywood smash hits.

But along with the wistful, often celebratory, look back at this land's past, more difficult aspects of its history also resurfaced. Some of these caused division, anger, even destruction. There were hints of this in the nineteenth century. The absence of the Oneida people from their lands struck Lafayette when he came to Utica in the 1820s. The dissonance between central New York's Yankee past and its immigrant present was the theme of Harold Frederic's masterpiece, *The Damnation of Theron Ware*, in the 1890s. But in the later decades of the twentieth century and the first two of the twenty-first, historical reckoning touched a powerful nerve. The Oneida land claim and the expansion of its businesses provoked reactions from activists ranging from lawsuits to death threats. The twentieth-century descendants of the Oneida Community burned as much evidence as they could of their ancestors' activities, particularly their sexual ones. Syracuse's recent decisions to reroute the I-81 and to remove its Columbus statue show a willingness to confront the past, but opponents argue that these actions will do little to change it and may bring negative consequences of their own.

Central New York now enters a new phase in its history. Its long era of post-industrial decline appears to be abating. Immigrants, many of them refugees, are bringing new life into old neighborhoods. The Oneida Indian Nation of New York is now one of the region's largest employers and landowners. Hopefully, the past will continue to play a role in the present, and the future, in a way that stirs us to live up to our ideals, and to learn from—and correct, as far as is possible—the wrongs that were done in previous generations as well as our own. What happens on this land is significant to America now and to what it will be in years to come.

Notes

Introduction

1. "At a Meeting of the Commissioners for Indian Affairs & their Associates, September 4, 1784," in Franklin B. Hough, ed., *Proceedings of the Commissioners of Indian Affairs, Appointed by law for the extinguishment of Indian Titles in the State of New York*, vol. 1 (Albany: Joel Munsell, 1861), 41.

2. Hough, *Proceedings of the Commissioners*, 1:45–47.

3. The term *sacred* is one of those included on the Native American Journalists Association's "Bingo Card" (see https://najanewsroom.com/bingo-card/), a tool it publishes to help "identify reliance on tropes or stereotypes when reporting in Indian Country." I have heard and read much that speaks of the sacred significance their homeland holds for Oneida people, both historically and in the present day, some of which his presented in this book. I am grateful to Joel Barkin, vice president of communications for the Oneida Indian Nation, who confirmed to me that the use of the term here is appropriate, and indeed for his help and guidance in many other ways in preparing this book.

4. Important references on Oneida archaeology include Peter Pratt, *Archaeology of the Oneida Iroquois, Vol. 1* (George's Mills, NH: Man in the Northeast, Inc., 1976); Anthony Wonderley, *Oneida Iroquois Folklore, Myth, and History* (Syracuse: Syracuse University Press, 2004); and Eric E. Jones, "Iroquois Population History and Settlement Ecology, AD 1500–1700" (PhD diss., Pennsylvania State University, 2008).

5. See Daniel K. Richter, *The Ordeal of the Longhouse: The Peoples of the Iroquois League in the Era of European Colonization* (Chapel Hill: University of North Carolina Press, 1992), Jon Parmenter, *The Edge of the Woods: Iroquoia, 1534–1701* (East Lansing: Michigan State University Press, 2010); Barbara Graymont, *The Iroquois in the American Revolution* (Syracuse: Syracuse University Press, 1972); Joseph T. Glatthaar and James Kirby Martin, *Forgotten Allies: The Oneida Indians and the American Revolution* (New York: Hill and Wang, 2006); David J. Norton, *Rebellious Younger Brother: Oneida Leadership and Diplomacy, 1750–1800* (De Kalb, IL: Northern Illinois University Press, 2009); Jack Campisi and Laurence M. Hauptman, eds., *The*

Oneida Indian Experience: Two Perspectives (Syracuse: Syracuse University Press, 1988); Laurence M. Hauptman, *Conspiracy of Interests: Iroquois Dispossession and the Rise of New York State* (Syracuse: Syracuse University Press, 1999); Laurence Hauptman and L. Gordon McLester III, eds., *The Oneida Indian Journey: From New York to Wisconsin* (Madison, WI: University of Wisconsin Press, 1999); and Karim Tiro, *The People of the Standing Stone: The Oneida Nation from the Revolution through the Era of Removal* (Amherst: University of Massachusetts Press, 2011).

6. See Alan Taylor, *The Divided Ground: Indians, Settlers, and the Northern Borderland of the American Revolution* (New York: Alfred A. Knopf, 2006) and *William Cooper's Town: Power and Persuasion on the Frontier of the Early American Republic* (New York: Alfred A. Knopf, 1996).

7. Whitney R. Cross, *The Burned-over District: The Social and Intellectual History of Enthusiastic Religion in Western New York* (Ithaca: Cornell University Press, 1950); Mary P. Ryan, *Cradle of the Middle Class: The Family in Oneida County, New York, 1790–1865* (Cambridge: Cambridge University Press, 1981); Milton C. Sernett, *Abolition's Axe: Beriah Green, Oneida Institute, and the Black Freedom Struggle* (Syracuse: Syracuse University Press, 1986); Milton C. Sernett, *North Star County: Upstate New York and the Crusade for African American Freedom* (Syracuse, Syracuse University Press, 2002).

8. Robert Allerton Parker, *A Yankee Saint: John Humphrey Noyes and the Oneida Community* (New York: G. P. Putnam's Sons, 1935); Maren Lockwood Carden, *Oneida: Utopian Community to Modern Corporation* (New York: Harper and Row, 1969); Constance Noyes Robertson, *Oneida Community: An Autobiography, Oneida Community, 1851–1876* (Syracuse: Syracuse University Press, 1981); Constance Noyes Robertson, *Oneida Community: The Breakup, 1876–1881* (Syracuse: Syracuse University Press, 1977); Spencer Klaw, *Without Sin: The Life and Death of the Oneida Community* (New York: Viking, 1993); Robert S. Fogarty, *Special Love/Special Sex: An Oneida Community Diary* (Syracuse: Syracuse University Press, 1994); Robert S. Fogarty, *Desire and Duty at Oneida: Tirzah Miller's Intimate Diary* (Bloomington: Indiana University Press, 2000); Lawrence Foster, *Free Love in Utopia: John Humphrey Noyes and the Origin of the Oneida Community* (Urbana: University of Illinois Press, 2001); Ellen Wayland-Smith, *Oneida: From Free Love to the Well-Set Table* (New York, Picador, 2016); Anthony Wonderley, *Oneida Utopia: Searching for Human Happiness and Prosperity* (Ithaca: Cornell University Press, 2017); Michael Doyle, *The Ministers' War: John W. Mears, the Oneida Community, and the Crusade for Public Morality* (Syracuse: Syracuse University Press, 2018).

9. James S. Pula, ed., *Ethnic Utica* (Utica: Ethnic Heritage Studies Center at Utica College, 2002); Philip A. Bean, *The Urban Colonists: Italian-American Identity and Politics in Utica, New York* (Syracuse: Syracuse University Press, 2010).

10. The essential work on the early phase of the Land Claim case is by the lawyer who represented the Oneidas in their first Supreme Court hearing, George Shattuck, *The Oneida Land Claims: A Legal History* (Syracuse: Syracuse University Press, 1991).

Also see Christopher Vescey, ed., *Iroquois Land Claims* (Syracuse: Syracuse University Press, 1988). One German-language book covers the Oneida land claim up to 2017, Harry Schüler, *Oneida Roulette: Irokesische Landruckforderungen Im Inter- Und Intra-Ethnischen Beziehungsgefuge* (Wiesbaden, Springer VS, 2018). On the rustbelt era, see Alexander R. Thomas, *In Gotham's Shadow: Globalization and Community Change in Central New York* (Albany: State University of New York Press, 2003).

11. William F. Galpin, *Central New York: An Inland Empire, comprising Oneida, Madison, Onondaga, Cayuga, Tompkins, Cortland, Chenango Counties and Their People*, 4 vols. (New York: Lewis Historical Publishing Co., 1941); Nelson Green, *History of the Mohawk Valley: Gateway to the West, 1614–1925, Covering the Six Counties of Schenectady, Schoharie, Montgomery, Fulton, Herkimer and Oneida*, 4 vols. (Chicago: S. J. Clarke, 1925); Harry F. Landon, *The North Country; A History, embracing Jefferson, St. Lawrence, Oswego, Lewis and Franklin Counties, New York*, 3 vols. (Indianapolis: Historical Publishing Company, 1932).

12. L. M. Hammond, *History of Madison County, State of New York* (Syracuse: Truair, Smith & Co., 1872), 101–103.

Chapter 1

1. Robert S. Feranec and Andrew L. Kozlowski, "Implications of a Bayesian Radiocarbon Calibration of Colonization Ages for Mammalian Megafauna in Glaciated New York State after the Last Glacial Maximum," *Quaternary Research* 85, no. 2 (2016): 262–270. The findings in this article are summarized by the same authors for non-specialist readers in *Ice Age Mammals Colonize New York: A STEM Lab Derived from Collections-Based Research at the New York State Museum*, New York State Museum Education Leaflet 37 (Albany: New York State Museum, 2017).

2. William A. Ritchie, *The Archaeology of New York State*, 2nd ed. (Garden City, NY: Natural History Press, 1969), 1–6; Jonathan C. Lothrop et al., "Current Archaeological Research on Paleoindian Sites in Central New York," in Eugene Domack, ed., *Oneida Basin, Glacial Lake Iroquois and Archaeological Contexts*, Guidebook for 79th Annual Reunion of the Northeastern Friends of the Pleistocene Field Conference, June 3–5, 2016.

3. Jonathan C. Lothrop et al., "Early Human Settlement of Northeastern North America," *PaleoAmerica* 2, no. 3 (2016): 192–251, DOI: 10.1080/20555 563.2016.1212178.

4. Francis P. McManamon, ed., *Archaeology in America: An Encyclopedia*, vol. 1 (Westport, CT: Greenwood Publishing Group, 2009), 53–55; Ritchie, *The Archaeology of New York State*, 36–40, 87–103.

5. Ritchie, *The Archaeology of New York State*, xxx–xxxi, 38–39, 157, 181, 207, 258–259. Dean Snow suggests that the White site may have been an early Owasco site from about 992 CE in *The Iroquois* (Cambridge, MA: Blackwell, 1994), 17.

6. McMahon, *Archaeology in America*, 1:53–55.

7. Snow, *The Iroquois*, 10–20; Engelbrecht, *Iroquoia*, 112. Recently, some archaeologists have disputed Ritchie's findings at the Owasco sites and their link to the origins of the Iroquois as well. See John P. Hart and Hetty Jo Brumbach, "The Death of Owasco," *American Antiquity* 68, no. 4 (2003): 737–752.

8. Snow, *The Iroquois*, 27–30, 35, 40–41; Ritchie, *The Archaeology of New York State*, 305; James A. Tuck, *Onondaga Iroquois Prehistory: A Study in Settlement Archaeology* (Syracuse: Syracuse University Press, 1971), 47–92.

9. Snow, *The Iroquois*, 46–49. Also see Robert E. Funk and Robert D. Kuhn, "Three Sixteenth-Century Mohawk Iroquois Village Sites," *New York State Museum Bulletin* 503 (2003), and Dean R. Snow, "Mohawk Valley Archaeology: The Sites," *Occasional Papers in Anthropology* 23 (2005).

10. Peter Pratt, *Archaeology of the Oneida Iroquois* (n.p., n.d.), 90–91; Snow, *The Iroquois*, 47

11. Eric E. Jones, "Using Viewshed Analysis to Explore Settlement Choice: A Case Study of the Onondaga Iroquois," *American Antiquity* 71, no. 3 (2006): 523–538; James W. Bradley, *Evolution of the Onondaga Iroquois: Accommodating Change, 1500–1655* (Lincoln, NE: University of Nebraska Press, 2005), 34–37.

12. Pratt, *Archaeology of the Oneida Iroquois*, 93–100, 107; Theodore Whitney, "The Buyea Site," *Bulletin of the New York State Archaeological Association* 50 (1970): 1–13; Eric E. Jones, "Population History of the Onondaga and Oneida Iroquois, A.D. 1500–1700," *American Antiquity* 75, no. 2 (2010), 397; Tuck, *Onondaga Iroquois*, 16; Anthony Wonderley, *Oneida Iroquois Folklore, Myth, and History* (Syracuse: Syracuse University Press, 2004), 5–6.

13. Wonderley, *Oneida Iroquois*, 1–4, 6, 24–31, 220.

14. Jones, "Population History," 401, 403; Anthony Wonderley and Martha L. Sempowski, *Origins of the Iroquois League: Narratives, Symbols, and Archaeology* (Syracuse: Syracuse University Press, 2019), 3.

15. Wonderley, *Oneida Iroquois*, 8, 135.

16. Guides to prehistoric Iroquois material culture include Ritchie, *Archaeology of New York State*; Pratt, *Archaeology of the Oneida Iroquois*; Wonderley, *Oneida Iroquois*; Funk and Kuhn, "Three Sixteenth-Century Mohawk Iroquois Village Sites"; Snow, "Mohawk Valley Archaeology: The Sites"; Tuck, *Onondaga Iroquois Prehistory*; Bradley, *Evolution of the Onondaga Iroquois*; William Englebrecht, *Iroquoia: The Development of a Native World* (Syracuse: Syracuse University Press), 2005. These studies use archaeological evidence to supplement descriptions from a range of earlier works going back to Lewis Henry Morgan's pioneering *League of the Ho-de-no-sau-nee, or Iroquois* (1851).

17. Pratt, *Archaeology of the Oneida Iroquois*, 12–13.

18. Snow, *The Iroquois*, 55–57; Pratt, *Archaeology of the Oneida Iroquois*, 12.

19. Daniel K. Richter, *The Ordeal of the Longhouse: The Peoples of the Iroquois League in the Era of European Colonization* (Chapel Hill: University of North Carolina

Press, 1992), 31–32, 39, 300 305. Also see Snow, *The Iroquois*, 57–60. Anthony Wonderley and Martha Sempowski's *Origins of the Iroquois League* (2019) provides the fullest and most recent summary of the formation of the League.

20. Wonderley, *Oneida Iroquois Folklore, Myth and History*, 57–84; Richter, *Ordeal of the Longhouse*, 8–10; Snow, *The Iroquois*, 2–4.

21. Samuel de Champlain, *Voyages of Samuel de Champlain, 1604–1618*, W. L. Grant, ed. (New York: Charles Scribner's Sons, 1907), 289–292.

22. Champlain, *Voyages*, 289–92.

23. Champlain, *Voyages*, 293–296.

24. Pratt, *Archaeology of the Oneida Iroquois*, viii–ix, 87–92, 148–151.

25. Champlain, *Voyages*, 292–293; David Hackett Fischer, *Champlain's Dream* (New York: Simon & Schuster, 2008), 330; Jones, "Population History," 389, 395, 397.

26. Champlain, *Voyages*, 292. The French original is in Champlain, *Voyages et descouvertures faites en la Nouvelle France, depuis l'année 1615, jusques à la fin de l'année 1618* (Paris: Claude Collet, 1618), 40. On site sequence, see Jones, "Population History" and "Using Viewshed Analysis." On the Cameron site, see Pratt, *Archaeology of the Oneida Iroquois*, 121–123. On the Pompey Center site, see Tuck, *Onondaga Iroquois Prehistory*, 176, and Bradley, *Evolution of the Onondaga Iroquois*, 133, 158. On the signage at Nichols Pond site, see J. T. Hall, "History Tested," *Syracuse New Times*, November 4, 2015, 10–11.

27. Champlain, *Voyages*, 165–166, 181–184, 276, 286; Fischer, *Champlain's Dream*, 145–147.

28. Fischer, *Champlain's Dream*, 117, 121, 152, 275, 310.

29. Champlain, *Voyages*, 276, 286; Fischer, *Champlain's Dream*, 322.

30. Samuel Eliot Morrison, *The European Discovery of America: The Northern Voyages, A.D. 500–1600* (Oxford: Oxford University Press, 1971), 224, 228; Eric J. Dolan, *Fur, Fortune, and Empire: The Epic History of the Fur Trade in America* (New York: W.W. Norton, 2010), 10–11; Snow, *The Iroquois*, 77–78; Richter, *Ordeal of the Longhouse*, 52.

31. Giovanni da Verrazano, *Verrazano's Voyage Along the Atlantic Coast of North America, 1524* (Albany: State University of New York, 1916), 8–12.

32. Bruce Trigger, *The Children of Aataentsic: A History of the Huron People to 1660* (Kingston, ON: McGill-Queen's University Press, 1987), 177–208, 214–224.

33. Richter, *Ordeal of the Longhouse*, 54–55.

34. Harmen Meyndertsz van den Bogaert, *A Journey Into Mohawk and Oneida Country, 1634–1635*, Charles T. Gehring and William A. Starna, trans. and eds. (Syracuse: Syracuse University Press, 1988), xix–xx, 1; Richter, *Ordeal of the Longhouse*, 56.

35. Van den Bogaert, *Journey*, 6–11, 19–20.

36. Pratt, *Archaeology of the Oneida Iroquois*, 37.

37. Van den Bogaert, *Journey*, 12–13.

38. Van den Bogaert, *Journey*, 13–14.

39. Lynn Ceci, "The Value of Wampum among the New York Iroquois: A Case Study in Artifact Analysis." *Journal of Anthropological Research* 38, no. 1 (1982): 97–107.

40. Van den Bogaert, *Journey*, 15–16.

41. Van den Bogaert, *Journey*, 12–13.

42. Gehring and Starna, "Introduction" in Van den Bogaerts, *Journey*, xxi–xxii.

Chapter 2

1. Cary F. Goulson, ed., *Seventeenth-Century Canada: Source Studies* (Toronto: Macmillan of Canada, 1970), 207–209, 219–224.

2. "Relation of what occurred in the Mission of the Fathers of the Society of Jesus, in the country of New France, From the Summer of the year 1653 to the Summer of the year 1654," in Reuben Gold Thwaites, ed., *The Jesuit Relations and Allied Documents*, vol. LXI (Cleveland: The Burrows Brothers, 1898), 32–43.

3. Thwaites, *Jesuit Relations*, LXI:72, 215–232; LXII:97, 123–124. Entries on Pierre-Joseph-Marie Chaumonot and Claude Dablon in George W. Brown et al., eds., *Dictionary of Canadian Biography*, vol. 1 (Toronto: University of Toronto & Université Laval, 1966), 205–207, 244; Richter, *The Ordeal of the Longhouse*, 108.

4. Thwaites, *Jesuit Relations*, LXII:12, 200–217; James W. Bradley, *Onondaga and Empire: An Iroquoian People in an Imperial Era*, New York State Museum Bulletin, no. 514 (Albany: State University of New York, 2020), 142; Jon Parmenter, *The Edge of the Woods: Iroquoia, 1534–1701* (East Lansing: Michigan State University Press, 2010); Bronwen McShea, *Apostles of Empire: The Jesuits and New France* (Lincoln: University of Nebraska Press, 2019).

5. Thwaites, *Jesuit Relations*, XLIII:62–280; "On the Preaching of the Faith to the Onneiouthronnon Iroquois," XLIV:28–32.

6. Thwaites, *Jesuit Relations*, XLIV:192–194.

7. Thwaites, *Jesuit Relations*, XLIV:205.

8. Richter, *Ordeal of the Longhouse*, 107–108, 109–111.

9. Thwaites, *Jesuit Relations*, XLIV:212–216; Bradley, *Onondaga and Empire*, 150–151.

10. Thwaites, *Jesuit Relations*, LI:123, 221–222.

11. Thwaites, *Jesuit Relations*, XLIV:223–224.

12. Thwaites, *Jesuit Relations*, XLV:204–205.

13. Thwaites, *Jesuit Relations*, XLVII:69–70, 174–177, 204–208.

14. Thwaites, *Jesuit Relations*, "Cruelties Practiced upon Some Frenchman Captured by the Iroquois in the Year 1662," L:55–67. Quoted pp. 59, 63.

15. E. B. O'Callaghan, ed., *Documents Relative to the Colonial History of New York*, vol. 3 (Albany: Weed, Parsons and Company, 1855), 250.

16. Dean R. Snow, Charles T. Gehring, and William A. Starna, eds., *In Mohawk Country: Early Narratives about a Native People* (Syracuse: Syracuse University Press, 1996), 188.

17. Jaap Jacobs, *New Netherland: A Dutch Colony in Seventeenth-Century America* (Leiden and Boston: Brill, 2005), 178–186; Tom Lewis, *The Hudson: A History* (New Haven: Yale University Press, 2005), 95–99.

18. Thwaites, *Jesuit Relations*, XLVII:216–217; L:209–210.

19. Thwaites, *Jesuit Relations*, LI:121–127, 232–232; LII:147–148; LIII:239–240.

20. Thwaites, *Jesuit Relations*, LIII:245–248, 251–252, 255–256.

21. Monte Bennett, "Glass Trade Beads from Central New York," in *Proceedings of the 1982 Glass Trade Bead Conference*, Research Records no. 16, ed. Charles F. Hayes (Rochester: Rochester Museum and Science Center, 1983), 57; Jones, "Population History," 396–397. Also see Eric E. Jones, "Iroquois Population History and Settlement Ecology, AD 1500–1700" (PhD diss., Pennsylvania State University, 2008), 291–293.

22. Thwaites, *Jesuit Relations*, LVI:33–34, 39–44; Bradley, *Onondaga and Empire*, 298.

23. Richter, *Ordeal of the Longhouse*, 119–120.

24. Thwaites, *Jesuit Relations*, LVII:111–125; LVIII:199–204.

25. Thwaites, *Jesuit Relations*, LVIX:239–240; LVX:181–182.

26. Pierre Millet, "Letter of Father Millet to Some Missionaries in Canada," in Thwaites, *Jesuit Relations*, LXIV:65–89.

27. Francis Jennings, *The Ambiguous Iroquois Empire: The Covenant Chain Confederation of Indian Tribes with English Colonies* (New York: W.W. Norton, 1984), 148–149; Bradley, *Onondaga and Empire*, 366–369, 372–373; Parmenter, "After the Mourning Wars: The Iroquois as Allies in Colonial North American Campaigns, 1676–1760," *The William and Mary Quarterly* 64, no. 1 (2007): 39–76.

28. Bradley, *Onondaga and Empire*, 373–374, 379–380, 387–389; Parmenter, "After the Mourning Wars," 45–47.

29. Thwaites, *Jesuit Relations*, VLXIV:87–106.

30. "His Excellency sent for the Sachims of the Five Nations to have a private conference & sayd, 4th July 1693," and "Major Peter Schuyler's Answer to the Five Nations, 3rd February 1694," in E. B. O'Callaghan, *Documents Relative to the Colonial History of New York*, 4:44, 88.

31. Thwaites, *Jesuit Relations*, LXIV:257–258.

32. "Count de Frontenac to Louis XIV, 1696," in E. B. O'Callaghan, *Documents Relative to the Colonial History of New York*, 9:639–640.

33. Chronicle attributed to Charles de Monseignat, "Relation de ce qui s'est passé de plus remarquable en Canada depuis le depart des vaisseaux de lannée derniere 1695 jusqu'au commencement de Novembre 1696," MS Can 35.4. Houghton Library, Harvard University, Cambridge, MA. Two different translations appear in O'Callaghan's documentary histories. The translation used here is in *The*

Documentary History of the State of New York, vol. 1 (Albany: Weed, Parsons & Co., 1849), 331–334. Also see *Documents Relative to the Colonial History of New York*, 9:653–654.

34. O'Callaghan, *The Documentary History of the State of New York*, 1:336, 338.

35. "Observations made by Robert Livingston Secretary for the Indian Affairs in his voyage to Onnondage in April 1700," in O'Callaghan, *Documents Relative to the Colonial History of New York*, 4:648; Bradley, *Onondaga and Empire*, 480–486, 492.

36. Jones, "Population History," 396; Jones, *Iroquois Population History*, 292–293; Richard Cole and Monte Bennett, "The Upper Hogan Site OND 5-4," *NYSAA Chenango Chapter Bulletin*, 15(2), 1974.

37. "Observations made by Robert Livingston Secretary for the Indian Affairs in his voyage to Onnondage in April 1700," in O'Callaghan, *Documents Relative to the Colonial History of New York*, 4:648–652.

38. "Journal of Capt. Johannes Bleeker Junior and Mr. David Schuyler's Journey to Onondage being sent thither by the Commissioners for the managing the Indian affairs, Albany 2nd June 1701," in O'Callaghan, *Documents Relative to the Colonial History of New York*, 4:890.

39. "Conference of Governor Hunter with the Indians, 1710," in O'Callaghan, *Documents Relative to the Colonial History of New York*, 5: 218, 220.

40. G. M. Waller, "New York's Role in Queen Anne's War, 1702–1713," *New York History* 33, no. 1 (1952), 40–53.

41. "Propositions made by ye sachims of Oneyde to his Excelly Robert Hunter . . . in Albany, 20 August 1710' in O'Callaghan, *Documents Relative to the Colonial History of New York*, 5:226–227.

42. Greg Rogers, "Petite Politique: The British, French, Iroquois, and Everyday Power in the Lake Ontario Borderlands, 1724–1760" (PhD diss., University of Maine, 2016), 32.

43. Dale Miquelon, "Ambiguous Concession: What Diplomatic Archives Reveal about Article 15 of the Treaty of Utrecht and France's North American Policy," *The William and Mary Quarterly* 67, no. 3 (2010): 459–486; Rogers, *Petite Politique*, 37.

44. Frank J. Klingberg, "The Noble Savage as Seen by the Missionary of the Society for the Propagation of the Gospel in Colonial New York, 1702–1750," *Historical Magazine of the Protestant Episcopal Church* 8, no. 2 (1939): 128–165.

45. Cynthia G. Falk, "Forts, Rum, Slaves, and the Herkimers' Rise to Power in the Mohawk Valley," *New York History* 89, no. 3 (2008): 221–234, 224; Philip Otterness, *Becoming German: The 1709 Palatine Migration to New York* (Ithaca: Cornell University Press, 2004).

46. Fintan O'Toole, *White Savage: William Johnson and the Invention of America* (London: Faber & Faber, 2005), 36–37, 41–44, 52–57.

47. "Answer made by the Six Nations . . . to His Excellency William Burnet Esq., 17 September 1724," in O'Callaghan, *Documents Relative to the Colonial*

History of New York, 5:717; Rogers, *Petite Politique*, 31, 41; Parmenter, *Edge of the Woods*, 74–75.

48. Klingberg, "Noble Savage," 161–162; Ernest Hawkins, *Historical Notices of the Church of England in the North American Colonies Previous to the Independence of the United States* (London: B. Fellowes, 1845), 290.

49. Harold William Blodgett, *Samson Occom* (Hanover, NH: Dartmouth College Publications, 1935), 54.

50. Monte R. Bennett, "The Primes Hill Site, MSV 5-2, An Eighteenth-Century Oneida Station," *NYSAA Chenango Chapter* 22, no. 4 (1988): 1–20, 4; O'Toole, *White Savage*, 51–55.

51. Richter, *Ordeal of the Longhouse*, 238–241; Jennings, *Ambiguous Iroquois Empire*, 288–290; Anthony F. C. Wallace, *The Tuscarora: A History* (Albany: State University of New York Press, 2012), 67–75.

52. Parmenter, "After the Mourning Wars," 57–62; Rogers, *Petite Politique*, 90–95; Daniel P. Barr, *Unconquered: The Iroquois League at War in Colonial America* (Westport, CT: Praeger, 2006), 114–116; Richard Berleth, *Bloody Mohawk: The French and Indian War and the American Revolution on New York's Frontier* (Hensonville, NY: Black Dome, 2010), 32; Samuel G. Drake, *A Particular History of the Five Years French and Indian War* (Albany: Joel Munsell, 1870), 98, 148.

53. Rogers, *Petite Politique*, 127, 129, 149, 151–154, 163; D. Peter MacLeod, *The Iroquois of Canada and the Seven Years' War* (Toronto: Dundurn Press, 1996), x–xi.

54. Barr, *Unconquered*, 117–122.

55. Frank Hayward Severance, *An Old Frontier of France: The Niagara Region and Adjacent Lakes under French Control*, 2 vols. (New York: Dodd, Mead and Company, 1917), 2:170; Rogers, *Petite Politique*, 169, 175–176.

56. "At a Meeting held at Burnetsfield July 7th, 1761," in *The Papers of Sir William Johnson*, James Sullivan, ed. (Albany: University of the State of New York, 1921), 3:432.

57. "Journal of Occurrences in Canada from October 1755 to June 1756, Capture of Fort Bull by M. De Léry, 1756," in O'Callaghan, *Documents Relative to the Colonial History of the State of New York*, 10:403; Jean-Claude Castex, *Dictionnaire des batailles terrestres franco-anglaises de la Guerre de Sept Ans* (Laval, QC: Les presses de l'Université Laval, 2006), 132.

58. Société Littéraire et Historique de Québec, *Mémoires sur le Canada, depuis 1749 jusqu'à 1760* (Quebec: T. Cary & Cie., 1838), 70–71; MacLeod, *Canadian Iroquois*, 23; Castex, *Dictionnaire des batailles terrestres*, 132.

59. "Capture of Fort Bull by M. De Léry, 1756," in O'Callaghan, *Documents Relative to the Colonial History of the State of New York*, 10:403–406.

60. O'Callaghan, *Documents Relative to the Colonial History of the State of New York*, 1:514–515, 10:405; MacLeod, *Canadian Iroquois*, 31–33; Castex, *Dictionnaire des batailles terrestres*, 131–133; Gilbert Hagerty, *Massacre at Fort Bull: The De Léry Expedition against Oneida Carry, 1756* (Providence, RI: Mowbray, 1971).

61. Parmenter, "After the Mourning Wars," 68.

62. David L. Preston, "'We Intend to Live Our Lifetime Together as Brothers': Palatine and Iroquois Communities in the Mohawk Valley," *New York History* 89, no. 2 (2008): 179–189.

63. "Summary of M. de Belletre's Expedition, the 28th November, 1757," in O'Callaghan, *The Documentary History of the State of New York*, 1:516–519; Castex, *Dictionnaire des batailles terrestres*, 231–233.

64. George Croghan, "A Summary of the Conduct of the Oneida Indians (Living at the Upper Town) Previous to the Attack of the French and their Indians upon the North Side of the German Flats, in the Province of New-York, in November, 1757," in O'Callaghan, *The Documentary History of the State of New York*, 1: 520–522.

65. Parmenter, "After the Mourning Wars," 70–71; Preston, "We Intend to Live Our Lifetime Together as Brothers," 182–184, 185; Karim Tiro, *The People of the Standing Stone: The Oneida Nation from the Revolution through the Era of Removal* (Amherst: University of Massachusetts Press, 2011), 22.

66. "Extract of a Letter from Albany, dated the 13th instant, being a relation of the murder committed at the German Flatts, near Fort Herchamer, by 80 Indians and 4 Frenchmen, *N. Y. Mercury*, May 22, 1758," in O'Callaghan, *The Documentary History of the State of New York*, 1:522–523; Nathaniel Soley Benton, *A History of Herkimer County* (Albany: J. Munsell, 1856), 58–59.

67. Parmenter, "After the Mourning Wars," 73–76; Barr, *Unconquered*, 126–129.

Chapter 3

1. "At a Meeting held at Burnetsfield July 7th, 1761," in Sullivan, *Papers of Sir William Johnson*, 3:432; Daniel R. Mandell, "'Turned Their Mind to Religion': Oquaga and the First Iroquois Church, 1748–1776," *Early American Studies* 11:2 (2013), 236.

2. Barr, *Unconquered*, 132–136.

3. Alan Taylor, *The Divided Ground: Indians, Settlers, and the Northern Borderland of the American Revolution* (New York: Alfred A. Knopf, 2006), 40–45.

4. Ruth L. Higgins, *Expansion in New York: With Especial Reference to the Eighteenth Century* (Columbus: Ohio State University, 1932), 29–32.

5. Higgins, *Expansion in New York*, 58–59; Samuel W. Durant, *History of Oneida County, New York* (Philadelphia: Everts & Fariss, 1878), 53–54.

6. Higgins, *Expansion in New York*, 56–69; Durant, *History of Oneida County*, 55–56.

7. Michael Berleth, *Bloody Mohawk* (Hensonville, NY: Black Dome, 2010), 21, 31–32, 100–101,144; Taylor, *Divided Ground*, 38–40, 48, 69–70; O'Toole, *White Savage*, 163–176.

8. "Johnson to Goldsbrow Banyar, November 24, 1768," in Sullivan, *Papers of Sir William Johnson*, 12:657; Hough, *Proceedings*, 1:237.

9. Silverman, *Red Brethren: The Brothertown and Stockbridge Indians and the Problem of Race in Early America* (Ithaca: Cornell University Press, 2010), 91–92.

10. "Johnson to Banyar, November 24, 1768," in Sullivan, *Papers of Sir William Johnson*, 12:659; Hough, *Proceedings of the Commissioners*, 1:45.

11. "Johnson to Banyar, November 24, 1768," "Henry Moore to William Johnson, November 13, 1768, "Johnson to Banyar, February 10, 1769," in Sullivan, *Papers of Sir William Johnson*, 12:658, 637, 697; Durant, *History of Oneida County*, 59–61.

12. Durant, *History of Oneida County*, 59.

13. Richter, *Ordeal of the Longhouse*, 257, 260.

14. Mandell, "Turned Their Minds to Religion," 212–217; Glatthaar and Martin, *Forgotten Allies*, 49; Tiro, *The People of the Standing Stone*, 16–17.

15. Pratt, *Archaeology of the Oneida Iroquois*, 8.

16. Glatthaar and Martin, *Forgotten Allies*, 49, 55–56; Richter, *Ordeal of the Longhouse*, 257; Taylor, *Divided Ground*, 55–56; Tiro, *People of the Standing Stone*, 16–17.

17. I have used the spellings of the corresponding villages of Canastota and Canaseraga Creek in use today. The two Tuscarora villages are labelled in a 1756 British map, "A colored map of the route between Albany and Oswego; drawn about 1756, on a scale of 2 miles to an inch," British Library, Cartographic Items Maps K.Top. 121.13. Various spellings are used in documents from the period. See Durant, *History of Oneida County*, 570; L. M. Hammond, *History of Madison County, State of New York* (Syracuse: Truair, Smith & Co., 1872), 575.

18. John Hall and Mary Ann Hall, *History of the Presbyterian Church in Trenton, N.J.* (Trenton, NJ: MacCrellish & Quigley, 1912), 127; Glatthaar and Martin, *Forgotten Allies*, 89, 16.

19. Mandell, "Turned Their Minds to Religion," 211–242.

20. Harold Blodgett, *Samson Occom* (Hanover, NH: Dartmouth College Publications, 1935), 54.

21. Blodgett, *Samson Occom*, 61–67.

22. Samuel Kirkland Lothrop, *Life of Samuel Kirkland, Missionary to the Indians* (Boston: Charles C. Little and James Brown, 1848), 143, 146–150.

23. Glatthaar and Martin, *Forgotten Allies*, 57–65; Taylor, *Divided Ground*, 66–68; Samuel Kirkland, *The Journals of Samuel Kirkland: 18th Century Missionary to the Iroquois, Government Agent, Father of Hamilton College* (Clinton, NY: Hamilton College, 1980); Hauptman and McLester III, *The Oneida Indian Journey*, 23.

24. Silverman, *Red Brethren*, 94; Glatthaar and Martin, *Forgotten Allies*, 70–72, 76–78; Taylor, *Divided Ground*, 67–68.

25. Berleth, *Bloody Mohawk*, 148, 169; Glatthaar and Martin, *Forgotten Allies*, 84–85.

26. David Levinson, "An Explanation for the Oneida-Colonist Alliance in the American Revolution," *Ethnohistory* 23, no. 3 (1976): 265–289; Preston, "We Intend to Live our Lifetime Together as Brothers," 187–188.

27. Berleth, *Bloody Mohawk*, 169.

28. Taylor, *Divided Ground*, 78; David J. Norton, *Rebellious Younger Brother: Oneida Leadership and Diplomacy, 1750–1800* (De Kalb, IL: Northern Illinois University Press, 2009).

29. Glatthaar and Martin, *Forgotten Allies*, 87–88, 96–97. Quote from "A Speech of the Chiefs and Warriors of the Oneida Tribe of Indians, to the four New-England Provinces, directed to Governur Trumbull, June 19, 1775" in Peter Force, ed., *American Archives: Consisting of authentick records, state papers, debates, and letters and other notices of publick affairs* (Washington, D.C.: U.S. Congress, 1837–53), ser. 4, vol. 2, 1117.

30. Glatthaar and Martin, *Forgotten Allies*, 108–112, 120–122, 126–129, 135; Taylor, *Divided Ground*, 82–86, 90–91; Barbara Graymont, *The Iroquois in the American Revolution* (Syracuse: Syracuse University Press, 1972), 86–110.

31. Glatthaar and Martin, *Forgotten Allies*, 137–138, 141–142, 145–146, 149; Graymont, *Iroquois in the American Revolution*, 115–116.

32. Graymont, *Iroquois in the American Revolution*, 117–118; Glatthaar and Martin, *Forgotten Allies*, 147–148, 158.

33. Glatthaar and Martin, *Forgotten Allies*, 152–160, 168–176; Berleth, *Bloody Mohawk*, 228–237, 242–243; Tiro, *People of the Standing Stone*, 48–49.

34. Berleth, *Bloody Mohawk*, 242–243.

35. Glatthaar and Martin, *Forgotten Allies*, 179–180.

36. Glatthaar and Martin, *Forgotten Allies*, 193–216; Graymont, *Iroquois in the American Revolution*, 163–164; Taylor, *Divided Ground*, 206.

37. Graymont, *Iroquois in the American Revolution*, 165–166, 175, 178–182, 185–190; Glatthaar and Martin, *Forgotten Allies*, 225–237. The fortification, sometimes called Fort Van Dyke, can be seen on the map by John Randel, Jr., "Plan of a Village at Oneida Castle, in Vernon in the County of Oneida. Laid out pursuant to instructions from the Surveyor General in November, 1813," in the New York State Archives, New York State Engineer and Surveyor, Survey maps of lands in New York State, ca. 1711–1913, Series A0273-78, Map #131B. There is no remaining structure, but the earthworks are still discernible. It is in a privately-owned wooded area with no signpost or historical marker.

38. Glatthaar and Martin, *Forgotten Allies*, 240, 242–243, 250; Tiro, *People of the Standing Stone*, 53–55.

39. Glatthaar and Martin, *Forgotten Allies*, 258–269; Tiro, *People of the Standing Stone*, 56–57.

40. Glatthaar and Martin, *Forgotten* Allies, 270–274; Tiro, *People of the Standing Stone*, 57–59.

41. Glatthaar and Martin, *Forgotten Allies*, 277–281, 284, 287–288.

42. "George Washington to Chastellux, 12 October 1783," in *The Writings of George Washington*, ed. Worthington Chauncey Ford, vol. 10 (New York: G.P. Putnam's Sons, 1891), 324–325. Quote from Berleth, *Bloody Mohawk*, 15.

43. Anthony Wonderley, "'Good Peter's Narrative of Several Transactions Respecting Indian Lands': An Oneida View of Dispossession, 1785–1788," *New York History* 84, no. 3 (2003): 244; Taylor, *Divided Ground*, 155.

44. "Peter Rykman to George Clinton, 23 August 1784" and "Jellis Fonda to George Clinton, 31 August 1784," in Hough, *Proceedings of the Commissioners*, 1:33, 35.

45. "The Commissioners met . . . , September 2, 1784," in Hough, *Proceedings of the Commissioners*, 1:39.

46. Taylor, *Divided Ground*, 158.

47. Taylor, *Divided Ground*, 158–160; Glatthaar and Martin, *Forgotten Allies*, 296–298.

48. Henry S. Manley, *The Treaty of Fort Stanwix, 1784* (Rome, NY: Rome Sentinel Company, 1932), 92–93.

49. Glatthaar and Martin, *Forgotten Allies*, 300–305; Taylor, *Divided Ground*, 145–146.

Chapter 4

1. Higgins, *Expansion in New York*, 105; Wonderley, "Good Peter's Narrative," 246; "At a Meeting of the Commissioners for Indian Affairs at the City of Albany, May 1785," in Hough, *Proceedings of the Commissioners*, 1:74–75. On the 1767 attempt see Sullivan, *Papers of Sir William Johnson*, 12:259.

2. Hough, *Proceedings of the Commissioners*, 1:73–75.

3. Wonderley, "Good Peter's Narrative," 246, 250.

4. Wonderley, "Good Peter's Narrative," 253; Taylor, *Divided Ground*, 163–165.

5. Wonderley, "Good Peter's Narrative," 257–259.

6. Wonderley, "Good Peter's Narrative," 258; Taylor, *Divided Ground*, 172–173.

7. "State Treaty with the Oneida Indians, 1788," in J. S. Whipple et al., *Report of the Special Committee to Investigate the Indian Problem of the State of New York, Appointed by the Assembly of 1888*, vol. 1 (Albany: Troy Press Company, 1889), 237–241; Wonderley, "Good Peter's Narrative," 261.

8. "State Treaty with the Oneida Indians, 1788," 1:237–241; Anthony Wonderley, "Chief Warriors, Pagan Priests, and Witch Killers: The Division of the Oneida Iroquois, 1789–1805," *New York History* 93, no. 2 (2012): 121–145, 127; Higgins, *Expansion in New York*, 105.

9. Wonderley, "Good Peter's Narrative," 271.

10. Laurence M. Hauptman, *Conspiracy of Interests: Iroquois Dispossession and the Rise of New York State* (Syracuse: Syracuse University Press, 1999), 70–73; Wonderley, "Good Peter's Narrative," 258, 263–264, 268–269; Taylor, *Divided Ground*, 172–173, 182–184, 217; Tiro, *People of the Standing Stone*, 78–84; J. David Lehman, "The End of the Iroquois Mystique: The Oneida Land Cession Treaties of the 1780s," *The William and Mary Quarterly* 47, no. 4 (1990), 544–546; Karim Tiro, "James Dean in Iroquoia," *New York History* 80, no. 4 (1999), 412–422.

11. Taylor, *Divided Ground*, 214–224.

12. Blodgett, *Samson Occom*, 162, 171, 185–188, 191, 206.

13. Blodgett, *Samson Occom*, 189, 195, 206–207, 211; Samuel Kirkland, *The Journals of Samuel Kirkland*, ed. Walter Pilkington (Clinton, NY: Hamilton College, 1980), 222–223.

14. Silverman, *Red Brethren*, 36–37, 75, 118–119; Lester G. Wells, "The Stockbridge Indians in New York State," *New York History* 27, no. 4 (1946), 476, 478.

15. Whipple et al., *Report of the Special Committee*, 1:278

16. Wells, "The Stockbridge Indians in New York State," 482–483, 479.

17. Census Office, *1st Census, 1790: Return of the Whole Number of Persons within the Several Districts of the United States* (Philadelphia: Childs and Swaine, 1793), 3.

18. Higgins, *Expansion in New York*, 102.

19. John Lincklaen, *Travels in the Years 1791 and 1792 in Pennsylvania, New York, and Vermont* (New York: G.P. Putnam's Sons, 1897), 67, 103; Higgins, *Expansion in New York*, 140–141; Durant, *History of Oneida County*, 59, 536; Pomroy Jones, *Annals and Recollections of Oneida County* (Rome, NY: Published by the author, 1851), 116, 439–441.

20. Higgins, *Expansion in New York*, 102–109.

21. Taylor, *Divided Ground*, 180; "On the 4th of September [1788] . . ." and "At a Treaty held at Fort Schuyler . . . with the Tribe or Nation of Indians called the Onondagoes . . . on the twelfth Day of September, in the Year one thousand seven hundred and eighty eight," in Hough, *Proceedings of the Commissioners*, 1:180–181, 198–201.

22. Taylor, *Divided Ground*, 189.

23. Higgins, *Expansion in New York*, 104–106.

24. Hauptman, *Conspiracy of Interests*, 78.

25. Harry F. Landon, *The North Country: A History, Embracing Jefferson, St. Lawrence, Oswego, Lewis and Franklin Counties, New York*, Vol. 1 (Indianapolis: Historical Publishing Company, 1932), 96–101; Simon Desjardins and Pierre Pharoux, *Castorland Journal: An Account of the Exploration and Settlement of Northern New York State by French Émigrés in the Years 1793–1797*, ed. and trans. John A. Galucci (Ithaca: Cornell University Press, 2010).

26. Higgins, *Expansion in New York*, p. 142–148; Harry F. Landon, *The North Country*, 1:88–89.

27. Landon, *The North Country*, 1:93–96; John C. Churchill, ed., *Landmarks of Oswego County* (Syracuse: D. Mason and Company, 1895), 490–491; Bob Peel, "Frenchman's Love Story," *Syracuse Herald American*, March 23, 1980; Desjardins and Pharoux, *Castorland Journal*, 26–27, 53–56.

28. Joachim Heinrich Campe, "Reise eines Deutschen nach dem See Oneida," *Sammtliche Kinder- und Jugend schriften von Joachim Heinrich Campe*, vol. 29–30 (Braunschweig: Schulbuchhandlung, 1830), 136; translation mine. The original German reads:

> Gegen uns über zeigte sich im See eine mit Bäumen und Gebüsch) wohlbewachsene Insel, auf welcher das Auge mit Wohlgefallen ruhete. Plötzlich sah ich von der Seite her, wo die Bäume dichter standen, einen stattlichen, großen und feinten jungen Mann mit einer schönen, ganz Europäisch und recht geschmactvoll gekleideten jungen Frau, die einen niedlichen, etwa drei-jährigen Knaben an der Sand hatte, auf uns zukommen. Vandek las die Verwunderung und Neugier, die dieser Unblick bei mir erregte, auf meinem Gesichte, und sagte, indem er die Ankommenden mir vorstellte, lächelnd: Herr und Frau von Wattines aus Flandern; jetzt unsere Mitbürger am Oneidasee!
>
> Es hätte keines Fingerzeigs bedurft, um mich, die Französische Herkunft dieser Personen vermuthen zu lassen. Ihre Sprache, ihre Kleidung und ihr Benehmen, Alles zeugte davon. Die natürlichste Vermuthung, die sich, nachher auch bestätigte, war, daß ich ein Paar jener unglücklichen Neufranken vor mir sähe, welche die Stürme der Französischen Staatsumwälzung aus ihrem Vaterlande geschleudert und bis hieher verschlagen hätten. Tiefe Spuren überstandenen schweren Kummers waren auf Beider edlen Gesichtern zu erkennen.

29. Harry F. Jackson, *Scholar in the Wilderness: Francis Adrian Van der Kemp* (Syracuse: Syracuse University Press, 1963), 122–128.

30. Lincklaen, *Travels*, 70, 112; Hammond, *History of Madison County*, 658–661.

31. Hamilton Child, ed., *Gazetteer and Business Directory of Madison County, N.Y. for 1868–9* (Syracuse: Journal Office, 1868), 29–30; Tiro, *People of the Standing Stone*, 148–149.

32. Taylor, *Divided Ground*, 301, 305–306, 308, 318–319; Hammond, *History of Madison County*, 487; Orasmus Turner, *History of the Pioneer Settlement of Phelps and Gorham's Purchase, and Morris' Reserve* (Rochester: William Alling, 1852), 475–476; Tiro, *People of the Standing Stone*, 103.

33. Henry J. Cookinham, *History of Oneida County, New York from 1700 to the Present*, vol. 1 (Chicago: S. J. Clarke), 71, 457; Taylor, *Divided Ground*, 385–387; Desjardins and Pharoux, *Castorland Journal*, 57.

34. "A treaty between the United States of America, and the tribes of Indians called the Six Nations, November 11, 1794," in Commissioner of Indian Affairs, *Treaties between the United States of America and the several Indian Tribes, from 1778 to 1837* (Washington, D.C.: Langtree and O'Sullivan, 1837), 48–51; Michael Leroy Oberg, *Peacemakers: The Iroquois, the United States, and the Treaty of Canandaigua* (Oxford: Oxford University Press, 2016), 8, 110, 133.

35. Letter to George Washington from the Oneida Indians, 7 April 1793, in *The Papers of George Washington*, Presidential Series, vol. 12, 16 January 1793–31 May 1793, ed. Christine S. Patrick and John C. Pinheiro (Charlottesville: University of Virginia Press, 2005), 422–424.

36. "A treaty between the United States, and the Oneida, Tuscarora, and Stockbridge Indians, dwelling in the country of the Oneidas, December 2, 1794," in Commissioner of Indian Affairs, *Treaties between the United States of America and the several Indian Tribes, from 1778 to 1837*, 52–53.

37. Lincklaen, *Travels*, 68, 70.

38. Jeremy Belknap and Jedediah Morse, *Report on the Oneida, Stockbridge, and Brothertown Indians, 1796* (New York: Museum of the American Indian, 1955), 13.

39. Wonderley, "Chief Warriors, Pagan Priests, and Witch Killers," 121–145; Oberg, *Peacemakers*, 108–109.

40. Blodgett, *Samson Occom*, 183; Lincklaen, *Travels*, 70; Jeremy Belknap, *Journal of a Tour from Boston to Oneida, June 1796* (Cambridge, MA: John Wilson and Son, 1882), 19–21.

41. Belknap and Morse, *Report*, 7, 9, 13–14; Belknap, *Journal of a Tour from Boston to Oneida*, 23.

42. Wonderley, "Chief Warriors, Pagan Priests, and Witch Killers," 138–145; Tiro, *People of the Standing Stone*, 111; Snow, *The Iroquois*, 180–181; Harold Blau, "The Iroquois White Dog Sacrifice: Its Evolution and Symbolism," *Ethnohistory* 11, no. 2 (1964): 97–119; Jones, *Annals and Recollections of Oneida County*, 864; Schoolcraft, *Notes on the Iroquois* (Albany: Erastus H. Pease and Company, 1847), 440; Taylor, *Divided Ground*, 380–382.

43. Wonderley, "Chief Warriors, Pagan Priests, and Witch Killers," 140–144; Wells, "The Stockbridge Indians in New York State," 485; Taylor, *Divided Ground*, 380–381.

44. Belknap and Morse, *Report*, 17, 20.

45. Wonderley, "Chief Warriors, Pagan Priests, and Witch Killers," 121–136; Taylor, *Divided Ground*, 196–198, 221–225; Julia K. Bloomfield, *The Oneidas* (New York: James Stewart, 1909), 149–150; Blodgett, *Samson Occom*, 188.

46. Norman K. Dann, *Peter Smith of Peterboro* (Hamilton, NY: Log Cabin Books, 2018), 21–26; Taylor, *Divided Ground*, 229–230.

47. Taylor, *Divided Ground*, 302.

48. Taylor, *Divided Ground*, 304–306; Whipple et al., *Report of the Special Committee*, 1:244–249.

49. Taylor, *Divided Ground*, 306–307; Hauptman, *Conspiracy of Interests*, 45.

50. Taylor, *Divided Ground*, 378–379. Quotes from Samuel Kirkland, *Journals*, June 23, 1805.

51. Samuel Kirkland Lothrop, *Life of Samuel Kirkland, Missionary to the Indians* (Boston: Charles C. Little and James Brown, 1848), 317–327, 339.

52. Lothrop, *Life of Samuel Kirkland*, 340–343.

53. Lothrop, *Life of Samuel Kirkland*, 348.

54. Belknap, *Journal of a Tour from Boston to Oneida*, 10–14.

55. Belknap, *Journal of a Tour from Boston to Oneida*, 15–24.

56. Lothrop, *Life of Samuel Kirkland*, 348–349, 356, 358–359.

57. "Samuel Kirkland to John Thornton Kirkland, President of Harvard College, 1810–1827, 5th December 1798," in Joseph D. Ibbitson and S. N. D. North, eds., *Documentary History of Hamilton College* (Clinton, NY: Hamilton College, 1922), 98.

58. "Samuel Kirkland to John Thornton Kirkland," 100–103.

59. Lothrop, *Life of Samuel Kirkland*, 357.

60. Elihu Root, "The Centenary of Hamilton College: Historical Address, June 17, 1912," in Ibbitson and North, *Documentary History of Hamilton College*, 16–18.

61. Lothrop, *Life of Samuel Kirkland*, p. 26; Ibbitson and North, *Documentary History of Hamilton College*, 112–113.

62. George Shattuck, *The Oneida Land Claims: A Legal History* (Syracuse: Syracuse University Press, 1991), 94–99; Whipple et al., *Report of the Special Committee*, 1:8, 249–252; Tiro, *People of the Standing Stone*, 109.

63. Karim Tiro, "'We Wish to Do You Good': The Quaker Mission to the Oneida Nation, 1790–1840," *Journal of the Early Republic* 26, no. 3 (2006), 369–370; Wonderley, "Chief Warriors, Pagan Priests, and Witch Killers," 138–139; Hammond, *History of Madison County*, 662.

64. Tiro, *People of the Standing Stone*, 112; Hammond, *History of Madison County*, 487; Hauptman, *Conspiracy of Interests*, 45–48.

65. Hammond, *History of Madison County*, 488–489, 662, 767–770; Tiro, *People of the Standing Stone*, 113.

66. "At a Treaty at the City of Albany . . . 1807," in Whipple et al., *Report of the Special Committee*, 1:264.

67. Whipple et al., *Report of the Special Committee*, 1:265; Hammond, *History of Madison County*, 507–509, 515; John L. Robertson, "The Birth of Canastota," *Canastota Bee-Journal*, July 26, 1960.

68. Tiro, *People of the Standing Stone*, 96, 118.

69. Tiro, *People of the Standing Stone*, 118–119; "At a Treaty at the City of Albany . . . 1809," in Whipple et al., *Report of the Special Committee*, 1:269–272.

70. John Randel, Jr., "Plan of a Village at Oneida Castle, in Vernon in the County of Oneida. Laid out pursuant to instructions from the Surveyor General in November, 1813," in the New York State Archives, New York State Engineer

and Surveyor, Survey maps of lands in New York State, ca. 1711–1913, Series A0273-278, Map #131B

71. "An Act relative to the Village of Oneida Castleton, and for other purposes, 1815," in New York State Legislature, *Laws of the State of New York, passed at the Thirty-Eighth session of the Legislature* (Albany: J. Buel, 1815), 259–260; "Report of the Commissioners of the Land-Office, on the Bill authorizing a re-appraisement of certain lands in Oneida Castleton, March 24, 1832," in *Documents of the Assembly of the State of New York, Fifty-Fifth Session, 1832*, vol. 3 (Albany: E. Croswell, 1932), no. 238; Melanie Zimmer, "Oneida Castle: Forsaken Capital," in *Forgotten Tales of New York* (Charleston, S.C.: The History Press, 2009).

72. Tiro, *People of the Standing Stone*, 119

73. "Map of Oneida Creek Tract, situate in Lennox, in the County of Madison. Purchased of the Oneida Indians 3rd March, 1810, the 27th February, 1811. Surveyed by order of the Surveyor General, in 1811. John Randall Jr., Deputy Surveyor," New York State Archives. State Engineer and Surveyor, Survey maps of lands in New York State, ca. 1711–1913. Series A0273-78, Map #157.

74. "At a Treaty at the City of Albany . . . 1810," in Whipple et al., *Report of the Special Committee*, 1:273.

75. Hammond, *History of Madison County*, 480; Child, *Gazetteer and Business Directory of Madison County, N.Y. for 1868–9*, 47.

76. Peter Silver, *Our Savage Neighbors: How Indian War Transformed Early America* (New York: W.W. Norton, 2008), 133, 234–235, 238, 264, 275, 282–283, 299.

77. Peter L. Bernstein, *Wedding of the Waters: The Erie Canal and the Making of a Great Nation* (New York: W.W. Norton, 2005), 97–99; Philip Lord, Jr., "The Covered Locks of Wood Creek," *The Journal of the Society for Industrial Archaeology* 27, no. 1 (2001), 5–15.

78. De Witt Clinton, "Private Canal Journal, 1810," in William W. Campbell, ed. *The Life and Writings of De Witt Clinton* (New York: Baker and Scribner, 1849), 27; Vivian C. Hopkins, "De Witt Clinton and the Iroquois." *Ethnohistory* 8, no. 2 (1961), 113–143.

79. Clinton, "Private Canal Journal, 1810," quoted, 52, 62–63.

80. Clinton, "Private Canal Journal, 1810," 173–174, 185–191; quoted, 174, 186–189, 190–191.

81. Bernstein, *Wedding of the Waters*, 158.

82. Nelson Greene, ed., *History of the Mohawk Valley: Gateway to the West, 1614–1925*, vol. 2 (Chicago: S. J. Clark, 1924), 1488–1489; Mary P. Ryan, *Cradle of the Middle Class: The Family in Oneida County, New York, 1790–1865* (Cambridge: Cambridge University Press, 1981), 10.

83. Gary M. Gibson, "The U.S. Brig *Oneida*: A Design and Operational History," *War of 1812 Magazine* 19 (2012), 13; Richard V. Barbuto, *New York's War of 1812: Politics, Society, and Combat* (Norman: University of Oklahoma Press, 2021), 47.

84. Tiro, *People of the Standing Stone*, 125–126.

85. Carl Benn, *The Iroquois in the War of 1812* (Toronto: University of Toronto Press, 1998), 155; Barbuto, *New York's War of 1812*, 202; Tiro, *People of the Standing Stone*, 126; Franklin B. Hough, *A History of Jefferson County in the State of New York from the Earliest Period to the Present Time* (Albany: Joel Munsell, 1854), 510–515; Ralph M. Faust, *The Story of Oswego, With Notes about Several Towns in the County* (Oswego: Palladium-Times Press, 1934), 92.

86. Bernstein, *Wedding of the Waters*, 185, 189, 213, 259; Gerard Koeppel, "Andrew Bartow and the Cement that Made the Erie Canal," *The New-York Journal of American History* 66, no. 1 (2005), 52–60.

87. Bernstein, *Wedding of the Waters*, 217, 235.

88. Moses Mears Bagg, *Memorial History of Utica, New York, From Its Settlement to the Present Time* (Syracuse: D. Mason and Co., 1892), 170.

89. Roger Haydon, ed., *Upstate Travels: British Views of Nineteenth-Century New York* (Syracuse: Syracuse University Press, 1982), 154; quote from Richard Weston, *A Visit to the United States and Canada in 1833* (Edinburgh: Richard Weston and Sons, 1836).

90. Noble E. Whitford, *History of the Canal System of the State of New York, Together with Brief Histories of the Canals of the United States and Canada*, vol. 1 (Albany: Brandow Printing Company, 1906), 914.

91. Bernstein, *Wedding of the Waters*, 262, 270, 314.

92. Whitford, *History of the Canal System of the State of New York*, 1:654–658.

93. Whitford, *History of the Canal System of the State of New York*, 1:506–554, 672–683.

94. John Warner Barber and Henry Howe, *Historical Collections of the State of New York* (New York: S. Tuttle, 1842), 363, reprinted from the *Utica Patriot*, March 19, 1816; Jones, *Annals and Recollections of Oneida County*, 866.

95. Schoolcraft, *Notes on the Iroquois*, 440–441.

96. Clinton, "Private Canal Journal, 1810," 187–190; Hauptman, *Conspiracy of Interests*, 45; Laurence M. Hauptman and L. Gordon McLester III, *The Oneida Indian Journey: From New York to Wisconsin, 1784–1860* (Madison, WI: University of Wisconsin Press, 1999), 23–26.

97. John A. Lomax and Alan Lomax, *American Ballads and Folk Songs* (New York: Macmillan, 1934), 543–546; W. B. Whall, *Ships, Sea Songs and Shanties* (Glasgow: James Brown, 1913), 1–3. The Shenandoah River in Virginia and Shenandoah National Park are not named after Shenandoah, but for the Senedo people. Notwithstanding, the names have often been conflated, even in congressional debates. See, for example, *Congressional Record: Containing the Proceedings and Debates of the Fifty-Seventh Congress, Second Session*, Vol. 36, Part 2 (Washington: Government Printing Office, 1903), 1996. Speaking of Shenandoah, Senator John Tyler Morgan of Alabama said, "The first man whom I call to the attention of the Senate is the man for whom those beautiful mountains and the beautiful river

beyond the Potomac were named." He was arguing for the admission to the Union as new states of Oklahoma and other territories with large Indian populations.

98. Michael Oberg, *Professional Indian: The American Odyssey of Eleazar Williams* (Philadelphia: University of Pennsylvania Press, 2015), 16, 53–54, 60–69; Jack Campisi, "The Oneida Treaty Period, 1783–1838," in Jack Campisi and Laurence M. Hauptman, eds., *The Oneida Indian Experience: Two Perspectives* (Syracuse: Syracuse University Press, 1988), 60; Tiro, *People of the Standing Stone*, 138–139; Tony Wonderley, "Sherrill's Lost Dauphin Hill, Kinsley Farm," *Oneida Dispatch*, March 1, 2016.

99. State of New York Legislature, *Legislative Documents of the Senate and Assembly of the State of New York, Fifty-Third Session, 1830*, vol. 1 (Albany: E. Croswell, 1830), no. 58, Jan 27, 1830; Whipple et al., *Report of the Special Committee*, 1:281–282.

100. Whipple et al., *Report of the Special Committee*, 1:284–285; Tiro, *People of the Standing Stone*, 140.

101. Whipple et al., *Report of the Special Committee*, 1:13; William Pool, *Landmarks of Niagara County, New York* (Syracuse: D. Mason and Company, 1897), 22; Wells, "The Stockbridge Indians in New York State," 489.

102. Tiro, *People of the Standing Stone*, 141–143, 152–153; Oberg, *Professional Indian*, 89, 91–101.

103. Jasper Parrish to Thomas McKinney, "State of Six Nations Population," October 11, 1824, American Indian Collection, Series I, Box 1, Folder 1, New-York Historical Society.

104. Laurence Hauptman and L. Gordon McLester III, *Chief Daniel Bread and the Oneida Nation of Indians of Wisconsin* (Norman: University of Oklahoma Press, 2002), 34–40; Tiro, *People of the Standing Stone*, 145, 232; Bernstein, *Wedding of the Waters*, 183; Hauptman and McLester III, eds., *The Oneida Indian Journey*, 12–13.

105. Glatthaar and Martin, *Forgotten Allies*, 3–5; Bagg, *Memorial History of Utica*, 167–169.

106. Whipple et al., *Report of the Special Committee*, 1:287; "Map of two tracts of land ceded to the State of New York by the First Christian Party of the Oneida Indians," New York State Archives, New York (State), State Engineer and Surveyor, Survey maps of lands in New York State, ca. 1711–1913. Series A0273-78, Map #278(4). Purchasers of the lots are listed in "Report of the Committee on Indian Affairs on the Petition of the Chiefs, &c., of the First Christian Party of Oneida Indians," in New York State Legislature, *Documents of the Senate of the State of New York, Seventy-Second Session*, 1849, vol. 2. (Albany: Weed, Parsons & Co., 1849), no. 46, Exhibit B.

107. Silverman, *Red Brethren*, 160–162.

108. "Copy of Maps 277A-277H," New York State Archives, New York (State), State Engineer and Surveyor, Survey maps of lands in New York State, ca. 1711–1913, Series A0273-78, Maps #277A-277H.

109. Christopher Geherin, "New Guinea: Racial Identity and Inclusion in the Stockbridge and Brothertown Indian Communities of New York," *New York History* 90, no. 3 (2009), 152, 158.

110. Silverman, *Red Brethren*, 172; Jones, *Annals and Recollections of Oneida County*, 503.

111. Tiro, *People of the Standing Stone*, 148–149.

112. Whipple et al., *Report of the Special Committee*, 1:298–302; Tiro, *People of the Standing Stone*, 150; "Report of the Surveyor-General, on the petition of the Orchard Party of Oneida Indians, March 6, 1834," in New York State Legislature, *Documents of the Senate of the State of New York, Fifty-Seventh Session, 1834*, Vol. 2 (Albany: E. Croswell, 1834), No. 88; John E. Smith, *Our County and its People: A Descriptive and Biographical Record of Madison County, New York* (Boston: The Boston History Company, 1899), 169.

113. Tiro, *People of the Standing Stone*, 148–150. On Han Yost as Moses Schuyler's father, see Schoolcraft, *Notes on the Iroquois*, 441.

114. Whipple et al., *Report of the Special Committee*, 1:291–292.

115. Whipple et al., *Report of the Special Committee*, 1:293–294.

116. Whipple et al., *Report of the Special Committee*, 1:296–297.

117. Whipple et al., *Report of the Special Committee*, 1:304.

118. Tiro, *People of the Standing Stone*, 193; Whipple et al., *Report of the Special Committee*, 1:311–12.

119. One exception is Tiro's *People of the Standing Stone*. Tiro mentions several of the post-1816 treaties, see pp. 140, 147, 149–151, 165–166.

120. Tiro, *People of the Standing Stone*, 162, 165.

121. Whipple et al., *Report of the Special Committee*, 1:312–314, 319–320, 328, 330; quote on 312. In 1840 Burchard was acting as attorney to the Oneida Indians, Case and Jenkins as commissioners of the Land Office of the State of New York, and Higinbotham as an agent on behalf of the Oneida Indians.

122. Whipple et al., *Report of the Special Committee*, 1:343–344, 348, 358, 362; "Map of the lands ceded to the people of the State of New York by the Orchard Party of the Oneida Indians by treaty of March 13, 1841," New York State Archives, Series A0273-78, Survey maps of lands in New York State, ca. 1711–1913, Map 434.

123. See A. E. Robertson and E. J. Murphey, Surveyors, "Map of Oneida County, New York: from actual surveys" (Philadelphia: Newell S. Brown, 1852); J. H. French, Surveyor, "Gillette's map of Oneida Co., New York: from actual surveys" (Philadelphia: John E. Gillette, 1858); "Map of Town of Vernon, Oneida County 1874," in D. G. Beers & Co., *Atlas of Oneida County, New York* (Philadelphia: D. G. Beers & Co., 1874); "Town of Vernon," in Century Map Company, *New Century Atlas: Oneida County, New York* (New York: Century Map Co., 1907).

124. Whipple et al., *Report of the Special Committee*, 1:37.

125. Population figures from 1842 are based on the numbers listed in the 1840–42 treaties. An 1845 census return showed a population of Oneidas in New

York State of 210, of whom 157 (31 families) resided on the reservation. At least 23 Oneidas were living on the Onondaga Reservation. See Schoolcraft, *Notes on the Iroquois*, 25, 32, 37.

Chapter 5

1. Clinton, "Private Canal Journal, 1810," 106–107, 110.
2. Whitney R. Cross, *The Burned-over District: The Social and Intellectual History of Enthusiastic Religion in Western New York* (Ithaca: Cornell University Press, 1950), 7–10, 42.
3. Bernstein, *Wedding of the Waters*, 338–339.
4. Charles Grandison Finney, *The Memoirs of Charles G. Finney: The Complete Restored Text*, Ricard A. Dupuis and Garth M. Rosell, eds. (Grand Rapids, MI: Academie Books, 1989), 156–171; quoted 157, 158.
5. Finney, *Memoirs*, 158, 160, 164.
6. Finney, *Memoirs*, 172–192; quoted 177.
7. Charles E. Hambrick-Stowe, "Charles G. Finney and Evangelical Anti-Catholicism," *U.S. Catholic Historian* 14, no. 4 (1996): 40.
8. Mary Ryan, *Cradle of the Middle Class: The Family in Oneida County, New York, 1790–1865* (Cambridge: Cambridge University Press, 1981), 75–104.
9. Milton C. Sernett, *Abolition's Axe: Beriah Green, Oneida Institute, and the Black Freedom Struggle* (Syracuse: Syracuse University Press, 1986), 31–36.
10. Sernett, *Abolition's Axe*, 36, 39–40.
11. Amos A. Phelps, "The Oneida Institute," Manuscript signed London 1843, Amos A. Phelps Correspondence, Boston Public Library, MS A.21 v.13, p.50, side 4.
12. Howard Alexander Morrison, "Gentlemen of Proper Understanding: A Closer Look at Utica's Anti-Abolitionist Mob," *New York History* 62, no. 1 (1981): 61–82.
13. Morrison, "Gentlemen of Proper Understanding," 66, 72–73; Fergus M. Bordewich, *Bound for Canaan: The Underground Railroad and the War for the Soul of America* (New York: Amistad, 2005), 175.
14. Lester Grosvenor Wells, "Indian Personal Name Entries in Peter Smith's Indian Blotter," *New York History* 28, no. 4 (1947): 466–469; Norman K. Dann, *Practical Dreamer: Gerrit Smith and the Crusade for Social Reform* (Hamilton, NY: Log Cabin Books, 2009), 17–19, 95–96; Octavius Brooks Frothingham, *Gerrit Smith: A Biography* (New York: G.P. Putnam's Sons, 1878), 5.
15. Dann, *Practical Dreamer*, 19–20; Frothingham, *Gerrit Smith*, 12–19.
16. Smith's "To the Proslavery Ministers of Madison County" (1843), criticized the US government for "wasting its wealth" on Indian wars in Florida, "consigning to banishment or slaughter whole tribes of Indians, whose only crime is that they have lands which slaveholders covet": Gerrit Smith, "To the Proslavery Ministers

of Madison County" (1843), Gerrit Smith Pamphlets and Broadsides [Smith 422], Syracuse University Library Special Collections, 2. Also see Dann, *Practical Dreamer*, 112; Frothingham, *Gerrit Smith*, 141, 298–299.

17. Dann, *Practical Dreamer*, 64–66, 278–281.

18. Gerrit Smith, "Church of Peterboro" (1843), Gilder Lehrman Institute of American History, Collection no. GLC04717.46; Frothingham, *Gerrit Smith*, 44, 63; Dann, *Practical Dreamer*, 50, 88.

19. Communication from Gerrit Smith to Edward C. Delavan on the reformation of the intemperate, 1833, Gerrit Smith Pamphlets and Broadsides [Smith 404], Syracuse University Library Special Collections, p. 2; Frothingham, *Gerrit Smith*, 48–49, 67–69.

20. Smith to Delavan, 1833, 5–6.

21. Census Office, 4th *Census, 1820* (Washington, D.C.: Gales and Stratton, 1821), 49–60.

22. Frothingham, *Gerrit Smith*, 115; Sernett, *North Star Country*, 169–171.

23. Dann, *Practical Dreamer*, 405–407.

24. "Speech of Mr. Gerrit Smith, in the meeting of the New-York Anti-Slavery Society: Held in Peterboro, October 22, 1835," Gerrit Smith Pamphlets and Broadsides [Smith 404], Syracuse University Library Special Collections.

25. Dann, *Practical Dreamer*, 415.

26. Jones, *Annals and Recollections of Oneida County*, 555, 631; Bordewich, *Bound for Canaan*, 151.

27. Bordewich, *Bound for Canaan*, 159; Dann, *Practical Dreamer*, 60.

28. Frothingham, *Gerrit Smith*, 70–71; Gerrit Smith, "Report from the County of Madison: To Abolitionists" (1843), Gerrit Smith Pamphlets and Broadsides [Smith 425], Syracuse University Library Special Collections.

29. Gerrit Smith, "Some of the Duties of an Abolitionist (And Every Whole Man is an Abolitionist)" (1841), Gerrit Smith Pamphlets and Broadsides [Smith 416], Syracuse University Library Special Collections.

30. Gerrit Smith "To the Proslavery Ministers of Madison County."

31. Sernett, *Abolition's Axe*, 81–82, 87; Jones, *Annals and Recollections of Oneida County*, 645, 812; Milton C. Sernett, *North Star Country*, 96.

32. Gerrit Smith, "Report from the County of Madison: To Abolitionists"; Jones, *Annals and Recollections of Oneida County*, 207–208; Milton M. Klein, *The Empire State: A History of New York State* (Ithaca: Cornell University Press, 2001), 386–390, 394–402.

33. Hamilton Child, ed., *Gazetteer and Business Directory of Madison County, N.Y. for 1868–9* (Syracuse: Journal Office, 1868), 25.

34. Bordewich, *Bound for Canaan*, 163–165, 177.

35. "Sands Higinbotham" (obituary), *Oneida Dispatch*, Sept. 18, 1868; available at https://www.findagrave.com/memorial/32074594/sands-higinbotham. Higinbotham is listed as a farmer in the 1850 US Federal Census and the 1855 and 1865 New

York State Censuses. He appears in the 1820 and 1830 censuses living in Vernon, but professions were not recorded.

36. John E. Smith, ed., *Our County and Its People: A Descriptive and Bibliographical Record of Madison County, New York* (Boston: Boston History Company, 1899), 309–311.

37. Smith, *Our County and Its People*, 289–291, 593; Hammond, *History of Madison County*, 524.

38. Smith. *Our County and Its People*, 207, 289–291, 304, 593; Hammond, *History of Madison County*, 523–525.

39. "Biography of Sands Higinbotham, Trustee of Hamilton College from 1836 to 1838," Hamilton College Archives, Biographies of the trustees of Hamilton College, 1812–1818, 1836–1869, Archives Oversize, Ham Col HF A6t.

40. Robert Allerton Parker, *A Yankee Saint* (New York: G.P. Putnam's Sons, 1935), 15–18; George Wallingford Noyes, ed., *Religious Experience of John Humphrey Noyes, Founder of the Oneida* Community (New York: Macmillan, 1923), 36.

41. John Humphrey Noyes, *Confession of Religious Experience* (Oneida, NY: Leonard and Company, 1849), 6; William Hepworth Dixon, *New America* (London: Hurst and Blackett, 1869), 356; Parker, *Yankee Saint*, 17–20; Spencer Klaw, *Without Sin: The Life and Death of the Oneida Community* (New York: Allen Lane, 1993), 23–24.

42. Douglas M. Strong, *Perfectionist Politics: Abolitionism and the Religious Tensions of American Democracy* (Syracuse: Syracuse University Press, 2001), 34; John B. Teeple, *The Oneida Family: Genealogy of a 19th Century Perfectionist Commune* (Cazenovia, NY: Oneida Community Historical Committee, 1985), x–xiii.

43. Noyes, *Confession of Religious Experience*, 18; Klaw, *Without Sin*, 26.

44. Klaw, *Without Sin*, 28–29; John Humphrey Noyes, *The Way of Holiness* (Putney, VT: J. H. Noyes and Company, 1838), 22.

45. Cross, *The Burned-Over District*, 240–241.

46. Klaw, *Without Sin*, 47. The words are Noyes's own from an article titled "The Secret History of Perfectionism" in which he denounced rival groups of Perfectionists.

47. Noyes, *Way of Holiness*, 102.

48. Noyes, *Way of Holiness*, 102–114.

49. George Wallingford Noyes, ed., *John Humphrey Noyes, The Putney Community* (Oneida, NY: G.W. Noyes, 1931), 1–4; Hubbard Eastman, *Noyesism Unveiled: A History of the Sect Self-styled Perfectionists with a Summary View of their Leading Doctrines* (Battleboro, VT: H. Eastman, 1849), 91–92. The letter appeared in the August 1837 edition of *The Battle-Axe and Weapons of War* (Philadelphia).

50. Yaacov Oved, *Two Hundred Years of American Communes* (New Brunswick, NJ: Transaction Books, 1988), 170.

51. John Humphrey Noyes, *History of American Socialisms* (Philadelphia: J. B. Lippincott and Company, 1870), 615; Wayland-Smith, *Oneida*, 47–49.

52. Constance Noyes Robertson, *Oneida Community: An Autobiography, 1851–1876* (Syracuse: Syracuse University Press, 1971), 10.

53. Parker, *Yankee Saint*, 120–121. Originally published on July 15, 1847, in Noyes's journal, *Spiritual Magazine*.

54. John Humphrey Noyes, *Male Continence* (Oneida, NY: Oneida Community, 1872), 11. These words are taken from Noyes's "Bible Argument," written in 1848 and reprinted in this twenty-four-page guide to this form of intercourse.

55. Eastman, *Noyesism Unveiled*, 187–191. The author reprints Mrs. Hall's personal testimony.

56. Klaw, *Without Sin*, 65–68; Foster, *Free Love in Utopia*, xiii.

57. Constance Noyes Robertson, *Oneida Community Profiles* (Syracuse: Syracuse University Press, 1977), 8, 14.

58. Parker, *Yankee Saint*, 160–161.

59. Parker, *Yankee Saint*, 160.

60. Parker, *Yankee Saint*, 163–176. Quote from a letter from John Humphrey Noyes to George Cragin, February 4, 1848, in George Wallingford Noyes, *John Humphrey Noyes, The Putney Community*, 388.

61. Dann, *Practical Dreamer*, 35.

62. Parker, *Yankee Saint*, 187–189; Doyle, *The Ministers' War*, 34–38.

63. Foster, *Free Love in Utopia*, xiii.

64. Raymond L. Cohn, "Nativism and the End of the Mass Migration of the 1840s and 1850s." *The Journal of Economic History* 60, no. 2 (2000): 375–376; Sernett, *North Star Country*, 154–155.

65. Dann, *Practical Dreamer*, 237–238.

66. It is unclear how long the term of the Utica and Syracuse Railroad's original agreement with Higinbotham to stop each train on his land was. Smith says the "contract was observed until the late Fifties": *Our County and Its People*, 61.

67. Bordewich, *Bound for Canaan*, 317–319.

68. James M. McPherson, *Battle Cry of Freedom: The Civil War Era* (Oxford: Oxford University Press, 1988), 80. Quotes from the Fugitive Slave Act 1850, printed in Holman Hamilton, *Prologue to Conflict: The Crisis and Compromise of 1850* (Lexington, KY: University of Kentucky Press, 1964), 204–208.

69. Bordewich, *Bound for Canaan*, 317–318; Sernett, *North Star Country*, 271.

70. Sernett, *North Star Country*, 270.

71. "The Texas Swindle and Slavery Bill," *Northern New York Journal*, September 11, 1850.

72. Sernett, *North Star Country*, 271.

73. "Mr. Webster's Prophesy," *Northern Journal*, October 15, 1851; Bordewich, *Bound for Canaan*, 324–325.

74. Bordewich, *Bound for Canaan*, 333–339.

75. "Oneida County Whig Convention," *New York Times*, October 1, 1852; "New York—Nominations for Congress and Assembly," *New York Times*, October 11, 1852; Cookinham, *History of Oneida County*, 1:111–112.

76. "Uncle Tom's Cabin," *Oneida Telegraph*, Oct. 9, 1852

77. "A New Book . . ." *Oneida Telegraph,* June 12, 1852.

78. "Kidnapping a Free Negro into Slavery," *Northern New York Journal*, January 26, 1853.

79. "The Kidnapping Case," *Oxford Times*, February 2, 1853.

80. "Position of Gerrit Smith," *Oneida Sachem*, June 24, 1854. On newspapers see Child, *Gazetteer and Business Directory of Madison County, N.Y. for 1868–9*, 27.

81. Foner, *Free Soil, Free Labor, Free Men: The Ideology of the Republican Party before the Civil War* (Oxford: Oxford University Press, 1979), 164.

82. "The Political Future," *Oneida Sachem*, March 14, 1857.

83. "The Dred Scott Case," *Oneida Sachem*, March 14, 1857.

84. Harry F. Jackson and Thomas F. O'Donnell, *Back Home in Oneida: Hermon Clarke and His Letters* (Syracuse: Syracuse University Press, 1965), 10, 16–17, 20–22.

85. Jones, *Annals and Recollections of Oneida County*, 191, 286, 301, 615, 826.

86. Jones, *Annals and Recollections of Oneida County*, 631.

87. Jones, *Annals and Recollections of Oneida County*, 710–711.

88. Foner, *Free Soil, Free Labor, Free Men*, 285–286; Phyllis F. Field, *The Politics of Race in New York: The Struggle for Black Suffrage in the Civil War Era* (Ithaca: Cornell University Press, 1982), 127.

89. Sernett, *North Star Country*, 152, 169, 171–179.

90. Sernett, *North Star Country*, 195–216; David S. Reynolds, *John Brown, Abolitionist: The Man Who Killed Slavery, Sparked the Civil War, and Seeded Civil Rights* (New York: Vintage Books, 2006), 89, 101, 430; McPherson, *Battle Cry of Freedom*, 204–207.

91. McPherson, *Battle Cry of Freedom*, 208–212.

92. Cadwallader Colden, *The History of the Five Indian Nations of Canada, which are dependent on the Province of New-York in America* (London: Printed for T. Osborne in Gray's-Inn, 1747); quoted p. 1.

93. Colden, *History of the Five Indian Nations*, v.

94. David Cusik, *Sketches of the Ancient History of the Six Nations* (Lewiston, NY: Cooley & Lathrop Printers, 1828), 16–17.

95. Henry R. Schoolcraft, *Notes on the Iroquois* (Albany: Erastus H. Pease and Company, 1847), vi–vii.

96. Schoolcraft, *Notes on the Iroquois*, 5, 15, 154, 219, 440; Richard G. Bremer, *Indian Agent and Wilderness Scholar: The Life of Henry Rowe Schoolcraft* (Mount Pleasant, MI: Clarke Historical Library, 1987), 1–5, 9, 13–15; Janet R. MacFarlane, et al., "Oneida Glass Factory Company." *New York History* 28, no. 1 (1947), 75–78.

97. Schoolcraft, *Notes on the Iroquois*, 75–76, 78, 81, 181–182, 185–186, 191–192, 442.

98. Lewis H. Morgan, *League of the Ho-de-no-sau-nee, or Iroquois* (1852) [what is this year, if it was published in 1904?], Herbert M. Lloyd, ed. (New York: Dodd, Mead and Company, 1904), 60, 136–137.

99. Taylor, *William Cooper's Town*, 36; Percy G. Adams, ed. *Crevecoeur's Eighteenth-Century Travels in Pennsylvania and New York* (Lexington, KY: University of Kentucky Press, 1961), xx–xxii, xxxiv.

100. Sophie von La Roche, *Erscheinung am See Oneida*, 3 vols. (Leipzig: Gräff, 1798); Victor Lange, "Visitors to Lake Oneida: An Account of the Background of Sophie von la Roche's Novel "Erscheinungen am See Oneida,'" *Symposium: A Quarterly Journal in Modern Literatures* 2, no. 1 (1948), 48–78; Nicole Jennifer Parry, ". . . *nicht die Menschen im Walde, Wilde genannt werden sollten*: Images of Aboriginal Peoples in the Works of Sophie von La Roche, Charles Sealsfield and Karl May" (PhD diss., University of Toronto, 2012), 28–69.

101. Taylor, *William Cooper's Town*, 36–40.

102. Taylor, *William Cooper's Town*, 53–54.

103. James Fenimore Cooper, *The Pioneers, or the Sources of the Susquehanna* (1823) in *The Leatherstocking Tales*, vol. 1 (New York: Literary Classics of the United States, Syndicate of the University of Cambridge, 1985), 461.

104. Cooper, *The Last of the Mohicans* (1826) in *Leatherstocking Tales*, 1:697–698.

105. Cooper, *The Pathfinder* (1840) in *Leatherstocking Tales*, 2:14.

106. Cooper, "Introduction to the First Edition," *The Last of the Mohicans* (New York: Penguin, 1986), 8.

107. *Oneida Sachem*, February 21, 1861, 2.

108. "War, War!" *Oneida Sachem*, April 18, 1861.

109. Frank Tomaino, "Mayors Series: City Elects Civil War Leader," *Utica Observer-Dispatch*, July 18, 2019; Kristen M. Trout, "'Showing the White Feather': The Civil War Ordeal of Col. William H. Christian," *Emerging Civil War*, June 28, 2016, https://emergingcivilwar.com/2016/06/28/showing-the-white-feather-the-civil-war-ordeal-of-col-william-h-christian/.

110. Eric Kennedy, "The Hard Luck Second Oneida," *The Waterville Times*, January 6 and 27, 2010; Frederick Phisterer, *New York in the War of the Rebellion, 1861–1865*, 3rd ed. Vol. 3 (Albany: J.B. Lyon Company, 1912), 2027.

111. Paul Taylor, *Glory Was Not Their Companion: The Twenty-Sixth New York Volunteer Infantry in the Civil War* (Jefferson, N.C.: McFarland and Company, 2005); Robert Tegart, "For the Support and Vindication of our National Flag": The 26th New York Volunteer Infantry," in James A. Pula, ed., *"With Courage and Honor": Oneida County's Role in the Civil War* (Utica: Ethnic Heritage Studies Center, Utica College, 2010), 91–122; Trout, "Showing the White Feather."

112. Phisterer, *New York in the War of the Rebellion*, 4:3111.

113. Phisterer, *New York in the War of the Rebellion*, 3111–3112.

114. *The Semi-Centennial of the Presbyterian Church of Oneida, N.Y.* (Rahway, N.J.: Merson Company Press, 1894).

115. Sernett, *North Star Country*, 229, 237; Schroeder, Patrick A., *The Highest Praise of Gallantry: Memorials of David J. Jenkins and James E. Jenkins of the 146th New York Infantry and Oneida Cavalry* (Daleville, VA: Schroder Publications, 2001); James S. Pula and Cheryl A. Pula, eds., *With Courage and Honor: Oneida County's Role in the Civil War* (Utica, NY: North Country Books, 2010).

116. "Madison County to Celebrate Pair of Civil War Soldiers as part of Black History Month Programming to Honor African-Americans," *Rome Sentinel*, February 7, 2020.

117. Donald M. Wisnoski, *The Opportunity is at Hand: Oneida County, New York Colored Soldiers in the Civil War* (Lynchburg, VA: Schroeder Publications, 2003).

118. Laurence Hauptman, *The Iroquois in the Civil War: From Battlefield to Reservation* (Syracuse: Syracuse University Press, 1992), 11, 68–83; Russell Horton, "Unwanted in a White Man's War: The Civil War Service of the Green Bay Tribes," *The Wisconsin Magazine of History* 88, no. 2 (2004): 18–27.

119. Laurence Hauptman, *An Oneida Indian in Foreign Waters: The Life of Chief Chapman Scanandoah* (Syracuse: Syracuse University Press, 2016), 19–20; Hauptman, *Iroquois in the Civil War*, 148–149.

120. Sidney David Brummer, *Political History of New York State During the Period of the Civil War* (New York: AMS Press, 1967), 234–239.

121. "Doings of Gov. Seymour," *New York Times*, July 15, 1853.

122. Sernett, *North Star Country*, 232–233.

123. Sernett, *North Star Country*, 226.

124. "Mr. Seymour at the Democratic State Convention, Albany, September 10, 1862, on receiving the Nomination of Governor," in Thomas M. Cook and Thomas W. Knox, eds., *Public Record: Including Speeches, Proclamations, Official Correspondence and Other Public Utterances of Horatio Seymour* (New York: I.W. England, 1868); quote on p. 55.

125. "Gov. Seymour and the Mass Meeting Today," *Syracuse Courier and Union*, October 28, 1863.

126. "Governor Seymour at a Democratic Meeting at Cooper Institute, New York, June 25, 1868," in Cook and Knox, *Public Record*, 329–332.

127. "'Our Ticket, Our Motto: This Is a White Man's Country; Let White Men Rule.' Campaign badge supporting Horatio Seymour and Francis Blair, Democratic candidates for President and Vice-President of the Unites States, 1868," Schomburg Center for Research in Black Culture, Photographs and Prints Division, The New York Public Library Digital Collections, 1868.

128. *Cazenovia Republican*, October 5, 1864.

129. *Watertown Daily Reformer*, February 2, 1865.

130. Parker, *Yankee Saint*, 49–50. Quotes from Noyes's letter to William Lloyd Garrison, 1837.
131. "Secession of the South," *The Circular*, Nov. 22, 1860.
132. "End of a Reprobate Government," *The Circular*, April 18, 1861.
133. "The Issue of the Hour," *The Circular*, April 18, 1861.
134. "The Lesson of the Riot," *The Circular*, September 3, 1863.
135. "About the War," *The Circular*, March 21, 1864.
136. "How the News was Taken at Mount Tom," *The Circular*, April 17, 1865.
137. "The President's Death," *The Circular*, April 17, 1865.
138. Robertson, *Oneida Community*, 112; originally printed in *The Circular*, May 29, 1865; Wonderley, *Oneida Utopia*, 134.
139. Parker, *Yankee Saint*, 210.
140. William T. Coggeshall, *The Journeys of Abraham Lincoln: From Springfield to Washington 1861, as President Elect; and from Washington to Springfield, 1865, as President Martyred* (Columbus: Ohio State Journal, 1865), 204.

Chapter 6

1. Gordon Hendricks, *Albert Bierstadt: Painter of the American West* (New York: H. N. Abrams, 1974), 11–46, 295, 321–322. Several paintings of Oneida County were advertised in the exhibition catalogues *Executor's Sale of Superb Modern Paintings: Two Choice Works by the Eminent Artist Albert Bierstadt, Esq.* (New York: James P. Silo, Auctioneer, 1892).

2. Hendricks, *Albert Bierstadt*, 188; William F. Helmer, *O.&W.: The Long Life and Slow Death of the New York, Ontario and Western Railway* (Berkeley, CA: Howell-North Press, 1959), 8–10, 55, 59. The painting is undated but the Haggin Museum suggests it was painted after 1875 because it is on a stretcher identical to that of another Bierstadt painting in the collection, *Forest Monarchs*, which bears the label "Wight & Gardner's Improved Canvas Stretchers, Patented January 19, 1875." It was normal practice for Bierstadt to paint his images from sketches or oil studies sometimes long after visiting the location he painted. Personal communication from Tod Ruhstaller, Haggin Museum CEO and Curator of History to the author, February 2, 2021.

3. Susan Fleming, "The Boston Patrons of Jean-Francois Millet," in Alexandra Murphy. ed., *Jean-François Millet* [exh. cat.] (Boston: Museum of Fine Arts, Boston, 1984), ix–xvii; Hendricks, *Albert Bierstadt*, 247–248, 261–262, 286–288.

4. Wager, *Our County and its People*, 2:16–18.

5. Hendricks, *Albert Bierstadt*, 167.

6. Hendricks, *Albert Bierstadt*, 233. Auction catalogues from 1891–92 include paintings titled *Oneida County, New York* and *Indian Summer, Oneida NY* by Bierstadt. See *Executor's Sale*, op. cit. and *Catalogue of the John C. Griswold collection of*

paintings: which include nineteen choice examples of the world-renowned artist Albert Bierstadt, N.A. with a few additions (New York: James P. Silo, Auctioneer, 1891), 8, 21.

7. Harriet McDoual Daniels, *Nine-Mile Swamp: A Story of the Loomis Gang* (Philadelphia: Penn Publishing Company, 1941); George W. Walter, *The Loomis Gang* (Prospect, NY: Prospect Books, 1953); E. Fuller Torrey, *Frontier Justice: The Rise and Fall of the Loomis Gang* (Utica, NY: North Country Books, 1992); E. Fuller Torrey, *Ride with the Loomis Gang* (Utica: North Country Books, 1997).

8. Ulysses Prentiss Hendrick, *A History of Agriculture in the State of New York* (Albany: J.B. Lyon Company, 1933), 295–300, 306, 335–343, 364–365, 433–436; David Maldwyn Ellis, "The Assimilation of the Welsh in Central New York," *New York History* 53, no. 3 (1972): 310; David Stradling, *The Nature of New York: An Environmental History of the Empire State* (Ithaca: Cornell University Press, 2010), 64.

9. US Bureau of the Census, *Historical Statistics of the United States, Colonial Times to 1970*, vol. 1 (Washington, DC: Department of Commerce, Bureau of the Census, 1975), 106.

10. Ellis, "The Assimilation of the Welsh in Central New York," 299–333.

11. Jones, *Annals and Recollections of Oneida County*, 307.

12. US Bureau of the Census, *Historical Statistics*, 1:106.

13. Durant, *History of Oneida County*, 330; Jones, *Annals and Recollections of Oneida County*, 577–578.

14. W.W. Clayton, *History of Onondaga County, New York* (Syracuse: D. Mason, 1878), 186–187.

15. Durant, *History of Oneida County*, 290; "St Patrick's Day in Utica," *Oneida Weekly Herald*, March 20, 1855.

16. Louis Dow Scisco, *Political Nativism in New York State* (New York: Columbia University Press, 1901), 48, 122–126; Thomas F. O'Connor, "Catholicism in the Fort Stanwix Country, 1776–1876," *Records of the American Catholic Historical Society of Philadelphia* 60, no. 2 (1949), 79–93.

17. Harold Frederic, *The Damnation of Theron Ware* (Chicago: Stone and Kimball, 1896); Bridget Bennet, *The Damnation of Harold Frederic: His Lives and Work* (Syracuse: Syracuse University Press, 1997), 21, 24, 31.

18. Foner, *Free Soil, Free Labor, Free Men*, 245–256, citing Jenkins to Hannibal Hamlin, Nov. 7, 1856.

19. Durant, *History of Oneida County*, 287, 337, 400.

20. Census Office, *9th Census, 1870*, vol. 1, *The Statistics and Population of the United States* (Washington, DC: Government Printing Office, 1872), 50–51.

21. Census Office, *9th Census, 1870*, 1:50–51, 215.

22. Census Office, *9th Census, 1870*, 1:215. Ward boundaries can be seen in D. G. Beers's *Atlas of Oneida County, New York* (Philadelphia: D.G. Beers and Co., 1874).

23. New York State Secretary's Office, *Census of the State of New York for 1875* (Albany: Weed, Parsons and Company Printers, 1877), 38. Ward boundaries

are shown on H. Wadsworth Clark, "Map of the City of Syracuse, published by Andrew Boyd for the Syracuse Directory 1873" (Syracuse: Gordon & Leis, Lithographers and Printers, 1873).

24. "New Council," *The Daily Observer* (Utica, NY), March 11, 1875; Durant, *History of Oneida County*, 303.

25. Syracuse Union, *Geschichte der Deutschen in Syracuse und Onondaga County* (Syracuse, NY: J. P. Pinzer, 1897), 159–181; Clayton, *History of Onondaga County*, 119.

26. Durant, *History of Oneida County*, 587.

27. Syracuse Union, *Geschichte der Deutschen*, 203–204; Durant, *History of Oneida County*, 345.

28. Census Office, *13th Census, 1910*, 11 vols. (Washington, DC: Government Printing Office, 1912–14), 1:781, 3:213, 216, 218, 231.

29. Census Office, *14th Census, 1920*, vol. 3 (Washington, DC: Government Printing Office, 1922), 701–702, 721, 726.

30. Philip Bean, *La Colonia: Italian Life and Politics in Utica, New York, 1860–1985* (Utica, NY: Utica College, Ethnic Heritage Studies Center, 2004); Bean, *The Urban Colonists: Italian American Identity and Politics in Utica, New York* (Syracuse: Syracuse University Press, 2010).

31. S. Joshua Kohn, *The Jewish Community of Utica, New York, 1847–1948* (New York: American Jewish Historical Society, 1959), 22, 23, 39, 44, 161–167; B. G. Rudolph, *From a Minyan to a Community: A History of the Jews of Syracuse* (Syracuse: Syracuse University Press, 1970).

32. Census Office, *14th Census, 1920*, 3:703, 721; Bean, *The Urban Colonists*, 216–217.

33. Joseph Hawley Murphy, "The Salt Industry of Syracuse—A Brief Review," *New York History* 30, no. 3 (1949): 304–315.

34. Michelle Stone, "German Immigrant Ancestors in Syracuse and Onondaga County, New York" (n.p., 2012), https://sites.rootsweb.com/~mstone/index.html; quote from a letter cited by Stone from Hans Knapp, *Viernheimer Auswandererbuch: Reißt euch los vom Tyrannenlande* (Viernheim: Hans Knapp, 1975).

35. Durant, *History of Oneida County*, 305–312.

36. Barbara A. Giambastiani, *Country Roads Revisited: The Cultural Imprint of Madison County* (Oneida, NY: Madison County Historical Society, 1984).

37. "President McKinley's Coffin," *New York Times*, September 15, 1901.

38. Cookinham, *History of Oneida County*, 2:524.

39. Biographical Review Publishing Company, *The Leading Citizens of Madison County* (Boston: Biographical Review Publishing Company, 1894), 5.

40. Biographical Review, *Leading Citizens*, 269–273.

41. Patricia A. Cooper, *Once a Cigar Maker: Men, Women, and Work Culture in American Cigar Factories, 1900–1919* (Urbana and Chicago: University of Illinois Press, 1987), 61.

42. Goldstein's US Passport Application, April 15, 1889. National Archives and Records Administration (NARA), Washington, DC, Roll: 324, Ancestry.com, *U.S. Passport Applications, 1795–1925* [database online]. Lehi, UT, USA: Ancestry.com Operations, Inc., 2007.

43. "Julius M. Goldstein, Prominent Oneidan, Dies at His Home," *Utica Observer-Dispatch*, January 16, 1938.

44. "Julius M. Goldstein of Oneida dies at 83," *New York Times*, January 16, 1938.

45. Anthony Wonderley, "Oneida's Forgotten Cigar Industry," *Madison County Historical Society* 44, no. 1 (2020), 4.

46. "Oneida," *Utica Free Press*, October 4, 1899; "State and Vicinity," *Brookfield Courier*, May 19, 1915; "Interesting Items," *Cazenovia Republican*, May 19, 1915.

47. "Oneida," *Utica Free Press*, October 4, 1899.

48. "J. M. Goldstein, 83, First Mayor, Dies," *Rome Sentinel*, January 17, 1938.

49. "Who Stole the Flag," *Oneida Evening Union*, August 8, 1898.

50. "Memorial Service for C. Will Chappell: Oneida is in Mourning," *Syracuse Post-Standard*, July 20, 1909.

51. "Miss Goldstein Bride of Jesse L. Oberdorfer," *Syracuse Post-Standard*, April 6, 1911. The wedding took place in the home of Adolph Guttman on Walnut Place. The *Syracuse Directory* of 1908 (Samson & Murdoch Co.), 908, 967, lists Guttman as a rabbi living at 102 Walnut Place.

52. "Oberdorfer Rites will be held on Wednesday: Notes Left by Former Brass Firm Executive Reveals Suicide by Poison," *Syracuse Journal*, August 20, 1935. The 1913 event was reported as an accident: "Oberdorfer has Narrow Escape," *Syracuse Journal*, February 10, 1913.

53. Dwight J. Stoddard, *Notable Men of Central New York* (Syracuse: Dwight J. Stoddard, 1903), 386–387.

54. Biographical Review, *Leading Men of Madison County*, 273.

55. "J. M. Goldstein, 83, First Mayor, Dies."

56. "Julius M. Goldstein, Prominent Oneidan, Dies at His Home"; "Oneida Now Has the Baby Lodge," *Oswego Daily Times*, March 8, 1902.

57. "Goldstein Rites Held Today," *Utica Daily Press*, January 18, 1938; "Julius Goldstein Dies; Cigar Manufacturer," *Syracuse Sunday American*, January 16, 1938.

58. Evamaria Hardin, "Archimedes Russell and Nineteenth-Century Syracuse," *The Courier* (Syracuse University Library Associates) 16, no. 3 and 4 (1979): 3–22.

59. Durant, *History of Oneida County*, 320–321; Bagg, *Memorial History*, 474.

60. Malio Cardarelli, "Carnegie Was No Friend of Utica Public Library," *Utica Observer Dispatch*, December 18, 2011. The previous building at 13 Elizabeth Street became the Utica School District Administration Building until it was razed in 1997. See Cardarelli, "Edgar Clark Utica Murals Finally Together Again," *Utica Observer-Dispatch*, December 1, 2013.

61. "Unveil Steuben Statue," *New York Times*, August 4, 1914.

62. Smith, *Our County and its People*, 354; Smith, *History of Chenango and Madison Counties, New York*, vol. 2 (Syracuse: D. Mason and Company, 1880), 591–592; Jocelyn Godwin, *The Spirit House, or Brown's Free Hall, in Georgetown, New York: A Short History* (Hamilton, NY: Upstate Institute at Colgate University, 2011).

63. Kevin Coffee, "The Success and Failure of Oneida Community Architecture," *American Communal Societies Quarterly* 12, no. 1 (2018): 4.

64. Janet R. White, "Designed for Perfection: Intersections between Architecture and Social Program at the Oneida Community," *Utopian Studies* 7, no. 2 (1996): 113–138; Coffee, "Success and Failure of Oneida Community Architecture," 3–27.

65. Robert S. Fogarty, "Oneida: A Utopian Search for Religious Security," *Labor History* 14, no. 2 (1973): 221.

66. Fogarty, "Oneida," 222; Kevin Coffee, "'The Oneida Community and the Utility of Liberal Capitalism," *Radical Americas* 4, no. 1 (2019): 3, 7.

67. John Taibi, *Railroading in the Stockbridge Valley* (Middletown, NY: O&W Railway Historical Society, 1996), Addendum, p. 3; Carden, *Oneida*, 117.

68. Klaw, *Without Sin*, 88.

69. Klaw, *Without Sin*, 181; Wonderley, *Oneida Utopia*, 98, 122–124.

70. Noyes, *The Berean*, 435.

71. John Humphrey Noyes, *Home Talks* (Oneida, NY: Oneida Community, 1875), 150.

72. Fogarty, *Special Love/Special Sex*; Wonderley, *Oneida Utopia*, 96–98.

73. Noyes, *American Socialisms*, 624.

74. Robertson, *Oneida Community*, 301–302; Oneida Community, *First Annual Report* (Oneida, NY: Oneida Community, 1849).

75. Emily Otis, letter to Beulah Hendee, November 9, 1864. Property of Syracuse University Special Collections.

76. *The Proceedings of the Women's Rights Convention held at Syracuse, September 8th, 9th, & 10th, 1852* (Syracuse: J. E. Masters, 1852), 38.

77. Gayle Veronica Fischer, "'She Ought to Be a *Female-man*': Dress Reform in the Oneida Community, 1848–1879," *Mid-America, An Historical Review* 77, no. 3 (1995): 258–261; Wonderley, *Oneida Utopia*, 229–230.

78. Wonderley, *Oneida Utopia*, 158; quoted from the Oneida Community's 1867 Handbook.

79. Pierrepont B. Noyes, *My Father's House: An Oneida Boyhood* (New York: Farrer & Rinehart, 1937), 66–67.

80. Jane Bailey, letter to Lily Cragin, undated. Property of Syracuse University Special Collections.

81. Noyes, *My Father's House*, 115.

82. Candace B. Bushnell, letter to Beulah Hendee, March 1, 1865. Property of Syracuse University Special Collections.

83. "The Oneida Community—What they do and how they live, Correspondence of the New York Tribune," *Rome Sentinel*, August 22, 1865.

84. Klaw, *Without Sin*, 191.
85. "Community Journal," *Oneida Circular*, November 3, 1873.
86. Wonderley, *Oneida Utopia*, 157
87. Doyle, *The Ministers' War*, 88–92.
88. Klaw, *Without Sin*, 84, 199–210; Wonderley, *Oneida Utopia*, 161–162, 168–174; Teeple, *The Oneida Family*, 189.
89. Monique Patenaude Roach, "The Loss of Religious Allegiance among the Youth of the Oneida Community," *The Historian* 63, no. 4 (2001): 787–806; Klaw, *Without Sin*, 216.
90. Fogarty, *Special Love/Special Sex*, 87.
91. Fogarty, *Desire and Duty*, 20–22.
92. Carden, *Oneida*, 98–101.
93. Doyle, *The Ministers' War*, 123–140.
94. Fogarty, *Desire and Duty*, 24; Doyle, *The Ministers' War*, 153–154, 160.

Chapter 7

1. "Un Caldo Appello alla Colonia Italiana," *La Gazzetta di Syracuse*, April 12, 1918.
2. Philip A. Bean, "The Great War and Ethnic Nationalism in Utica, New York, 1914–1920," *New York History* 74, no. 4 (1993): 382–413.
3. "For their Country's Sake," *Madison County Times* (Chittenango, NY), October 25, 1918, 3; "Reopen Syracuse Camp in Spring if War Continues," *Syracuse Post-Standard*, September 19, 1918; Arthur F. Thompson, Report of Influenza Epidemic at Syracuse Recruit Camp, Syracuse, NY—September 12 to October 15, 1918, RG 112 Records of the Office of the Surgeon General (Army). October 16, 1918, http://hdl.handle.net/2027/spo.0560flu.0014.650.
4. Robert V. Bruce, *1877: Year of Violence* (Indianapolis: Bobbs-Merrill Company, 1959), 203, 285; David Stowell, *Streets, Railroads, and the Great Strike of 1877* (Chicago: University of Chicago Press, 1999); David O. Stowell, "Albany's Great Strike of 1877," *New York History* 76, no. 1 (1995): 31–55.
5. "Militia Put Down Utica Strike Riots," *New York Times*, April 5, 1912; Philip A. Bean, "Leftists, Ethnic Nationalism, and the Evolution of Italian-American Identity and Politics in Utica's "Colonia," *New York History* 87, no. 4 (2006): 423–474; Philip A. Bean, *The Urban Colonists: Italian-American Identity and Politics in Utica, New York* (Syracuse: Syracuse University Press, 2010); James S. Pula, ed., *Ethnic Utica* (Utica, NY: Oneida County Historical Society, 2002).
6. James S. Pula and Philip Bean, "The Anatomy of Immigrant Strikes: A Comparison of Polish and Italian Textile Workers in Central New York," *The Polish Review* 41, no. 3 (1996): 273–292.
7. "Violent 1919 Strike Caused Chaos in Rome," *Rome Sentinel*, March 31, 2019.

8. Jan Voogd, *Race Riots and Resistance: The Red Summer of 1919* (New York: Peter Lang, 2008), 69.

9. "Platform Crashes at Heflin Meeting of 10,000 Klansmen," *New York Times*, June 17, 1928; David M. Chalmers, *Hooded Americanism: The History of the Ku Klux Klan*, 3rd ed. (New York: F. Watts, 1981), 257–265.

10. Bean, *The Urban Colonists*, 318–328; Rocco LaDuca, "Day 1: The Mob Files," *Utica Observer-Dispatch*, May 3, 2009; Alexander R. Thomas, *In Gotham's Shadow: Globalization and Community Change in Central New York* (Albany: State University of New York Press, 2003); George Schiro, *Americans by Choice: History of the Italians in Utica* (Utica: Thomas J. Griffiths Sons, 1940).

11. Mortimer F. Barrus, a plant pathologist at Cornell University set up a field laboratory in Oneida and took a series of remarkable photographs of Italian workers' life in seasonal camps and at work picking beans on Burt Olney's Canning Farm in the summer of 1909. These are housed in the Cornell University, Plant Pathology Herbarium (CUP) Collection, accession numbers 005940a-h; 005943b, 005944b-k, 005945b-c, 005644d.

12. Madison County Farmland Protection Board, "Madison County Agriculture and Farmland Protection Plan," July 2005, 13; Dorris Lawson. *Italians in Canastota* (Canastota, NY: Canastota Publishing Company, 1976); Joseph D'Amico, *The Italian Farmers of Canastota* (Charleston, SC: CreateSpace Publishing, 2010); Mike Milmo, "Hoo-ray for 'Sweet Sandwich,'" *Chittenango-Bridgeport Times*, April 13, 1983, 4.

13. Richard Goldstein, "Carmen Basilio Dies at 85; Took Title from Robinson," *New York Times*, November 7, 2012; Lou O'Neil, "Sports," *Long-Island Star Journal*, September 21, 1957, 6; Obituary of Joseph Basilio, *Rome Daily Sentinel*, August 12, 1974; Ron Yassen, dir., *Fighting the Mob: The Carmen Basilio Story* (ESPN, 2000); Mark Allen Baker, *Title Town USA: Boxing in Upstate New York* (Charleston, SC: The History Press, 2010).

14. Marlene Park, "City and Country in the 1930s: A Study of New Deal Murals in New York," *Art Journal* 39, no. 1 (1979): 37–47.

15. Jan DeAmicis, "Slavery in Oneida County, New York," *Afro-Americans in New York Life and History* 27, no. 2 (2003): 69–134; Jan DeAmicis, "'To Them That has Brot Me Up': Black Oneidans and their Families, 1850–1920," *Afro-Americans in New York Life and History* 21, no. 2 (1997): 19–38; S. David Stamps and Miriam Burney Stamps, *Salt City and its Black Community: A Sociological Study of Syracuse, New York* (Syracuse: Syracuse University Press, 2008), 27–37.

16. Stamps and Stamps, *Salt City and its Black Community*, 37–40; K. Animashaun Ducre, *A Place We Call Home: Gender, Race, and Justice in Syracuse* (Syracuse: Syracuse University Press, 2013); Matt Mulcahy, "The Map: Segregated Syracuse," WSTM, February 24, 2021, cnycentral.com/news/the-map-segregated-syracuse/the-map-segregated-syracuse-see-first-documented-association-of-race-and-redlining.

17. Census Office, *14th Census, 1920*, 3:687.

18. Census Office, *16th Census, 1940*; *Population: Characteristics of the Nonwhite Population by Race* (Washington, DC: Government Printing Office, 1943), 6.

19. Census Bureau, *1970 Census of Population, Advance Report* (1971), PC(V2)-34: New York, 4.

20. Robert Samuels, "In Syracuse, A Road and Reparations," *Washington Post*, October 20, 2019; Matt Mulcahy, "The Map: Segregated Syracuse . . . still," February 22, 2021, https://mmulcahy.exposure.co/the-map; Robert Searing, "1938: Pioneer Homes Give Syracuse Families a Chance at a 'Decent' Place to Live," Syracuse.com, May 20, 2021, https://www.syracuse.com/living/2021/05/1938-pioneer-homes-gives-syracuse-families-a-chance-at-a-decent-place-to-live.html; Stamps and Stamps, *Salt City and its Black Community*, 63.

21. Stamps and Stamps, *Salt City and its Black Community*, 80–87, 94; Alana Semuels, "How to Decimate a City," *The Atlantic*, November 20, 2015, https://www.theatlantic.com/business/archive/2015/11/syracuse-slums/416892/.

22. Syracuse-Onondaga Planning Agency, "Onondaga County Trends 2007 Summary," 2007, http://www.ongov.net/planning/documents/county_trends_summary_2007.pdf.

23. "Cornhill's History and Notable Residents," *Utica Observer-Dispatch*, December 31, 2015.

24. Semuels, "How to Decimate a City."

25. Dick Case, "Book Serves up the Life of Syracuse's 'Aunt Jemimah,'" *Syracuse Post-Standard*, November 3, 2002.

26. "Alex Haley Honored at his 'Roots'—Hamilton College," *New York Times*, May 30, 1977; "Rome Woman Recalls Working as Secretary to 'Roots' Writer Haley," *Rome Sentinel*, September 21, 2014.

27. Stamps and Stamps, *Salt City and its Black Community*, 124–128, 156–160; "Racial Violence Besets Syracuse," *New York Times*, August 17, 1967; Johnathan Croyle, "1967: After Claims of Police Brutality Downtown Syracuse Witnesses Scenes of Rioting and Looting," Syracuse.com, June 10, 2020, https://www.syracuse.com/living/2020/06/1967-after-claims-of-police-brutality-downtown-syracuse-witnesses-scenes-of-rioting-and-looting-vintage-photos.html.

28. Semuels, "How to Decimate a City."

29. Patrick Lohman and Catie O'Toole, "Afternoon Syracuse Black Lives Matter protest draws hundreds," Syracuse.com, July 18, 2016, https://www.syracuse.com/news/2016/07/afternoon_syracuse_black_lives_matter_protest_draws_hundreds.html.

30. Galpin, *Central New York*, 1:69–82; Cookinham, *History of Oneida County*, 1:442–446, 450–452.

31. Frank Tomaino, "Utica's 1950s Boom Era Began with Chicago Pneumatic," *Utica Observer-Dispatch*, May 10, 2018.

32. Frank Tomaino, "Utica's 1950s Boom Era," *Utica Observer-Dispatch*, May 10, 2018.

33. Ronald W. Schatz, "The Barons of Middletown and the Decline of the North-Eastern Anglo-Protestant Elite," *Past & Present* 219 (2013): 165–200; "Rand Strike Data Admitted by Court," *New York Times*, November 11, 1937.

34. Johnathan Croyle, "An Historical Timeline of the Lockheed Martin Plant in Salina," Syracuse.com, September 26, 2019, https://www.syracuse.com/living/2019/09/an-historical-timeline-of-the-lockheed-martin-plant-in-salina-photos.html?outputType=amp.

35. John Henry Thompson, ed., *Geography of New York State* (Syracuse: Syracuse University Press, 1966), 485.

36. Charley Hannagan, "New Process Gear Stops Production This Week after 124 Years," Syracuse.com, August 20, 2012, https://www.syracuse.com/news/2012/08/new_process_gear_closes_this_w.html; Johnathan Croyle, "Throwback Thursday: General Motors announces plans to close Salina plant in 1992," Syracuse.com, December 8, 2017, https://www.syracuse.com/vintage/2017/12/throwback_thursday_general_motors_announces_plans_to_close_salina_plant_in_1992.html.

37. Michael Luo and Lydia Polgreen, "Layoffs by Carrier Corp. Strike Syracuse in Heart," *New York Times*, October 7, 2003.

38. J. R. Short et al., "Reconstructing the Image of an Industrial City," *Annals of the Association of American Geographers* 83, no. 2 (1993): 213.

39. Thompson, *Geography of New York State*, 469; Census Bureau, *1970 Census of Population, Preliminary Report* (1971), PC(P2)-214, Utica-Rome, N.Y.

40. "The Thruway and Utica-Rome Tomorrow!" New York State Archives, New York State Thruway Authority, Motion pictures of Thruway construction and related matters, approximately 1951–1967, 14512-91, Box 2, 16mm, black & white, sound, 1951.

41. Noble E. Whitford, *History of the Barge Canal of New York State* (Albany: J. B. Lyon Co., 1922), 219, 480, 491–492.

42. New York State Department of Commerce, *New York State Vacationlands* (Albany: State of New York, 1959), 80–81.

43. Stradling, *Nature of New York*, 156; Jack Henke, *Sylvan Beach on the Lake Oneida: A History* (Lakemont, NY: North Country Books, 1975).

44. Eric Schmitt, "Boom Time for Army Base and its Region," *New York Times*, November 30, 1989, B1.

45. Thompson, *Geography of New York State*, 480, 482.

46. Carden, *Oneida*, 114, 116.

47. Anthony Wonderley, "Sherrill's Lost Dauphin Hill, Kinsley Farm," *Oneida Dispatch*, March 1, 2016. The church building was moved to Vernon, where it served as a Unitarian chapel and then as a town hall until it was razed in the 1960s and replaced with the current fire station.

48. Carden, *Oneida*, 130, 145, 150, 153, 173; Wonderley, *Oneida Utopia*, 196–198, 204–206.

49. Carden, *Oneida*, 114–116, 145–173.

50. Carden, *Oneida*, 175.

51. Jane Kinsley Rich, *A Lasting Spring: Jessie Catherine Kinsley, Daughter of the Oneida Community* (Syracuse: Syracuse University Press, 1983), xvi–xvii;

Katherine Rushworth, "Mansion House Exhibit Shows Creative Force of Oneida Community," Syracuse.com, July 11, 2010, https://www.syracuse.com/cny/2010/07/mansion_house_exhibit_shows_creative_force_of_oneida_community.html; Ellen Wiley Todd, *The "New Woman" Revised: Painting and Gender Politics on Fourteenth Street* (Berkeley: University of California Press, 1993), 43–48.

52. Wonderley, *Oneida Iroquois*, 38–49, 53.

53. Wayland-Smith, *Oneida*, 230–232.

54. Foster, *Free Love in Utopia*, xi–xii; Wayland-Smith, *Oneida*, 254–260.

55. Wolfgang Saxon, "Pierrepont Trowbridge Noyes, 78, Former Head of Oneida Tableware," *New York Times*, April 11, 1992, 33; Thompson, *Geography of New York State*, 485; Carden, *Oneida*, 181.

56. Constance L. Hays, "Why the Keepers of Oneida Don't Care to Share the Table," *New York Times*, June 20, 1999; Wayne Myers, "Company began as a Religious Commune," *Oneida Dispatch*, September 11, 2004, 1, 7.

57. Sean Kirst, "Turning Point to a Prolonged War," *Syracuse Post-Standard*, August 3, 2014, 1, 8.

58. "Vietnam War: Archive of American Gold Star Casualties," www.honorstates.org.

59. "Negroes Boycott Syracuse Drills," *New York Times*, April 22, 1970; Pat Putnam, "End of a Season at Syracuse," *Sports Illustrated*, September 28, 1970; David Marc, *Leveling the Playing Field: The Story of the Syracuse 8* (Syracuse, Syracuse University Press, 2015); Johnathan Croyle, "1970: Remembering the 'Syracuse 8,' the SU Football Players Who Risked Their Playing Careers for Change," Syracuse.com, July 1, 2020, https://www.syracuse.com/living/2020/07/1970-remembering-the-syracuse-8-the-su-football-players-who-risked-their-playing-careers-for-change.html.

60. "Syracuse U. Students Stage R.O.T.C. Sit-in," *New York Times*, February 20, 1970.

61. John Robert Green, *Syracuse University*, Vol. 5: *The Eggers Years* (Syracuse: Syracuse University Press, 1998), 23–44.

62. Thompson, *Geography of New York State*, 474–475, 484–485, 487.

63. Thompson, *Geography of New York State*, 479.

64. U.S. Congress, House Committee on Ways and Means, *Hearings before the Committee on Ways and Means on Tariff and Trade Proposals, Part 7* (Washington: U.S. Government Printing Office, 1968), 3503–3506.

65. Johnathan Croyle, "An Historical Timeline."

66. Agis Salpukas, "GE's Plants a Symbol of TV Output Decline in Northeast," *New York Times*, May 28, 1977.

67. Michael Luo and Lydia Polgreen, "Layoffs by Carrier Corp. Strike Syracuse in Heart," *New York Times*, October 7, 2003.

68. "Allied's Plan to Leave Shocks Syracuse Area," *New York Times*, April 29, 1985.

69. "Chicago Pneumatic Move," *New York Times*, February 29, 1996.

70. U.S. Census Bureau, "Patterns of Metropolitan and Micropolitan Population Change: 2000 to 2010 Tables," Chapter 1, https://www.census.gov/data/tables/time-series/dec/c2010sr-01.html.

71. Megan Carpentier, "When General Electric Jobs Left Schenectady So Did a Way of Life," *The Guardian* (UK), November 6, 2016.

72. Aaron Atteridge and Claudia Strambo, "Closure of the Kodak Plant in Rochester, United States: Lessons from Industrial Transition," Stockholm Environment Institute Briefing, June 2021. https://cdn.sei.org/wp-content/uploads/2021/06/closure-of-the-kodak-plan-in-rochester.pdf.

73. Paul Zielbauer, "Oneida County Seeks Fines from Woodstock '99 Organizers," *New York Times*, July 10, 1999.

74. "Mayhem at Woodstock Festival Has Led to 39 Arrests So Far," *New York Times*, August 5, 1999; Alona Wartofsky, "Woodstock '99 Goes Up in Smoke," *Washington Post*, July 27, 1999; Harmon Leon, "Woodstock 50 Is Cancelled—Why It's Time to Leave the Festival Alone," (New York) *Observer*, January 8, 2019.

75. Michael Streissguth, *City on the Edge: Hard Choices in the American Rust Belt* (Albany: State University of New York Press, 2020).

76. Brian Hiatt, "Did Woodstock '99 Kill Rock?" *Rolling Stone*, July 26, 2019, https://www.rollingstone.com/music/music-features/was-woodstock-99-end-of-rock-863958/.

77. William A. Hoglun, "Abandoned Farms and the 'New Agriculture' in New York State at the Beginning of the Twentieth Century," *New York History* 34, no. 2 (1953): 185–203.

78. Paul Abrahams, "Agricultural Adjustment during the New Deal Period the New York Milk Industry: A Case Study," *Agricultural History* 39, no. 2 (1965), 92–101.

79. "Russians to Vie with Farmers in Oneida County on Milk Yield," *New York Times*, December 5, 1959, 1; Max Frankel, "Rattle of Pails Fades in Soviet," *New York Times*, January 24, 1960.

80. Richard D. Lyons, "Conservative Sects Find Home in New York," *New York Times*, October 3, 1981; "Inexpensive Land Lures Amish, Mennonites to Region," *Utica Observer-Dispatch*, March 10, 2013; Jennifer Ellen Ifft and Yawen Gao, "Old Order Amish Settlements and New York Farmland Markets," *Journal of ASFMRA* (2019): 100–107.

81. Carly Fox et al., *Milked: Immigrant Dairy Farmworkers in New York State* (Workers' Center of Central New York and the Worker Justice Center of New York, 2017).

82. Office of the New York State Comptroller, "A Profile of Agriculture in New York State," August 2019, https://www.osc.state.ny.us/files/reports/special-topics/pdf/agriculture-report-2019.pdf; United States Department of Agriculture, "2017 Census of Agriculture: County Profiles, Oneida County, New York," https://www.nass.usda.gov/Publications/AgCensus/2017/Online_Resources/County_Profiles/.

83. Kristine McKenna, 'The Truth Behind 'Brother's Keeper,'" *Los Angeles Times*, February 11, 1993; Dick Case, "On the Farm, Ward Boys Shrug off the Fuss," *Syracuse Herald-American*, February 16, 1992.

84. Lionel D. Wyld, *Low Bridge! Folklore and the Erie Canal* (Syracuse: Syracuse University Press, 1962), 104–107.

85. Lionel D. Wyld, *Walter D. Edmonds, Storyteller* (Syracuse: Syracuse University Press, 1982), 1–44.

86. Walter D. Edmonds, *Drums along the Mohawk* (Boston: Little, Brown and Company, 1936), 461, 463.

87. "Gen. Herkimer's 40-mile March to be Marked," *New York Times*, May 26, 1912, 9.

88. "Neighboring News," *Cazenovia Republican*, September 26, 1912, 5.

89. "Sign was Removed," *Norwich Sun*, November 2, 1916.

90. Joan M. Zenzen, "Administrative Histories: Writing about Fort Stanwix National Monument," *The Public Historian* 31, No. 2 (2009): 56–57; Joan M. Zenzen, *Fort Stanwix National Monument: Reconstructing the Past and Partnering for the Future* (Albany: State University of New York Press, 2009).

91. United States Department of the Interior, National Parks Service, "Fort Stanwix National Monument: A Masterplan," 1967.

92. "Upstate Fort to be Rebuilt," *New York Times*, August 29, 1974, 66; John Menutt, "Colonial Ft Stanwix Undergoing Restoration," *New York* Times, August 2, 1970, 56.

93. "Bicentennial Barge Is Popular Upstate," *New York* Times, August 5, 1976.

94. Roger Segelken, "Exhibit Tour Keeps Historic Sprit Alive," *Syracuse Herald-American*, August 1, 1976; "Bicentennial Barge is Popular Upstate," *New York* Times, August 5, 1976.

95. Roger Segelken, "Rome Lays Siege to First Flag Title," *Syracuse Herald-American*, July 31, 1977.

96. Hauptman, *An Oneida Indian in Foreign Waters*, 1–20.

97. Hauptman, *An Oneida Indian in Foreign Waters*, 18, 24–25, 32, 35–36.

98. John Tashuda, "The Oneida Land Claim, Yesterday and Today," *Buffalo Law Review* 46 (1998): 1001–1009; *United States v. Boylan*, 265 F. 165 (2nd Cir. 1920); Hauptman, *An Oneida Indian in Foreign Waters*, 17, 21, 68–69.

99. Hauptman, *An Oneida Indian in Foreign Waters*, 70–71, 73–74, 83–84, 88, 90–91; Shattuck, *Oneida Land Claims*, 11.

100. Hauptman, *An Oneida Indian in Foreign Waters*, 78; Shattuck, *Oneida Land Claims*, 43–44; Schüler, *Oneida Roulette*, 108–109.

101. William T. Hagan, "To Correct Certain Evils: The Indian Land Claims Cases," in Christopher Vescey and William A. Starna, eds., *Iroquois Land Claims* (Syracuse: Syracuse University Press, 1988), 28.

102. Hauptman, *An Oneida Indian in Foreign Waters,* 95, 111; Shattuck, *Oneida Land Claims*, 234; Karim M. Tiro, "Claims Arising: The Oneida Nation of

Wisconsin and the Indian Land Claims Commission, 1951–1982," *American Indian Law Review* 32, no. 2 (2007): 518–520, 522–523.

103. Shattuck, *Oneida Land Claims*, 6–14.

104. Shattuck, *Oneida Land Claims*, 10–11, 24, 26–27, 34.

105. Shattuck, *Oneida Land Claims*, 51–52, 58, 75; Allan van Gestel, "The New York Indian Land Claims: The Modern Landowner as Hostage," in Vescey and Starna, *Iroquois Land Claims*, 131.

106. Harold Faber, "Oneida Indians Win Two Victories in Fight to Regain New York Lands," *New York Times*, July 17, 1977.

107. Van Gestel, "The New York Indian Land Claims," 126, 133n22.

108. Shattuck, *Oneida Land Claims*, 66–67, 70 76; "Suit by Oneida Indian Nation Bids New York Cede 6 Million Acres' *New York Times,* March 4, 1978.

109. Van Gestel, "The New York Indian Land Claims," 127.

110. Harold Faber, "Oneida Indians Win Two Victories."

111. Nina Dale, "The County of Oneida v. Oneida Indian Nation: The Continuing Saga of American Indian Territorial Wars," *Pace Environmental Law Review* 4, no. 1 (1986): 232.

112. Dale, "The County of Oneida v. Oneida Indian Nation," 245.

113. Wonderley, *Oneida Iroquois*, 214, 218.

114. "'Cold War' Pits Indian vs. Indian and Both Against City of Oneida," *New York Times,* August 2, 1976; "Divided Oneida Tribe Seeks to End Feud," *New York Times*, December 29, 1986; Johnathan Croyle, "From the Archives: When the Oneida Bingo Hall Burst into Flames," Syracuse.com, February 22, 2016, https://www.syracuse.com/vintage/2016/02/from_our_archives_the_oneida_b.html; Schüler, *Oneida Roulette*, 139–140, 146–147.

115. Kliph Nesteroff, "How Charlie Hill Became the First Native American Comedy Star," *Esquire*, February 11, 2021.

116. William Glaberson, "Struggle for Oneidas' Leadership Grows Bitter as Casino Succeeds," *New York Times*, June 17, 1996.

117. Beverly Gage, "Indian Country, NY," *The Nation*, November 27, 2000; Oneida Indian Nation 2019 Annual Report.

118. "Indian Tribes Make Own Cigarettes to Avoid NY Tax," *New York Times*, February 23, 2012; John Berry, "Oneida Nation, Banking on Tax-exempt Status, Buys Cigarette Factory," Syracuse.com, September 17, 2009, https://www.syracuse.com/news/2009/09/oneida_nation_banking_on_taxex.html.

119. Francis X. Clines, "Where Profit and Tradition Mingle; Oneida Nation's CEO Runs New York's First Indian Casino," *New York Times*, August 2, 1994.

120. William Glaberson, "Struggle for Oneidas' Leadership Grows Bitter"; David W. Chen and Charlie Leduff, "Bad Blood in Battle over Casinos; Issue Divides Tribes and Families as Expansion Looms," *New York Times*, October 28, 2001; Theresa Vargas and Annys Shin, "Oneida Indian Nation Is the Tiny Tribe Taking on the NFL and Dan Snyder over Redskins Name," *Washington Post*, November 16, 2013.

121. Francis X. Clines, "Where Profit and Tradition Mingle"; John Woodrow Cox, "Tribe Fighting Redskins Name Plans 'Oz' Casino despite Author's Racist Past," *Washington Post*, February 6, 2015.

122. William Glaberson, "Struggle for Oneidas' Leadership Grows Bitter"; City of Sherrill v. Oneida Indian Nation of NY, 544 US 197, Supreme Court 2005.

123. Vargas and Shin, "Oneida Indian Nation Is the Tiny Tribe"; Wonderley, *Oneida Iroquois*, 218–219.

124. David W. Chen and Charlie Leduff, "Oneida Indian Leadership in Flux after U.S. Flip-Flop' *New York Times*, September 19, 1993; "N.Y. Oneida Say Wis. Tribe Is Meddling," *The Capital Times* (Madison, Wisconsin), July 31, 1993; "Halbritter Defines Land Claim Dispute," *Syracuse Post-Standard*, June 25, 1994, B-4(C); David Tobin, "Group Can't Affiliate Itself with N.Y. Oneidas' *Syracuse Post-Standard*, July 6, 1994; "Oneida Faction Breaks Rank with Tribe," *Syracuse Herald Journal*, August 23, 1994; Mary Margaret Earl, "Vernon Oneidas Seek Independence," *Syracuse Herald Journal*, August 2, 1994; "Bad Blood in Battle over Casinos; Issue Divides Tribes and Families as Expansion Looms," *New York Times*, October 28, 2001; Glenn Coin, "Oneidas Evict Four Families," *Syracuse Post-Standard*, July 30, 2003, B5; David Melmer, "Wisconsin, New York Oneida Tribes Dispute Land Claim," *Chicago Tribune*, February 15, 2004; "Life and Times of a Clan Mother," *Utica Observer-Dispatch*, December 3, 2009; Joanne Shenandoah in Wilma Mankiller, ed., *Every Day is a Good Day: Reflections by Contemporary Indigenous Women* (Golden, CO: Fulcrum Publishing, 2011); Schüler, *Oneida Roulette*, 146–147, 160–173.

125. "Judge Excludes Landowners from Oneida Lawsuit," *New York Times*, September 27, 2000, p. B2.

126. Stephen W. Haggas, "Questions and Answers Concerning the Indian Land Claim Actions," January 5, 1999, https://ocgov.net/oneida/landclaim/important information.

127. Ezra Rosser, "Protecting Non-Indians from Harm? The Property Consequences of Indians," *Oregon Law Review* 87, no. 1 (2008): 198–202; "New York Rally Planned to Protest Land Claim by Oneidas," *New York Times*, January 30, 1999; Schüler, *Oneida Roulette*, 180.

128. Michelle Breidenbach, "Group Threatens to Kill Indians, Others," *Syracuse Post-Standard*, November 5, 1999; Gage, "Indian Country, NY."

129. "Rally Planned to Protest Land Claim by Oneidas," *New York Times*, January 30, 1999.

130. Gage, "Indian Country, NY."

131. Peter Applebome, "Land, Taxes and a Dispute as Old as the United States, *New York Times,* January 9, 2005.

Epilogue

1. Gage, "Indian Country, NY."

2. "Turning Stone Allowed to Continue Operating," *Syracuse Post-Standard*, June 14, 2007; "Ruling Lets Turning Stone Casino Stay Open," *Rochester Democrat and Chronicle*, June 14, 2007.

3. Quote from Justice Ginsberg's opinion in *City of Sherrill v. Oneida Indian Nation of N. Y.*, 544 U.S. 197 (2005).

4. Matthew L. M. Fletcher, "The Supreme Court's Indian Problem," *Hastings Law Journal* 59 (2008): 602.

5. "Ruth Bader Ginsburg Wants Trump to Appoint a Native American Woman to the Supreme Court," *The Buffalo Chronicle*, May 5, 2020.

6. *City of Sherrill v. Oneida Indian Nation of N. Y.*, 544 U.S. 197 (2005).

7. "Oneidas Win Agreement to Put Land into Federal Trust," *Syracuse Post-Standard*, May 21, 2008, A1, A6.

8. Quote from Justice Ginsberg's opinion in *City of Sherrill v. Oneida Indian Nation of N. Y.*, 544 U.S. 197 (2005).

9. Elizabeth Cooper, "State, Counties File Land-Into-Trust Suit," *Utica Observer-Dispatch*, June 20, 2008.

10. Glenn Coin, "Federal Judge Agrees with Oneidas in 3 Related Lawsuits," *Syracuse Post-Standard*, September 30, 2009.

11. Shaila K. Dewan, "After 5 Days, Oneida Deal is Unraveling," *New York Times*, February 22, 2002; Charles V. Bagli, "Deal by Wisconsin Oneidas May Clear Way for Casino," *New York Times*, November 19, 2003.

12. Ken Belson, "Judge says Oneida Indians Deserve a Right for Redress," *New York Times*, May 22, 2007.

13. Glenn Coin, "Oneidas' Land Claim Denied," *Syracuse Post-Standard*, August 10, 2010, A1, A9.

14. Glenn Coin, "Land Claim Appeal Won't be Heard," *Syracuse Post-Standard*, October 18, 2011, A3–4.

15. "State Grants Oneida Indians Exclusive Territory for Casino," *New York Times*, May 17, 2013, A17.

16. Glenn Coin, "Oneida Nation, State Agree on Wide-ranging Deal on Gaming, Taxing, Land," Syracuse.com, May 16, 2013, https://www.syracuse.com/news/2013/05/oneida_nation_state_agree_on_h.html; Glenn Coin and Michelle Breidenbach, "How Gov. Cuomo, the Oneida Indian Nation and Two Counties Made Historic Deal in Record Time," Syracuse.com, May 16, 2013, https://www.syracuse.com/news/2013/05/how_gov_coumo_the_oneida_india.html; "State Grants Oneida Indians Exclusive Territory for Casino," A17.

17. *Upstate Citizens for Equality, Inc. v. United* States, 841 F.3d 556 (2d Cir. 2016).

18. "Upstate Citizens Lament Supreme Court Decision," *Rome Sentinel*, December 1, 2017.

19. Claudia Tenney, "A Rotten Deal with 'Casino Oneidas,'" *New York Post*, May 29, 2013.

20. Elizabeth Cooper, "Is Tenney's Tweet Racist? Oneida Nation Objects to 'Spray Tan' Comment," *Utica Observer-Dispatch*, April 10, 2015.

21. John Woodrow Cox, "Tribe Fighting Redskins Name Plans 'Oz' Casino despite Author's Racist Past," *Washington Post*, February 6, 2015.

22. Annys Shin and Dan Steinberg, "Daniel Snyder Defends Redskins Name in Emotional Letter to Fans," *Washington Post*, October 9, 2013; Theresa Vargas and Susan Svrluga, "NFL Executives Meet with Oneida Indian who Supports Redskins Name," *Washington Post*, November 8, 2013; Ariel Sabar, "The Anti-Redskin," *The Atlantic*, October 2015.

23. Ray Halbritter, "The Terrible R-word that Football Needed to Lose," *CNN Opinion*, July 14, 2020.

24. Patrick Howley, "Anti-Redskins Indian Leader not a Legitimate Member of His Tribe," *Daily Caller*, October 14, 2013; Mike Florio, "Oneida Indian Nation Fires Back at Attacks on Ray Halbritter," *NBC Sports*, October 15, 2013.

25. Dennis Zotigh, "A Light at the Museum: Bringing a Massive Bronze to Life," *American Indian* 13, no. 3 (2017).

26. "Museum of the American Revolution Receives $10M Donation from Oneida Indian Nation," Museum of the American Revolution Press Release, July 11, 2012.

27. Margaret Splain, "We Need to Learn to Forgive Each Other," *Syracuse Post-Standard*, February 7, 2000, 13.

28. Michelle York, "Saving Oneidas' Language, One Long Word at a Time," *New York Times*, July 18, 2005, B6.

29. Monica Marie Zorilla, "Oneida Indian Nation Leader Ray Halbritter Launches Standing Arrow Productions, Will Adapt Sally Jenkins Book," *Variety*, February 22, 2021; "Oneida Indian Nation Plans Beach Project," *Rome Sentinel*, May 21, 2021; Oneida Indian Nation, 2021 Annual Report.

30. *Lilly v. Oneida Ltd. Employee Benefits Administrative Committee et al.*, United States District Court Northern District of New York, 2nd Circuit (2008).

31. Jolene Walters, "Kallet Says Plant Will Never Reopen," *Oneida Dispatch*, September 11, 2004, 1, 3.

32. Wayland-Smith, *Oneida*, 265.

33. *Lilly v. Oneida Ltd. Employee Benefits Administrative Committee et al.*

34. Office of the New York State Comptroller, "Special Report: Central New York Region Economic Profile," November 2016; Office of the New York State Comptroller, "Special Report: Mohawk Valley Region Economic Profile," July 2018.

35. New York State Department of Health, New York State Opioid Annual Report, 2019.

36. Charles A. Schumer, "War on Heroin Is Raging in Oneida County and Feds Need to Get More Involved," Press Release, February 17, 2015.

37. Geoff Herbert, "Syracuse Named One of the 'Worst Cities for Black Americans' to Live," Syracuse.com, November 28, 2017, https://www.syracuse.com/news/2017/11/syracuse_worst_cities_black_americans.html; Mark Weiner, "Syracuse's Poverty Rate Spikes among Hispanics, despite Declines in NY and Nation," Syracuse.

com, September 13, 2018, https://www.syracuse.com/politics/2018/09/syracuses_poverty_rate_spikes_among_hispanics_despite_declines_in_ny_and_nation.html.

38. Ron Johns, "Protesters Call for Action in 2005 Death of Walter Washington Jr. at Hands of Utica Police," *Utica Observer-Dispatch*, September 30, 2020.

39. H. Rose Schneider, "Protests Condemn Death of Utica Teen, Columbus Statue," *Utica Observer-Dispatch*, October 11, 2020.

40. Chris Baker, "What Happens at Columbus Circle When (or If) the Statue Comes Down," Syracuse.com, June 14, 2021, https://www.syracuse.com/news/2021/06/what-happens-at-columbus-circle-when-or-if-the-statue-comes-down.html.

41. Marisa Schultz, "GOP Congresswoman Calls Dem Opponent's Family 'Thuggish' Criminals," *New York Post*, September 28, 2018; Samantha Madison, "Tenney Memo Calls Brindisi's Family 'Criminals,' 'Thuggish,' " *Utica Observer-Dispatch*, September 20, 2018; Doug George-Kanentiio, "Lawmaker Goes Silent on Native Human Rights," indianz.com, August 23, 2018, https://www.indianz.com/News/2018/08/23/doug-georgekanentiio-lawmaker-goes-silen.asp.

42. Shane Goldmacher and Tyler Pager, "Trump Mocks Gillibrand and Cuomo in his First Visit to Upstate N.Y. as President," *New York Times*, August 13, 2018; Luke Perry, *Donald Trump and the 2018 Midterm Battle for Central New York* (Cham: Palgrave MacMillan, 2019).

43. Rick Moriarty, "Economist: Central NY Economy Improving, but Challenges Remain," Syracuse.com, January 22, 2020, https://www.syracuse.com/business/2020/01/economist-central-ny-economy-improving-but-challenges-remain.html.

44. Jesse McKinley, "General Electric Comes Back to Utica and Brings Jobs along with It," *New York Times*, August 20, 2015.

45. Stacy Cowley, "Setting a Made-in-the-U.S.A. Table: Yes, Do Stick a Fork in It," *New York Times*, October 21, 2015; "Sherrill Manufacturing Ramps up Production," *Rome Sentinel*, March 18, 2020.

46. "Oneida County Economy Continues Growth, Federal Agency Says," *Rome Sentinel*, December 19, 2019.

47. Teri Weaver, "Syracuse's I-81 project gets $800M in NY budget, with latest plan coming this summer," Syracuse.com, April 9, 2021; Robert Samuels, "In Syracuse, A Road and Reparations," *Washington Post*, October 20, 2019.

48. Paul Zielbauer, "Looking to Prosper as a Melting Pot; Utica, Long in Decline, Welcomes an Influx of Refugees," *New York Times*, May 7, 1999; Susan Hartman, "A New Life for Refugees, and the City They Adopted," *New York Times*, August 10, 2014; Susan Hartman, "How Refugees Transformed a Dying Rust Belt Town," *New York Times*, June 2, 2022; Alissa Scott, " 'Town that Loves Refugees': Is It Reality or Perception in Utica?" *Utica Observer-Dispatch*, February 27, 2017.

49. Chris Baker, "Refugees in Syracuse: Benefit or Burden? Here's What the Numbers Say," Syracuse.com, February 27, 2017, https://www.syracuse.com/poverty/2016/03/refugees_in_syracuse_benefit_burden.html.

Bibliography

Newspapers

American Socialist, Oneida, NY
Brookfield Courier, Brookfield, NY
The Buffalo Chronicle, Buffalo, NY
Canastota Bee-Journal, Canastota, NY
The Capital Times, Madison, WI
Cazenovia Republican, Cazenovia, NY
Chicago Tribune, Chicago, IL
Chittenango-Bridgeport Times, Chittenango, NY
The Communist, St. Louis, MO
Daily Observer, Utica, NY
La Gazzetta di Syracuse, Syracuse, NY
The Guardian, UK
Labor: A Cosmopolitan Newspaper, New York, NY
Long Island Star Journal, Long Island City, NY
Los Angeles Times, Los Angeles, CA
Madison County Times, Chittenango, NY
New York Post, New York, NY
New York Times, New York, NY
Northern Journal, Lowville, NY
Northern New York Journal, Watertown, NY
Norwich Sun, Norwich, NY
Oneida Community Circular, Oneida, NY
Oneida Dispatch, Oneida, NY
Oneida Evening Union, Oneida, NY
Oneida Telegraph, Oneida, NY
Oneida Sachem, Oneida, NY
Oneida Weekly Herald, Utica, NY

Oswego Daily Times, Oswego, NY
Oxford Times, Oxford, NY
Rochester Democrat and Chronicle, Rochester, NY
Rome Sentinel, Rome, NY
Syracuse Courier and Union, Syracuse, NY
Syracuse Herald American, Syracuse, NY
Syracuse Journal, Syracuse, NY
Syracuse Post-Standard, Syracuse, NY
Syracuse.com (*Syracuse Post-Standard*)
Utica Daily Press, Utica, NY
Utica Free Press, Utica, NY
Utica Observer-Dispatch, Utica, NY
Washington Post, Washington, DC
Waterville Times, Waterville, NY
Watertown Daily Reformer, Watertown, NY

Other Sources

Abrahams, Paul. "Agricultural Adjustment during the New Deal Period the New York Milk Industry: A Case Study." *Agricultural History* 39, no. 2 (1965): 92–101.

Ackley, Kristina. "Haudenosaunee Genealogies: Conflict and Community in the Oneida Land Claim." *American Indian Quarterly* 33, no. 4 (2009): 462–478.

Adams, Percy G., ed. *Crevecoeur's Eighteenth-Century Travels in Pennsylvania and New York*. Lexington, KY: University of Kentucky Press, 1961.

Atlas of Oneida County, New York. Philadelphia: D. G. Beers & Co., 1874.

Bagg, Moses Mears. *Memorial History of Utica, New York, From its Settlement to the Present Time*. Syracuse: D. Mason and Co., 1892.

Baker, Mark Allen. *Title Town USA: Boxing in Upstate New York*. Charleston, SC: The History Press, 2010.

Barbagallo, Tricia A. "Black Beach." *New York State Archives* 5, no. 1 (2005): 18–22.

Barber, John Warner, and Henry Howe. *Historical Collections of the State of New York*. New York: S. Tuttle, 1842.

Barnes, Erica, and Jason Emerson. *The Bear Tree and Other Stories from Cazenovia's History*. Syracuse: Syracuse University Press, 2021.

Barr, Daniel P. *Unconquered: The Iroquois League at War in Colonial America*. Westport, CT: Praeger, 2006.

Bean, Philip A. "The Great War and Ethnic Nationalism in Utica, New York, 1914–1920." *New York History* 74, no. 4 (1993): 382–413.

———. *La Colonia: Italian Life and Politics in Utica, New York, 1860–1985*. Utica, NY: Utica College, Ethnic Heritage Studies Center, 2004.

———. "Leftists, Ethnic Nationalism, and the Evolution of Italian-American Identity and Politics in Utica's 'Colonia.'" *New York History* 87, no. 4 (2006): 423–474.

———. *The Urban Colonists: Italian-American Identity and Politics in Utica, New York.* Syracuse: Syracuse University Press, 2010.

Belknap, Jeremy. *Journal of a Tour from Boston to Oneida, June 1796, with Notes by John Dexter.* Cambridge, MA: John Wilson and Son, 1882.

Belknap, Jeremy, and Jedediah Morse. *Report on the Oneida, Stockbridge, and Brothertown Indians, 1796.* New York: Museum of the American Indian, 1955.

Bennett, Monte R. "Glass Trade Beads from Central New York." In *Proceedings of the 1982 Glass Trade Bead Conference*, Research Records no. 16. Ed. Charles F. Hayes, 51–58. Rochester: Rochester Museum and Science Center, 1983.

Bennett, Monte R. "The Primes Hill Site, MSV 5-2, An Eighteenth-Century Oneida Station." *NYSAA Chenango Chapter* 22, no. 4 (Jan. 1988): 1–20.

Bennet, Bridget. *The Damnation of Harold Frederic: His Lives and Work.* Syracuse: Syracuse University Press, 1997.

Benton, Nathaniel Soley. *A History of Herkimer County.* Albany: J. Munsell, 1856.

Berleth, Richard. *Bloody Mohawk: The French and Indian War and the American Revolution on New York's Frontier.* Hensonville, NY: Black Dome, 2010.

Benn, Carl. *The Iroquois in the War of 1812.* Toronto: University of Toronto Press, 1998.

Bernstein, Peter L. *Wedding of the Waters: The Erie Canal and the Making of a Great Nation.* New York: W.W. Norton, 2005.

Blau, Harold. "The Iroquois White Dog Sacrifice: Its Evolution and Symbolism." *Ethnohistory* 11, no. 2 (1964): 97–119.

Blodgett, Harold William. *Samson Occom.* Hanover, NH: Dartmouth College Publications, 1935.

Bloomfield, Julia K. *The Oneidas.* New York: James Stewart, 1909.

Bogaert, Harmen Meyndertsz van den. *A Journey into Mohawk and Oneida Country, 1634–1635.* Translated and edited by Charles T. Gehring and William A. Starna. Syracuse: Syracuse University Press, 1988.

Bordewich, Fergus M. *Bound for Canaan: The Underground Railroad and the War for the Soul of America.* New York: Amistad, 2005.

Bradley, James W. *Evolution of the Onondaga Iroquois: Accommodating Change, 1500–1655.* Syracuse: Syracuse University Press, 1987.

———. *Onondaga and Empire: An Iroquoian People in an Imperial Era.* New York State Museum Bulletin, no. 514. Albany: State University of New York, 2020.

Bremer, Richard G. *Indian Agent and Wilderness Scholar: The Life of Henry Rowe Schoolcraft.* Mount Pleasant, MI: Clarke Historical Library, 1987.

Brown, George W. et al., eds. *Dictionary of Canadian Biography.* Volume 1. Toronto: University of Toronto & Université Laval, 1966.

Bruce, Robert V. *1877: Year of Violence.* Indianapolis: Bobbs-Merrill Company, 1959.

Brummer, Sidney David. *Political History of New York State during the Period of the Civil War*. New York: AMS Press, 1967.

Campbell, William W., ed. *The Life and Writings of De Witt Clinton*. New York: Baker and Scribner, 1849.

Campe, Joachim Heinrich. "Reise eines Deutschen nach dem See Oneida." *Sammtliche Kinder- und Jugend schriften, von Joachim Heinrich Campe*, vol. 29–30, Braunschweig: Schulbuchhandlung, 1830.

Campisi, Jack, and Laurence M. Hauptman, eds., *The Oneida Indian Experience: Two Perspectives*. Syracuse: Syracuse University Press, 1988.

Castex, Jean-Claude. *Dictionnaire des batailles terrestres franco-anglaises de la Guerre de Sept Ans*. Laval, QC: Les presses de l'Université Laval, 2006.

Ceci, Lynn. "The Value of Wampum among the New York Iroquois: A Case Study in Artifact Analysis." *Journal of Anthropological Research* 38, no. 1 (1982): 97–107.

Census Office. *1st Census, 1790: Return of the Whole Number of Persons within the Several Districts of the United States*. Philadelphia: Childs and Swaine, 1793.

———. *4th Census, 1820*. Washington, DC: Gales and Stratton, 1821.

———. *9th Census, 1870*. Vol. 1, *The Statistics and Population of the United States*. Washington, DC: Government Printing Office, 1872.

———. *13th Census, 1910*. 11 vols. Washington, DC: Government Printing Office, 1912–14.

———. *14th Census, 1920*. Vol. 3. *Population, 1920*. Washington, DC: Government Printing Office, 1922.

———. *16th Census, 1940. Population: Characteristics of the Nonwhite Population by Race*. Washington, DC: Government Printing Office, 1943.

———. *19th Census*, 1970. *1970 Census of Population, Advance Report* (1971). Washington, DC: Government Printing Office, 1971.

Champlain, Samuel de. *Voyages et descouvertures faites en la Nouvelle France, depuis l'année 1615, jusques à la fin de l'année 1618*. Paris: Claude Collet, 1618.

———. *Voyages of Samuel de Champlain, 1604–1618*. W.L. Grant, ed. New York: Charles Scribner's Sons, 1907.

Chalmers, David M. *Hooded Americanism: The History of the Ku Klux* Klan. 3rd ed. New York: F. Watts, 1981.

Child, Hamilton, comp. *Gazetteer and Business Directory of Madison County, N.Y. for 1868–9*. Syracuse: Journal Office, 1868.

Churchill, John C. ed., *Landmarks of Oswego County*. Syracuse: D. Mason and Company, 1895.

Clayton, W. W. *History of Onondaga County, New York*. Syracuse: D. Mason, 1878.

Coffee, Kevin. "The Oneida Community and the Utility of Liberal Capitalism." *Radical Americas* 4, no. 1 (2019): 1–22.

———. "The Success and Failure of Oneida Community Architecture." *American Communal Societies Quarterly* 12, no. 1 (Jan 2018): 3–27.

Coggeshall, William T. *The Journeys of Abraham Lincoln: From Springfield to Washington 1861, as President Elect; and from Washington to Springfield, 1865, as President Martyred*. Columbus: Ohio State Journal, 1865.

Cohn, Raymond L. "Nativism and the End of the Mass Migration of the 1840s and 1850s." *The Journal of Economic History* 60, no. 2 (2000): 361–383.

Colden, Cadwallader. *The History of the Five Indian Nations of Canada, which are dependent on the Province of New-York in America*. London: Printed for T. Osborne in Gray's-Inn, 1747.

Cole, Richard, and Monte Bennett. "The Upper Hogan Site OND 5-4." *NYSAA Chenango Chapter Bulletin* 15, no. 2 (1974).

Cook, Thomas M., and Thomas W. Knox, eds. *Public Record: Including Speeches, Proclamations, Official Correspondence and Other Public Utterances of Horatio Seymour*. New York: I. W. England, 1868.

Cooper, Patricia A. *Once a Cigar Maker: Men, Women, and Work Culture in American Cigar Factories, 1900–1919*. Urbana and Chicago: University of Illinois Press, 1987.

Commissioner of Indian Affairs, *Treaties between the United States of America and the several Indian Tribes, from 1778 to 1837*. Washington, DC: Langtree and O'Sullivan, 1837.

Cookinham, Henry J. *History of Oneida County, New York: From 1700 to the Present Time*. 2 vols. Chicago: S. J. Clarke, 1912.

Cooper, James Fenimore. *The Last of the Mohicans*. New York: Penguin, 1986.

———. *The Leatherstocking Tales*. Blake Nevius, ed. 2 vols. New York: Literary Classics of the United States, Syndicate of the University of Cambridge, 1985.

Countryman, Edward. *The American Revolution and Political Society in New York, 1760–1790*. Baltimore: Johns Hopkins University Press, 1981.

Cross, Whitney R. *The Burned-over District: The Social and Intellectual History of Enthusiastic Religion in Western New York*. Ithaca: Cornell University Press, 1950.

Cusik, David. *Sketches of the Ancient History of the Six Nations*. Lewiston, NY: Cooley & Lathrop Printers, 1828.

Dale, Nina. "The County of Oneida v. Oneida Indian Nation: The Continuing Saga of American Indian Territorial Wars." *Pace Environmental Law Review* 4, no. 1 (1986): 221–251.

D'Amico, Joseph. *The Italian Famers of Canastota*. Charleston, SC: CreateSpace Publishing, 2010.

Daniels, Harriet McDoual. *Nine-Mile Swamp: A Story of the Loomis Gang*. Philadelphia: Penn Publishing Company, 1941.

Dann, Norman K. *Peter Smith of Peterboro: Furs, Land and Anguish*. Hamilton, NY: Log Cabin Books, 2018.

———. *Practical Dreamer: Gerrit Smith and the Crusade for Social Reform*. Hamilton, NY: Log Cabin Books, 2009.

DeAmicis, Jan. "Slavery in Oneida County, New York." *Afro-Americans in New York Life and History* 27, no. 2 (2003): 69–134.

———. "'To Them That has Brot Me Up': Black Oneidans and their Families, 1850–1920." *Afro-Americans in New York Life and History* 21, no. 2 (1997): 19–38.

Desjardins, Simon, and Pierre Pharoux, *Castorland Journal: An Account of the Exploration and Settlement of Northern New York State by French Émigrés in the Years 1793–1797*. Edited and translated by John A. Galucci. Ithaca: Cornell University Press, 2010.

Dixon, William Hepworth. *New America*. London: Hurst and Blackett, 1869.

Dolan, Eric J. *Fur, Fortune, and Empire: The Epic History of the Fur Trade in America*. New York: W.W. Norton and Company, 2010.

Doyle, Michael. *The Ministers' War: John W. Mears, the Oneida Community, and the Crusade for Public Morality*. Syracuse: Syracuse University Press, 2018.

Drake, Samuel G. *A Particular History of the Five Years French and Indian War*. Albany: Joel Munsell, 1870.

Ducre, K. Animashaun. *A Place We Call Home: Gender, Race, and Justice in Syracuse* Syracuse: Syracuse University Press, 2013.

Durant, Samuel W. *History of Oneida County, New York, with Illustrations and Biographical Sketches*. Philadelphia: Everts & Fariss, 1878.

Eastman, Hubbard. *Noyesism Unveiled: A History of the Sect Self-styled Perfectionists with a Summary View of their Leading Doctrines*. Battleboro, VT: H. Eastman, 1849.

Edmonds, Walter D. *Drums along the Mohawk*. Boston: Little, Brown and Company, 1936.

Ellis, David Maldwyn. "The Assimilation of the Welsh in Central New York." *New York History* 53, no. 3 (1972): 299–333.

Englebrecht, William. *Iroquoia: The Development of a Native World*. Syracuse: Syracuse University Press, 2005.

Falk, Cynthia G. "Forts, Rum, Slaves, and the Herkimers' Rise to Power in the Mohawk Valley." *New York History* 89, no. 3 (2008): 221–234.

Faust, Ralph M. *The Story of Oswego, With Notes about several Towns in the County*. Oswego, NY: Palladium-Times Press, 1934.

Feranec, Robert S., and Andrew L. Kozlowski. "Implications of a Bayesian Radiocarbon Calibration of Colonization Ages for Mammalian Megafauna in Glaciated New York State after the Last Glacial Maximum." *Quaternary Research* 85, no. 2 (2016): 262–270.

———. "Ice Age Mammals Colonize New York: A STEM Lab Derived from Collections-Based Research at the New York State Museum." *New York State Museum Education Leaflet* 37. Albany: New York State Museum, 2017.

Field, Phyllis F. *The Politics of Race in New York: The Struggle for Black Suffrage in the Civil War Era*. Ithaca: Cornell University Press, 1982.

Finney, Charles Grandison. *The Memoirs of Charles G. Finney: The Complete Restored Text*. Edited by Ricard A. Dupuis and Garth M. Rosell. Grand Rapids, MI: Academie Books, 1989.

Fischer, David Hackett. *Champlain's Dream: The European Founding of North America*. New York: Simon and Schuster, 2009.

Fischer, Gayle Veronica. "'She Ought To Be a *Female-man*': Dress Reform in the Oneida Community, 1848–1879." *Mid-America, An Historical Review* 77, no. 3 (1995): 237–265.

Fletcher, Matthew L. M. "The Supreme Court's Indian Problem." *Hastings Law Journal* 59 (2008): 579–642.

Fleming, Susan. "The Boston Patrons of Jean-Francois Millet," in *Jean-François Millet*, exhibit catalog. Edited by Alexandra Murphy. Boston: Museum of Fine Arts, Boston, 1984.

Fogarty, Robert S., ed. *Desire and Duty at Oneida: Tirzah Miller's Intimate Memoir*. Bloomington: Indiana University Press, 2000.

———. "Oneida: A Utopian Search for Religious Security." *Labor History* 14, no. 2 (1973): 202–227.

———., ed. *Special Love/Special Sex: An Oneida Community Diary*. Syracuse: Syracuse University Press, 1994.

Foner, Eric. *Free Soil, Free Labor, Free Men: The Ideology of the Republican Party before the Civil War*. Oxford: Oxford University Press, 1979.

Force, Peter, ed. *American Archives: Consisting of authentick records, state papers, debates, and letters and other notices of publick affairs*. Series 4, Vol. 2. Washington, DC: US Congress, 1837–53.

Foster, Lawrence. *Free Love in Utopia: John Humphrey Noyes and the Origin of the Oneida Community*. Urbana: University of Illinois Press, 2001.

Frederic, Harold. *The Damnation of Theron Ware*. Chicago: Stone and Kimball, 1896.

Frothingham, Octavius Brooks. *Gerrit Smith: A Biography*. New York: G.P. Putnam's Sons, 1878.

Funk, Robert E., and Robert D. Kuhn. "Three Sixteenth-Century Mohawk Iroquois Village Sites." *New York State Museum Bulletin* 503 (2003).

Geherin, Christopher. "New Guinea: Racial Identity and Inclusion in the Stockbridge and Brothertown Indian Communities of New York." *New York History* 90, no. 3 (2009): 141–166.

Giambastiani, Barbara A. *Country Roads Revisited: The Cultural Imprint of Madison County*. Oneida, NY: Madison County Historical Society, 1984.

Gibson, Gary M., "The U.S. Brig *Oneida*: A Design and Operational History." *War of 1812 Magazine* 19 (2012): 1–82.

Glatthaar, Joseph T., and James Kirby Martin, *Forgotten Allies: The Oneida Indians and the American Revolution*. New York: Hill and Wang, 2006.

Godwin, Jocelyn. *The Spirit House, or Brown's Free Hall, in Georgetown, New York: A Short History.* Hamilton, NY: Upstate Institute at Colgate University, 2011.

Goulson, Cary F., comp. *Seventeenth-Century Canada: Source Studies.* Toronto: Macmillan of Canada, 1970.

Graymont, Barbara. *The Iroquois in the American Revolution.* Syracuse: Syracuse University Press, 1972.

Green, John Robert. *Syracuse University.* Vol. 5: *The Eggers Years.* Syracuse: Syracuse University Press, 1998.

Greene, Nelson, ed. *History of the Mohawk Valley: Gateway to the West, 1614–1925.* 4 Vols. Chicago: S. J. Clark, 1924.

Hagerty, Gilbert. *Massacre at Fort Bull: The De Léry Expedition against Oneida Carry, 1756.* Providence, RI: Mowbray Co., 1971.

Hall, John, and Mary Ann Hall, *History of the Presbyterian Church in Trenton, N.J.* Trenton, NJ: MacCrellish & Quigley, 1912.

Hambrick-Stowe, Charles E. "Charles G. Finney and Evangelical Anti-Catholicism." *U.S. Catholic Historian* 14, no. 4 (1996): 39–52.

Hammond, Luna M. *History of Madison County, State of New York.* Syracuse: Truair, Smith & Co., 1872.

Hardin, Evamaria. "Archimedes Russell and Nineteenth-Century Syracuse." *The Courier* (Syracuse University Library Associates), 16.3 and 16.4 (1979): 3–22.

Hart, John P., and Hetty Jo Brumbach, "The Death of Owasco." *American Antiquity* 68, no. 4 (2003): 737–752.

Hauptman, Laurence M. *Conspiracy of Interests: Iroquois Dispossession and the Rise of New York State.* Syracuse: Syracuse University Press, 1999.

———. *An Oneida Indian in Foreign Waters: The Life of Chief Chapman Scanandoah.* Syracuse: Syracuse University Press, 2016.

———. *The Iroquois in the Civil War: From Battlefield to Reservation.* Syracuse: Syracuse University Press, 1992.

Hauptman, Laurence, and L. Gordon McLester III. *Chief Daniel Bread and the Oneida Nation of Indians of Wisconsin.* Norman: University of Oklahoma Press, 2002.

Hauptman, Laurence and L. Gordon McLester III, eds. *The Oneida Indian Journey: From New York to Wisconsin.* Madison, WI: University of Wisconsin Press, 1999.

Haydon, Roger, ed. *Upstate Travels: British Views of Nineteenth-Century New York.* Syracuse: Syracuse University Press, 1982.

Hawkins, Ernest. *Historical Notices of the Church of England in the North American Colonies, Previous to the Independence of the United States.* London: B. Fellowes. 1845.

Hendrick, Ulysses Prentiss. *A History of Agriculture in the State of New York.* Albany: J.B. Lyon Company, 1933.

Hendricks, Gordon. *Albert Bierstadt: Painter of the American West.* New York: H.N. Abrams, 1974.

Henke, Jack. *Sylvan Beach on the Lake Oneida: A History.* Lakemont, NY: North Country Books, 1975.

Helmer, William F. *O.&W.: The Long Life and Slow Death of the New York, Ontario and Western Railway*. Berkeley, CA: Howell-North Press, 1959.

Higgins, Ruth L., *Expansion in New York: With Especial Reference to the Eighteenth Century*. Columbus: Ohio State University, 1932.

Hoglun, William A. "Abandoned Farms and the 'New Agriculture' in New York State at the Beginning of the Twentieth Century." *New York History* 34, no. 2 (1953): 185–203.

Hopkins, Vivian C. "De Witt Clinton and the Iroquois." *Ethnohistory* 8, no. 2 (1961): 113–143.

Horton, Russell. "Unwanted in a White Man's War: The Civil War Service of the Green Bay Tribes." *The Wisconsin Magazine of History* 88, no. 2 (2004): 18–27.

Hough, Franklin B. *A History of Jefferson County in the State of New York from the Earliest Period to the Present Time*. Albany: Joel Munsell, 1854.

———, ed., *Proceedings of the Commissioners of Indian Affairs, Appointed by law for the extinguishment of Indian Titles in the State of New York*. 2 vols. Albany: Joel Munsell, 1861.

Ibbitson, Joseph D., and S. N. D. North, eds., *Documentary History of Hamilton College*. Clinton, NY: Hamilton College, 1922.

Ifft, Jennifer Ellen, and Yawen Gao. "Old Order Amish Settlements and New York Farmland Markets." *Journal of ASFMRA* (2019): 100–107.

Jackson, Harry F. *Scholar in the Wilderness: Francis Adrian Van der Kemp*. Syracuse: Syracuse University Press, 1963.

Jackson, Harry F., and Thomas F. O'Donnell. *Back Home in Oneida: Hermon Clarke and his Letters*. Syracuse: Syracuse University Press, 1965.

Jacobs, Jaap. *New Netherland: A Dutch Colony in Seventeenth-Century America*. Leiden: Brill, 2005.

Jennings, Francis. *The Ambiguous Iroquois Empire: The Covenant Chain Confederation of Indian Tribes with English Colonies*. New York & London: W.W. Norton, 1984.

Johnson, William. *The Papers of Sir William Johnson*. 14 vols. Albany: University of the State of New York, 1921–65.

Jones, Eric E. "Iroquois Population History and Settlement Ecology, AD 1500–1700," PhD diss., Pennsylvania State University, 2008.

———. "Population History of the Onondaga and Oneida Iroquois, A.D. 1500–1700." *American Antiquity* 75, no. 2 (2010): 387–407.

———. "Using Viewshed Analysis to Explore Settlement Choice: A Case Study of the Onondaga Iroquois." *American Antiquity* 71, no. 3 (2006): 523–538.

Jones, Pomroy. *Annals and Recollections of Oneida County*. Rome, NY: Published by the author, 1851.

Kirkland, Samuel. *The Journals of Samuel Kirkland: 18th Century Missionary to the Iroquois, Government Agent, Father of Hamilton College*. Edited by Walter Pilkington. Clinton, NY: Hamilton College, 1980.

Klaw, Spencer. *Without Sin: The Life and Death of the Oneida Community*. New York: Allen Lane, 1993.

Klein, Milton M. *The Empire State: A History of New York State.* Ithaca: Cornell University Press, 2001.

Klingberg, Frank J. "The Noble Savage as Seen by the Missionary of the Society for the Propagation of the Gospel in Colonial New York, 1702–1750." *Historical Magazine of the Protestant Episcopal Church* 8 no. 2 (1939): 128–165.

Koeppel, Gerard. "Andrew Bartow and the Cement that Made the Erie Canal." *The New-York Journal of American History* 66, no. 1 (2005): 52–60.

Kohn, S. Joshua. *The Jewish Community of Utica, New York, 1847–1948.* New York: American Jewish Historical Society, 1959.

Kurczewski, Frank E. "Historic and Prehistoric Changes in the Rome, New York Pine Barrens." *Northeastern Naturalist* 6, no. 4 (1999): 327–340.

Landon, Harry F. *The North Country; A History, Embracing Jefferson, St. Lawrence, Oswego, Lewis and Franklin Counties, New York.* 3 Vols. Indianapolis: Historical Publishing Company, 1932.

Lange, Victor. "Visitors to Lake Oneida: An Account of the Background of Sophie von la Roche's Novel 'Erscheinungen am See Oneida.'" *Symposium: A Quarterly Journal in Modern Literatures* 2, no. 1 (1948): 48–78.

Lawson, Dorris. *Italians in Canastota.* Canastota, NY: Canastota Publishing Company, 1976.

The Leading Citizens of Madison County. Boston: Biographical Review Publishing Company, 1894.

Lehman, J. David. "The End of the Iroquois Mystique: The Oneida Land Cession Treaties of the 1780s." *The William and Mary Quarterly* 47, no. 4 (1990): 523–547.

Levinson, David. "An Explanation for the Oneida-Colonist Alliance in the American Revolution." *Ethnohistory* 23, no. 3 (1976): 265–289.

Lewis, Tom. *The Hudson: A History.* New Haven: Yale University Press, 2005.

Lincklaen, John. *Travels in the Years 1791 and 1792 in Pennsylvania, New York, and Vermont.* New York: G. P. Putnam's Sons, 1897.

Lomax, John A., and Alan Lomax. *American Ballads and Folk Songs.* New York: Macmillan, 1934.

Lord, Philip, Jr. "The Covered Locks of Wood Creek," *The Journal of the Society for Industrial Archaeology* 27, no. 1 (2001): 5–15.

Lothrop, Jonathan C., Darrin L. Lowery, Arther E. Spiess, and Christopher J. Ellis. "Early Human Settlement of Northeastern North America," *PaleoAmerica* 2, no. 3 (2016): 192–251.

Lothrop, Jonathan C., Michael Beardsley, Mark Clymer, Susan Winchell-Sweeney, and Meredith H. Younge. "Current Archaeological Research on Paleoindian Sites in Central New York." In Eugene Domack, ed., *Oneida Basin, Glacial Lake Iroquois and Archaeological Contexts,* Guidebook for 79th Annual Reunion of the Northeastern Friends of the Pleistocene Field Conference, June 3–5, 2016, Verona, New York.

Lothrop, Samuel Kirkland. *Life of Samuel Kirkland, Missionary to the Indians*. Boston: Charles C. Little and James Brown, 1848.

MacLeod, D. Peter. *The Iroquois of Canada and the Seven Years' War*. Toronto: Dundurn Press, 1996.

MacFarlane, Janet R., Isaac Taintor, G. B. Shearman, and S. B. Shearman. "Oneida Glass Factory Company." *New York History* 28, no. 1 (1947): 75–78.

Mandell, Daniel R. "'Turned their Mind to Religion': Oquaga and the First Iroquois Church, 1748–1776." *Early American Studies* 11, no. 2 (2013): 211–242.

Mankiller, Wilma, ed. *Every Day is a Good Day: Reflections by Contemporary Indigenous Women*. Golden, CO: Fulcrum Publishing, 2011.

Manley, Henry S. *The Treaty of Fort Stanwix, 1784*. Rome, NY: Rome Sentinel Company, 1932.

Marc, David. *Leveling the Playing Field: The Story of the Syracuse 8*. Syracuse, Syracuse University Press, 2015.

McManamon, Francis P., ed. *Archaeology in America: An Encyclopedia*. 4 vols. Westport, CT: Greenwood Publishing Group, 2009.

McPherson, James M. *Battle Cry of Freedom: The Civil War Era*. Oxford: Oxford University Press, 1988.

McShea, Bronwen. *Apostles of Empire: The Jesuits and New France*. Lincoln: University of Nebraska Press, 2019.

Meyers, Jeffrey. *Edmund Wilson: A Biography*. Boston: Houghton Mifflin Company, 1995.

Miquelon, Dale. "Ambiguous Concession: What Diplomatic Archives Reveal about Article 15 of the Treaty of Utrecht and France's North American Policy." *The William and Mary Quarterly* 67, no. 3 (2010): 459–486.

Monseignat, Charles de. "Relation de ce qui s'est passé de plus remarquable en Canada depuis le depart des vaisseaux de lannée derniere 1695 jusqu'au commencement de Novembre 1696." MS Can 35.4. Houghton Library, Harvard University, Cambridge, MA.

Morgan, Lewis H. *League of the Ho-de-no-sau-nee, or Iroquois*. Edited by Herbert M. Lloyd. New York: Dodd, Mead and Company, 1904.

Morrison, Howard Alexander. "Gentlemen of Proper Understanding: A Closer Look at Utica's Anti-Abolitionist Mob." *New York History* 62, no. 1 (1981): 61–82.

Morrison, Samuel Eliot. *The European Discovery of America: The Northern Voyages, A.D. 500–1600*. Oxford: Oxford University Press, 1971.

Murphy, Joseph Hawley. "The Salt Industry of Syracuse: A Brief Review." *New York History* 30, no. 3 (1949): 304–315.

New York State Department of Commerce. *New York State Vacationlands*. Albany: State of New York, 1959.

New York State Legislature. *Documents of the Assembly of the State of New York, Fifty-Fifth Session, 1832*. Albany: E. Croswell, 1832.

———. *Legislative Documents of the Senate and Assembly of the State of New York Fifty-Third Session, 1830*. Albany: E. Croswell, 1830.

———. *Documents of the Senate of the State of New York, Fifty-Seventh Session, 1834*. Albany: E. Croswell, 1834.

———. *Documents of the Senate of the State of New York, Seventy-Second Session,* 1849.

———. *Laws of the State of New York, passed at the Thirty-Eighth session of the Legislature*. Albany: J. Buel, 1815.

New York State Secretary's Office. *Census of the State of New York for 1875*. Albany: Weed, Parsons and Company, 1877.

Norton, David J. *Rebellious Younger Brother: Oneida Leadership and Diplomacy, 1750–1800*. De Kalb, IL: Northern Illinois University Press, 2009.

Noyes, George Wallingford, ed. *John Humphrey Noyes, The Putney Community*. Oneida, NY: G. W. Noyes, 1931.

———, ed. *Religious Experience of John Humphrey Noyes, Founder of the Oneida Community*. New York: Macmillan, 1923.

Noyes, John Humphrey. *The Berean: A Manual for the Help of Those Who Seek the Faith of the Primitive Church*. Putney, VT: Office of the Spiritual Magazine, 1847.

———. *Confession of Religious Experience*. Oneida, NY: Leonard and Company, 1849.

———. *History of American Socialisms*. Philadelphia: J. B. Lippincott and Company, 1870.

———. *Home Talks*. Oneida, NY: Oneida Community, 1875.

———. *Male Continence*. Oneida, NY: Oneida Community, 1872.

———. *The Way of Holiness*. Putney, VT: J. H. Noyes and Company, 1838.

Noyes, Pierrepont B. *My Father's House: An Oneida Boyhood*. New York: Farrer & Rinehart, 1937.

Oberg, Michael Leroy. *Peacemakers: The Iroquois, the United States, and the Treaty of Canandaigua, 1794*. Oxford: Oxford University Press, 2016.

———. *Professional Indian: The American Odyssey of Eleazar Williams*. Philadelphia: University of Pennsylvania Press, 2015.

O'Callaghan, E. B., ed. *Documentary History of the State of New York*. 4 vols. Albany: Weed, Parsons & Co., 1849–51.

———, ed. *Documents Relative to the Colonial History of New York*. 15 vols. Albany: Weed, Parsons & Co., 1853–87.

Oneida Community. *First Annual Report*. Oneida, NY: Oneida Community, 1849.

O'Connor, Thomas F. "Catholicism in the Fort Stanwix Country, 1776–1876." *Records of the American Catholic Historical Society of Philadelphia* 60, no. 2 (1949): 79–93.

O'Toole, Fintan. *White Savage: William Johnson and the Invention of America*. London: Faber & Faber, 2005.

Otterness, Philip. *Becoming German: The 1709 Palatine Migration to New York*. Ithaca: Cornell University Press, 2004.

Oved, Yaacov. *Two Hundred Years of American Communes*. New Brunswick, NJ: Transaction Books, 1988.

Park, Marlene. "City and Country in the 1930s: A Study of New Deal Murals in New York." *Art Journal* 39, no. 1 (1979): 37–47.

Parker, Robert Allerton. *A Yankee Saint: John Humphrey Noyes and the Oneida Community*. New York: G. P. Putnam's Sons, 1935.

Parmenter, Jon. "After the Mourning Wars: The Iroquois as Allies in Colonial North American Campaigns, 1676–1760." *The William and Mary Quarterly* 64, no. 1 (2007): 39–76.

———. *The Edge of the Woods: Iroquoia, 1534–1701*. East Lansing: Michigan State University Press, 2010.

Patrick, Christine S., and John C. Pinheiro, eds. *The Papers of George Washington, Presidential Series*, Vol. 12: *16 January 1793–31 May 1793*. Charlottesville: University of Virginia Press, 2005.

Pratt, Peter. *Archaeology of the Oneida Iroquois, Vol. 1*. George's Mill, NH: Man in the Northeast, Inc., 1976.

Parrish, Jasper. "State of Six Nations Population, October 11, 1824." American Indian Collection, Series I, Box 1, Folder 1, New-York Historical Society.

Parry, Nicole Jennifer. ". . . *nicht die Menschen im Walde, Wilde genannt werden sollten*: Images of Aboriginal Peoples in the Works of Sophie von La Roche, Charles Sealsfield and Karl May." PhD diss., University of Toronto, 2012.

Perry, Luke. *Donald Trump and the 2018 Midterm Battle for Central New York*. Cham, Switzerland: Palgrave MacMillan, 2019.

Pertusati, Linda. *In Defense of Mohawk Land: Ethnopolitical Conflict in Native North America*. Albany: State University of New York Press, 1997.

Phelps, Amos A. "The Oneida Institute, 1843." Amos A. Phelps Correspondence, Boston Public Library, MS A.21 v.13, 50.

Phisterer, Frederick. *New York in the War of the Rebellion, 1861–1865*. 3rd ed. 5 vols. Albany: J. B. Lyon Company, 1912.

Pool, William. *Landmarks of Niagara County, New York*. Syracuse: D. Mason and Company, 1897.

Preston, David L. "'We Intend to Live Our Lifetime Together as Brothers': Palatine and Iroquois Communities in the Mohawk Valley." *New York History* 89, no. 2 (2008): 179–189.

Pula, James S. ed. *Ethnic Utica*. Utica, NY: Oneida County Historical Society, 2002.

Pula, James S., and Philip Bean, "The Anatomy of Immigrant Strikes: A Comparison of Polish and Italian Textile Workers in Central New York," *The Polish Review* 41, no. 3 (1996): 273–292.

Pula, James S., and Cheryl A. Pula, eds. *With Courage and Honor: Oneida County's Role in the Civil War*. Utica, NY: North Country Books, 2010.

Reynolds, David S. *John Brown, Abolitionist: The Man Who Killed Slavery, Sparked the Civil War, and Seeded Civil Rights*. New York: Vintage Books, 2006.

Rich, Jane Kinsley. *A Lasting Spring: Jessie Catherine Kinsley, Daughter of the Oneida Community*. Syracuse: Syracuse University Press, 1983.

Richter, Daniel K. *The Ordeal of the Longhouse: The Peoples of the Iroquois League in the Era of European Colonization*. Chapel Hill, NC: University of North Carolina Press, 1992.

Ritchie, William A. *Archaeology of New York State*. 2nd ed. Garden City, NY: Natural History Press, 1969.

Roach, Monique Patenaude. "The Loss of Religious Allegiance among the Youth of the Oneida Community." *The Historian* 63, no. 4 (2001): 787–806.

Robertson, Constance Noyes. *Oneida Community: An Autobiography, 1851–1876*. Syracuse: Syracuse University Press, 1981.

———. *Oneida Community Profiles*. Syracuse: Syracuse University Press, 1977.

———. *Oneida Community: The Breakup, 1876–1881*. Syracuse: Syracuse University Press, 1977.

Roche, Sophie von La. *Erscheinung am See Oneida*. 3 vols. Leipzig: Gräff, 1798.

Rogers, Greg. "Petite Politique: The British, French, Iroquois, and Everyday Power in the Lake Ontario Borderlands, 1724–1760," PhD diss., University of Maine, 2016.

Rosser, Ezra. "Protecting Non-Indians from Harm? The Property Consequences of Indians." *Oregon Law Review* 87, no. 1 (2008): 175–220.

Rudolph, B. G. *From a Minyan to a Community: A History of the Jews of Syracuse*. Syracuse: Syracuse University Press, 1970.

Ryan, Mary P. *Cradle of the Middle Class: The Family in Oneida County, New York, 1790–1865*. Cambridge: Cambridge University Press, 1981.

Schatz, Ronald W. "The Barons of Middletown and the Decline of the North-Eastern Anglo-Protestant Elite." *Past & Present* 219 (2013): 165–200.

Schiro, George. *Americans by Choice: History of the Italians in Utica*. Utica: Thomas J. Griffiths Sons, 1940.

Schoolcraft, Henry R. *Notes on the Iroquois*. Albany: Erastus H. Pease and Company, 1847.

Schroeder, Patrick. A. *The Highest Praise of Gallantry: Memorials of David J. Jenkins and James E. Jenkins of the 146th New York Infantry and Oneida Cavalry*. Daleville, VA: Schroder Publications, 2001.

Schüler, Harry. *Oneida Roulette: Irokesische Landruckforderungen Im Inter- Und Intra-Ethnischen Beziehungsgefuge*. Wiesbaden, Springer VS, 2018.

Scisco, Louis Dow. *Political Nativism in New York State*. New York: Columbia University Press, 1901.

The Semi-Centennial of the Presbyterian Church of Oneida, N.Y. Rahway, N.J.: Merson Company Press, 1894.

Sernett, Milton C. *Abolition's Axe: Beriah Green, Oneida Institute, and the Black Freedom Struggle*. Syracuse: Syracuse University Press, 1986.

———. *North Star County: Upstate New York and the Crusade for African American Freedom*. Syracuse, Syracuse University Press, 2002.

Severance, Frank Hayward. *An Old Frontier of France: The Niagara Region and Adjacent Lakes under French Control.* 2 vols. New York: Dodd, Mead and Company, 1917.

Shattuck, George. *The Oneida Land Claims: A Legal History.* Syracuse: Syracuse University Press, 1991.

Short, J. R., L. M. Benton, W. B. Luce, and J. Walton. "Reconstructing the Image of an Industrial City." *Annals of the Association of American Geographers* 83, no. 2 (1993): 207–224.

Silver, Peter. *Our Savage Neighbors: How Indian War Transformed Early America.* New York: W.W. Norton, 2008.

Silverman, David J. *Red Brethren: The Brothertown and Stockbridge Indians and the Problem of Race in Early America.* Ithaca: Cornell University Press, 2010.

Smith, Gerrit. "Church of Peterboro." Peterboro, 1843.

———. "On the Reformation of the Intemperate, 1833." Gerrit Smith Pamphlets and Broadsides [Smith 404]. Syracuse University.

———. "Report from the County of Madison: To Abolitionists." Peterboro, NY, 1843.

———. "Some of the Duties of an Abolitionist (And Every Whole Man is an Abolitionist)." Peterboro, NY, 1841.

———. "Speech of Mr. Gerrit Smith, in the meeting of the New-York Anti-Slavery Society: Held in Peterboro, October 22, 1835." Peterboro, NY, 1835.

———. "To the Proslavery Ministers of Madison County." Peterboro, NY, 1843.

Smith, John E. *History of Chenango and Madison Counties, New York.* 2 vols. Syracuse: D. Mason and Company, 1880.

Smith, John E., ed. *Our County and Its People: A Descriptive and Bibliographical Record of Madison County, New York.* Boston: Boston History Company, 1899.

Snow, Dean R. "Mohawk Valley Archaeology: The Sites." *Occasional Papers in Anthropology* 23 (2005).

———. *The Iroquois.* Cambridge, MA: Blackwell, 1994.

Snow, Dean R., Charles T. Gehring and William A. Starna, eds. *In Mohawk Country: Early Narratives about a Native People.* Syracuse: Syracuse University Press, 1996.

Société Littéraire et Historique de Québec. *Mémoires sur le Canada, depuis 1749 jusqu'à 1760.* Quebec: T. Cary & Cie., 1838.

Stamps, S. David, and Miriam Burney Stamps. *Salt City and Its Black Community: A Sociological Study of Syracuse, New York.* Syracuse: Syracuse University Press, 2008.

Stoddard, Dwight J. *Notable Men of Central New York.* Syracuse: Dwight J. Stoddard, 1903.

Stowell, David O. "Albany's Great Strike of 1877." *New York History* 76, no. 1 (1995): 31–55.

———. *Streets, Railroads, and the Great Strike of 1877.* Chicago: University of Chicago Press, 1999.

Stradling, David. *The Nature of New York: An Environmental History of the Empire State*. Ithaca: Cornell University Press, 2010.

Streissguth, Michael. *City on the Edge: Hard Choices in the American Rust Belt*. Albany: State University of New York Press, 2020.

Strong, Douglas M. *Perfectionist Politics: Abolitionism and the Religious Tensions of American Democracy*. Syracuse: Syracuse University Press, 2001.

Syracuse Union. *Geschichte der Deutschen in Syracuse und Onondaga County*. Syracuse: J. P. Pinzer, 1897.

Taibi, John. *Railroading in the Stockbridge Valley*. Middletown, NY: O&W Railway Historical Society, 1996.

Tashuda, John. "The Oneida Land Claim, Yesterday and Today." *Buffalo Law Review* 46 (1998): 1001–1009.

Taylor, Alan. *The Divided Ground: Indians, Settlers, and the Northern Borderland of the American Revolution*. New York: Alfred A. Knopf, 2006.

———. *William Cooper's Town: Power and Persuasion on the Frontier of the Early American Republic*. New York: Alfred A. Knopf, 1996.

Taylor, Paul. *Glory Was Not Their Companion: The Twenty-Sixth New York Volunteer Infantry in the Civil War*. Jefferson, NC: McFarland and Company, 2005.

Teeple, John B. *The Oneida Family: Genealogy of a 19th Century Perfectionist Commune*. Cazenovia, NY: Oneida Community Historical Committee, 1985.

Thomas, Alexander R. *In Gotham's Shadow: Globalization and Community Change in Central New York*. Albany: State University of New York Press, 2003.

Thompson, John Henry, ed. *Geography of New York State*. Syracuse: Syracuse University Press, 1966.

Thwaites, Reuben Gold, ed., *The Jesuit Relations and Allied Documents*. 73 vols. Cleveland: Burrows Brothers, 1896–1901.

Tiro, Karim M. "Claims Arising: The Oneida Nation of Wisconsin and the Indian Land Claims Commission, 1951–1982." *American Indian Law Review* 32, no. 2 (2007): 509–524.

———. "James Dean in Iroquoia." *New York History* 80, no. 4 (1999): 391–422.

———. *The People of the Standing Stone: The Oneida Nation from the Revolution through the Era of Removal*. Amherst: University of Massachusetts Press, 2011.

———. " 'We Wish to Do You Good': The Quaker Mission to the Oneida Nation, 1790–1840." *Journal of the Early Republic* 26, no. 3 (2006): 353–376.

Todd, Ellen Wiley. *The "New Woman" Revised: Painting and Gender Politics on Fourteenth Street*. Berkeley: University of California Press, 1993.

Torrey, E. Fuller. *Frontier Justice: The Rise and Fall of the Loomis Gang*. Utica, NY: North Country Books, 1992.

———. *Ride With the Loomis Gang*. Utica: North Country Books, 1997.

Trigger, Bruce. *The Children of Aataentsic: A History of the Huron People to 1660*. Kingston, ON: McGill-Queen's University Press, 1987.

Tuck, James A. *Onondaga Iroquois Prehistory: A Study in Settlement Archaeology*. Syracuse: Syracuse University Press, 1971.

Turner, Orasmus. *History of the Pioneer Settlement of Phelps and Gorham's Purchase, and Morris' Reserve*. Rochester: William Alling, 1852.

US Bureau of the Census. *Historical Statistics of the United States, Colonial Times to 1970*. 2 vols. Washington, DC: Department of Commerce, Bureau of the Census, 1975.

US Congress. *Congressional Record: Containing the Proceedings and Debates of the Fifty-Seventh Congress, Second Session*. Washington, DC: Government Printing Office, 1903.

Verrazano, Giovanni da. *Verrazano's Voyage Along the Atlantic Coast of North America, 1524*. Albany: State University of New York, 1916.

Vescey, Christopher, ed. *Iroquois Land Claims*. Syracuse: Syracuse University Press, 1988.

Voogd, Jan. *Race Riots and Resistance: The Red Summer of 1919*. New York: Peter Lang, 2008.

Wager, Daniel E., ed. *Our County and its People: A Descriptive Work on Oneida County, New York*. 2 vols. Boston: Boston History Company, 1896.

Wallace, Anthony F. C. *The Tuscarora: A History*. Albany: State University of New York Press, 2012.

Waller, G. M. "New York's Role in Queen Anne's War, 1702–1713." *New York History* 33, no. 1 (1952): 40–53.

Walter, George W. *The Loomis Gang*. Prospect, NY: Prospect Books, 1953.

Washington, George. *The Writings of George Washington*. Vol. 10. Edited by Worthington Chauncey Ford. New York: G. P. Putnam's Sons, 1891.

Wayland-Smith, Ellen. *Oneida: From Free Love Utopia to the Well-Set Table*. New York: Picador, 2016.

Wells, Lester G. "Indian Personal Name Entries in Peter Smith's Indian Blotter." *New York History* 28, no. 4 (1947): 466–469.

———. "The Stockbridge Indians in New York State," *New York History* 27, no. 4 (1946): 476–491.

Whall, W. B. *Ships, Sea Songs and Shanties*. Glasgow: James Brown, 1913.

Whipple, J. S. et al. *Report of the Special Committee to Investigate the Indian Problem of the State of New York, Appointed by the Assembly of 1888*. 2 vols. Albany: Troy Press, 1889.

White, Janet R. "Designed for Perfection: Intersections between Architecture and Social Program at the Oneida Community." *Utopian Studies* 7, no. 2 (1996): 113–138.

Whitford, Noble E. *History of the Barge Canal of New York State*. Albany: J.B. Lyon Co., 1922.

———. *History of the Canal System of the State of New York, Together with Brief Histories of the Canals of the United States and Canada*. 2 vols. Albany: Brandow Printing Company, 1906.

Whitney, Theodore. "The Buyea Site." *Bulletin of the New York State Archaeological Association* 50 (1970): 1–13.

Wisnoski, Donald M. *The Opportunity Is at Hand: Oneida County, New York Colored Soldiers in the Civil War.* Lynchburg, VA: Schroeder Publications, 2003.

Wonderley, Anthony. "Chief Warriors, Pagan Priests, and Witch Killers: The Division of the Oneida Iroquois, 1789–1805." *New York History* 93, no. 2 (2012): 121–145.

———. "'Good Peter's Narrative of Several Transactions Respecting Indian Lands': An Oneida View of Dispossession, 1785–1788." *New York History* 84, no. 3 (2003): 237–273.

———. *Oneida Iroquois Folklore, Myth, and History.* Syracuse, NY: Syracuse University Press, 2004.

———. "Oneida's Forgotten Cigar Industry." *Madison County Historical Society* 44, no. 1 (2020): 4.

———. *Oneida Utopia: Searching for Human Happiness and Prosperity.* Ithaca: Cornell University Press, 2017.

Wonderley, Anthony, and Martha L. Sempowski, *Origins of the Iroquois League: Narratives, Symbols, and Archaeology.* Syracuse: Syracuse University Press, 2019.

Wyld, Lionel D. *Low Bridge! Folklore and the Erie Canal.* Syracuse: Syracuse University Press, 1962.

———. *Walter D. Edmonds, Storyteller.* Syracuse: Syracuse University Press, 1982.

Zenzen, Joan M. "Administrative Histories: Writing about Fort Stanwix National Monument." *The Public Historian* 31, no. 2 (2009), 55–65.

———. *Fort Stanwix National Monument: Reconstructing the Past and Partnering for the Future.* Albany: State University of New York Press, 2009.

Zimmer, Melanie. *Forgotten Tales of New York.* Charleston, SC: The History Press, 2009.

Index

10th Mountain Division, 215–16

A Current Affair, 227
Abenaki People, 53
Abolitionism, 8, 13, 14, 131–34, 137–40, 148, 149–55, 164, 165, 192, 209–10, 253
Abolitionist, The (Cazenovia), 139
Adams, John, 96
Adirondack Park, 213
Adirondacks, 3, 154, 184, 214
African Americans, xiv–xv, 8, 9, 14, 54, 121, 131, 133, 136–37, 150, 152, 153, 154, 163–65, 201, 204, 206, 207–10, 220–21, 243–44, 252–53, 254–55
Agriculture, 16, 20, 65, 68, 87, 89, 93, 99, 102, 105, 107, 112, 159, 172, 174, 190, 226–27, 255
Agwrondougwa (Good Peter), 66–67, 68, 72, 76–77, 82–83, 85, 97, 98, 104
Akwesasne (Saint Regis), 52, 53, 85
Albany, NY, xiii, 4, 6, 20, 144, 203, 213, 230; canal and rail era in, 7, 116, 141–42, 228; Civil War Era, 133, 134, 140, 150, 152, 161, 167, 174; colonial city, 44–47, 49–55, 57, 61–63, 65, 70, 72, 74, 75, 118; in the Early Republic, 82, 88, 92, 93, 95, 100–101, 103, 105, 107–108, 111, 113, 114, 120; as Fort Orange (Dutch rule), 29, 32, 33, 36
Albany-Oswego Corridor, 4–5, 7, 10, 46–47, 52, 53, 57, 62, 65, 111, 257, 100–101, 110, 257
Alcohol, 28, 32, 40–41, 46, 49, 52, 67–68, 80–81, 97, 118, 120, 157, 188, 257
Alexandria Bay, NY, 215
Algonquin People, 19, 22, 27, 28, 36, 40, 53, 65
Allen, Emily Hope, 218
Allen, Henry C., 207, 212, 222
Allies in War, Partners in Peace (Sculpture), 250
American Anti-Slavery Society, 132, 137
American Colonization Society, 133, 137
American Federation of Labor, 183
American Revolution, xiii, 1, 3, 5–6, 11, 13–14, 49, 66, 69–78, 70, 78, 80, 87, 88, 92, 93–96, 101, 103, 114, 118, 120, 123, 157, 158, 159, 160, 242, 257–58, 259
American Tragedy, An (Dreiser), 214

325

Amherst, Jeffery, 50
Amish People, 226
Andastogué People, 41
Andover Theological Seminary, 142
Andrews, Rev. William, 49
Andros, Edmund, 39
Angerstein, John, 93
Anglicanism, 47, 48, 49, 51, 63, 66–67, 69
Annals and Recollections of Oneida County (Jones), 137, 153, 174, 225
Anthony, Susan B., 192
Antietam, 162
Anti-Federalists, 96
Appalachian Mountains, 4, 17, 60, 78, 117
Architecture, 186–89, 212–13
Arenias, 31
Armory Square, Syracuse, 224
Arnold, Benedict, 74
Articles of Confederation, 96
Atahensic, 21
Atlantic Ocean, 4, 5, 10, 15, 16, 21, 27–29, 30, 31, 46, 49, 57, 114, 203
Auburn, NY, 236
Augusta, Town of, NY, 225
Aupaumut, Hendrick, 121
Ava, Town of, NY, 225

Bahamas, 171
Bailey, Jane, 194
Bakus, Azel, 118
Bakus, Billy, 205
Banyar, Goldsbrow, 64
Baptists, 130, 182
Barbé-Marbois, François, 158
Barclay, Rev. Henry, 49, 50
Barge Canal, 7, 213–14, 228, 230
Barkin, Joel, 249, 261
Barneveld, NY, 90
Bartow, Andrew, 116

Basilio, Carmen, 205, 243
Battle of Barren Hill, 75
Battle of Chippewa, 115
Battle of Fredericksburg, 162
Battle of Gettysburg, 162–63
Battle of Long Island, 72
Battle of Oriskany, 5, 6, 66, 73–74, 97, 230. *See also* Oriskany, NY
Battle of Saratoga, 6, 74
Battle of Second Bull Run, 162
Battle-Axe and Weapons of War, 145
Baum, L. Frank, 14, 249
Bavaria, Kingdom of, 176
Beardsley, Samuel, 133, 139, 164
Beaver Wars, 4, 28, 32, 35–36, 37–39, 42–46, 156
Beech Tree, 72, 98
Beecham, William, 176
Belestre, Francois-Marie Picote de, 55–56, 65
Belknap, Jeremy, 97–99, 103–105, 111
Bendix Aviation, 211
Big Tree, 229
Binghamton, NY, 16, 117, 158
Bingo, 238–39
Biographical Review Company, 182
Black Cap, 92
Black Lives Matter, 14, 210, 252
Black River, 3, 55, 93, 114, 117, 213, 215
Black River Canal, 117, 176, 228
Bleecker Street Presbyterian Church, Utica, 133
Bleeding Kansas, 154
Bloomer, Amelia, 192
Bloomfield, Joseph, 71
Bogaert, Harmen Mendertsz van den, 29–32, 39
Bond, Schoeneck & King, 236
Book of Common Prayer, 49
Boon, Gerrit, 90, 92, 97
Boonville, NY, 92, 117, 161, 162, 228

Bosnian Americans, 255
Boston Massacre, 69
Boston, MA, 69, 70, 71, 93, 102–104, 133, 182
Bouckville, NY, 15
Boylan vs. George, et al. (1909), 232–33
Boylan, Julia, 232
Boylan, Patrick, 232
Boylston, Thomas, 93
Bradstreet, John, 57
Brant, Joseph, 60, 63, 68, 69, 70, 72–73, 75, 76, 77, 80
Brant, Molly, 63
Bread, Daniel, 120
Breckenridge, John, 155
Brewerton, NY, 3, 16, 57
Bridgeport, NY, 138
Bridgewater, NY, 63
Brindisi, Anthony, 253
Bristol, England, 27
Brook Farm, 145, 190
Brookfield, Town of, NY, 225
Broome County, NY, 16
Brother's Keeper, 227
Brothertown People, 87–90, 119, 120, 121–22, 159, 170, 225
Brown, Grace, 214
Brown, Jim, 209, 214
Brown, John (abolitionist), 8, 132, 154–55
Brown, John (governor), 93
Brown, Timothy, 188
Bruyas, Jacques, 40–42
Bryan v. Itasca County, 238
Buchanan, James, 153
Buck's Island, 2
Buffalo, NY, 7, 112, 116, 120, 123, 140, 142, 150, 152, 161, 164, 167, 179, 180, 213, 230
Bumppo, Natty, 159–60
Burchard, Nathan, 125

Bureau of Indian Affairs, 246
Burgoyne, John, 6, 72, 74
Burnet, William, 49
Burnetsfield. *See* German Flats
Burt Olney Plant, Oneida, NY, 204
Burt, Jonathan, 147, 149
Bushnell, Candice, 194
Butler, John, 71, 72, 75
Buyea Site, 19

Cabot, John, 27
Cady, Asa Waterman, 115
Cady, Daniel, 134
California, 169, 190, 216, 223
Cameron Site, 25
Campe, Joachim, 94
Campisi, Jack, 236
Canada, xiv, 2, 15, 19, 26, 27, 119, 170, 198, 218, 219; under British rule, 3, 70, 72, 78, 79, 80, 83, 84, 93, 111, 113, 114, 117, 257; in the era of New France, 25, 28–29, 35, 37–38, 43, 46, 52, 57; Oneidas of the Thames removal to, 14, 110, 125, 127, 147, 157; and the Underground Railroad, 140, 150, 157
Canada Creek, 2
Canajoharie, 62, 103
Canandaigua, NY, 96, 97
Canaseraga, nr. Chittenango, NY, 66, 86–87, 95, 96–97, 98, 107
Canastota Reservation, 108, 116
Canastota Tract, 107–108
Canastota, NY, 15, 25, 66, 116, 137, 141, 150, 178, 182, 184, 205, 213, 214, 229, 243
Captain Peter, 97–98, 104
Carey, Elisha, 116
Caribbean, 27, 91
Carlisle Indian Industrial School, 231, 250

Index | 327

Carousel Center (Destiny USA), 224
Carrier Corporation, 212, 221
Carrier Dome, 224
Carter, Jimmy, 236
Cartier, Jacques, 28
Case, Salmon, 125
Castorland, NY, 93
Cataraqui, 43
Catawba People, 51
Catholicism, 66, 131; immigrants and, 141, 148, 174–77, 179, 202, 206; Jesuit Mission and, 35, 42, 46, 52
Catskills, 169
Cayuga County, NY, 147
Cayuga Lake, 18
Cayuga People, 4, 6, 17, 18, 37, 43, 45, 71, 72, 75, 79, 82, 86, 92, 93, 96, 99, 246
Cazenove, Theophilius, 92
Cazenovia College, 212
Cazenovia Lake, 3, 19, 92
Cazenovia Republican, 165
Cazenovia, NY, 8, 107, 139, 149, 182
Chad Hanna (Edmonds), 229
Champlain, Samuel de, 22–26, 28, 29, 54
Change the Mascot Campaign, 12, 250
Chaplin, William, 149–50
Chappell, C. Will, 182–86
Chappell, Chase, Maxwell & Company, 182
Charles E. Hancock Airport, 212
Charlesbourg-Royal, 28
Charleston, SC, 155
Charlotte, NC, 222
Chassanis, Peter, 93
Chaumonot, Fr. Joseph, 36, 37
Chaussegros de Léry, Gaspard-Joseph, 53, 54
Chenango Canal, 117, 176, 177, 180

Chenango County, NY, 16, 92, 117, 152, 169, 226, 253
Chenango River, 171, 213
Chenango Twenty Townships, 92
Cherokee People, 124, 237
Cherry Valley, NY, 75, 77, 81
Chicago Pneumatic Tool Company, 211, 222
Chicago, IL, 116, 180
Chickasaw People, 237
Childs Commission Drainage Ditch, 205
China, 99
Chingachgook, 159–60
Chittenango Creek, 95, 116
Chittenango Falls, 3, 215
Chittenango, NY, 66, 95, 105, 115, 116, 105, 115, 147, 205, 213, 249
Choctaw People, 51, 237
Christian Perfection (Wesley), 142
Christian, William H., 161–62
Chrysler, 211
Chung, Connie, 227
Church of England. *See* Anglicanism
Church of Peterboro, 135
Cicero, NY, 93
Circular, The, 166, 190, 195, 196
City of Sherrill v. Oneida Indian Nation of New York, 246
Civil War, 8, 13, 114, 129, 131, 132, 155, 161–67, 170, 171, 172, 177, 210, 258
Civilian Conservation Corps, 215
Clark's Mills, NY, 153
Clarke, Hermon, 153, 164
Cleveland, OH, 116
Clinton Square, Syracuse, 151, 210
Clinton, DeWitt, 13, 98, 111–13, 116, 118, 129, 250
Clinton, George (colonial governor), 51

Clinton, George (state governor), 1, 78–80, 82–83, 85–87, 92, 96, 100, 123
Clinton, James, 75–76
Clinton, NY, 90, 117
Clock, Conrad, 95, 107
Clovis culture, 15
Cobleskill, NY, 75
Coburn, Alexander, 175
Cohoes Falls, NY, 141
Colbert, Claudette, 229
Cold War, 9, 213, 216, 226, 244
Colden, Cadwallader, 156
Cole, Thomas, 198–99, 224
Colgate University, 139, 196, 212
Collins Site, 41
Columbia University, 196
Columbus Monument Corporation, 253
Columbus, Christopher, 27, 206, 253, 260
Compagnie du Canada, 26
Conaghquieson, 56, 59, 65
Congregationalism, 63, 130, 132, 139, 173, 197
Conkling, Roscoe, 162, 210
Connecticut, 39, 63, 67, 83, 88, 108, 130, 132, 142, 228
Constantia, NY, 95
Constitution of the United States, 6, 96, 165, 235, 237
Continental Congress, 69, 71
Cook, Louis (Colonel Louis), 83, 85, 86
Cooper, James Fenimore, 11, 13, 138, 156, 158–60, 160, 228, 259
Cooper, Polly, 250
Cooperstown, NY, 159
Copp, John, 75
Corbally, John, 221
Cornelius, Wilson, 233
Cornhill, Utica, 208

Cornwallis, Charles, 77
Cortland County, NY, 253
Cortland, NY, 214
Cosby Patent, 62, 90, 99
Cosby, William, 62
Costner, Kevin, 250
County of Oneida v. Oneida Indian Nation of New York State (Oneida II), 237, 238, 241
Course of Empire, The (Cole), 198–99
Covenant Chain, 43
Cowaselon Creek, 122
Cowasselon Tract, 119
Coxe, William, 64
Coxe's Patent, 64, 90
Cragin, Mary, 146
Crittenden Compromise, 164
Croghan, George, 56
Crouse Memorial College, 186
Crouse-Hinds Company, 233
Cuomo, Andrew, 247–48
Cuomo, Mario, 239
Cusic, Cornelius, 164
Cusik, David, 156–57

Dablon, Fr. Claude, 36
Daily Reformer (Watertown), 165
Dairy Famers' Union, 226
Damnation of Theron Ware, The (Frederic), 175, 259
Danforth, Joshua, 133
Darwin, Charles, 196
Daughters of the American Revolution, 118, 229
De Ferrière, Angel, 107–108, 110, 113, 119, 121–22
De Marco, Tony, 205
De Ruyter, NY, 138
Dean, James, 82, 83, 85, 100, 101, 103, 118
Decker, George, 232
Declaration of Independence, 154

Deerfield, MA, 47, 119
Deerfield, NY, 255
Deganawido, 21
Dekayenensere Isaac (Old Isaac), 66–67, 68, 72
Delaware People, 22
Delaware River, 37
Dellius, Godefridus, 44
Delta Lake, 214
Democratic Party, 22, 124, 133, 151–53, 155, 164, 165, 175, 175, 183, 220, 253, 254
Denny, Abraham, 118
Denny, Louis, 107, 112, 113
Denny, Polly, 107
Denonville, Marquis de, 43
Department of the Interior, 246, 247
Detroit, MI, 46, 59, 93, 116
Devan, Henry, 147
Devereux, Nicholas, 176
DeWitt, NY, 211, 220
Donnacona, 28
Dougherty Site, 19
Douglas, Stephen, 155
Douglass, Frederick, 150, 164–65
Dow, Lorenzo, 130
Doxtater, Lydia, 218
Dreiser, Theodore, 214
Drum, Hugh A., 215
Drums along the Mohawk, 11, 228–29, 230, 244
Dryden, NY, 93, 116
Durant, Samuel W., 176
Durhamville, NY, 116, 141, 171, 213
Düsseldorf, 169
Dutch West India Company, 29
Dwight, Timothy, 104

East Syracuse, NY, 212
Eastman-Kodak, 223
Edmonds, Walter D., 11, 218, 228–29
Edwards, Jonathan, 66

Eighth Lake, 215
Elm, Abraham, 164
Emancipation Proclamation, 165
Embargo Act (1803), 113
Emerson, Ralph Waldo, xiii, 70, 124
Enchanted Forest, 215
England, 27, 28, 39, 40, 43, 45–47, 48, 49, 71
Episcopalianism, 119, 122, 185
Erie Canal, 7, 10, 11, 13, 93, 111, 113, 115–17, 120–21, 123, 125, 130, 132, 140, 141, 142, 147, 163, 171, 179, 207, 212, 213–14, 228, 230, 258
Erie People, 22
Erscheinung am See Oneida (Von La Roche), 158
Essex County, NY, 154
Evening on Oneida Lake (Bierstadt), 168, 170
Everett, Edward A., 233
Everson Art Museum, 213

Fairmont, NY, 220
Falcone Brothers, 204
Fayetteville, NY, 192, 215, 224
Federalists, 96
Fenner, Town of, NY, 163
Filkins, John L., 172
Finger Lakes, 16, 129
Finney, Charles G., 8, 130–31, 132, 135, 225
First Hundred Years, The (Edmonds), 218
First Pagan Purchase. *See under* New York State, Oneida Land Acquisitions (1809)
Fish Creek, 57, 85, 108, 111, 170
Fitzhugh, Ann Carrol, 135
Fletcher, Benjamin, 44
Flint, 22
Florence, Town of, NY, 135, 225

Florida, 223
Floyd, General William, 154
Floyd, George, 250
Folwer, David, 67
Fonda, Henry, 229
Forbes, Eli, 67
Ford, John, 229
Fort Bull, 53–56, 230
Fort Craven, 57
Fort de la Présentation, 52
Fort Drum, 215–16
Fort Frontenac, 45, 53, 57, 78. *See also* Kingston, ON
Fort Herkimer, 78, 81, 82. *See also* German Flats
Fort Hunter, 48–49, 50, 53, 62, 66–67
Fort Newport, 53
Fort Niagara, 5, 48, 52, 57, 67, 70, 71, 75–80, 92, 111
Fort Orange. *See* Albany, NY
Fort Oswego, 48, 62, 78, 79. *See also* Oswego, NY
Fort Schuyler. *See* Fort Stanwix
Fort Stanwix: and 1768 Line of Property, 57, 63–64, 68, 80; during American Revolution, 5–6, 71–74, 75, 95, 257; State Conference at (1784), 1–2, 78–79, 80, 236; twentieth-century reconstruction of, 13, 230, 244; US conference at (1784), 6, 79–80, 158, 233. *See also* Treaty of Fort Stanwix (1788)
Fort Sumter, 155, 166
Fort Ticonderoga, 72
Fort Williams, 53, 54, 55
Fourier, Charles, 145, 196
France, 120, 158, 169, 202; in American Revolution, 6, 86; early exploration in America, 26–28; in French and Indian War, 5, 52, 57, 59, 63; and Jesuit mission, 36–38; in Napoleonic era, 68, 94, 112–13; wars with England, 43, 46–48, 51. *See also* New France
Francis, Job, 157
Franklin, Benjamin, 86
Frederic, Harold, 175, 259
Free Soil Party, 150–52
Freemasonry, 131, 185
Fremont, John, 153
French and Indian War (1754–63), 5, 11, 52–57, 62, 107, 118, 159
French Revolution, 91, 94, 107
Frenchman Island, 94, 158
Friend of Man, 138
Frontenac, Comte de, 44–47
Fugitive Slave Act (1850), 149–51, 154
Fur Trade, 4, 26–27, 28, 31–32, 50–51, 93, 134

Gale, George Washington, 132
Galpin, William F., 12
Garakontié, 41
Garfield, James, 198
Garrison, William Lloyd, 133, 165
Gazzetta di Syracuse, 202
General Electric, 211, 221–23, 231, 254
General Motors, 211
Genesee Road, 96, 100, 105, 107, 108. *See also* Seneca Turnpike
Genesee River, 18
Geneva, NY, 112
Genoa, NY, 147
Geography of New York State (Thompson), 216
George III, 60, 64, 70
George, Ray, 250
George-Kanentiio, Doug, 253
Georgetown, NY, 188, 225
German Americans, 176–78, 179–80, 183, 202–206. *See also* Palatine Germans

German Flats, 49, 51, 55, 56, 57, 59, 62, 65, 69, 71, 73, 75, 82, 90, 118
German-American Alliance, 229
Germany, 49, 158, 169, 173, 176–78, 180, 186, 202
Gillet, Moses, 130–31
Gillette, Chester, 214
Ginsburg, Ruth Bader, 246, 247
Ginseng, 99
Glenwood Cemetery, Oneida, 184
Globe Malleable Iron Works, 204
Globe Woollen Company, 180
Goff Site, 19
Goldstein, Julius, 182–86
Gompers, Samuel, 183
Good Peter. *See* Agwrondougwa
Grand Army of the Republic, 163
Grant, Ulysses S., 165, 182
Grasshopper, 72, 75
Great Awakening, 68, 130
Great Fugitive Slave Law Convention, 149–50
Great Migration, 207
Great Peace of Montreal (1701), 46, 47
Green Bay, WI, 119, 120, 122
Green Lakes, 215
Green, Beriah, 132–34, 137–38, 150, 210
Greenhalgh, Wentworth, 39, 41, 42
Griffiss Air Force Base, 216, 223, 224, 225, 230
Guatemala, 226
Guiteau, Charles, 198
Gulf of Mexico, 59
Gulf of Tonkin Incident, 220

Haiti, 87
Halbritter, Arthur Raymond "Ray," 12, 238–42, 245, 248–50, 253
Haley, Alex, 209
Hall of Languages, Syracuse University, 197

Hall, Harriet, 146–47
Hamilton College, 102–105, 118, 134, 137, 141, 170, 195, 209, 212
Hamilton, Alexander, 102
Hamilton, Erastus, 188–89, 198
Hamilton, NY, 150
Hamilton-Oneida Academy. *See* Hamilton College
Hampton Normal and Agricultural Institute, 231
Han Yost, 99, 122
Handsome Lake, 99
Hann Yerry, 72, 97
Hanna, Richard, 253
Hannibal, NY, 93
Hanyoust Family, 232–34
Harper, John, 81, 82
Harper's Ferry, 8, 182, 155
Harvard Law School, 239
Harvard University, 228
Hasenclever, Peter, 64
Hasheesh Eater, The (Ludlow), 170
Haudenosaunee (Iroquois), xiv, 1, 4–6, 27, 99, 241, 253; in age of colonial empires, 23–27, 28–33, 35–46, 47–58, 64, 107, 212; during American Revolution, 69–80, 257; in American Wars, 115, 164; Confederacy, 4, 11, 21–22, 51, 52, 74, 156; and Everitt Commission, 233; origins and archaeology, 16–22; removal from homelands, 81, 86, 100, 124, 127; writing about, 11, 156–60, 229, 259. *See also* Mohawk, Oneida, Onondaga, Cayuga, Seneca People
Haudenosaunee of the Grand River, 115
Hauptman, Laurence, xiv
Hawley, Gideon, 66
Hendee, Beulah, 192
Henderson Bay, 53

Henry VII of England, 27
Henry, William "Jerry," 150–52, 164, 192, 210
Herchheimer, Georg, 49
Herkimer County, NY, 162, 211
Herkimer, Nicholas, 56, 73, 207
Herkimer, NY, 49, 62, 229. *See also* German Flats
Herrington, Anna Short, 209
Hiawatha, 21
Higginsville, NY, 117
Higinbotham, Niles, 142, 184
Higinbotham, Sands, 121, 125, 140–42, 148, 195
Hill, Charlie, 239
Hispanic Americans, 252
History of Oneida County (Durant), 176
History of the Five Indian Nations (Colden), 156
Hitchcock, Luke, 99
Hitler, Adolf, 186
Holland Land Company, 90, 92, 107
Holland Patent, NY, 198
Hollywood, 11, 229, 259
Home Owners' Loan Corporation, 208
Homer, NY, 93
House of Representatives, 151
Howe, William, 72
Howlett Hill Site, 17
Hubbard, Melvin Henry, 182
Hudson Bay, 59
Hudson River, 4, 7, 15, 32, 49, 88, 111, 113, 117
Hudson River School, 160, 169
Hudson Valley, 5, 40, 99, 171, 175, 223
Hudson, Henry, 29
Hudson, NY, 161
Hughes, Charles Evans, 232
Hunter, Robert, 47
Huron (Wyandot) People, 17, 23–26, 28, 35

Ice Age, 15
Ifshin, David, 220
Il Pensiero Italiano, 202
Ilion, NY, 211
Illinois, 160
Immigration, 8–9, 12–13, 172–80, 184–86, 201–207, 210, 243, 255, 258–60; German, 49, 164, 167, 176–78, 179–80, 202–203; Irish, 115, 141, 148, 167, 174–77; Italian, 179, 202–205, 253; Jewish, 179, 184, 204, 208; Polish, 179, 202–203; Refugee, 255, 260; Welsh, 173–74, 202
Indian Claims Commission, 233–34
Indian Gaming Regulatory Act (1988), 239
Indian Nonintercourse Act (1790), 6, 96, 100, 101, 127, 235, 243
Indian Removal Act (1830), 124
Indian Volunteers Regiment, 114
Indiana, 119, 121
Inland Lock and Navigation Company, 111, 114, 115–16, 213
Inlet, NY, 214
International Boxing Hall of Fame, 205
Interstate 81, 208, 231, 252, 254, 260
Ireland, 49, 148, 173–74, 175–76, 202, 222
Ithaca, NY, 205

Jackson, Andrew, 124, 133
Jamesville, NY, 204
Jefferson County Iroquois, 28
Jefferson County, NY, 130, 163, 176, 216, 226
Jefferson, Thomas, 113, 121
Jenkins, Sally, 250
Jenkins, Timothy, 122, 125, 139, 148, 149, 152, 175
Jerry Rescue. *See* Henry, William "Jerry"

Jervis, John, 115
Jesuit Order, 35–38, 41–43, 46, 47, 68, 157, 174, 212
Jesuit Relations, 37, 38, 39, 40, 42
Jigonhsasee, 21
Johnson, Anna, 218
Johnson, Guy, 69–70, 71, 77
Johnson, Lyndon, 220, 235, 253
Johnson, Philip, 213
Johnson, Sir William, 49, 51, 52, 56, 59, 60, 63–64, 67, 68–69
Johnstown, NY, 49, 75
Jones, Pomroy, 11, 137, 139, 153, 174, 225

Kahn, Lawrence, 247
Kahnawake, 41, 46, 71, 83, 119
Kallet, Peter, 219, 251
Kanaghwaes, 72
Kanonwalohale, 5, 10, 65–69, 71, 72, 74–77, 87–90, 93, 95, 97–99, 101–103, 105, 107–109, 112, 118, 216, 242. *See also* Oneida Castle, NY
Kansas, 124, 154
Kansas-Nebraska Act, 152
Karen people, 255
Kayendalongwea, William, 72
Kellogg, Minnie, 233
Kellogg, Rebecca, 66
Kennedy, John F., 253
Kennedy, Robert F., 229
Kent State, 220
Kenwood, NY, 218
King George's War, 51, 52
King William's War, 45
Kingsbury, Alison Mason, 206
Kingston, ON, 45, 53, 114, 151. *See also* Fort Frontenac
Kinsley, Jessie Catherine, 218
Kirkland, Town of, NY, 153

Kirkland, Samuel, 68–72, 79, 80, 82, 83, 85, 86, 89, 95, 97, 100, 101–105, 112, 117, 118, 130, 139, 209
Kirkpatrick, William, 50, 99
Klock, George, 63
Know-Nothing Party, 148, 174, 177
Korean War, 213
Krasnaya, Russia, 226
Ku Klux Klan, 204, 207, 253

La Famine, 43
La Fayette, Marquis de, 74–75, 79, 83, 120, 259
La Guardia, Fiorello, 226
La Luce, 202
Lachine, QC, 43
Lairdsville, NY, 147
Lake Champlain, 26, 72
Lake Erie, 116, 123
Lake Iroquois, 15, 78
Lake Ontario, 3, 5, 6, 7, 15, 28, 30, 32, 48, 50, 53, 55, 57, 72, 78, 93, 94, 111, 114, 117, 215
Lamoka Lake, 16
Land Claims, Oneida. *See under* Oneida People
Last of the Mohicans, The (Cooper), 159, 160
Latourette, James, 142, 144
Laurentide Ice Sheet, 15
Le Mercier, François, 38
Le Moyne College, 205, 212
Le Moyne, Simon, 38, 211, 212
Leading Citizens of Madison County, 182, 183, 184
League of the Ho-de-no-sau-nee, or Iroquois (Morgan), 158
Leatherstocking Tales (Cooper), 11, 13, 158–60, 228
Lefèbvre de la Barre, Antoine, 43

334 | Index

Lenape People, 27
Lenox, Town of, NY, 110, 148, 149
Lewis County, NY, 93, 136, 162, 176, 225, 254
Lewiston, NY, 156
Lexington and Concord, MA, 69
Libbey, Inc., 219
Liberty Party, 138, 150–51
Lille, France, 94
Limekiln Lake, 215
Lincklaen, John, 90, 95, 97, 98, 107
Lincoln, Abraham, 8, 155, 160, 164, 166, 167, 254
Line of Property (1768), 1, 2, 3, 60, 63, 64, 82, 87, 89. *See also under* Fort Stanwix
Little Niagara, 52
Little, Floyd, 220
Liverpool, NY, 211
Livingston Lease, 83–86
Livingston, John, 83–86, 92
Livingstone, Robert, 46–47, 48, 62
Locklear, Arlinda, 247
Loguen, Jermain Wesley, 133, 150, 154, 155, 210
London, England, 77, 93, 175
Long Island, 88, 154
Loomis Gang, 171–72
Loomis, "Plumb," 172
Loomis, "Wash," 171
Loomis, George Washington, 171
Louis XIV of France, 44, 49
Louisbourg, 57
Low Bridge, Everybody Down, 228
Lowville, NY, 93, 151, 161, 225
Ludlow, Fitz Hugh, 170
Lyons, NY, 129

MacNeish, Richard, 16
Macomb, Alexander, 93
Macomb's Great Purchase, 93

Madison and Onondaga Abolitionist, 139
Madison Barracks, 215
Madison County Eagle, 138
Madison County Historical Society, 184
Madison County, NY, 3, 7, 15, 89–90, 116, 117, 148, 216, 225, 227, 240; antebellum and Civil War Years in, 8, 132, 136, 138–39, 150, 151, 163, 167; Euro-American settlement of, 8, 66, 95, 110; Oneida Land Claims and, 235, 237, 245; Oneida Reservations in, 125–27, 230–33, 235, 237–38, 246; Oneida settlements in, 18, 20, 25, 30, 46, 157; post Civil War era, 169, 171, 173, 176, 178, 182, 184–85, 188, 204, 206
Madison, James, 79
Mahican People, 22, 29
Maine, 236
Mallett, Rhoda, 171
Manchot, Chief, 42
Manhattan, 29, 31
Manlius, NY, 224
Mansion House. *See* Oneida Community
Marble Hill, 98, 123, 218, 241, 250
Marble Hill Oneidas, 123, 218, 241, 250. *See also* Oneida People, Orchard Party
Marshall, Town of, NY, 225
Maryland, 136, 149, 162
Massachusetts, 5, 39, 70, 78, 89, 102, 119, 123, 142, 45, 148, 169
Matt, Francis Xavier, 180
Matteson, Orasmus B., 151, 152
May, Samuel, 192
McClellan, George, 165
McDonald, John, 103

Index | 335

McKinley, William, 182
McNab Site, 19
McQuade, James, 161–62
Mears, John W., 195–96, 197, 198
Mennonites, 226
Menominee People, 120–21
Merrell Soule Company, 211
Merwin, Abigail, 145
Methodists, 122, 130, 142, 150, 175, 197, 255
Mexican Cession, 149
Mexican War, 149, 161
Mexico, 149, 226
Miami People, 45
Miller, Kenneth Hayes, 218
Miller, Tirzah, 198
Millet, Pierre, 41–44
Milton J. Rubenstein Museum of Science and Technology, 224
Milwaukee, WI, 116
Mississauga People, 52, 73
Mississippi River, 57, 78, 124, 139
Mohawk and Malone Line, 214
Mohawk Language, 18, 49, 63
Mohawk People, 1, 4, 5, 8, 17, 18, 22, 26, 32, 36, 37, 39, 40, 43, 44, 45, 46, 48, 49, 50, 51, 52, 62–63, 65, 66, 68–69, 70, 73, 77, 79, 83, 89, 114, 159
Mohawk River, 4, 13, 15, 29, 32, 46, 48, 50, 57, 61, 62, 73, 91, 99–103, 108, 110, 113, 132, 214
Mohawk Valley, 4, 6, 18, 50, 56, 70, 71, 77, 95, 124, 226, 230
Mohawk Valley Community College, 212
Mohawk Valley Formula, 211
Mohawk Valley Resource Center for Refugees, 255
Mohegan People, 67, 88, 89
Mohican People, 89, 159

Montreal, QC, 28, 36, 37, 39, 41, 45, 46, 47, 55, 57, 70, 71, 72, 93, 111, 117, 156
Moon Site, 19
Morgan, Lewis Henry, 158, 160, 259
Morgan's Rangers, 229
Mormons, 148
Morrisville, NY, 138, 171
Morse, Jedediah, 103–105, 111
Moscow, 226
Mostly Canallers (Edmonds), 228
Muckland, 15, 204–205
Munnsville, NY, 30, 46, 121, 227
Munson-Williams-Proctor Institute, 213
Museum of the American Revolution, 250
My Father's House (Noyes), 218
Myanmar, 255

Nanticocke People, 65
National Casket Company, 182
National Football League, 12
National Museum of the American Indian, 250
National Women's Rights Convention, 192
Native American Rights Fund, 237
Netherlands, 28
Neutral People, 22
New Amsterdam. *See* New York City
New Deal, 205
New England, xiii, 7, 40, 47, 63, 66, 70, 72, 78–79, 87, 89, 90, 124, 129, 130, 140, 144, 148, 153, 171, 173, 178, 202, 220
New France, 26, 36, 40, 43, 44, 45, 49
New Guinea Plot, 121
New Hampshire, 151
New Harmony, IN, 145

New Hartford, NY, 90, 153, 224, 248
New Haven, CT, 142, 144
New Jersey, 50, 71
New Military Tract, 93, 96, 100
New Netherland, 36, 39–40, 50
New Sweden, 28, 37
New York and Oswego Railroad, 195
New York Anti-Slavery Society, 132, 133, 137
New York Central Railroad, 7, 13, 142, 169, 214
New York City, 7, 29, 40, 72, 93, 120, 111, 116, 117, 133, 140, 142, 164, 169, 170, 172, 175, 178, 179, 180, 213, 214, 226, 227, 230
New York Harbor, 27, 40, 49, 116
New York Indian Census of 1845, 157
New York Indian Commission, 1–3, 78–79, 82–83, 92
New York Mercury, 54
New York Mills, NY, 113, 153, 179, 203
New York Post, 248
New York Referendum on Black Suffrage 1860, 154; earliest habitation of, 15–18
New York State, xiii–xiv, 4, 11, 11–15, 135, 199, 223, 226, 240; abolition of slavery in, 136, 207; dispossession of Native peoples by, 1–3, 6–7, 10, 78–80, 81–87, 90, 96, 100–101, 105–10, 120–24, 127, 142, 257, 259; Oneida Land Claims Cases and, 233–34, 235–38, 241–43, 244, 245–48; Referendum on Black Suffrage (1860), 154
New York State Conservation Department, 215
New York State Department of Commerce, 215
New York State Museum, 20
New York State Parks, 215
New York State Thruway, 7, 13, 14, 29, 213, 239
New York State Vacationlands, 215
New York State, Oneida Land Acquisitions, 81–122, 141; 1785, 81; 1788, 6, 83–86, 86, 87, 88; 1789, 116, 141; 1795, 6, 101, 116, 141, 235; 1798, 105–107; 1802, 107; 1807, 107–108; 1809, 108, 116; 1810–11, 108–109, 141; 1815, 119; 1817, 119; 1824, 121; 1826, 122; 1829, 122; 1834, 122
New York Times, 152, 175, 182, 184, 203, 222, 242
New York Tribune, 167, 194
New York, Ontario and Western Railway (O&W), 169, 214
New York, Province of, 1, 39–40, 44, 46–52, 61–62, 156
Newfoundland, 27
Newhouse Communications Center, 220
Newhouse trap, 190, 216–17
Newhouse, Sewell, 190
Niagara County, NY, 119
Niagara Falls, NY, 154, 169, 190, 216–17
Niagara Mohawk Building, Syracuse, 212
Niagara River, 112
Nichols Pond, 19, 25
Nicks Lake, 215
Niew Rotterdam. *See* Constantia, NY
Niklasko, 72
Nine Mile Swamp, 171
Nioure, 53
Nipissing People, 53
Nixdorf, Harriet, 184
Nixon, Richard, 220, 221, 225, 235
North Carolina, 27

Index | 337

North Star, 150
North Syracuse, NY, 220
Northern Journal (Lowville, NY), 151
Northern New York Journal (Watertown, NY), 152
Northrop, Solomon, 152
Norwich, NY, 16, 92
Notable Men of Central New York, 183, 185
Notes on the Iroquois (Schoolcraft), 157
Nowadaga Creek, 62
Noyes, George Wallingford, 218–19
Noyes, Harriet (née Holton), 145
Noyes, John Humphrey, 142–50, 166, 190–93, 197–98, 216, 218, 231, 243, 251
Noyes, Pierrepont B., 193–94, 217–19
Noyes, Pierrepont T., 219
Noyes, Theodore, 197

Oberdorfer Brass, 185
Oberdorfer, Jesse L., 185
Oberg, Michael, xiv
Occom, Samson, 67–68, 87–89
Ogden, David, 138
Ogdensburg, NY, 52, 53
Ogilvie, John, 49, 50
Ohio, 154, 180, 220
Ohio territory, 59, 79, 102, 115
Ohio Valley, 52
Oklahoma, 124
Old Forge, NY, 214
Old Fort Schuyler, 57, 62, 92, 95, 103
Old Oneida, 65, 67, 72, 77, 97, 98, 102, 103
Olmstead, Frederick Law, 188
Oneida Association, 131
Oneida Carry, 5, 10, 46, 50, 51, 53, 55, 57, 60, 63, 70, 78, 103, 111, 114, 251

Oneida Castle, NY, 5, 65, 108, 109, 110, 139, 152, 217, 229. *See also* Kanonwalohale
Oneida Community, 8, 10, 12, 13, 125, 140, 142–50, 165–66, 188–92, 193–98, 216–17, 231, 243, 258, 259
Oneida County Executive, 241
Oneida County v. Oneida Indian Nation of New York State, 237
Oneida County, NY, 10, 130, 147–48, 157, 202, 207, 216, 223, 225, 226, 228, 252, 254; antebellum and Civil War years in, 133, 136–37, 151–54, 161–63, 167; Euro-American settlement of, 66, 91, 92, 95, 120, 140; Oneida Land Claims and, 237, 239, 241–42, 248; Oneida Reservations in, 125, 127, 230; Post Civil War era, 170–79, 181
Oneida Creek, 10, 19, 25, 65, 89, 103, 108, 110, 112, 116, 117, 122, 123, 142, 147, 156, 167, 218, 231
Oneida Creek Tract, 108, 116
Oneida Depot. *See* Oneida, NY
Oneida Dispatch, 163
Oneida Evening Union, 184
Oneida Glass Factory, 157
Oneida Independent Company Cavalry, 163
Oneida Indian Nation of New York, 12, 240, 244, 249, 250, 253, 256, 260
Oneida Indian Nation of New York v. County of Oneida, New York, et al. (Oneida I), 235, 237
Oneida Indian Territory, 238–40
Oneida Institute, 131–32, 137, 138, 150
Oneida Lake, 2–4, 6, 10, 15, 16, 19, 157, 204, 215, 247; in age of

338 | Index

colonial empires, 23, 25, 29, 30, 32, 36, 46, 50, 52, 56, 65; in the early Republic, 85, 93, 94–95, 98–99, 105–106, 108, 110, 114; canals and, 117, 140, 213; in literature and art, 158–59, 168–70

Oneida Lands, New York acquisition of. *See* New York State, Oneida Land Acquisitions

Oneida Language, 18, 66, 68, 97, 99, 102, 158, 231, 250, 256

Oneida Limited, 10, 13, 140, 216–19, 246, 251, 254

Oneida Manufacturing Society, 111

Oneida Nation Enterprises, 12, 240, 243–45, 250, 256

Oneida People: and 1784 Conferences at Fort Stanwix, 1–3, 78–80; American Revolution and, 1, 5, 11, 14, 68–78, 120; and death of Shenandoah, 117–19; DeWitt Clinton, the Erie Canal and, 112–13, 116, 120; eighteenth-century settlements of, 64–66, 98–99; emigration to Wisconsin, 7, 119–21, 122–24; emigration to Canada, 7, 124–25, 147; encroachments within 1788 Reservation, 95–96; in era of New France, 4, 36–56; and the French and Indian War, 5, 52–60; land claims, 9–10, 12, 14, 101, 201, 233–38, 239, 240, 241–44, 245–47; land dispossession by New York State, xiv, 6–7, 81–88, 100–101, 105–10, 119, 121, 122–24, 125; and the Line of Property (1768), 63–64; Orchard Party, 122, 123, 125, 127, 241; origins and archaeology, 16–22, 50; Presbyterian Mission and, 66–68, 97; and the province of New York, 47–52, 61–62; Stockbridge and Brothertowns among, 87–90; at time of first contact with Europeans, 3–4, 22–32; and Tuscarora people, 50–51; and the US government, 6, 96–97, 105; visited by Belknap and Morse (1796), 103–105; in the War of 1812, 114–15; writing about, 11, 156–60

Oneida People of the Thames (Ontario), 7, 9, 14, 124–25, 147, 233–38, 250

Oneida People of Wisconsin, 7, 9, 14, 119–21, 122–24, 164, 233–38, 239

Oneida Presbytery, 138

Oneida Regiments (Civil War), 8, 161–63

Oneida Reservation (1788), 6, 7, 10, 83–85, 86, 90, 93, 95, 101, 105, 112, 116, 122, 159, 188, 216, 233, 237, 241

Oneida Reservation (1840, "Windfall"), 125, 127, 142, 230

Oneida River, 3, 4, 10, 30

Oneida Sachem, 152, 153, 161, 174

Oneida Square, Utica, 252

Oneida Standard, 153

Oneida Telegraph, 152

Oneida Weekly Herald, 175

Oneida, NY, 10, 29, 116, 117, 12–13, 140–42, 148, 152, 158, 161, 163, 167, 169, 173, 178, 182–86, 197, 204, 210, 214, 227

Oneida People of New York: in the 21st century, 245–51, 256; and Indian Gaming, 9, 14, 238–40, 244, 249; land claims, 9–10, 233–38, 241–43, 245–49; reservations after 1840, 125–27, 141–42, 230–33

Onion Fields, The (Kingsbury), 205–206

Index | 339

Onondaga County Community College, 212
Onondaga County, NY, 17, 157, 163, 164, 175, 179, 207, 208, 252, 255
Onondaga Lake, 25, 36, 44, 45, 92, 112, 113, 179, 180, 211, 212, 222
Onondaga People, 2, 4, 6, 8, 17, 18, 19, 21, 22, 26, 31, 35, 36, 38, 43, 44, 45, 46, 47, 51, 52, 71, 74, 75–76, 79, 82, 86, 92, 93–94, 96, 99, 229, 233
Onondaga Reservation, 7, 86, 92, 93, 231, 233, 238
Onondaga River, 2
Oquaga, 59, 64, 65, 66, 67, 68, 69, 72, 75, 76, 81, 158
Orchard Reservation, 98, 125, 126, 157, 230
Oriska, 50, 65, 73, 74, 98
Oriskany Patent (1705), 2, 61–63, 71, 90
Oriskany, NY, 161. *See also* Battle of Oriskany
Osborn, Amos, 170–71
Osborn, Rosalie, 170–71
Oswegatchie, 52, 53
Oswego Canal, 135, 177
Oswego County, NY, 95, 136, 151, 163, 226
Oswego Falls, 156
Oswego River, 4, 135
Oswego, NY, 46, 47, 48, 52, 53, 54, 55, 57, 70, 71, 72, 73, 94, 112, 114, 135, 140, 151, 154, 169, 170. *See also* Fort Oswego
Otis, Emily, 192
Otsego County, NY, 159, 176
Otsego Lake, 159
Otsiquette, Peter, 83, 85
Ottawa People, 9
Ottawa River, 26
Oved, Yaakov, 145

Owasco culture, 16–17
Owego Creek, 3
Owen, Robert, 145, 196
Owlville Cluster, 15
Oxford Times, 152
Oxford, NY, 92

Palatine Germans, xiii, 49, 51, 55–57, 60, 62, 69, 95, 229
Palmyra, NY, 148
Panic of 1837, 135
Paris, France, 83, 93
Paris, Town of, NY, 153
Passamaquoddy People, 236
Pataki, George, 245, 247
Paterelli, Michael, 205
Paterson, David, 247
Pathfinder, The (Cooper), 160
Pei, I.M., 213, 220
Pendleton, Nathan, Jr., 121
Penet, Peter, 85, 86–87, 95, 97, 99
Penet's Square, 87
Pennsylvaniam 16, 60, 84, 90, 231
Penobscot People, 236
People of the Standing Stone: The Oneida Nation, the War of Independence, and the Making of America (2017), 250
Perkins, Reuben, 108
Peterboro, NY, 8, 132, 134, 136, 137, 147, 150, 154, 163, 226
Peterman v. Pataki, 245
Petersburg Tract, 100–101
Philadelphia, PA, 77, 92, 102, 132, 145, 250
Phillips, Melvin, 241
Pickering, Timothy, 96, 97, 102
Pierce, Franklin, 151–52
Pioneer Homes, 208
Pioneers, The (Cooper), 159
Point Peninsula culture, 16, 17
Point Place Casino, 249

Poland, 183
Pompey Center, NY, 19, 25
Pompey, NY, 19, 93
Pontiac, 59
Pontiac's Rebellion, 60
Port Ontario, NY, 94
Port, Edmund, 236
Portugal, 27
Powell & Goldstein Cigar Company, 182
Powell, John C., 182
Powless, 73
Pratt, Peter, 25
Presbyterianism, 50, 63, 66–69, 87, 119, 130, 132, 135, 137, 138–39, 141, 162, 173, 195, 197
Prime's Hill, 46, 50, 56, 64, 65, 157
Proceedings of the Commissioners of Indian Affairs (1861), 2
Proclamation of 1763, 60
Prussia, 183
Putney Community, 146–47
Putney, VT, 142, 147

Quaker Oats Company, 209
Quakers, 105, 112
Quebec, 22, 26, 28, 36, 38, 44, 57, 156
Queen Anne, 48
Queen Anne's War, 47, 48, 62, 64

Rand, James, Jr., 211
Raquette Lake, 215
Real All-Americans, The (Jenkins), 250
Reed, Jacob, 81
Remington Rand, 211
Remsen, NY, 173
Rensselaer County, 140
Rensselaer Family, 40
Republican Party, 141, 152–55, 162, 164–65, 173, 175, 184, 204, 210, 220, 253

Reserve Officers Training Corps, 220
Rhode Island, 39, 88, 140
Rigaud de Vaudreuil, Philippe de, 44–45
Ritchie, William A., 16
Robbins, Alberto, 163
Roberts, Warren, xiii
Robertson, Miles, 217
Robinson, Sugar Ray, 205
Rochester, NY, 116, 140, 148, 150, 154, 161, 182, 192, 213, 223
Rockefeller, Nelson, 235
Rockwell, William Hanyoust, 232–33, 238
Rolling Stone, 225
Rome Haul (Edmonds), 228
Rome Iron Mill Company, 211
Rome Manufacturing, 204
Rome Sentinel, 194, 229
Rome Turney Radiator Company, 211
Rome Wire, 204, 211
Rome, NY, 2, 4, 10, 53, 130–31, 161, 186, 213, 214, 216, 221–22, 251; Erie Canal and Railroads in, 115–17, 141; Fort Stanwix Reconstruction, 12, 229–30; immigrants and, 173–74, 176, 178, 204; industry and strikes, 203–204, 209, 210–12; Woodstock '99 in, 223–24, 225. *See also* Oneida Carry
Roosevelt, Nicholas, 93
Roosevelt, Theodore, 184
Roots (Haley), 209
Royal Blockhouses (Oneida Lake), 57, 111, 250
Russell, Archimedes, 186
Russia, 166, 266

Sabine, Joseph, 151
Sackets Harbor, NY, 3, 114–15, 215
Saint François Xavier du Sault. *See* Kahnawake

Sainte-Marie de Gannentaha, 36, 37
Salina, NY, 211
Salmon River, 3, 43, 94
Salt Company of Onondaga, 180
Sandy Creek, 3
Sangerfield, Town of, NY, 170
Sangertown Square, 224
Saratoga, NY, 51, 74, 152. *See also* Battle of Saratoga
Sardino, Thomas, 221
Sargeant, John, 89, 94, 104, 112
Saucy Nick, 95
SavOn, 239, 246
Scanandoah, Albert "Doc," 233
Scanandoah, Chapman, 231–34
Scanandoah, Mary, 232–33
Scanandoah, William, 232–33
Schenectady, NY, 5, 43, 57, 62, 77, 78, 80, 81, 82, 85, 103, 111, 95, 134, 141, 213, 223, 231
Schermerhorn, John, 124
Schiller and Goethe Statue, Syracuse, 206
Schoharie Creek, 48, 62
Schoolcraft, Henry, 118, 157, 160, 259
Schoolcraft, Lawrence, 157
Schumer, Chuck, 252
Schuyler Family, 40
Schuyler, Moses, 122, 125
Schuyler, Philip, 71, 74, 100, 101, 103, 111
Schuyler, Pieter, 44, 47, 61–62
Scononda Creek, 157, 190
Scotland, 66, 102–104
Scott, Dred, 153
Scriba, Georg, 93–94
Scriba's Patent, 93–94
Seale, Bobby, 221
Seber, John, 95
Second Great Awakening, 148, 225
Selkirk Shores, 215

Seminole People, 249
Seneca Falls Convention, 192
Seneca People, 4, 17, 18, 43, 45, 60, 72, 73, 75, 76, 79, 82, 96, 99, 192, 237
Seneca River, 115
Seneca Turnpike, 13, 96, 98, 110, 117, 119, 121, 122, 125, 140, 142. *See also* Genesee Road
Servis, Peter, 64
Servis' Patent, 64, 90
Seven Days' Battle, 162
Seven Years' War. *See* French and Indian War
Seymour, Horatio, 164
Shako:wi Cultural Center, 98, 240
Shattuck, George, 234–37
Shawnee People, 65, 99
Shenandoah, Joanne, 239
Shenandoah, John, 68, 70, 72, 76–77, 83, 96, 97, 98, 104, 112, 113, 117–19, 121, 157, 229, 250
Shenandoah, Maisie, 238
Sherman, Willett, 157
Sherrill Manufacturing, 254
Sherrill, NY, 98, 99, 107, 110, 119, 125, 190, 218, 229, 230, 241, 246, 251, 254. *See also* Old Oneida
Shipman, David, 159
Side Cut Canal, 117, 140
Silversmith, 98
Sinavis, Thomas, 72
Skanawadi, 157
Sketches of the Ancient History of the Six Nations (Cusik), 156
Sky Holder, 22
Slavery, xiv, 8, 13–14, 95, 121, 129, 131–34, 136–40, 149–55, 163–66, 167, 207–10, 253, 258, 259
Smith, Gerrit, 8, 13, 132, 134–40, 148–52, 154, 192, 210, 226
Smith, Peter, 99–100, 101, 118, 132, 134, 159, 207

Smith-Coulter Farm, 205
Smithfield Turnpike, 122
Snow, Dean, 17
Snyder, Dan, 249
Society for the Propagation of Christian Knowledge, 66, 102–104
Society for the Propagation of the Gospel in Foreign Parts, 48
Society of Jesus. *See* Jesuit Order
Soenrese, 42
Solegwaston, Isaac, 104
Solvay Process Company, 211, 212, 233
Somali Bantu People, 255
Somalia, 255
Sons of the American Revolution, 229
Sotomayor, Sonia, 247
South Carolina, 166, 209
South Dakota, 14
Spanish Flu, 203
Spanish-American War, 184, 231
Spaulding, Philander, 232
Spencer, Elihu, 66
Spencer, Joshua A., 151
Spencer, Thomas, 70
Spirit House, 188
Spiritual Magazine, 146
Spiritualism, 188
Spitzer, Eliot, 248
Splain, Margaret, 250
Sqorhea, 29
St. Anne's Church, Fort Hunter, 48–49
St. John de Crèvecoeur, J. Hector, 158
St. Lawrence Iroquoians, 22, 28
St. Lawrence River, 1, 2, 3, 4, 5, 7, 15, 16, 26, 28, 52, 57, 70, 93, 117, 257
St. Leger, Barry, 6, 72, 73
St. Patrick's Day, 175
St. Regis. *See* Akwesasne
Standing Arrow Productions, 250
Stanton, Elizabeth Cady, 134, 192

State Tower, Syracuse, 212
Steam Cotton Mills Company, 153
Sterling Site, 65
Steuben, Friedrich Wilhelm von, 90, 173, 187
Steuben, NY, 173
Stevenson, John, 163
Stockbridge People, 87–90, 98, 103–104, 119–22, 159
Stockbridge, MA, 88
Stockbridge, Town of, NY, 41, 66, 89–90, 98, 103–104, 119, 216
Stone Arabia, NY, 49, 51, 62
Stowe, Harriet Beecher, 152
Stuyvesant, Peter, 37
Sullivan, John, 75–76
SUNY Albany, xiii
SUNY College of Environmental Science and Forestry, 212
SUNY Morrisville, 212
SUNY Polytechnic Institute, 254
Susquehanna culture, 16
Susquehanna River, 1, 2, 3, 64–65, 81, 117
Susquehanna Valley, 51
Susquehannock People, 22, 118
Sweden, 28
Sylvan Beach, NY, 111, 170, 215, 250
Syracuse 8, 220
Syracuse Chilled Plow Company, 210–11
Syracuse Union, 177
Syracuse University, 186, 197, 209, 212, 220, 221, 224
Syracuse, NY, 4, 7, 8, 9, 14, 17, 18, 220–21, 234, 249, 252–55; African Americans in, 150–51, 164–65, 201, 207–10, 252, 254; architecture, 186, 188–89, 212–13; Civil War Era in, 137, 140, 150, 154, 161, 163, 164–65, 192; Erie Canal and railroads in, 116, 140, 141–42; industry and

Index | 343

Syracuse, NY, *(continued)*
immigration, 167, 172–80, 185, 202–204, 206, 210–11, 231; post WWII Boom and Bust, 210, 211–13, 221–22, 224

Tadodaho, 21
Taft, William Howard, 184
Tagawaron, 65
Tarenyawagon, 156–57
Tayaheure, Jimmy, 72
Tecumseh, 99
Tekakwith, Kateri, 41–42
Tennessee, 150
Tenney, Claudia, 245, 248–49, 253
Tenskwatawa, 99
Teotonharason, Madeleine, 36
Texas, 223
Thames River, Ontario, 125. *Also see* Oneida People of the Thames
Thirty Years' War, 36
Thomas, Clarence, 248
Thompson, Jacob, 234
Thompson, John, 216, 221
Thousand Islands, 22–23, 215
Thurston Site, 30
Tin Pan Alley, 259
Tioga, NY, 75
Tiononderoge, 62
Tipperary Hill, Syracuse, 174
Tonight Show with Johnny Carson, 239
Toronto, 52
Tousard, Louis de, 75
Towner, James, 197
Treaty of Canandaigua (1794), 6, 96, 100, 234
Treaty of Fort Stanwix (1788), 10, 83–86, 100, 102
Treaty of New Echota (1835), 124
Treaty of Paris (1783), 77–78
Treaty of Utrecht (1713), 48, 51, 62

Treaty of Westminster (1674), 40
Trump, Donald, 254, 258
Tshejoana, 157
Tubman, Harriet, 154
Tug Hill Plateau, 3, 135, 225
Turning Stone Casino, 12, 14, 239–40, 242, 245, 246, 248, 249, 255
Tuscarora People, 50–51, 59, 65, 66, 68, 72, 74, 79, 80, 82, 87, 88, 98, 103, 119, 160, 164
Tuscarora Reservation, 156
Tuscarora War, 51
Tuttle Site, 19
Twelve Years a Slave (Northrop), 152
Two Kettles Together, 73

Unadilla River, 63, 81
Unadilla, NY, 75
Uncle Tom's Cabin (Stowe), 152
Underground Railroad, 8, 139, 150, 258
United States Freedom Fighters, 242
United States v. Boylan (1920), 233
Updike, Fritz, 229
Upstate Citizens for Equality, 238, 242–43, 245, 247, 248
Upstate Medical University, 212
US Supreme Court, 12, 201, 232–33, 235, 237–39, 241, 243, 244, 246–48
USS *Hornet*, 163
USS *Maddox*, 220
USS *Marietta*, 231
USS *Oneida*, 114
USS *Superior*, 115
USSR, 213, 255
Utah, 229
Utica Chamber of Commerce, 11, 229
Utica Citizens' Corps, 161
Utica College, 212

Utica Cotton Mills, 153
Utica Demokrat, 177
Utica Deutsche Zeitung, 177
Utica Globe, 203
Utica Insane Asylum, 162
Utica Morning Herald, 175
Utica Observer, 153
Utica Observer-Dispatch, 242
Utica Standard and Democrat, 137
Utica Steam Cotton Mills, 180
Utica, NY, 10, 120, 130–31, 148, 211, 220–22, 224, 226, 229, 253–55; African Americans in, 201, 207–10, 252–53; antebellum and Civil War era, 8, 132–34, 137, 139, 140, 152–53, 161–62, 164, 210; early settlement of, 57, 62, 90, 91–92, 95, 99, 103, 108, 111, 115, 140–42; industry and immigration, 8, 111, 113, 116, 117, 167, 172–81, 202–204, 206, 210; refugee resettlement in, 255

Valentine, William, 229
Valley Forge, 75, 250
Valley Mills, NY, 89
Van Buren, Martin, 133
Van der Kemp, Francis Adrian, 94
Van Eps, Abraham, 95
Van Schaick, Goose, 75, 94
Vandenburgh, Origen, 151
Vermont, 8, 142, 145, 146
Vernon Center, NY, 139
Vernon, Town of, NY, 66, 95, 109, 121, 127, 134, 140, 148–49, 157, 247, 248
Verona Beach State Park, 215
Verona, Town of, NY, 108, 116, 11, 239, 242, 247, 248
Verrazano, Giovanni da, 27
Vietnam War, 220

Virgil, NY, 93
Virginia, 51, 60, 77, 162, 231
Von la Roche, Sophie, 158
Voyage dans la haute Pensylvanie et dans l'état de New York (St. John de Crèvecoeur), 158

Walker, Benjamin, 173
Wall Street Crash, 210
Wallingford, CT, 167, 190, 216
Walsh, Ben, 253
Walton, William, 64
Wampanoag People, 237
Wampsville, NY, 163, 188
Wampum, 30–31, 44, 47, 55, 59, 67
War of 1812, 7, 113–15, 123, 215
War of the Spanish Succession, 48
Ward Brothers, 227
Ward, Delbert, 227
Ward, Samuel Ringgold, 133
Ward, William (Bill), 227
Warren, Peter, 49
Washington Post, 240
Washington Redskins, 12, 249
Washington, D.C., 119, 121, 136, 139, 160, 162, 166, 250
Washington, George, 71, 75, 77, 86, 90, 96, 102, 105, 115, 117, 118, 210, 250
Waterman, Delia (Dolly), 234
Watertown, NY, 93, 150, 152, 158, 165, 215
Waterville, NY, 153, 170–71
Watson, Elkanah, 85
Way of Holiness, The (Noyes), 144
Webster, Daniel, 151
Wemple, Abraham, 82
Wemple, Myndert, 95, 96, 188
Wenro People, 22
Wesley, John, 142
West End Brewing Company, 180

Western, Town of, NY, 154, 225
Wheaton, Charles, 151
Wheelock, Eleazar, 63, 67–68
Whig Party, 139, 141, 150–52
White River, 121
White Skin, 72, 77
White, Hugh, 90, 132
Whitesboro, NY, 132, 137, 138
Whitestown, NY, 90, 98, 103, 153, 158, 161
Wilkinson, Jemima, 129
Wilkinson, Parker B., 163
Williams, Eleazar, 2, 119, 122, 217
Wilson, Woodrow, 187
Winder, Mary, 234
Windfall Reservation. *See* Oneida Reservation (1840)
Winnebago (Ho-Chunk) People, 120, 121
Wisconsin, xiv, 7, 14, 120, 121, 122, 123, 127, 124, 140, 157. *See also* Oneida People of Wisconsin
Witmer, G. Robert, Jr., 243

Wöchentlicher Syracuse Demokrat, 177
Women's Rights Movement, 192–93, 258
Wonderful Wizard of Oz, The (Baum), 14, 249
Wood Creek, 2, 4, 46, 50, 53, 54, 61, 62, 73, 78, 100, 103, 108, 110, 111, 112, 114, 115, 117
Wood, Frank, 209
Woodstock '99, 223–24, 225, 244
Woolsey, Melanchton Taylor, 114
World Trade Center, 251
World War I, 114, 118, 179, 202–203, 206, 207, 210
World War II, 114, 208, 210, 216

Y Cyfaill, 173
Y Drych, 173
Yale, 104, 142, 144, 170, 196, 197
Yankee Stadium, 205
Yellow Brick Road Casino, 249
Yorktown, VA, 6, 77
Yugoslavia, 255